THE PENGUIN HISTORY OF BRITAIN
General Editor: David Cannadine

A Monarchy Transformed

THE PENGUIN HISTORY OF BRITAIN

MARK KISHLANSKY

A Monarchy Transformed

BRITAIN 1603–1714

ALLEN LANE
THE PENGUIN PRESS

ALLEN LANE
THE PENGUIN PRESS

Published by the Penguin Group
Penguin Books Ltd, 27 Wrights Lane, London w8 5tz, England
Penguin Books USA Inc., 375 Hudson Street, New York, New York 10014, USA
Penguin Books Australia Ltd, Ringwood, Victoria, Australia
Penguin Books Canada Ltd, 10 Alcorn Avenue, Toronto, Ontario, Canada m4v 3b2
Penguin Books (NZ) Ltd, 182–190 Wairau Road, Auckland 10, New Zealand

Penguin Books Ltd, Registered Offices: Harmondsworth, Middlesex, England

First published 1996
1 3 5 7 9 10 8 6 4 2

Maps drawn by Nigel Andrews

Set in 10.75/13.75 pt Monotype Sabon
Typeset by RefineCatch Limited, Bungay, Suffolk
Printed in England by Clays Ltd, St Ives plc

A CIP catalogue record for this book is available from the British Library

ISBN 0–713–99068–6

To Eddie and his godfather,
for their inspiration

Contents

List of Maps

Preface

I was first introduced to the political history of seventeenth-century Britain thirty years ago in an undergraduate survey course. Since then I have never wanted to study anything else. I found it the most fascinating combination of personalities, events and problems that I had ever encountered. I still do. In those days history was taught as a narrative, and for those, like me, who didn't know the story of the seventeenth century it was nothing short of amazing. I heard a sequence of lectures describe the collapse of an entire system of government; the creation of a revolutionary new one based on zeal and Utopian vision; its failure; the restoration of the older system; yet another collapse, followed by a foreign invasion; still another revolution; and finally Britain's absorption into and domination of the European state system. Each chapter was more remarkable than the last, a wheel of transformation in perpetual motion.

Over the past thirty years the movement of that wheel has become blurred. The mid-1960s inaugurated a quarter-century of scholarly productivity probably unrivalled in recorded time, and most of it was devoted to microscopic examination by highly trained professionals. Learned monographs, passionate historiographical debates, self-consciously debunking essays have filled a cornucopia of writing on the Stuart period of British history. Historians have learned much more about seventeenth-century politics and are much more secure in what they know now than in those days when they could confidently generalize about the movements of entire social classes or the causes of the English Revolution. If local archives, the British Museum and the Public Records Office are not exactly the Garden of Eden, the fruit to be found in them has nevertheless proved irresistible. But, as in Eden, our gains in knowledge have come with the loss of innocence. They have also come at the cost of coherence, and this has deprived students and general readers of a glimpse of the wonders that the seventeenth century holds.

My intention in this book is to recreate that fascination for another generation. Of course, I cannot tell the story as it was told to me: most of my professional life has been involved in making it difficult to put Humpty-Dumpty back together again (a seventeenth-century nursery rhyme about the siege of Gloucester, by the way). The running joke of *1066 and All That*, one of the great historical satires, was that Britain was destined to be 'top nation' and that everything memorable about its history contributed to a foreordained goal. Much writing about what were then called the Puritan and the Glorious Revolutions was predicated on the same assumption, and not even the advent of Marxist historiography, beginning in the 1940s, challenged this notion that history is a process rather than a story. That challenge has come over the last two decades and, paradoxically, it has made it difficult to create a narrative about the seventeenth century without highlighting all of the exceptions, the culs-de-sac and the dead ends. Modern historians may once again believe that history is a story, but they no longer concede that it has a beginning, middle or end. This makes the task of writing narrative more challenging than ever, especially for those brought up on a steady diet of analysis, nourished only by questions that begin with 'Why?' In this book I am equally interested in addressing 'Who?', 'What?', 'Where?' and 'When?'

With apologies to colleagues whose work I admire in other contexts, I believe that no synthesis of modern scholarship can result in a single, coherent, up-to-date narrative, and I have not chosen to provide one. There are a number of excellent detailed surveys of the period which give full play to historiographical interpretation; acknowledge contradiction, complexity and just plain muddle; and invite readers either to resolve the matters themselves or to remain for ever mystified. This work is intended only as an introduction, to stimulate curiosity rather than to satisfy it. It assumes no foreknowledge on the part of its audience, though those with some background may discover the many things going on below the surface. I have tried to invigorate the drama of the period with drama, the personalities with personality. If readers can understand why for generations the history of the seventeenth century has held Britons in thrall, then this book will have succeeded in all it sets out to do.

Every historical narrative is in some senses arbitrary, and this one is no exception. Considerations of space, of intended audience and of my own interests have necessarily shaped the chapters that follow. Beyond the opening chapter, there is nothing on social, economic or women's history; beyond the analytic discussion in Chapter 2, little on local history and administration. The first can be explained on the grounds that another series treats social history exclusively; the second on the decision to explain events from the centre and to maintain an even narrative across the entire century. The admirable studies of English counties under the early Stuarts have few analogues for the reigns of their successors and none for Ireland and Scotland. There is also no treatment of intellectual life here – of literature, philosophy, science or the fine arts. A cursory inclusion seemed potentially more offensive than exclusion, and I was insufficiently skilled to weave these developments into the core of political history. Though power operates on a cultural as well as a political level, it is hard to instance this at any given moment.

The narrative chapters all begin with the description of a dramatic event – a device that will not be to everyone's taste, especially those who already know the details. My intention is to engage readers by confronting them with how a particular historical moment unfolds, how outcomes are not predetermined, and how events and personalities galvanize a political nation. I hope, as well, that these descriptions create the pleasure of a good story. They are followed by a brief analytic section that highlights the themes of the ensuing chapter.

The title of this book, A Monarchy Transformed, is intended to convey an impression of the three themes that are interwoven within it. In the first place, and of paramount importance for the subsequent political history of the western world, the constitutional position of the English monarch was far different at the end of the century from at the beginning. Though the form of monarchical government survived its testing time, its practice had been revolutionized. Secondly, the particular history of the Stuart monarchy was one of continual mutation as the challenges of one generation overwhelmed the capacities of the next. Thirdly, the estate that the Stuarts had inherited was far different from the one they bequeathed: an empire in America; a toehold in South Asia; strategically important Mediterranean ports; and, of course, union with Scotland and political control over most of Ireland. The significance of these changes is mostly evident at the end of the dynasty, though both the North American plantations and East Indian trading began much earlier. The interconnected histories of England, Scotland and Ireland were omnipresent, complicated by the regal union of England and Scotland and the military occupation of Ireland. In the pages that follow I have been concerned to uncover more of the background of those moments when Irish, Scottish and English history intersected than has been conventional in such surveys, but I have done it from a decidedly English point of view. However disappointing it was to James I, Great Britain existed only during the last seven of the years covered in this book, and to survey the history of Scotland adequately during the other 104 years requires that Scottish institutions and personalities be treated in their own integrity and that a parallel narrative be composed. Ireland, of course, presents even more complex problems, for to include it in a history of Britain is to accept a view of its conquest that is both contentious and inadequate. Therefore my overall treatment of Ireland and Scotland is cursory at best, reflecting what I judged to be the demands of telling a coherent story in a limited space.

In a general book of this nature it did not seem advisable to follow scholarly conventions. I hope there are no statements so contentious as to require footnotes, and that those alert to what is borrowed will also know from where it came. Suggestions for further reading at the end will acknowledge many of the secondary works from which I have drawn as well as provide guidance to one of the most highly developed of all historiographical traditions. Discussions of financial matters must be understood to be approximate. Detailed descriptions of the size of royal debts and income are valuable comparatively and in the trends they suggest, but it cannot be assumed that they are accurate, even though they represent the laborious conclusions of the ablest historians. Quotations, which are in most cases unattributed, have been modernized, conflated, and removed from their original contexts, as I have used them only to give flavour to the narrative and not as evidence for any statement. Similarly, I have decided to identify most peers and office-holders with a single title except when, like Buckingham or Marlborough, they receive extended treatment. Usually that title was the last one they received, as for the Jacobean Earl of Somerset or the Caroline Earl of Clarendon. But occasionally, as with the Marquis of Hamilton, it is more sensible to use the title they held at the time when they were a principal actor. This saves readers from having to remember that Sir Thomas Osborne was at various times in these chapters Viscount Latimer, Earl of Danby, Marquis of Carmarthen and Duke of

Leeds. I have called him Danby. This means, however, that on occasion some people are called by titles that they have, by strict chronology, not yet received. Similarly there are rare cases in which I have narrated events out of sequence, summarizing, for example, the entire legislative achievements of a parliament before focusing on a single one. In both these matters I have preferred to sacrifice exactitude for gains in brevity and clarity. Similarly, I have always reckoned years to begin on 1 January rather than 25 March.

Though books bear the names of their authors, they are nurtured and cared for by many before they see the light of day. Such a large number of scholars, students and friends have read and commented upon portions of this manuscript that a list of their names might rival the index. I would like to thank them all collectively. The historians who have corrected slips, errors and insupportable interpretations have done so, as they have revealed in their correspondence, as a labour for the benefit of their students. They have insisted upon the clarification of things which they understand perfectly well but upon which experience has proved beginners need guidance. In this context, I shall refrain from taking sole responsibility for any errors that remain, though I certainly shall take responsibility for correcting them subsequently. At Penguin Books Mr Peter Carson and his staff, including Andrew Kidd and Caroline Knight, have been a joy to work with. Jeanne Thiel lived with the creation of this book and tolerated its constant intrusion into the quietude of her summer bicycle rides with the good cheer that has always characterized her acceptance of my obsession with the seventeenth century. My son, Matthew, endured the writing of this book with quizzical bemusement. I hope he will discover that the book answers the question he posed when he first heard that I had agreed to write the Penguin history of the seventeenth century: 'Was the seventeenth century decisive in the history of penguins?' Matthew, the seventeenth century was decisive for everything!

Cambridge, Massachusetts
1996

Prologue

It is astonishing to reflect on the achievements of Britain's seventeenth century. The period that coincided with the rule of the Stuarts (1603–1714) introduced so much that defined the nation for decades to come, and so much that remains vibrant today. The modern business world was born; science came of age; literature matured as never before or after; feudal forms withered; torture, witchcraft and heresy died away. A Scot, a Dutchman and finally a German sat on the throne of xenophobic England. In 1707 England and Scotland formed the union of Great Britain. The British empire, source of so much wealth in the eighteenth century, pride in the nineteenth, and trouble thereafter, began. For the first time in history Britannia ruled the waves, and for the first time in centuries her army was as feared as her navy. Britons peopled a new continent on the Atlantic Ocean and established a new trading partner on the Indian Ocean. In 1603 Britain was an isolated archipelago; in 1714 it was among the intellectual, commercial and military centres of the world.

In seventeenth-century Britain merchants founded the East India Company to trade in the Spice Islands and the Royal African Company to partake of the lamentable slave trade. Both created unimaginable wealth for participants and investors alike. The Stuarts inaugurated nearly every element of modern commerce and finance. The Bank of England was founded in 1694, the Bank of Scotland in 1695. Cheques, banknotes and milled coins made possible an economy based on money. The creation of the Stock Exchange and the national debt made possible an economy based on credit. The excise and the land tax revolutionized government finance. Insurance companies were born – the Sun and Lloyd's were the first – to protect against the devastation of fire, and then to spread risk in business ventures. British merchants plied their trade around the globe as Virginia, Massachusetts Bay,

Barbados and Nova Scotia were settled and Calcutta was established. Newspapers came into existence and were so astoundingly popular that weeklies were succeeded by dailies and dailies by morning and evening editions. They advertised an amazing assortment of new products, such as tobacco, sugar, rum, gin, port, champagne, peppermint and Cheddar cheese. Tea, coffee and chocolate produced a revolution not only in habits of consumption but also in diet as these caffeine-laced beverages were gradually substituted for soporific beer. The consumption of coffee became such a craze among the well-to-do that the first coffee-houses opened and were soon in competition with the more exclusive gentlemen's clubs, which began at the same time. Urban dwellers, especially, experienced a transformation of their daily lives.

In seventeenth-century Britain the prototype of a steam engine was created, and coke was produced and then used to manufacture iron – one of the miracle products of the age. The cooking hob and the pressure cooker were invented – to the consternation of those who had turned spits or boiled beef for hours. There was a veritable revolution in personal hygiene as the water closet appeared in fashionable homes and the commode became an indispensable piece of furniture. Among the smart set at the end of the reign of the Stuarts, men carried umbrellas to keep waistcoated suits dry, women to protect their hoop skirts, neither of which costumes had ever been seen before. Britain became smaller as coach services provided springed carriages for travel along the early turnpike roads, which charged tolls based on statute miles first calculated by John Ogilby. The beginning of the postal service and the introduction of the penny post in London transformed communication.

Not even the Renaissance could boast so prodigious an outburst of intellectual creativity as was found in Stuart Britain. Francis Bacon laid the foundations for scientific experimentation and the inductive method. The modern disciplines of biology, chemistry and physics all trace their origins to the breakthrough findings of seventeenth-century Britons: William Harvey, who discovered the circulation of blood; Robert Boyle, who posited the existence of the chemical elements; and Isaac Newton, who propounded the theory of gravity. And these were but the shooting stars in a firmament so vast that the Royal Society was created to survey it. The botanist John Ray originated the basic principles of plant classification; the mathematician William Napier invented logarithms; and the astronomer Edmund Halley predicted the return of the comet that bears his name. William Oughtred devised the multiplication sign in mathematics, John Newton the binomial theorem in algebra, and Isaac Newton the differential calculus. Among the technological wonders of the age, Robert Hooke invented the microscope, the quadrant, the marine barometer and the spring balance for watches; Boyle perfected the air pump and created the first vacuum; and Newton constructed a reflecting telescope. In medicine – a profession that was still organized in guilds – the College of Physicians issued the first *Pharmacopoeia* to describe the properties of drugs; Peter Chamberlen invented the forceps; diabetes was first diagnosed; kidney stones were operated upon; the pulse was first counted; and a successful blood transfusion was made. Astonishingly, plague disappeared from the British Isles.

New recreations appeared which gave pleasure for ever after. Enthusiasts organized cricket matches which became so popular that the first cricket club was then founded. James I introduced golf into England and established the Royal Blackheath Golf Club in 1608. Izaak Walton codified knowledge about fishing in *The Compleat Angler*. Cribbage was invented. Charles II brought the sport of yachting back from his exile, and Queen Anne inaugurated sweepstakes in horse racing and then established the most famous of all competitions, the Ascot Races.

In seventeenth-century Britain dazzling prodigy houses were built by architects such as Inigo Jones, Sir Christopher Wren, Nicholas Hawksmoor and Sir John Vanbrugh. Each one was more astounding than the last: Hatfield, Audley End, Wilton, Castle Howard, Chatsworth and Blenheim. At Oxford, visitors marvelled at the construction of the Bodleian Library, the Sheldonian Theatre and the Ashmolean Museum; at Cambridge, Sir Christopher Wren constructed the imposing Trinity College Library. In the wilderness in another Cambridge, John Harvard founded a college. In London, Inigo Jones laid out Covent Garden, which quickly came to house a vegetable market, and Charles II welcomed the public into St James's Park. In 1666, fire destroyed 80 per cent of the old City; and architects and planners then created modern London, with fifty-one new churches and Wren's domed St Paul's Cathedral as the crowning achievement. In the suburbs, Holland House, Kensington Palace, and Chelsea and Greenwich Hospitals were all imposing additions to a spreading capital.

Some forms of entertainment were meant to astonish. Inigo Jones and Ben Jonson created masques for the early-seventeenth-century court, with singing, dancing and fireworks. More developed entertainment followed. Opera began, imported first from Italy and then transformed by Henry Purcell, who orchestrated *Dido and Aeneas*, and Handel, who composed his *Rinaldo*. Sadler's Wells Theatre opened for musical entertainment and a violinist gave the world's first public concert. Thomas Ravenscroft introduced the round as a method of teaching children to harmonize with rhyming ditties like 'Three Blind Mice'. John Bull produced the earliest version of 'God Save the King'.

Nothing was more astonishing in seventeenth-century Britain than the production of literature. Though little more than 5 million people in the entire world spoke English, the language was immortalized by the poets, playwrights and pamphleteers of the seventeenth century. Shakespeare, Jonson, Donne and Herbert dominated the beginning; Defoe, Addison, Swift and Pope the end. In between, Milton wrote *Paradise Lost* and Bunyan *Pilgrim's Progress*. The most widely read work in the English language is the King James Bible, the next are the plays of Shakespeare; they were printed within a decade of each other. In a five-year period beginning in 1603, theatre-goers could attend an incredible run of opening nights that included *Measure for Measure*, *Sejanus*, *Othello*, *King Lear*, *Macbeth*, *Volpone*, *Antony and Cleopatra*, *Coriolanus* and *Pericles*. Sixty years later the flow of masterpieces still continued. In a five-year period beginning in 1667 Milton published *Paradise Regained* and *Samson Agonistes*, Dryden wrote *The Conquest of Granada*, Aphra Behn's *Oroonoko* was performed, and Samuel Pepys completed his diary. If tragedy reached its height under James I, comedy reigned supreme after the Restoration, when drawing-room farces and comedies of manners such as *Marriage à la Mode*, *The Country Wife* and *The Way of the World* were all performed and actresses first graced the stage.

In seventeenth-century Britain the writing of political theory reached heights unattained since the Golden Age of Athens. Filmer wrote *Patriarcha*, Hobbes *Leviathan*, Harrington *Oceana* and Locke *Two Treatises of Government*, each a masterpiece. King James republished *The True Law of Free Monarchies*; Henry Parker articulated the first theory of parliamentary sovereignty; the Levellers created the *Agreement of the People*; and Henry Ireton wrote the *Heads of the Proposals*. The *Instrument of Government* became the first and only written constitution ever adopted in England. John Lilburne, Henry

4

Neville, Marchmont Nedham, John Milton and Algernon Sidney all contributed to the development of republican theory.

New ideas, new forms of entertainment, new theories of government abounded. The religious beliefs of seventeenth-century Britons were shaken to the core. The episcopal church, which came to be called Anglican by the second half of the century, was buffeted by high-church Arminians in the 1630s and by low-church latitudinarians in the 1690s. In the early decades it navigated away from the rocks of Puritanism, in the late decades from the shoals of Catholicism. Outside the Anglican church, all was ferment. The Baptists were established; George Fox founded the Quakers; and Jews were readmitted to England. A Presbyterian church was created for a time. In 1650 the Commonwealth made adultery a capital offence; in 1672 Parliament debarred Catholics and dissenters from civil office. As early as 1624, Lord Herbert of Cherbury wrote the first work of deism, *De Veritate*, though it was decades before a limited religious freedom was established.

No history can account for such dazzling achievements. It is perhaps as well to gaze upon so bright a firmament rather than try to measure the gaseous compounds of each star. And among all these constellations none burned hotter nor were more instantly recognized in seventeenth-century Britain than the revolutions in government that led to the trial and execution of one Stuart monarch and the deposition and exile of another. In the mid-century, the monarchy, the House of Lords, and the episcopal church were all abolished and a government in the name of the people was established. England enforced its will upon Scotland and Ireland through conquest and occupation. In 1688 the leaders of the English political nation deserted a native Catholic monarch and rallied to a foreign Protestant one, again dividing the Stuart kingdoms and resulting in the long-term suppression of Irish Catholicism. It was these events which most affected the lives of those who lived through them, which had such momentous consequences for the archipelago and the continent, and which have lived in memory ever since as the defining moments in the political history of Britain.

I

The Social World

At the beginning of the seventeenth century most British people were farmers. Over 80 per cent of the English population lived in the countryside, and the proportions in Scotland and Ireland were higher. Their lives were governed by the inexorable rhythms of the seasons, their fortunes by the fertility of the earth and the vagaries of the weather.

Soil and climate largely determined the form of agriculture, but this varied so considerably even within regions that exceptions were the rule. In lowland England, east of a diagonal that ran roughly from the Tees in the north to Weymouth in the south-west, farming generally consisted of raising foodstuffs, corn crops for bread and beer, peas and beans for winter storage, and animal fodder. Here the land was rich, with heavy clays and lush meadows. In this zone, rainfall was concentrated in late autumn and early spring, nutrifying the ground after harvest and the seeds after planting. In the north-west, including all of Wales, Scotland and most of Ireland, animal husbandry predominated. These were the uplands, and here the soil was thin and the climate harsh, more suited to tending flocks of sheep than stalks of grain. Among the Gaelic Irish, cattle were still considered a measure of wealth. In the English midlands, a zone stretching south towards the Sussex downs and west through Oxfordshire, the land was suitable for both activities and farmers could choose to plough their land up for crops or lay it down for pasture as their sense of the market-place dictated. Though corn and sheep dominated the seventeenth-century agricultural economy, there were pockets of other activities. Horses and oxen were bred in Wales and the west midlands, mainly for transport and labour. Kent and Sussex were notable for orchards and the speciality hops that were brewed into 'great beer'. In the fens and the Cotswolds dairying produced much of the butter and cheese that could be bought at markets.

Ecology determined social organization as much as it did economic life. Though the north-western zone contained the greatest portion of English land, it held less than a third of the people. They were dispersed in widely scattered settlements, for many acres were needed to maintain flocks and to scratch out subsistence from the small oat and barley crops that the thin soils yielded. Kin was more important than the community, especially in remote areas which experienced little in-migration. Most of Scotland and Ireland were organized around clans, but in Scotland, the Highland and Lowland zones marked out significant variations in landholding, social structure and economic activity. Throughout this north-western zone, parishes were large, as were the estates of the local gentry and aristocracy, which were measured in miles rather than acres. This relative isolation reinforced traditional values, as the aid of kin and neighbours was often a matter of survival. The wealthy practised an open-handed hospitality long after it had gone out of fashion in the south, while the concept of good lordship remained an aristocratic code. In return, tenants followed the dictates of their lords with a near-feudal loyalty, making possible the raising of aristocratic armies and the survival of pockets of Catholicism. The south-east was dotted with villages rather than homesteads. The steeple was in plain view of closely built dwellings which were centred on either the churchyard or the green. Fields, meadows and commons surrounded the village and were the site of communal agricultural activities, though each family owned its own land and harvested its own crops. Kinship was comparatively weak, and the social structure of the village was determined more by wealth and standing than by blood. As the English settled parts of Ireland and North America, they made every effort to replicate these patterns of geography, society and culture.

In both ecological zones, the parish was the primary unit of community organization. An administrative unit of the church, the parish penetrated deeply into the lives of the families who composed it. The parish defined the social boundaries of the Christian community, and there was commonly an annual ceremony in which its physical boundaries were perambulated. Strangers were defined as those outside the parish, especially when it was coterminous with the village. The rituals that marked the passage of life – baptisms, communions, marriages and burials – were all performed within the parish. The minister was the visible presence of the church who brought religion to the people.

Religion suffused parish culture, though popular religion might be expressed in a variety of ways that revealed the overlap between pagan and animist beliefs with Roman Catholicism and then Protestantism. Sunday services as well as the holy days of the religious calendar were crucial markers of the rhythms of labour as well as occasions of sociability and celebration. Throughout the seventeenth century parishes became part of wider networks of exchange as transportation and communication improved and as towns pulled them into contact with each other.

The growth of towns was one of the enduring legacies of the sixteenth century. In large concentrations of population, the dominance of the exchange of commodities and wage labour characterized a different form of economic life. Urban development resulted from two factors: increased population, beginning in the sixteenth century, and increased agricultural efficiency, beginning in the seventeenth. In England the total number of inhabitants grew from over 3 to over 4 million between 1550 and 1600, and from 4 to 5 million during the seventeenth century. Though the estimates are speculative, Ireland and Scotland may both have had almost 1 million people in 1600, but, while Scotland's population stagnated thereafter, Ireland's doubled by 1700. The North American colonies grew from a few thousand to a quarter of a million.

Population increase, however, was not spread evenly across this period. In England, there were two distinct demographic epochs: an unrelenting upward spiral that began before 1550 and lasted for a full century, and population decline and stagnation from 1650 to 1700. The rise occurred despite harvest failures in the 1560s, 1590s, 1610s and 1640s and major outbreaks of plague in 1563, 1625 and 1665; the decline despite improved agricultural productivity and the disappearance of plague after 1665. Ireland's population, too, suffered severe episodes of plague, the worst occurring in 1649–53. But its population history was, like North America's, one of sustained growth. The mid-century recovery took nearly thirty years, but beginning in the 1670s the upward pressure was unrelenting. Though Scotland's demographic regime resembled Ireland's, with high birth and death rates, its population history was more like England's, with growth into the early seventeenth century and stagnation thereafter.

Population increase had a profound effect upon economic and social life. At the most basic level, there were more mouths to feed by the labour of a smaller proportion of the population, and this necessitated fundamental change. The sixteenth-century agrarian economy was predominantly a subsistence economy. Farmers produced a variety of grains and legumes, raised a small number of animals, and gathered what grew wild with the aim of providing all that their families needed to survive. They were neither dependent upon markets nor oriented towards them. The techniques they used to ensure survival were time-tested and conservative.

In the fertile lowland zone of England, although farming was a communal enterprise, the villagers collectively determined which fields would be planted and which would lie fallow, how many animals could be grazed on the commons, and what amounts of fish and wood could be extracted from ponds and forests. These were normally guided by the custom of the manor and the practical experiences of each generation. Land was held in small strips scattered throughout the village fields, and an average holding of roughly thirty acres might be divided into twenty or more strips. This subdivision allowed each family to participate in the range of uses to which the land was put, having some strips in fields of barley, some in peas and some in grass. Strips also tended to even out local variations in fertility and protect against the freak appearance of storms and insects. Though the size of the overall plot owned by families varied significantly from place to place – larger in the infertile uplands, smaller in the bounteous fens – the amount of land necessary for subsistence was the unit to which holdings gravitated in every village. In England there was an active land market, and individual strips were sold, exchanged or bequeathed with the object of accumulating subsistence-sized plots that would allow the families of two children to remain in the village. Thus one generation would get ahead so that the next might start out even.

The merit of subsistence agriculture was that it allowed the largest number of families in the village to ride the crests and troughs of nature and survive all but the worst ecological disasters. Common ploughing meant that the village could survive with fewer expensive oxen and ploughshares, and communal foddering maximized fertilization; though both necessarily reduced yields. Taxation was mostly in kind and therefore self-regulating to shortage and surplus. Subsistence agriculture cannot be measured by its efficiency, since there is a natural limit to the use of increased quantities of highly perishable commodities. Mutual dependence bred cooperation if it did not eliminate competition, though it would be inaccurate to view the agrarian community as idyllic. Alcoholism was rampant, domestic violence was common, and feuds and grudges were endemic. Manorial and church courts told the same story of theft, trespass, adultery and defamation in small as was writ large in quarter sessions and the central court of Star Chamber.

While there remains no adequate explanation for the surge in the population of the British Isles before 1650, the subsequent stagnation can be accounted for mainly by the fact that women delayed their first marriages longer than in previous generations, thereby shortening the period in which they could bear children, and a higher percentage of women never married at all. In England and Scotland first marriages occurred late in life for both sexes throughout the period. The mean for males, which remained constant in the seventeenth century, was 28 years; the mean for women rose from 25.6 to 26.2 by mid-century. This allowed a typical woman a fertile period of about nineteen years, during which, if both she and her husband remained alive, she would commonly have nine pregnancies, of which six or seven might result in births. At least a third of her offspring would perish as infants or children, leaving three or four to survive to their tenth year. Thus completed British families, which lived in nuclear units of parents and children, were commonly composed of five or six people, while the average for all families was just over four. Households would not be much larger, as servants and apprentices replaced children moving to other households. Irish women married much younger, at 22 or 23, as did those in New England, where families were larger.

This pattern of nuclear families and compact households was evident in lowland Scotland and the North American colonies as well. But in these places the demographic regimes were different. Scottish communities were susceptible to famine during the whole of the seventeenth century; population growth was checked by comparatively high mortality rates, and life expectancy was considerably lower than in England. The harvest failures in 1696, 1698 and 1699 resulted in both starvation and the emigration of tens of thousands of Scots. In North America, demographic patterns were determined by location. In the New England colonies, population mushroomed as a surplus of land and a dearth of disease produced a salubrious environment. Infant mortality was lower than at any time before the advent of modern medicine, life expectancy higher. Twenty per cent of the first generation of male New Englanders reached the age of eighty. In the Chesapeake the demographic regime was murderous, as festering swamps, a torrid climate and contagious diseases decimated wave after wave of immigrants. Two-thirds of those who arrived in Virginia between 1619 and 1622 were dead by 1623. There and in Maryland and Carolina, labour had to be imported for plantation work – either black slaves or white indentured servants. More than three-quarters of white males who arrived in the Chesapeake owed labour service, and they were the largest category of immigrants, creating a gender imbalance that gradually declined across the century from 6 to 2.5 males for each female.

Despite these variations, the family was the primary unit of British society and served a number of functions, ranging from the ordering of social and economic life to the provision of bodily and psychological comfort. As a unit of social organization, the family was frequently compared to 'a little commonwealth' in which the structures and obligations of governance replicated in miniature those of the nation at large. In this model of 'domestic economy', which encompassed the household as well as the family, husbands were responsible for the conduct of their wives, parents for the moral upbringing of their children, masters for the training of their servants. These structured relationships mirrored the hierarchical nature of society and defined personal relationships as a series of interlocking roles. Adult men were at the apex, their obligation to rule sanctioned by God's injunction to Adam, but the superordinate role of women as parents and employers, especially within the household, was clearly established. This was no more than a reflection of the realities of a world in which most women would be widowed and become head of their domestic units. But the prescription to obedience in the family – echoed in biblical readings, church services and the adages of folk wisdom – should not suggest that all families were orderly or that all members accepted the roles assigned them. The dictates of personality, of experience and of necessity all combined to make each family unique. Indeed, the all too frequent invocation of the ideal type suggests that experience was far from it.

As a mode of economic organization, the family was the primary unit of production. Most marriages were made on economic calculations, with the timing dependent upon inheritance or the completion of apprenticeship or domestic service. Marriage contracts, especially among the wealthy, were complex prenuptial agreements that specified the dowry the woman would bring as wife and the portion she would receive as widow. By the late seventeenth century the marriage market was no metaphor: dowries were advertised in newspapers. Love matches were not unknown and were becoming more common, but prevailing wisdom held that love was an emotion acquired within marriage rather than before. Thus elopements were prosecuted as abduction if the girl's father was not influential enough to bring a charge of rape. Divorce was proscribed by law and rare in practice.

In its economic role, the family was also a patriarchal hierarchy of responsibilities and functions that incorporated women and children. All members of the family laboured in specified roles that were the product of physical limitations and cultural assumptions. Men ploughed, reaped with scythes, herded animals, wove cloth, worked with tools, and manufactured. Women planted, reaped with sickles, tended animals, spun thread, worked with food products, and sold goods. Children gathered, swept grain after harvest, watched animals, and learned crafts, cookery or trades as befitted their futures. The patriarchal nature of the family economy was most clearly seen in patterns of inheritance which privileged males over females and eldest sons over all. Most English families practised primogeniture, which passed land and the bulk of accumulated wealth to the eldest son while setting aside portions of one kind or another for his siblings. Younger males were often provided with skills through apprenticeships; females were provided with dowries to improve their marital prospects. These practices were replicated by the English who settled in Ireland, and contrasted with the Gaelic traditions of partible inheritance, which divided the land among the surviving males.

Customs like primogeniture – once described as a system that 'if it did not drown all the kittens but one, threw all but one into the water' – suggest strains in the interpersonal relations within families. Sibling rivalries were an in-built characteristic of the unequal life chances that resulted from the lottery of birth order. Indeed, younger children were likely to be sent from home by the age of ten to begin service or training. Though nuclear families predominated, many were amalgamations of earlier unions and included step-parents, half-siblings and all the complications they imply. There can be no doubt that children were favoured over all other kin or household members and that they were the special care of their parents, but parent–child relationships were not as emotively affectionate as they were to become. This probably had less to do with psychological distancing because of the high incidence of child mortality than with cultural assumptions about the rearing of children and the economic necessity of setting them to work. Theories that stressed the stain of original sin and the proclivity of children towards evil long resisted humanist arguments to the contrary. Corporal punishment was common at all levels of society, and it would be surprising if people who ordinarily struck farm animals sought other means to correct obstinate children. 'Teach the child to fear the rod and cry softly' was the credo of John Wesley's mother at the end of the seventeenth century.

Yet, for all of this, children were the means by which the family survived. Lineage and longevity were especial values of the seventeenth century, and in this context the family served the purpose of cultural continuity. Much estate planning was done to ensure the long-term survival of a particular family, with land passed directly to grandchildren through a device known as the strict settlement or through long leases that lasted three generations. Continuity rather than callousness was the reason why a second child was named after his father once an identically named first child had died.

The surplus population created by the demographic upsurge of the sixteenth and early seventeenth centuries put pressure on family relationships in another way. Villages became incapable of providing a livelihood for their large progenies, and this resulted in increased geographical mobility, especially among women. Whether English communities had ever been geographically stable remains an open question, but throughout the early modern period there was continuous migration by those who sought betterment or subsistence. The pattern of motivation changed over time. In the period of demographic expansion most were 'hardship' migrants, commonly without skill or money. After 1650 a larger proportion were moving to better themselves and were prepared for the occupations into which they entered. It was not uncommon for more than half of a village's families to have disappeared over the course of two generations. Migration was an ever-present factor within both Scottish and Irish society, and it was from these societies that the bulk of New World immigrants derived after the initial settlements.

In the first decades of the sixteenth century and the last decades of the seventeenth, migrants who moved to towns generally found greater economic opportunity. But during most of the period towns were unable to sustain the run-off of rural population. Indeed, those who migrated to towns seeking subsistence were more likely to find death, for the confluence of epidemic disease, improper sanitation, inadequate shelter, and violence was lethal. Mortality rates were much higher in towns, and without a constant stream of migrants towns would have been unable to sustain their populations, let alone increase in size.

Towns did not grow numerically over this period, but more crossed the threshold from agricultural to exchange economies. In England over 600 communities could lay claim to being towns – mostly small markets of around 1,000 inhabitants. There were few regional centres with over 5,000 people and fewer provincial capitals like Norwich, Bristol, York and Exeter with populations ranging from 10,000 to 30,000. But these sectors grew such that in 1600 three times as many towns had populations over 5,000 as had had in 1500, and the trend continued despite the fact that, after another half-century of growth, population declined and then levelled off by 1700. Moreover, in England, twice as many people lived in cities of 10,000 or more in 1600 than had a century earlier; in Scotland 50 per cent more did. In both places this number would double again over the course of the seventeenth century – in England, largely as a result of London's explosive growth.

London was a world of its own. It was the political, legal, social and economic capital of England. The city and its environs were the site of royal government, of the law courts, of aristocratic palaces and gentry town houses, and of one of the greatest ports in Europe. At its financial centre was the Royal Mint; at its commercial heart was the Royal Exchange. London was a magnet that attracted everything, 'drawing to it all the animal and vital spirits' of the state. Officially dispersed throughout the land, the church hierarchy gravitated so often to London that the bishops too built palaces on the banks of the Thames. London was the centre of cultural life even though the official centres of learning were at Cambridge and Oxford, which mostly served as finishing-schools for the wealthy and seminaries for the church. The Stationers' Company regulated the book trade and controlled the nation's printing-presses from London. And there in the early seventeenth century Gresham's College taught the new science and mathematics that were excluded from the church-dominated curriculum of the universities. Theatres flourished on the south bank, attracting as many as 20,000 spectators a week until they were closed in mid-century,

England and Wales: Principal Towns in the Seventeenth Century

only to be reopened after the Restoration in more respectable districts where they were twice as popular.

London's growth was phenomenal. The 40,000 inhabitants who lived mostly within the walled city in 1500 had increased to over 200,000 a century later, sprawling into Westminster and over thirty new suburban parishes, and that larger population tripled in the next hundred years, perhaps reaching 600,000 in the 1690s despite distressingly high death rates and emigration to North America. By then, one in nine English people lived in London, and it was the largest city in the western world. There was no equivalent in Ireland or Scotland. Dublin did not reach 10,000 inhabitants before the middle of the seventeenth century, and Edinburgh, though the second largest urban centre in Britain by 1700, had a population of only 40,000.

Growth placed great strains on the agrarian regime. While the strengths of subsistence agriculture outweighed its weaknesses, its shortcoming was that it was not well suited to either innovation or expansion, which were made necessary by the unrelenting pressure of population increase in England. At first, excess sons and daughters were easily absorbed. More land was put into cultivation, and market towns grew with the influx of labour. But the natural limits to growth were quickly reached, and, despite famine and epidemics in the 1610s and 1620s, population continued to increase. The first manifestation of crisis was inflation. The growing towns needed ever greater quantities of foodstuffs, and, as demand outstripped supply, prices rose. Basic agricultural commodities were four times more expensive in 1600 and six times more expensive by 1650 than they had been in 1500. Grains led the way, but livestock and their by-products did not lag far behind. Only the price of textiles and industrial goods grew more slowly, doubling during the sixteenth century.

Though such increases seem modest by modern standards, they did not occur in a modern, flexible economy. Local variations could be even worse than national trends, for the primitive state of transportation restricted the movement of goods despite the abundance of internal waterways and natural harbours. The surplus production of one area was rarely available to alleviate the undersupply of another, and government regulation against 'middlemen', however well-intended, exacerbated the problem. Towns did all they could to secure their food supply, buying up agricultural land, entering into contracts for future deliveries, and regulating production and distribution.

Inflation not only created misery: it upset notions about economic behaviour predicated on the relative stability of prices and values. On many manors, rents could not be raised and land was held for long terms. Leases for ninety-nine years assumed that the value of land would hold steady from generation to generation, or at least that it was as likely to go down as to go up. Taxation levied 'in kind' made a similar assumption about commodities, and it was a grim joke that the value of a tithe – the 10 per cent tax paid to the church – from a failed harvest at the beginning of the seventeenth century was worth more than from a bumper crop a century earlier.

For 150 years the cost of everything rose but labour, because, while there were more mouths to feed, there were also more hands to work. As commodity prices sky-rocketed, real wages dropped like a stone. The most reliable figures are so appalling that their accuracy has long been doubted. Across the sixteenth century, to take one example, the real wages of workers in the English building trades halved, and they continued their decline during the next fifty years. Agricultural wages, with the exception of highly skilled reapers, may have fallen even further, and those of casual labour of the kind that kept most immigrants afloat in cities sank furthest. It was not until after the civil wars of the 1640s that real wages recovered significantly, and by then the structure of both the agrarian and the urban economy was undergoing fundamental change.

This precipitous decline in real wages and standards of living was mitigated by the fact that the wages of both agricultural and industrial labourers were supplemented by 'diet', a specified menu of food that was allocated by employers according to a scale graduated by gender, skill and responsibility. With food prices soaring, the provision of 'diet' was increasingly valuable. It is also important to realize that only a small segment of the population was wholly dependent upon wages for its subsistence. In rural communities wages were normally supplemental to agricultural activity, and even in most urban areas families kept garden plots and livestock – a fact attested by the passage of tethering ordinances and the appointment of hog-reeves in many seventeenth-century towns. Nevertheless, mitigation was not alleviation. In lowland Scotland, a diet rich in meat, cheese and butter in the sixteenth century gave way to one overwhelmingly composed of oats. The lot of ordinary people worsened steadily for nearly a century, and there was much misery throughout the land.

But it is an ill wind that blows no one any good. Rising prices and falling wages were a bonanza for producers of surpluses. Much land was held by great magnates, corporate institutions, the church and the crown. These owners now had an incentive to exploit estates that were under-utilized. Manorial demesne land – that part of the manor that was reserved for the use of the lord – came to be leased at competitive rents. Innovations in agricultural techniques increased yields. Nitrogen-fixing crops helped reduce the period in which land had to lie fallow; flooding meadows in the winter and draining them in the spring allowed for early spring grasses, which meant more animals could survive winter and provide manure for spring planting. Scientific animal breeding and new feed crops like turnips produced hardier stocks at lower costs. Such adaptations came in slowly, and expensive ones like meadow flooding and draining were suitable only to large estates. But they bespoke a new attitude towards agrarian production that could be seen on much smaller estates which now began to orient themselves towards market production, especially in the Thames valley and the ring of counties around London. In Ireland, the development of a land registry, better security of tenure and the conversion to cash rents had a similar effect in stimulating the growth of a market economy. Although Irish economic development was hampered by a lack of capital and by the political upheavals of near-constant warfare, the seventeenth century was characterized by growth and diversification.

The vitality of growing market-places for agricultural surplus meant that local communities were no longer compelled to diversify their output. They could specialize in what best suited their estates and purchase the rest. Specialtiy cropping, especially of luxuries like wheat, whose low yield made it expensive for the farmhouse table, was one result of the new market-oriented agriculture. Land consolidation was another. Dispersed strips that were prized because they spread risk now became detested because they inhibited gain. Hedges and closes began to appear in what were once open fields, and within them individual farmers used their own animals to fertilize their own crops. Enclosures took many forms, from the rational exchange of strips to create unified plots to the forcible eviction of tenants to create unified estates. In the sixteenth and seventeenth centuries there was more of the former, as those families who edged ahead of their neighbours snapped up whatever land came on to the market. Where conventionally the village was composed of a few medium-sized holders and a large number of smallholders, the seventeenth-century village became more polarized. A few owners of comparatively large amounts of land – three or more times the amount necessary for subsistence – dominated a group of small-holders and an even larger number of landless cottagers possessing an acre or two as a garden. This diminution of holdings was especially pronounced in the upland zone, where there were fewer towns to absorb migrants. There the first decades of the seventeenth century brought famine, as the land could not support the level to which population had grown.

The emergence of these large holders into the ranks of the yeomanry further accelerated the transition from subsistence to commercial agri-culture. They derived no benefit from communal ploughing or man-œuvring and eyed their portion of the village common greedily. While smallholders and agrarian labourers continued locked in a struggle for survival with nature, yeoman farmers had the leisure to dominate vil-lage governance and to begin to cut a figure in their county. In one Staffordshire village three-quarters of all constables were drawn from this group. The puzzling fact that there was no equivalent development in early modern Scotland is one of the crucial factors in explaining the differential growth of English and Scottish agriculture.

What was true for the English yeoman was true *a fortiori* for manorial lords. The value of land rose steadily, and rents, though com-plicated by the nature of land tenancies, may have kept pace with agricultural inflation and have risen 500 per cent by 1640. Those who had bought the lands of the dissolved monasteries at bargain rates benefited most. Their returns increased no matter how they managed their estates: they could sell at higher prices, mortgage at greater values, or farm for better profits. The late sixteenth and early seven-teenth century was long remembered as an age of conspicuous con-sumption. Peers built prodigy houses of hundreds of rooms surrounded by sculptured gardens and acres of deer-park for recreation. Ordinary gentlemen replaced their timbered mansions with stone piles erected according to the latest architectural tastes. Mansions sprang up in ex-clusive parts of town to house the county élites, who were more peri-patetic in their horse-drawn coaches. In London, Covent Garden and portions of the West End were laid out as town houses for the gentry, many of whom spent an increasing part of their year in the capital for the social season, the sessions of the law courts or meetings of Parliament. Lords of manors had always been rich, but never before was so much of their wealth liquid. While some of the profits of agriculture were ploughed back into the land, much went to support the 'port and bearing of a gentleman', as the lifestyle of the leisured orders was described.

Great wealth could be made by careful attention to estate management, but greater wealth could be found at court, at the bar or in mercantile ventures. Profits from the land indirectly supported all three. The period was characterized by a rising gentry whose numbers were increasing more quickly than the rest of the population and whose wealth, power and prestige were greatly enhanced. Unlike the peerage, who were defined by rank and whose mobility was dependent upon the monarch, who alone could create titles, the gentry were more amorphous. Their order ran the gamut from knights to minor squires and was dynamic throughout the period. Families of middling fortune in one generation could become county magnates in the next and pass finally into the peerage, as was the case with the Spencers of Althorp. Others of the same stock, through misfortune or miscalculation, could fade into oblivion, as was the case with their Catholic Tresham neighbours. It was the gentry who benefited most from the expansion of the legal profession and court office, as both became the preserve of heirs awaiting their inheritances and younger sons seeking their fortunes. London teemed with the offspring of the landed élite, and in many families it was the son sent into law, office or trade who made the mark. The eldest son of Lord Keeper Nicholas Bacon settled comfortably at Redgrave in Suffolk, while the youngest son, Francis Bacon, turned his legal training into an earldom. Sir Ralph Verney could support only two of three sons from his Buckinghamshire estates. The youngest, John, was sent into trade, where he made the fortune that sustained the family at Claydon for the next 300 years.

Though overseas trade was not yet a significant sector of the economy at the beginning of the seventeenth century, its growth and transformation made Britain one of the great commercial powers of Europe a hundred years later. From the mid sixteenth century England's chief commodity was cloth, which a century later still accounted for over 80 per cent of the goods exported. For Ireland, the export of cattle and their by-products underpinned what little international trade there was. The English cloth trade was controlled by the broadcloth monopoly of the Merchant Adventurers' Company and was centred in London and the Low Countries, where the woven, unfinished cloth was shipped.

The monopoly ensured the profits of those allowed into the trade as well as a steady revenue to the crown in customs and loans. Cloth exports were subject to the normal fluctuations of early modern commerce, but a series of calamities permanently lessened their value. Beginning in the middle of the sixteenth century, near-constant European warfare decreased demand by increasing price. The silting of Antwerp harbour disrupted the Adventurers' conventional trading arrangements, while the Dutch revolt against Spain rendered alternatives perilous. Coincidentally, heavy English broadcloth was falling out of fashion as lighter and cheaper fabrics, known as 'new draperies', were developed. Volume and revenue stagnated throughout the late sixteenth century, recovered briefly thereafter, and then declined precipitously with the outbreak of the Thirty Years War in 1618.

The decline of the traditional English cloth trade encouraged the development of new products and markets. Lighter weaves were exported to Mediterranean ports, and new draperies were soon competing with broadcloth as London's chief export. In Europe, Spain and Portugal were becoming as important outlets for textiles as Holland; outside Europe, new ventures were created to exploit markets in the Atlantic and Indian oceans. Beginning in the 1660s the balance of the English export trade shifted decisively. Textile shipments to Europe were now evenly divided between traditional markets in Holland and Germany and new markets in Spain and the Mediterranean. Moreover, the geographical expansion of markets for English goods coincided with the success of England's burgeoning long-distance trade. By the end of the century, England had replaced Holland as the great entrepôt for transshipping. Salt fish, tobacco and sugar from the Atlantic; calicoes, pepper and spices from the East Indies – all passed through London on their way to European destinations. By 1700, re-exports, which were negligible at the beginning of the seventeenth century, had grown to almost a third of the goods shipped from England, while cloth had fallen to less than a half. Exports from Ireland to England, gauged by customs receipts, increased tenfold in the early seventeenth century as the Irish economy adapted to commercial forms.

England's rise to commercial prominence had more to do with imports than exports. Here three developments were crucial: the creation of new companies organized along new economic principles; the rise of the shipping industry; and the protection offered to English vessels by government regulation.

While exports were dominated by cloth throughout the seventeenth century, the import trade developed in every imaginable direction. Imports catered primarily to the rich, and there was an insatiable demand for luxury goods. In the late sixteenth century, monopoly companies were founded to open trade with the Baltic, Muscovy and Africa. They were funded through the pooling of stock which was at first related to specific expeditions and ultimately came to represent a share in the worth of the company itself. The most important of these joint-stock companies was the East India Company, founded in 1601 to trade in the Far East. From modest beginnings, the East India Company flourished, buying spices, silk and cotton calico prints and selling them at huge profits in London. Originally a group of aggressive young merchants frozen out of the export trade, the directors of the East India Company soon became the London mercantile establishment. Shares of the company were traded on the Royal Exchange, allowing both large and small investors to participate in the boom in imports. This was not limited to the Asian trade. Across the Atlantic, a new cash crop took the English market by storm. Tobacco began as an expensive luxury crop but was soon affordable to everyone. In 1640 only 500 tons were shipped for English consumption from America's eastern seaboard; twenty years later imports had grown to 4,500 tons and by 1700 had reached 11,000 tons. Ireland, too, shared the addiction, importing over 1,500 tons by 1700, when per-capita consumption achieved a level not seen again until the mid nineteenth century.

The rise of a successful long-distance carrying trade necessitated a concomitant growth in English shipping. At the beginning of the seventeenth century the English mercantile fleet was small, antiquated and expensive. It could not compete with the Dutch for the bulk carrying trade, with the Portuguese for the long-distance trade, nor with the French for the Mediterranean trade. Most ships had been built to hold cloth for the easy run to Holland, and while they were manœuvrable and seaworthy, as the Spanish had discovered in 1588, they were hardly the basis of a modern merchant marine. This changed decisively with the outbreak of the Thirty Years War. Alone among the maritime powers, England stayed neutral, and it now paid merchant syndicates to invest in new ships. By 1640 not only had the total tonnage of English ships nearly tripled, the number of large ships had increased tenfold. Though the largest ships were built for the East India Company – the 1,000-ton *Trade's Increase* sank on her maiden voyage –

some of the new merchant ships were located in ports outside London, and after the Restoration the Atlantic trade catapulted Bristol into prominence.

The incentive to build and invest in large trading vessels came with protection. Beginning in the 1650s, a series of Navigation Acts was passed by English parliaments to restrict the use of foreign-owned ships in trade to and from England. The problem could be seen most dramatically in the coal trade, where nearly four times as many foreign as English-owned vessels shipped from Newcastle. The Navigation Act of 1661 enumerated a series of commodities that could be shipped only in English bottoms, and restricted both the North American and the European re-export trade entirely to colonial or English-built ships. Though it took a series of trade wars with the Dutch to make them stick, the Navigation Acts created the conditions for a further boom in English shipbuilding. Tonnage doubled between 1640 and 1700.

Mercantile activity on this scale naturally meant an increase in the number of merchants and an upsurge in their wealth. Directors of the great trading companies were as rich as any peer of the realm, though their fortunes were in capital rather than land. 'An estate's a pond, but a trade's a spring,' Daniel Defoe held. Some few bought their way into the aristocracy when earldoms could be purchased for £10,000; others shipped their daughters to the countryside with the same passion for prestige as they moved pepper for profit. But, increasingly, successful merchants scorned the traditional ethos that valued land, lineage and leisure over money. If it was true that at the end of the sixteenth century the gentry could buy the aristocracy, it was true that at the end of the seventeenth century the professional classes of doctors, lawyers, merchants and financiers could buy the gentry. Their knighthoods came from service rather than genealogy as the locus of power shifted from the arms of the aristocracy to the purses of the professionals, a group that was not fully integrated into the structure of English society.

Viewed analytically, England was hierarchically organized and patriarchally dominated. At its apex was a small élite – less than 3 per cent of the population – who were variously described as *nobilitas*, gentlemen or worthies. Though numerically few, they were finely gradated into ranks, which were divided into orders and redivided into place. Though there were only sixty-one members of the titular nobility in 1600, they were split into the five separate ranks of dukes, earls, marquises, viscounts and barons. Earls would duel over who was to come first in a procession, and purchasers of titles paid extra to have their patents backdated. The questing of the gentry was no different, and country gentlemen were known to refuse to sit on the bench of justices if their name was not placed high enough on the commission of the peace. In 1611 the crown created the hereditary rank of baronet by which knights of sufficient wealth and three generations' standing could distinguish themselves from the parvenus. The knightly orders of the Garter and the Bath expanded to satisfy the same impulse. In 1603 demand was so great that James I created more knights in four months than Elizabeth I had in forty-four years. The distinction became so debased that Charles I was able to raise significant revenue by taxing those of the next generation who refused to accept it. The seventeenth-century variation of the oldest joke in the world had as its punchline 'That was no gentleman, that was a knight.'

The precision of these distinctions was significant, for it created the impression of stability which was otherwise constantly belied. The Tudors had turned the peerage into an aristocracy of service, and for the few who were the fourteenth Earl Arundel or the eleventh Earl of Northumberland there were many more who were the first of their lines. The Stuarts continued the pattern with a vengeance, nearly tripling the size of the titular aristocracy both by selling titles in the second quarter of the seventeenth century and by rewarding office-holders in the later decades. By 1714 over three-quarters of the English peerage had been created by the Stuarts. Recruitment into the peerage was a matter of necessity, for, even with collateral descent to brothers and nephews, male lines on average lasted no longer than three generations. But the composition of the gentry was equally fluid. In seventeenth-century Lancashire, for example, there was approximately the same number of gentry families in 1640 as there had been in 1600: 774. But less than 500 of these were the same families, nearly 300 having lost gentry status and over 200 others having gained it in less than two generations. Over a longer period, more than 80 per cent of the gentry families of Dorset and Lincolnshire in 1640 had not been gentry in those counties in 1500; in Warwickshire the turnover was above 90 per cent. Only the county of Kent, with its large indigenous gentry and its practice of partible inheritance, appears to have been an exception.

Faced with flux, analysts stressed fixity. Theorists further elaborated the medieval cosmological order of the great chain of being which made a place for everything and had everything in its place, from God to inanimate objects. The pews of churches came to be allocated in strict adherence to the social ordering of the village, with the governing families seated in front and the labouring families standing behind. The official genealogies of the royal heralds were supplemented by the assiduous and mainly bogus researches of individual families, who characteristically traced their ancestry to before the Norman Conquest. The gentry began to name their children after their maternal grandfathers, and among the members of the Long Parliament were Symonds D'Ewes, Harbottle Grimston, Framlingham Gaudy and Bulstrode Whitelocke. Identification with the land was particularly strong, and a sentimental attachment began to develop for one's county. Newly created peers chose their titles from their estates, newly risen gentry named their houses after themselves, as did the Eliots of Port Eliot, the Edgcumbes of Mount Edgcumbe and the Godolphins of Godolphin – all Cornish neighbours.

It is hard to determine whether distinctions of status were invidious. They had legal standing not only in the regulation of rights and responsibilities but also in sumptuary legislation that governed what could be worn or consumed by different orders of people. Thus social distinction was constantly on display in dress, demeanour and deportment, and it was continually reinforced by deference which ranged from modes of speech and forms of address to the doffing of caps and ceding the right of way. This was not simply practised across the great divides but was also a way of life among the upper orders. Nowhere was deference more elaborate than at court, where bowing one's head and bending one's knee were forms of salutation and the rules of conduct in the presence of the monarch necessitated that courtiers of the highest rank back out of a chamber with their eyes averted. Nor was deference reserved for relationships in the public sphere. When, in the late seventeenth century, the Duchess of Somerset tapped her husband with a fan to gain his attention he rebuked her by saying, 'Madam, my first duchess was a Percy and she never took such a liberty.'

Below the ranks of the élite, distinctions of status quickly blurred. At one level this was because most commentators were either members of or aspirants to the élite orders. Their modes of classification were generally bipolar: gentle and common; the better and the meaner sort; those who worked with their hands and those who didn't; even, in Gregory King's sophisticated construction of 1688, 'increasing' or 'decreasing the wealth of the kingdom'. Hierarchy created practical and functional distinctions among the élite that did not operate with the same strength among the masses. Nevertheless, we should not conclude that those who lived on the margins of subsistence did not have their own systems of differentiation. Judging from marriage patterns, forms of celebration and testimony in church courts, they too believed that their world was hierarchically ordered. Yeoman and husbandman – who were likely to be addressed as goodman, to use the masculine form – were the cream of village society, clearly distinguished from cottagers and labourers by their wealth and the responsibilities they were given. In the towns, where people lived among a broader cross-section of the social structure, there developed the category of the 'middling sort' – tradesmen, shopkeepers, successful artisans – whose title, like that of the husbandman and goodwife, was often prefixed with the word 'honest'. Nevertheless their status was indistinct and correlated mostly to wealth. The old forty-shilling-freeholder definition of a yeoman had disappeared both with inflation and with the transformation of the landholding system. In its place came the recognition of others.

Commentators categorized the vast majority of the population simply as labourers or the poor. Successive legislative acts distinguished on the basis of character, and divided the masses into the labouring poor, the impotent poor and the idle poor. Agricultural labourers always made an important adjunct to what by landowners could do, especially at harvest time, when gathering crops ahead of the arrival of destructive storms was a constant anxiety. But population increase and the consolidation of large holdings with its concomitant subdivision of small ones meant that a greater part of every rural community became composed of labourers. A large number were servants in husbandry – fulfilling the same role in agriculture that apprentices did in trades – on annual contracts. They were young men and women awaiting their inheritances or their marriages who worked for small wages and board. Others were casual labourers hired seasonally but allowed the use of abandoned sheds for shelter. In the towns, labour also divided between skilled and casual, with the difference that casual labour, especially lifting and carrying, knew no season and was subject to no contract.

Increasing population and urban migration so expanded the labour pool that by the end of the sixteenth century there was a perception that England had a significant problem of poverty. There was, of course, nothing new about poverty. A subsistence agrarian economy could expect to have over a quarter of its population chronically poor and another quarter cyclically poor at some point in its life cycle. Demographic and agricultural change probably pushed these portions to their upper limits. Numbers are hard to come by: in one rural Essex parish in the early seventeenth century two-thirds of the population was either below or at the poverty level; in 1570 Norwich entitled over 2,300 inhabitants to receive poor-relief, a minimum number for the truly destitute in that city. Norwich's scheme for collective charity through a poor rate was intended to prevent public begging. In London, travellers reported hordes of beggars and claimed it was impossible to walk the streets without tripping over them. One observer estimated their number at over 12,000 in the City alone. Even in the 1660s, when population pressure had begun to ease, one-third of all households were exempt from the Hearth Tax on grounds of poverty. Beggars were the most visible sign of poverty within towns, vagabonds the most visible on the roads between them. The great Scottish subsistence crisis of the 1690s may have forced as many as 200,000 people to beg actively. The numbers of those on the tramp in search of work was also increasing in England, and they were travelling long distances by seventeenth-century standards – commonly forty miles or more. Vagabonds had become so numerous by the seventeenth century as to constitute a new class of poor.

The most common descriptive terms for these two categories of the poor were the impotent and the idle – 'God's poor and the Devil's', as one analyst succinctly put it. The impotent poor were those who, by contemporary lights, were deserving of relief. They were poor through no fault of their own – such as the mentally or physically incapacitated, orphans, and widows with small children. The impotent poor were easily recognized in the village community and in the majority of urban areas. Widows normally formed the largest part of the category, for they were not uncommon in early modern society and their misfortune was unpredictable. It was for this group that poor-relief was originally designed – a civic responsibility to replace the institutions of the Catholic church. The idle poor were those who were deemed poor by choice – 'sturdy beggars' or 'masterless men' in contemporary parlance. They were capable of earning their bread but, it was believed, preferred to beg it, or worse.

The so-called 'idle poor' were composed of two very different groups whose existence was often conflated in the hysteria over disorder that gripped English society in this period. The smallest part of the idle poor were 'vagrants' who populated the underworld of crime and vice: brutes and bawds, cut-purses and cat-burglars, muggers and murderers. Scots labelled their behaviour 'sorning', begging with menace. They were masterless in a literal sense. Among these vagrants were others who, while not criminal, were nevertheless tarred with the brush of 'vagrancy' by contemporaries. Abandoned wives and unmarried mothers were among the most common of the wandering poor – the wives searching for their husbands; the unmarried fleeing a life of shame. While some of these women turned to crime – generally prosti-tution – most were just destitute. But the largest component of the so-called 'sturdy beggars' were migrants seeking economic betterment, and it was not until the middle of the seventeenth century that these poor people were accepted for what they were – labourers searching for honest employment rather than fleeing it.

The poor were treated as they were regarded. Elizabethan legislation made both impotent and idle poor the responsibility of the parishes in which they were born: the impotent to be cared for, the idle to be corrected. If either were found outside their native parish they were to be escorted back, usually after some form of corporal punishment which ranged from the shame of the stocks to the pain of the lash. Such regulations were largely ineffective, for, while no parish welcomed the arrival of someone else's poor, neither did it wish the return of its own. Moreover, in the more anonymous urban parishes enforcement placed too great a burden upon officials. Thus national legislation became draconian. The Statute of Artificers in 1563 introduced whipping; an act of 1572 mandated branding and mutilation. The brand – a V, for vagrant – made it possible for authorities to identify recidivists, who were to be dealt with more harshly. Capital punishment was prescribed for those who were convicted a third time, though this solution to vagrancy was rarely invoked. As contemporaries became aware of the problem of structural unemployment, they began to create mandatory workhouses called Bridewells on the model of the London hospital set aside for the poor. Bridewells were a sticking-plaster to a haemorrhage, providing cheap labour for employers and permanent dependency for the small number of poor people who could be admitted to them. Those who couldn't were to be provided with out-relief, a form of sup-plemental income. Overall, this legislation did little to alleviate either the problem of poverty or the plight of the poor, but it did establish the principle of public welfare and it was sufficiently successful that by the end of the seventeenth century the better off were complaining about their taxes and rates in one parish had increased sixty times in two generations. Scottish society dealt with its poor more informally, using voluntary collections rather than compulsory ratings. In Scotland, poor-relief was still regarded as a function of the church rather than the state.

Poverty and vagrancy were thought to be symptomatic of a deterioration of public order that was widely perceived at the beginning of the seventeenth century. Belief that England was overpopulated led to schemes to expand the plantation of Ireland and to increase emigration to North America. Belief that public discipline was breaking down led to increasing prosecution of crime and the expansion of the powers of local justices of the peace to suppress disorder. Whether perception matched reality is difficult to determine. Waves of enforcement had the paradoxical effect of heightening anxiety, which in turn powered new waves of enforcement. In the decades before the Civil War, prosecution of all categories of crime from murder to licensing infractions increased. There were twice as many felony indictments in Cheshire in the 1620s as there had been forty years earlier, and three times as many as there would be forty years later. Juries, which for centuries had nullified the rigours of the law by failing to convict the guilty or by minimizing the gravity of their offences, now exacted a full measure. The county of Devon averaged nearly 25 executions a year in the first decade of the seventeenth century, London 150 a year for the first quarter of the century. Petty crime was prosecuted with as much vigour as felony, and the commissions of the peace in some counties doubled in size to keep pace with the workload. Presentment of victimless crimes like swearing, disorderly conduct, adultery and fornication overwhelmed ecclesiastical and county courts. For a time, the regulation of inns and alehouses became an obsession of local communities, which preferred to identify alcoholism with passing strangers. Indeed, regulatory prosecutions accounted for the bulk of legal business. In a four-year period the Essex sessions handled 3,500 cases, 700 of which were presentments of individuals who failed to attend church.

Crime was an obvious threat to the social order, and authorities were always alert for conspiracies that could lead to riot or revolt. Though there were some worrying moments like the Oxfordshire riots in 1596, when dearth threatened, and the Midland Revolt of 1607, which was sparked by enclosures, threats to the larger political order were inconsequential until the conflagration of the mid-century. But threats to the political order in small – the authority of husbands over wives in the family; the control of the younger generation in town or village – were ever-present. Some of these were matters that ultimately ended in courts, but there were also traditional means of social control designed to maintain the male-dominated gender system and restrict sexual activity to monogamous marriages. Civic leaders saw sexual promiscuity as a threat to the effective functioning of the community on a number of levels: it led to unwed mothers and bastard children, created jealousies and feuds within the village, and gave women independence. They viewed sexual restraint as the lid on all other forms of social discipline: if lifted it would loose a Pandora's box of sin and degradation. The lid strained with so much pushing and pulling, for, with no effective means of birth control and with marriages delayed until the mid-twenties, sexual frustration ran high. It is remarkable how successful English communities were in enforcing female chastity. Though out-of-wedlock births peaked in the first decade of the seventeenth century, they were still only 3 per cent of the total. Moreover, a portion of these were the result of prenuptial relations rather than promiscuity, for it was not uncommon for intercourse to follow betrothal and not unknown for false promise or bad luck to prevent the wedding.

One element in this success, of course, was supervision. In nucleated villages people lived cheek by jowl, with little or no privacy during their entire lives. Given the interdependency necessary for survival, they were brought up to mind each other's business. Dwellings were commonly a single room, beds were shared, and even those who had separate chambers usually had neither passageways nor doors to close them off. In wood/pasture communities, distance achieved the same result as propinquity. Scattered homesteads limited contact between adolescents to Sunday services and chaperoned events. Equally important were the moral and cultural strictures that valued honesty and reputation – code-words for the chastity of maids and the fidelity of wives. The community practised a variety of shaming rituals to enforce these norms. Alleged whores might be set in carts and paraded through the parish; horns might be placed outside the homes of adulterers. Riding rituals were usually designed to shame the husband of an unfaithful wife, on the principle that it had been his duty to exercise control. Some of these utilized straw figures or neighbours to make the point; others might force the actual individuals concerned to ride facing the animal's tail while jeering crowds playing rough music accompanied the perambulation. These occasions, known as skimmingtons in the west of England, usually resulted from the belief that the wife had beaten her husband – an inversion of the social order even more dangerous than adultery. Conversely, those who made false accusations also suffered, and this further reinforced the importance of reputation. Scolds, as these women were called, were placed in mechanical ducking-stools and publicly dunked in pools or ponds for their slanders.

Shaming rituals were traditional means by which communities exercised social control outside the judicial system, but they were particularly successful in the early seventeenth century because they combined elements of festive culture with the emergence of a moral and religious austerity that came to be called Puritanism. Puritanism was much more than a social movement. It derived from a multiplicity of impulses and satisfied a variety of needs, and must be viewed in the first instance as an expression of religious fundamentalism. Its doctrine was a logical outgrowth of advanced Protestant dogma, its liturgy a coherent interpretation of Calvinism. Thus it would be reductionist to identify the origins of Puritanism with the dramatic upsurge of population and the obsession with disorder that it generated. But it would also be myopic to dismiss the timing as coincidental. As a lay movement, Puritanism reached its height in the two generations preceding the Civil War, when concerns about social dislocation and moral collapse also peaked. Moreover, as a lay movement, the strongest Puritan impulses were towards a reformation of manners, which for some took the form of severe self-abnegation and for others the form of repressive authoritarianism. Though Puritanism appealed to men and women of every walk of life, it flourished in towns especially among the 'industrious sort' – those who had succeeded by effort which they attributed to grace.

Puritans separated themselves into communities of the godly which practised a strict moral discipline. Their beliefs divided humanity into the few who were predestined to be the elect of God and the many who were predestined to be damned for all eternity. They also rent the community of the parish and engaged in a struggle for control of local religion. Though none could know the mind of God, those who were his saints – as Puritans described the elect – might well be distinguished by their blameless conduct, strict moral code and exacting self-discipline. Though most Puritans shared a basic ecclesiology, Puritanism was more a lifestyle than it was a theology; indeed it was a catch-all category that encompassed a wide range of doctrinal positions, many of them incompatible with each other. Puritans could be identified by what they were even more than by what they believed, and critics parodied them mercilessly for their speech, dress and demeanour. Ben Jonson's Zeal-of-the-Land Busy in *Bartholomew Fair* was the ideal stereotype, instantly recognizable by his pomposity and self-righteousness, his doomsday prognostications and his self-appointed officiousness. Small wonder that Puritans were reviled and much of their conduct proscribed. As explicit critics of corrupt worship and public immorality, they were implicit critics of church and state.

Yet, wherever they came into positions of authority, Puritans infused their communities with discipline and enforced orderliness on their neighbours. Godly magistrates had a greater responsibility for the enforcement of biblical injunctions than of purely civic regulations, and Puritan preachers thundered against blasphemy, adultery and Sabbath-breaking, while Puritan justices prosecuted crimes against persons and property and enforced compulsory church attendance with an Old Testament rigour. The increasing activity of local sessions was as much a result of these attitudes as of the 'stacks of statutes' passed in Parliament. In those towns which Puritans came to dominate, they quickly manifested the new attitudes by putting the poor to work, enforcing corporate regulations, and repairing churches and charitable institutions. In Dorchester, for example, the magistrates erected a new hospital to house the children of the poor, set them at work and instruct them in true religion. The programme of poor-relief was financed by doubling the parish rate and using funds collected in one parish to alleviate burdens in another. The town's Puritan minister, John White, was a whirlwind of activity, conducting services, lecturing, and overseeing the hospital, Bridewell and free school. His successes could be measured in increasing church attendance and decreasing premarital sexual activity. His failures could be measured by the divisiveness his activities engendered. Zealous constables and beadles waged an unrelenting war with the town's miscreant population, somewhat swelled by a successful brewery from whose profits the reformers paid for their ambitious programmes.

Puritan attitudes were not restricted to reforming clerics and godly magistrates: they were absorbed into the codes of the élites in quite unexpected ways. Some elements of Puritanism might be thought egalitarian, especially those which stressed the equality of all believers and which blurred the lines between cleric and layman. The one could be seen as an attack upon the hierarchical social order, the other as an assault upon the episcopacy. But Puritanism was also élitist, and its stress upon election reinforced many of the values that humanist writers had been inculcating among the educated classes for generations. The ideal of the well-ordered household – essential when it became as large as did many gentlemen's estates – now acquired a patina of devotion as well. Conduct books that stressed piety within the context of the daily lives of men of estate and affairs were published in profusion for the edification of the landed élites. Evidence from surviving libraries shows that they were bought and read, and wills often list them as prize possessions specifically bequeathed where it was thought they would do the most good. Indeed, it was the gentry who allowed Puritanism to grow, appointing ministers to the many livings that had fallen into lay hands since the Reformation, sponsoring lectureships and itinerant preaching, protecting those who fell foul of ecclesiastical authorities. Similarly, in the largest towns Puritanism flourished among the wealthy. London's merchant community had a large share of Presbyterians, and especially among the self-made there was a tendency to reckon the Lord's blessings in the counting-house as well as the pew. For gentlemen and merchants alike the Puritan programme of social control, shorn of some of its zealousness and inflexibility, complemented their own needs as governors, magistrates, businessmen and landowners. It befitted a society that was undergoing profound social and economic change – change that its political institutions could absorb only slowly and fitfully.

2

The Political World

Seventeenth-century Britain was a kingdom, the dominion of a monarch. Dominion was a potent word, for its root, *dominus*, denoted lordship in heaven as on earth. In theory, the king of England, Scotland and Ireland held absolute power over the lives and property of his subjects, in the first cases by hereditary descent, in the case of Ireland by conquest. '[Kings] make and unmake their subjects; they have power of raising, and casting down; of life, and of death.' The king or queen could levy taxes, pardon criminals, declare war or settle peace. He or she licensed all manufacture, regulated all markets, governed all trade. The king could open his ports to immigrants or close them to émigrés. He could naturalize aliens or legitimize bastards. He alone created or dissolved corporations. All charters, including Magna Carta, were royal grants of *privileges* – that is, private laws given from the king's absolute rights. The sovereign's word was law, promulgated as statute with the advice of his parliament or as proclamation with the advice of his council. He could choose his counsellors at will, command them to serve him, and ignore their recommendations with impunity. His power to summon and dissolve parliaments was unquestioned, as was his freedom to accept or reject the bills that passed the Houses. He created all bishops, all judges, all peers, because the monarch was the apex of church, law and aristocracy.

The monarch was addressed as Majesty or Highness, to signify his position atop the political hierarchy. All bowed before the king, but the king bowed only before God – most notably in the coronation ceremony, when he received the crown. He was called 'liege lord' or 'dread sovereign' by his greatest subjects, to express their vassalage and his awe-inspiring authority. Monarchs were likened to God – 'even by God himself they are called gods', as James I averred – equated with the sun and designated the fount of wisdom and justice. Each image represented an incontestable universal good, leaving competitors to be identified with the devil, darkness and drought. The most common metaphorical associations of the monarchy were with fathers of families and with the head of the body. As father, the king was the guardian of his subjects, a natural ruler and instinctual protector. As head of the body politic, the king directed all of the other parts to provide nourishment and safety. These homologies reinforced hierarchy and interdependence while demonstrating how monarchy emulated the natural order. 'The prince's command is like a thunderbolt; his command upon our allegiance is like the roaring of a lion.' None of this was lip-service.

The formal theory of royal power in Britain stressed the divine right of kings. It had no less an authority than King James, the first of the Stuart dynasty, who as James VI of Scotland wrote a conventional defence of kingship in *The True Law of Free Monarchies* (1598). In it James demonstrated that monarchy derived its authority directly from God – 'it is the true pattern of divinity' – and that its practice was strengthened because it was congruent with the laws of nature and the customs of the realm. James cited the oft-repeated verses from the Book of Samuel where the Lord told the Israelites that a monarch had the right to turn their property and their children to his own uses. He lectured his subjects that, as he ruled as God's regent, only God could judge him. This was, of course, a potent sanction, for, as James realized, 'the highest places are often the sliddriest'. The divine right of kings was also supported by the biblical account of Creation. This was classically elaborated by Sir Robert Filmer, who wrote *Patriarcha* in the 1620s, though it was not published until 1680, after his death. Like James, Filmer simply codified commonly held views about the origins of kingship, in this case by analogizing them to the powers granted Adam to rule his family. God made Adam an absolute ruler and gave him dominion over the fruits of the earth, command over his wife, and the power of life and death over his helpless infants. All government was thus patriarchal – the rule of the father over his family, over his tribe or over his nation.

These patriarchal explanations, particularly of the origins and nature of kingship, were rarely questioned in Britain at the beginning of the seventeenth century. Royal authority was too commonly on display, royal power too firmly embedded in the ordinary activities of government to require much speculation about origins and first principles. The royal arms were everywhere, the king's head was stamped on every newly minted coin. 'God save the King' served for greetings and partings and was prayed in every church on every Sunday. Law ran in the king's writ, justice in the king's name. Every transfer of property, every testamentary bequest took place in royal courts. Every patent began in the king's name 'by the Grace of God'.

But what was illimitable in theory was restricted in practice. At his coronation, the monarch swore 'to confirm to the people of England the laws and customs to them granted', reasserting all of the privileges yielded by his predecessors. These considerably limited the king's ability to suspend the operation of law, to tax without consent, or to imprison without cause. Over the centuries, through the operation of common law and the accretion of statute, the English monarchy had developed a 'settled course' that was sometimes described as 'mixed monarchy', to distinguish it from Continental forms of absolutism that were labelled tyranny. Even critics of crown policy defended their positions by exalting the nature of the British monarchy.

Alongside these conventional ideas about the divine origins of monarchy were others which, though neither contradictory nor incompatible, derived from different explanations. They imagined that monarchy was a contract between ruler and ruled. Contractual theories were associated with creation myths that began in a state of nature which preceded government. Different theorists hypothesized it in different ways. One account – that of Thomas Hobbes – described the state of nature as 'a war of every man with every man' in which life was 'mean, nasty, brutish, and short'. In order to escape this chaos, people surrendered all their power to a sovereign in exchange for protection of their lives and the safeguarding of their property. The sovereign held absolute power – that is, the accumulation of all the power his subjects had surrendered. In another contractual theory, associated with John Locke, the state of nature was pictured as a little Eden. Groups of people came together voluntarily to form societies of mutual benefit. They entrusted limited power to a sovereign who ruled on their behalf, serving their larger needs and acting as representative of their individual interests. Thus in Hobbes's view government was formed out of necessity, in Locke's it was formed out of convenience.

Both opinions were current before these great thinkers erected systematic theories of government around them, and they led to a variety of conclusions, for it was not the contract but the conditions under which it was made that mattered. Contractual thinkers like Hobbes concluded that monarchical power was absolute, while contractual thinkers like Locke concluded that it was conditional. But even this was not the contrast that it seemed. Since it was commonplace to believe that contracts were religious obligations – that is, covenants sworn before God – all contracts necessarily rested upon divine right. As it was also commonplace to believe that the ruler was restricted by God's commandment to govern for the benefit of his people, all divine right rested upon conditions. Therefore later ideas which could be segregated in theory around concepts such as absolutism and constitutionalism were intertwined in practice and there was a vast middle ground of common assumption and belief. If *The True Law of Free Monarchies* was the classic statement of divine-right absolutism, it was an equally classic statement of contractualism, as its subtitle indicated: 'Or the Reciprocal and Mutual Duty Betwixt a Free King and his Natural Subjects'.

Constitutionalist thinking about the nature of English government rested upon the common law. This was an ineffable amalgam of custom and precedent – what the Romans might have called the *mors maiorum*: the ways of our ancestors. By the seventeenth century common-law thought had been highly developed and revolved around two important, if variant, principles. First it was held that the common law was a reflection of natural law and therefore inherently equitable. According to Sir Edward Coke, the greatest of the common lawyers, this made common law the superior form of law in England and its courts the highest judicature. Secondly, Coke argued that an understanding of the common law was an artificial process of reasoning acquired through training and study and was therefore the preserve of the common lawyers. The common law was not simply the practice of equity as any reasonable person could understand it, nor the compiling of precedents as any experienced person might remember them. On more than one occasion these principles seemed reducible to the position that the common law was what Sir Edward Coke said it was, but behind them was the belief that the common law was a living law that metamorphosed over centuries. The English constitution was not just unwritten: it could not be reduced to writing.

Thus the constitutionalist position was that monarchical power was limited by the evolution of its practice. However divine its origins and God-like its authority, successive monarchs had granted privileges and yielded to principles that established a balance between the prerogatives of princes and the liberties of subjects. Those privileges had been confirmed in charters, elucidated in statutes, and established by custom. What they were, and what they meant, like the common law itself, was not always easy to determine. But that they existed was indisputable and undisputed. When a group of parliamentarians dominated by common lawyers thought to instruct James I on the traditions of the English monarchy they pointed to conditions in Europe, where it could truly be said 'the prerogatives of princes do daily grow, the liberties of the subject are at an everlasting stand'. In England, even after the rule of the most stable and powerful dynasty in centuries, Elizabeth Tudor might easily have argued the opposite.

James I was prescient when he said 'it were dangerous to submit the power of a king to definition'. Difficulties over interpreting the prerogatives of princes and the liberties of subjects always came at the extremes: in all-or-nothing debates that were rarely applicable to practical problems. Pushed to limits, absolutists could only argue that the king could do no wrong and in the last resort his power was limited by God alone. Shoved to the wall, constitutionalists could only argue that the subject had an absolute right to his life and property that was protected by the common law. When push came to shove, these extreme positions emerged in a debate over obedience and resistance. It was, of course, in the interest of kings to argue that subjects owed them absolute obedience, and such strictures were the common stuff of sermons, biblical exegeses and everyday political discourse. An official homily on obedience was read in every parish church, and it left little to the imagination. 'Let us mark well and remember that the high power and authority of kings are the ordinances not of man, but of God. We may not resist, nor in any wise hurt, an anointed king.' Treason was a capital crime, and was broadly construed to encompass intentions, words and deeds. Since the mid sixteenth century, each successive Treason Act added new offences, and executions were public events *pour encourager les autres*. The contention that kings could be judged only by God was intended to refute any arguments that suggested that there were circumstances in which they could be judged by subjects.

Such arguments had been developing throughout the sixteenth century as a result of the Protestant Reformation. Reformers believed that defence of true religion conformed to a higher law than that promulgated by kings. If the biblical injunction 'Render unto Caesar the things which are Caesar's' governed obedience in civic matters, its corollary, 'and unto God the things that are God's', governed in spiritual matters. Thus developed the theory that it was the duty of lesser magistrates – those who also derived their authority from God – to resist the destruction of true churches. This logic backed both the Dutch revolt against Spain and the Huguenot rising against the kings of France. Ultimately the same argument was espoused by Catholic theorists to preach rebellion against Protestant princes. In the Jesuit version of what was becoming a formal theory of resistance, individuals were empowered to oppose the imposition of heresy. As redactions of resistance theory increased – some of the most potent were those of the Scottish Presbyterians against whom James VI wrote – the restrictions upon individual action diminished. By the beginning of the seventeenth century some resistance theorists held that the tyranny that could be opposed was not limited to matters of conscience nor the opposers to lesser magistrates. These ideas ultimately developed into a full-blown theory of parliamentary sovereignty in the 1640s. Principles such as *singulas major, universalis minor* – 'greater than any but less than all': the assertion that, while the king was the most powerful individual, his power was less than that of the community as a whole – were grafted on to a doctrine of coordination which claimed that the king must govern with his parliament and that the power of any two of the three elements of king, Lords and Commons was superior to the remaining element. These doctrines allowed Parliament to fight a civil war against the king while claiming that it was not fighting against the monarchy. But these doctrines were unstable and ultimately resulted in the abolition of the monarchy and the creation of a commonwealth. When the monarchy was restored after 1660 it became treason to publish these principles.

Even the most limited interpretation of royal power, however, assumed that seventeenth-century government was the king's government. The different personalities and circumstances of the ruler defined each reign. James I and Charles II were inattentive to business; Charles I and James II were absorbed by it. James I avoided foreign entanglements; William III and Queen Anne embraced them. These were personal inclinations that defined the terms of government while they ruled. So were the ways in which they made use of their favourites in managing affairs of state. Governmental leaders neither emerged through a political process nor rose to power through the possession of particular offices. James I's favourite was Lord Chamberlain, Charles

I's Lord Admiral, Charles II's Lord Chancellor, and Anne's Lord Treasurer. James I advanced Scots, William III Dutchmen. Charles I elevated his Archbishop of Canterbury to the highest powers; James II tossed his into prison. After 1689 there was always a pretender to the British crowns, which forced William and Mary and Queen Anne occasionally to look over their shoulders. *Le Roy le veult* – 'It is the will of the king' – the phrase by which statutes became law, pertained to all government.

There were of course institutions that provided stability from monarch to monarch as well as administrators who carried out day-to-day business. None was more important than the Church of England, of which the king was the supreme governor. The English church was episcopal in structure, with archbishops for the two dioceses of York and Canterbury and twenty-six bishoprics in England and Wales. James I restored bishops to the Scottish church and expanded their number in the Church of Ireland, the minority Protestant church. The appointment of bishops and thus the control of the leading personnel of the church was entirely in the hands of the monarch. Though, as the century progressed, bishops were chosen more for their administrative capacities than for their piety – no one in the late century rivalled the eloquence of Lancelot Andrewes – there were always a number of outstanding divines in the English church.

Bishops were responsible for the oversight of their dioceses, and most conducted regular visitations to inspect the physical state of their parishes and correct the spiritual state of their parishioners. The bishops oversaw a parish clergy that numbered about 8,600 in the seventeenth century. Like the bishops, many were royal appointees, for the crown was the largest ecclesiastical patron, owning perhaps a third of the advowsons – the right to appoint clergymen to livings – in England and Wales. At the beginning of the seventeenth century there was an upsurge in the quality of ministers as the universities produced more graduates than there were vacant livings and an intense devotionalism swept the land. Ministers were in the forefront of the movement for a 'Puritan' reformation, just as bishops were for an 'Arminian' one. The upheavals of the mid-century, when over a quarter of ministers were deprived of their livings, and then of the Restoration period, when another 10 per cent were discharged, should not be exaggerated, for the established church maintained its role in local communities despite these dislocations. But a steady erosion in the income of parish clergy had a lasting impact upon the profession of clergyman, which declined in both popularity and status by the end of the Stuart era.

The church was ever-present in the life of the nation, the key local institution. The parish was the primary unit of self-identification – far stronger than town or county – and, not surprisingly, religious controversy both generated and replicated divisions within communities. It was the task of the crown to establish doctrine and liturgy and to enforce its acceptance. In the early seventeenth century it was believed that church and nation were coterminous, and the principal dynamic of religious dispute was reformation. Catholics were officially proscribed (though not eradicated), and Protestants who dissented from established practice were persecuted. After 1660, the prinvcipal dynamic of religious dispute was toleration, as a number of unsuccessful efforts were made to relax the penalties against Catholics and Protestant dissenters. These efforts mostly followed the private desires of individual monarchs, with both Charles II and James II striving for leniency towards Catholics and William III attempting to alleviate the disabilities against Protestants.

But in the seventeenth century government was not yet divided between the private life of the king and the public life of the monarchy. Nowhere was the blending of these two elements more apparent than at court. Though the court was the locus of power in the Stuart monarchy, it had no formal political function. At the beginning of the seventeenth century it combined the king's domestic life and his political life, and not until the end of the century did the court signify the royal household alone. The court was composed of all those who attended the monarch, either by duty or by design. Most were office-holders – thousands of officials and servants who served the monarchy, from the Master of Wards to the Mistress of Wardrobe. Others came in search of favour – 'cutting a figure' as it was called – hoping to become one of the fortunate few from the importunate many. The court was the centre for the ceremonial aspects of kingship, the place where the king was on display, and it therefore developed rituals so elaborate that publishers found profit in printing guidebooks to court etiquette. In earlier times, peers and greater gentry had been required to pay court to the monarch, but by the seventeenth century it was all kings could do to keep them away. Orders that gentlemen depart London were continually renewed to no effect, and the court grew exponentially during the reigns of the Stuarts – in tandem with the fortunes to be made out of royal service.

In response, monarchs found it necessary to order the court so as to separate their personal lives from their civic responsibilities. James I did this by creating a separate administration for his bedchamber, which he staffed almost entirely with Scots. Charles I went further, strictly dividing the Privy Chamber from the public rooms in the Palace of Westminster. Entry to the Chamber was restricted to a small group of officials who acted as conduits even to important officers of state. At court, the politics of access was vitally significant and changed from monarch to monarch. As James I used his Scots, Charles II used his mistresses, and Anne her maids of honour. Nevertheless, that part of the court that comprised the royal household numbered over 1,000 in the reign of Charles I and grew by 30 per cent after the Restoration, before being scaled back by Queen Anne.

On its public side, the court contained the great officers of state and the Privy Council. It is this that is commonly referred to as royal government and analysed in terms of institutional and bureaucratic development. Yet, like the private side of the court, of which it was a logical extension, this public, governmental, side was very much a product of the character of the monarch. It is still premature to speak of departments of state in referring to the institutional divisions of the king's government, and it is impossible to produce a flow chart of organizational power. As the public activities of the king involved collecting and disbursing revenue, dispensing justice and regulating social and economic activity, his officers served these functions. But they did not develop along functional lines so that one set of institutions was a treasury, another law courts, and a third a police force. Rather they evolved as separate jurisdictions each containing its own treasury, law courts and enforcement personnel. The fortunes of these offices waxed and waned, though it was generally agreed that by the seventeenth century the three most important were the Lord Treasurer, the Lord Chancellor and the Secretary.

Given the Stuarts' financial problems, the Lord Treasurer, who presided over the Exchequer, was becoming the key royal official. The Exchequer gradually gained control over the audit of revenue, though separate courts like the Court of Wards and separate receivers like the Privy Purse remained independent. The Treasurer was the king's principal adviser on financial matters, an office of great frustration throughout most of the century, but a position of power. Even so, the Treasurer was far from indispensable, and the office was left vacant after Salisbury's death in 1612 and the Exchequer was run by a committee for a time under Charles II.

The Lord Chancellor was gradually becoming the most important legal officer in the realm through his control of the great seal, his role as Speaker of the House of Lords, and his position as judge in Chancery. Once the preserve of churchmen, the Chancellorship was now the property of the common lawyers. It was the position from which the Earl of Clarendon directed the restoration of Charles II and the Earl of Nottingham built the Tory party after 1690.

The office of Secretary of State was also gaining power in the seventeenth century, as the volume of business which passed through the Secretaries' hands increased. The Secretary was in constant attendance upon the king, controlled the signet, and was thus responsible for all royal correspondence and Privy Council administration. During the course of the seventeenth century the office was formally divided into northern and southern departments – the first to handle affairs in the north of Europe, the second to deal with the Mediterranean nations – and the number of clerks and under-officers increased correspondingly.

The Treasurer, Chancellor and Secretaries were by no means the only senior officers of state, but they were the most important public officials who sat on the Privy Council and advised the king. From a small body of a dozen officers under Queen Elizabeth, the Privy Council grew steadily under the Stuarts to over thirty in the reign of James I, forty in the reign of Charles I, and more than sixty in the reign of Charles II. After that it became so unwieldy that a smaller cabinet council developed to handle the most important matters of state and to manage Parliament. Like the court, the Privy Council had few formal functions. It sat as the Court of Star Chamber to hear special cases; it exercised vast, if unspecified, administrative authority; and it discussed foreign policy. There seems to have been little structure to the Council's activity. Charles I created specialized committees of the Council; during the Interregnum there were committees of trade, which Charles II expanded and which ultimately gave way to the boards of the late seventeenth century. But these did little to discipline the Privy Council's work, which remained a jumble of the momentous and the inconsequential.

The king's principal officers and his special advisers comprised the Council. Among the officers who routinely sat in Council and might be considered *ex officio* members, half were from the household side of government, half from the public side. The Archbishop of Canterbury represented the church, and the Lord Lieutenant of Ireland government in Dublin. The peerage dominated the Privy Council, which reflected its control of court office as well as the way in which the political sphere coincided with the social hierarchy. It is difficult to generalize about the independence of the Council as a body or of privy counsellors as individuals. Court office confirmed prestige, conferred honour, and made one either rich or richer. Such considerations must have damped down free spirits and encouraged conformity. Yet the same factional infighting that dominated the court and the House of Lords was present in the Council, and alternative policies were fully aired in Council debates.

The king's servants numbered in the thousands even before the Restoration, when revenue departments like the Customs and Excise expanded. As there were no formal requirements for office, places were filled by patrimony, patronage or purchase. Patrimonial succession was a powerful ideology, and it could be seen at work in office-holding. The son of Elizabeth's chief minister, Lord Burghley, became James I's chief minister, the Earl of Salisbury. Successive Dukes of Buckingham were Masters of the Horse; successive Dukes of Ormond were Lord Lieutenants of Ireland. These, however, were exceptions, as the British bureaucracy was more open than its Continental counterparts. Family ties also commonly bound patronage, as more remote relations became clients of their successful kinsmen. The first Duke of Buckingham found employment for his siblings, in-laws, nieces, nephews and cousins in a grand efflorescence of nepotism. But even on a smaller scale patronage was an important means of sponsored mobility through which many able officials were recruited. In Queen Anne's reign close to half of all household officials had a relative in service. Finally, offices could increasingly be purchased outright and, as property, were difficult either to abolish or to reform. Even the greatest offices of state were for sale: the first Earl of Manchester paid £15,000 to be made Lord Chief Justice and later paid £20,000 to be made Lord Treasurer. Both were thought bargains, for the fees and perquisites attached to such places made many a seventeenth-century fortune.

Whether the purchase of places and the profits to be made from them corrupted Stuart government is an open question. Official salaries were nominal, so users bore the real costs of office through fees and gifts. Contemporaries complained ceaselessly of the high costs of lawsuits and suspected that cases were drawn out to increase the incomes of clerks and judges, but there were few allegations of bribery. The crown generally chose its public officials from the wealthiest families in the kingdom, which on the whole made them less susceptible to small-scale temptation. Those who handled finance had a bad reputation, and James I's treasurers Dorset – whose family name, Sackville, was pronounced 'Sack fill' by pundits – and Suffolk were shameless. Shady deals were more common than peculation, as those at the centre of power could use their influence to gain profitable contracts or to bully their way on to syndicates. But what the king gave with one hand he often took with the other. Court officers had to maintain their establishments out of allowances commonly in arrears and not infrequently defaulted upon. Ambassadors paid the cost of their embassies; those whose homes fell in the path of royal progresses hosted the king and his entourage. The king tapped great officers of state for large loans of uncertain duration. For all the royal favour that was showered upon the first Duke of Buckingham, he died nearly bankrupt from financing military expeditions that he was chosen to lead.

Not all royal government was located at Westminster. There were entirely separate administrations for Scotland and Ireland. Government of Scotland was complicated by the wholehearted manner in which the Stuarts abandoned their lifelong habitat for their newly acquired one. It is an understatement to observe that James VI fled south: he cast but one backward glance – a four-month visit in 1617 – and his son, Charles I, was nearly eight years on the English throne before he found time for a Scottish coronation. Both early and later Stuarts were willing to let Scotland govern itself, not even bothering to place English confidants on the royal council, the episcopal bench or the courts of law. Powerful Scottish noblemen, whether service peers like the Maitlands or landed ones like the Argylls, were the true governors during the seventeenth century. The Scottish Estates – the equivalent of a parliament – the distinctive legal system based on Roman Law and the Scottish privy council were all allowed to operate without overt interference from Westminster. Only the church was a matter of conflict, and that brief – though tragic.

Once James VI & I failed to achieve the incorporative union of England and Scotland he desired, he encouraged a process of integration designed to Anglicize Scottish nobles by providing them with English lands, wives and offices the better to dazzle the less fortunate or the more insular who remained at home. However, he could establish

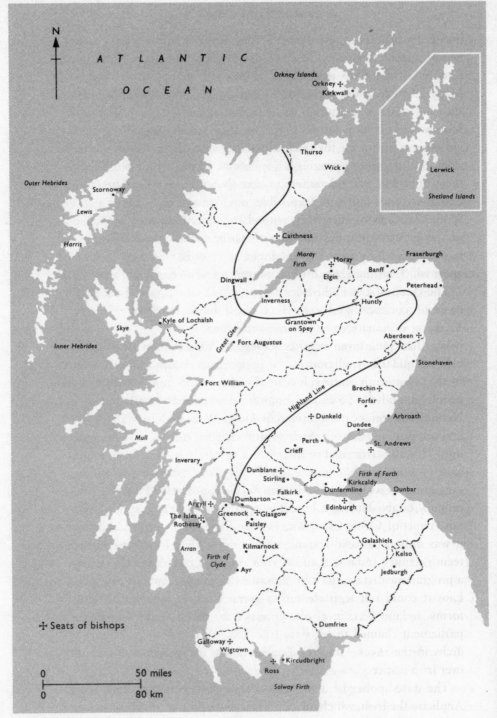

Scotland: Principal Towns in the Seventeenth Century

no similar process in reverse: no English nobleman married a Scottish heiress or took possession of a Scottish estate. Moreover, even the most favoured of the Scots in England maintained their Scottish identities. Many English brides were second wives, and much English wealth slithered north to maintain ancient Scottish estates. The Anglicized Scots were known as 'amphibians' for their ability to live in both environments, if not for the thick skins necessary to repel abuse on both sides. As the century progressed, it became more difficult for kings or their ministers to understand or manipulate Scottish affairs. Only Cromwell and James II were able briefly to impose their will on Scotland, achieving their aims with characteristic brutality. At the end of the century the minister Robert Harley opined that he 'knew no more of Scotch business than of Japan'. Paradoxically, it was this drift apart which ultimately led to the incorporative union of 1707.

The claim of the English king to the Irish crown was made on the basis of conquest and an act of the English parliament in 1541. Mythical explanations of a time when Brutus ruled a united archipelago had long given way to distinctive developments of language, culture and latterly religion. If it is premature to speak of an Irish state by the seventeenth century, it is wholly appropriate to speak of an Irish people, as did the Scots and English who wished to rule over them. Neither Tudor nor Stuart monarchs sought confirmation of their rights and responsibilities from the Irish or their delegates. Indeed, it was not until James II attempted to use Ireland as a launching pad for an invasion of England that one of these monarchs actually set foot in a kingdom over which they laid claim to rule. Thus Ireland was ruled by a military establishment, a Lord Lieutenant or Viceroy, and the prerogative court of Castle Chamber. Though there was an Irish parliament, it was only occasionally summoned – three times in the early seventeenth century and not at all between 1666 and 1689 – and then to pass a programme dictated to it by Westminster. In conformity to Poynings' Law, it could not legislate on its own. Whatever the constitutional forms, Ireland was, in effect, governed by martial law. The English parliament claimed to legislate Irish law – abolishing the Irish monarchy in the 1650s – and the English courts claimed final jurisdiction over Irish justice.

The stated policy of a succession of English administrators was to Anglicize the Irish, which meant to introduce English forms of law and commerce, and the Protestant religion. The benign form of this policy was to attempt to convert Gaelic chieftains into English lords; the malignant was to appropriate their estates on trumped-up charges and flimsy excuses. In return, Gaelic and Catholic 'old English' leaders participated in an uninterrupted series of revolts against the imposition of English authority. Though bloody and costly, most were resolved in England's favour. Throughout the sixteenth century, the grip of Tudor monarchs over Ireland tightened, until only Ulster remained entirely in Irish hands. The plantation of Ulster with Scots and English settlers was to be the major objective of early Stuart and Cromwellian policy in Ireland. It was a policy that could be enforced only by military might and achieved only by nearly two decades of warfare. But it was achieved, and by 1660 most of Ireland's land was owned by 'new English' settlers who had arrived in the previous half-century, though most of it was worked by a Catholic peasantry living in near-feudal conditions. Charles II allowed the Duke of Ormond – an amphibian of a different kind: born Catholic in Ireland, raised Protestant in England, champion of the royalist cause among both 'old' and 'new English' – to govern Ireland by his own lights, and he was vastly more successful than had been the Earl of Strafford, who had been given free rein by Charles I. James II attempted to restore both power and property to the dispossessed Catholic majority – a policy which ultimately failed on the battlefield. After 1689 Catholic Ireland was ruled by the ascendancy, Protestant Anglo-Irish families with a total monopoly on political power.

The complexities of governing three kingdoms – as well as colonies in America – were real, but hardly unmanageable. Throughout the sixteenth century, England had demonstrated that it could enforce its will upon its neighbours, occupying Ireland and neutralizing Scotland. It had also demonstrated, through the incorporation of Wales, that it was flexible enough to contain more than one culture within its polity. There was nothing inherently destabilizing about one king ruling three kingdoms. Moreover, unlike the Habsburgs' possessions in Europe, the Stuart kingdoms were surrounded by nothing more inhospitable than water. Foreign troops could not constantly probe weakly defended borders or easily capture strategic strongholds. French incursions into Scotland and even the recent Spanish landing in Ireland were diplomatic rather than military manœuvres. An invasion force considerable enough to conquer England might just as easily land in England itself, as William III was to demonstrate. The behaviour of the Stuart monarchs suggests that they saw their multiple kingdoms as a matter of prestige rather than of power. Little attempt was ever made to extract revenues from the periphery to the centre, even in times of acute fiscal distress. The principle that Ireland and Scotland, and the American colonies afterwards, should pay the cost of their own administration can only be described as minimalist, and government in Ireland and Scotland followed a pattern of benign neglect punctuated by periods of malignant attention.

In one regard only did the different natures of the three Stuart kingdoms pose intractable difficulties, and that was in religion. Each society contained the same multiplicity of beliefs, but each was differently proportioned. Dispossessed or not, the mass of Irish people were Roman Catholic, the flood of Scottish settlers after 1611 were Presbyterian, and the adherents to the established English episcopal church were a distinct minority. In Scotland, the official church was rigorously Presbyterian – opposed to an episcopal hierarchy, giving more power to laymen in ecclesiastical governance, and worshipping austerely. Catholicism survived in the Highlands and among certain noble families, but support for episcopacy, though on the upswing, was exiguous. In England, the established episcopal church dominated, but there were pockets of Roman Catholicism and a tiny, though vocal, coterie of radical Protestants who wished their church closer to Scottish than English practice. Attempts by members of the differing groups to alter these balances inevitably created crisis. In Ireland, the callow 'new English' confiscated land to nourish an episcopal church that had neither roots nor branches. They lorded over the Catholic 'old English', depriving them of political power, social prestige and access to justice on the basis of their religion alone. In Scotland, the struggle between kirk-type and cathedral-type Protestants gouged deep scars in late-seventeenth-century society. In England, the efforts of Puritans to reform the episcopal church in the early seventeenth century and of Catholics to coexist alongside it after 1660 were both responsible for political upheaval. Efforts by the crown to achieve even a modicum of conformity, either by tolerance or by intolerance, fared no better. No religious policy could possibly satisfy these competing interests, and complaints were just as loud when the crown opted for diversity as when it insisted on uniformity. In an era of religious bigotry, it was a multiplicity of faiths rather than of kingdoms that was inherently dangerous.

Beyond separate kingdoms, Stuart monarchs had to deal with separate jurisdictions within England, patchwork remnants of crown properties and administrative problem spots. The Duchy of Lancaster governed the widely scattered estates originally possessed by that royal family; the Duchy of Cornwall (with its extensive mining interests) governed the property of the Prince of Wales. The Cinque Ports – harbour towns in Kent and Sussex most likely to absorb the shock of a French invasion – had their own Lord Warden, while Cheshire, which continued to claim the special status of a palatine with jurisdiction separate from the royal courts, had its own chamberlain and court of sessions. There was a separate council situated at York – the Council of the North – which had legal and administrative powers in all of England north of the Humber, and another situated at Ludlow – the Council in the Marches of Wales – which controlled the western border counties and all of Wales. These were prerogative courts that heard civil and criminal cases, and they did not submit to the jurisdiction of the common-law courts at Westminster. This made them the target of attacks, especially when Coke was Lord Chief Justice, and both were abolished by the Long Parliament along with the rest of the king's prerogative courts.

The chief vehicles of royal government in the localities were the sheriffs, Lord Lieutenants and justices of the peace. They served as proxies for the king in administrative, military and judicial matters respectively. Each of the fifty-one English and Welsh counties had its own officials, drawn from its local élites, and in this sense, if in no other, there was a county community. That the chief officers of the crown were local worthies had important consequences for English government. It bound the centre and localities together in mutually reinforcing ways. The crown lent its prestige to those it chose as office-holders; office-holders used their local standing to extend the power of the crown. Rival families like the Wentworths and Savilles in Yorkshire or the Phelips and Pouletts in Somerset contested in both court and country. In the later seventeenth century these contests allowed the government to reward and punish political opponents and to build political parties. Yet, because they were responsible for enforcing royal policy, local power-brokers could mitigate the rigours of inappropriate rules and regulations – a strength the crown did not always recognize. The final, and not inconsiderable, advantage of the English system of local government was that it was free to the crown. Members of the élites competed ferociously for appointments that not only carried no remuneration but also involved considerable cost. This allowed local government to expand without regard to the fiscal restraints on the crown.

The sheriff was the crown's agent of enforcement in the county. He received all judicial writs – ranging from the summons of members to Parliament to the distraint of cows – and enforced all judgements. He arrested alleged criminals and produced them for trial, though the jails in which they were held were private enterprises. He appointed the under-sheriffs and the constables who carried out this work, and in a large county he might have as many as 100 officials under his supervision. Anciently, the sheriff held a monthly court in the shire town, but this practice had become irregular as his business expanded and as the courts of sessions developed. The shire court was now associated mainly with the meeting of assizes, the twice-yearly legal sessions presided over by royal judges on circuit which heard the county's cases of serious crimes. The sheriff hosted assizes – he was responsible for everything from accommodation and entertainment to briefing the judges on the scheduled cases – and he empanelled the grand and petty juries from among the reluctant freeholders of the county. The other event that necessitated a formal meeting of the shire court was the selection of members to Parliament. As parliaments were summoned by writ, it was the sheriff's responsibility to endorse the writ with the names of those chosen by the assembly of county freeholders and return it to the Lord Chancellor.

The monarch chose sheriffs on the recommendation of the Lord Chancellor, who offered three names from which the king 'pricked' one with a stylus. The Chancellor gathered nominations from local peers or central office-holders who knew the county personnel. The process was haphazard, and those not appointed one time were generally chosen the next, as the term of office was a single year. Charles I used political criteria for selecting sheriffs only once, 'pricking' outspoken members of Parliament to keep them home during the parliament of 1626. In the early seventeenth century gentlemen still sought the shrievalty – in his second term as sheriff of Norfolk, in 1601, Bassingbourne Gaudy delighted in having all of his cloaks remade with the Gaudy crest quartered with that of the county – but it was a burdensome office. Responsible for collecting fines and enforcing judgements, the sheriff had to make up any shortfall from his own pocket. Entertainment at assizes was expensive, as were trips to London – sometimes for years afterwards – to settle accounts. Beginning in the 1630s sheriffs collected ship money, and after that the prestige of the office disappeared under the weight of its burdens. During the Interregnum, all local officials came from lower in the social scale, but the shrievalty remained depressed after the Restoration. Except in times of crisis it became the preserve of parish gentry; in Hampshire before 1680 most sheriffs were actually drawn from the ranks of esquires.

While the shrievalty was losing prestige, the lieutenancy was gaining it. The Lord Lieutenant and his deputies were responsible for raising and training the county militia and keeping them in a state of readiness to suppress rebellion or invasion. Traditionally, local military power had been the preserve of the aristocracy, who lived in fortified castles and kept armed retainers. But by the seventeenth century military power had become the preserve of the monarch, who controlled all warships, artillery and siege equipment. Old castles were no match for new cannonry, and the aristocracy had replaced their fortifications with luxurious palaces. In return the crown rewarded them with the office of Lord Lieutenant, which by the seventeenth century had become restricted to the aristocracy. With peers as Lord Lieutenants, the greatest county gentry jostled to be made deputy lieutenants, and the lesser gentry to be militia captains.

Basing appointments on social standing necessarily affected the readiness of the militia. Not even routine annual musters were held in most counties during the first decade of the century, and it was difficult to say whether there was more rust on the equipment or on the men supposedly trained to use it. Charles I made every effort to reform the workings of the lieutenancy, but paradoxically he allowed the office to become both a life tenancy and a family heirloom. Still, manpower and training improved sporadically, and most county bands grew during the 1630s – though hardly enough to save the king once civil war began.

If the lieutenancy was useful to contain neither rebellion nor invasion – the northern trained bands had hardly mustered before the Scots overran them in 1640 – it came to serve an important political function after the Restoration. For military control the later Stuarts kept up professional soldiers like the Grenadiers and the Coldstream Guards, but for social control they kept up the lieutenancy. In the 1660s the king granted Lord Lieutenants and deputy lieutenants police powers to regulate their counties. They led the commissions that enforced the Corporation Act, had broad scope to search for arms, and could imprison 'disorderly persons' – which, during the tensions of the 1670s and '80s, generally meant religious dissenters. It was the task of the lieutenants, as one deputy put it, 'to inquire into men's principles'. Statutes that established military levies, defined the roles of under-officers, and mandated drill also enhanced the power of the lieutenancy. The peers and gentry who composed the lieutenancy now had the authority and the means to maintain order in their counties and prevent another civil war. In the same way, the crown had means of disciplining the county élites. As membership in the lieutenancy became a mark of prestige and a base of power, exclusion from it signalled the opposite. Predictably, numbers expanded at the top as in some counties deputy lieutenancies doubled or tripled, while the number of joint Lord Lieutenants rose. The later Stuarts showed no hesitation in using their power of appointment and dismissal aggressively, and they frequently purged the lieutenancy in response to political and religious conflicts.

The commission of the peace underwent a similar transformation beginning in the 1580s. Justices of the peace became the mainstay of English local justice in the sixteenth century, and their importance grew steadily thereafter. They enforced over 300 statutes which regulated people, places and things. They heard all criminal cases, binding serious matters over to sessions of assizes and handling petty crime themselves. Their largest responsibilities were in administrative and regulatory law, where they oversaw everything from houses of correction to highway repairs. Increasingly, their case-load included matters that had once been moral offences: illegitimate births, the regulation of drunkenness through the licensing of alehouses, and failure to attend church. The entire bench met together four times a year at quarter sessions, each lasting two or three days, during which they dispatched hundreds of cases with enviable efficiency. Between sessions, the justices heard complaints, and the warrant of any two of them was sufficient either to dismiss or to bind over. By the later seventeenth century this out-of-sessions work had evolved into petty sessions. Criminal trials at sessions took place without lawyers, and JPs acted the roles of prosecutors and defence attorneys. They were not infrequently acquainted with the circumstances of the case and the parties involved, and this was thought advantageous in achieving justice.

The Lord Chancellor, normally on recommendation from the Lord

Lieutenant or other central officials with knowledge of local circumstances, named JPs. Like the lieutenancy, the commission of the peace mirrored the county's social hierarchy, with peers and their sons placed first, baronets and knights next, and greater and lesser gentry following. The commission of the peace so clearly defined local standing that gentlemen sent agents to London to plead for higher positions than those accorded their neighbours, or to lobby to be included. Clerks were more commonly bribed to leave an enemy out than to put a friend in, and tampering with the document itself was not unknown. Fathers were particularly anxious for their sons, and a place on the bench was soon seen as a hereditary right. Under these pressures the compact Elizabethan bench grew into a sprawling Jacobean one. Not even the reforms of Charles I's Lord Keeper Coventry could do much to arrest the trend. Between 1600 and 1703, to govern roughly the same population, the total number of JPs tripled to 3,700. In the early seventeenth century appointments remained apolitical and the Chancellor took special care to ensure that county societies riven by faction were unified on their bench. By the later seventeenth century the commissions fell victim to the same pressure as the lieutenancies, and in just three years James II, using religious and political criteria, replaced over 80 per cent of the justices that he had appointed at his accession.

The combination of social distinction and legal responsibility represented by the commission ensured that some justices would be more active than others. Many looked upon the appointment as a simple honorific and rarely attended sessions or took examinations. Others arrived at the justices' dinner to hear the latest gossip, meet friends and relatives, and conduct personal business. The arrangement of many marriages began and ended at quarter sessions. The sessions of the peace became social events on the calendar of the greater gentry, with horse racing, sporting events, and less savoury entertainment the chief attractions. As there was an informal social side to sessions, so there was an informal political side. The quarterly meeting together of so many community leaders made sessions an ideal occasion for them to share their concerns and express opinions about events of moment. Sessions were an especially good occasion for reconciling feuding families and settling rancorous disputes, and the shire's magistracy sealed pacts by their presence. It was also at quarter sessions that the gentry commonly determined who should represent the county in Parliament or drew up petitions of grievances to be sent to the crown. When they acted in concert in these ways, the gentry most closely approximated a county community.

Though the informal aspects of sessions turned the meetings of justices into an event of county-wide significance – a vigorous competition developed among towns to host them – they were centrally concerned with the enforcement of law. Many JPs took their responsibilities seriously and served with distinction. They kept notebooks of their out-of-sessions work and heard depositions throughout the year. They formed part of the quorum of the bench, the central core that ensured that the increasing amount of work ordered by the Privy Council was accomplished. They complained continually of the 'stacks of statutes' laid upon them, of the shortage of active justices, and of the difficulties of enforcement. But acceptance of the role of magistrate penetrated throughout the ranks of the gentry. The fashion of sending sons to the Inns of Court for a year of study developed in anticipation of their appointment to the bench. Publishers prospered by commissioning handbooks with titles like *The Country Justice* to explain the complexities of the office. Many, though by no means most, justices combined their zeal for office with the godliness that was identified with Puritanism. Communities seeking the suppression of alehouses appealed to these justices just as publicans seeking licences avoided them. Many JPs sat on the bench for years on end. In Essex during the first half of the century justices averaged ten years of service each, while five of them sat for over thirty years.

The role of the justices of the peace in enforcing the policies of the centre in the localities made them ideal spokesmen for the localities in the centre. This fitted them perfectly as representatives to Parliament, the great council of the realm that advised the monarch on policy, made statute law, and granted the extraordinary revenue of the crown. No institution of royal government underwent so profound a change in the seventeenth century as did Parliament. From an intermittent assembly summoned on specific occasions, Parliament became the principal organ of royal government, as necessary for rule as the king himself.

Before the 1620s, Parliament might be described as an event. The king summoned it to confirm his succession and for advice on extraordinary occasions generally connected to war. Parliament existed to do the king's business. Over the centuries its role in the legislative process had expanded and its function as a representative of the interests of the nation had matured. But it remained a royal council, summoned and dissolved at will, its agenda developed and controlled by the Privy Council, its decisions subject to the approval of the crown. During the forty-five-year reign of Queen Elizabeth ten parliaments were called, no session lasted longer than five months, and in total Parliament met less than 6 per cent of the time. The first Stuarts summoned their parliaments more frequently – there were seven by 1628 – but in twenty-four of the thirty-seven years before 1640 no parliaments were in session.

Parliament was not an oppositional institution in the early seventeenth century because it was hardly an institution at all. This changed dramatically with the Civil War. The Long Parliament sat in continuous session for thirteen years, during which it not only developed institutional coherence but also made the claim to be the fundamental authority of the nation after the execution of Charles I. The passage of a Triennial Act, which mandated a session once every three years, assured the frequency of post-Restoration parliaments, as did the even greater need of the later Stuarts for war finance. In the first twenty years of his reign Charles II held sessions in some part of every year but one, though many were brief and without legislative consequence. Rather than do without parliaments, Charles II and his heirs learned how to manage them. After the Revolution of 1688 parliamentary sessions lengthened and more bills were passed – a total of 1,750 acts between the accession of William III and the death of Queen Anne.

Parliament consisted of three elements: king, Lords and Commons. Each first acted independently of the other, and they then joined together to turn bills into statutes. The king was an integral and necessary part of Parliament, and the common lawyers developed a theory that his powers were never stronger than when he appeared as 'king-in-Parliament', promulgating the laws agreed to by the representatives of his people. Whether or not this was the case, the king set parliaments in train both by summoning them to meet at Westminster and by providing their agenda in a speech made either in person or by the Lord Chancellor. Monarchs could attend sessions of the House of Lords, as Charles I did in the 1620s, whispering to Buckingham during debates, and Queen Anne did at the beginning of the eighteenth century, hidden demurely behind a screen. They might summon the members of the Houses to Whitehall to lecture them on their proceedings, as James I was wont to do, or send them notes, as Charles II preferred. As the monarch called his council of Parliament to him, so he sent it away. This could take the form of adjournment, prorogation or dissolution. Before the dissolution of Parliament, all of the bills that had passed both Houses were submitted to the king's pleasure, private legislation being accepted with the phrase 'It will be as you wish', public acts with the phrase 'The king wills it.' Though the crown had the power to veto bills, it was rare for legislation the king opposed to pass both Houses.

Traditionally the House of Lords was the more significant of the two chambers. It was composed of the peers of the realm and the twenty-six bishops of the Church of England. Membership was an appurtenance of title and, while they might act for the welfare of the nation, the lords were not representatives. Peerages proliferated as the exigencies of the Stuarts eradicated the parsimony of the Tudors. In 1600 there were only 55 lay peers eligible to sit in the Lords; in 1660, after James I had exchanged titles for cash and Charles I titles for loyalty, there were 120; by 1700, at the end of the reign of William III, there were 170. Allowing for this remarkable growth – the aggregates mask considerable demographic attrition – the Upper House achieved institutional continuity through the experience of its members. Moreover, many lords sat on the Privy Council, where they originated the parliamentary agenda.

The House of Lords had both judicial and legislative functions. As a judiciary it received private petitions, acted as a court of appeal on writs of error from King's Bench, and, after 1621, tried cases of impeachment against royal ministers. As a legislature it drafted bills to be presented to the Commons or amended bills presented by them. Like the Lower House, the Lords read each bill three times, improving it in committee or letting it die. Bills which aroused opposition were rarely completed, and before the 1680s most decisions made in the Upper House were unanimous. Peers who objected to the passage of a bill could enter a personal protest against it, though this was rarely necessary. The influence of the House of Lords diminished in the seventeenth century under the humiliation of titles for sale, an eleven-year abolition, the infusion of Charles II's bastards and William III's Dutchmen, and Anne's creation of twelve peers to form a political majority, yet its power remained co-equal with that of king and Commons and no legislation that it rejected could become law, though by the end of the seventeenth century the lords had lost their power to amend money bills.

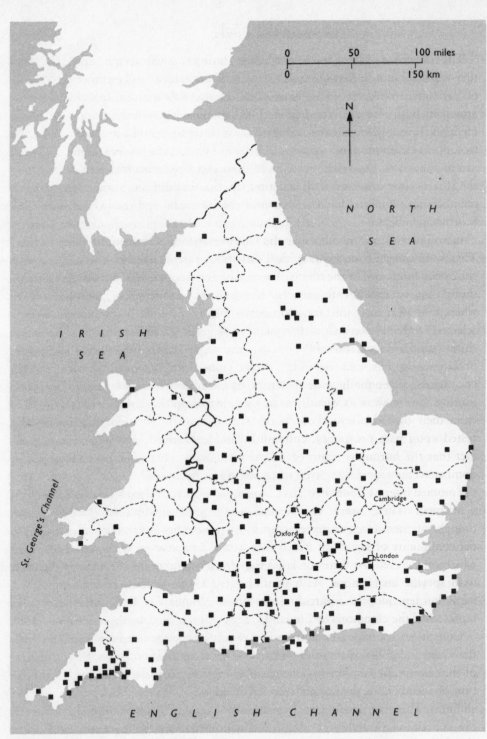

England and Wales: Parliamentary Boroughs

The transformation of the Lower House during the seventeenth century was so complete that by Anne's reign both Parliament and member of Parliament were synonymous with the House of Commons. It had grown in both size and prestige during the sixteenth century, when Henry VIII used Parliament to confirm the Reformation and Elizabeth to support the monarchy in times of crisis. In 1500 there were less than 300 members; by 1600 there were more than 450. Uncharacteristically, the Stuarts slowed this growth, and after Charles II added six new seats membership remained fixed at 513 until the Union of 1707 added 45 Scottish members.

In complex ways, members of the Commons were representatives. They were chosen from geographical districts, either as knights of the shire or as burgesses of the towns. There was no residency requirement, though by the seventeenth century shire knights were rarely selected where they were not substantial property-holders. The boroughs that selected burgesses were so diverse as to defy generalities. Their franchises could be as narrow as the ownership of a few pieces of property or as open as all the householders of the community. Those selected encompassed an equally wide spectrum. The great urban areas, whose leading citizens were as wealthy as any gentleman, increasingly picked from their own denizens. Poor ports, whose right to representation rested upon past prosperity, commonly chose outsiders. Despite the fact that the boroughs returned 80 per cent of members, the gentry dominated the Commons. Even in the later seventeenth century, when the monied interest flourished, over three-quarters of MPs were landed gentlemen. These were experienced county administrators who thought of themselves as representatives of those who chose them, of the community of gentry of which they were a part, and of the crown which they served. At times of crisis they might come to Westminster with specific instructions, with petitions to present or tasks to perform, but few adopted a parochial viewpoint. Members of Parliament represented the commons of England.

Constituencies selected members in a variety of ways which reflected the social and political environment and which changed over the course of the century. By law, knights of the shire were chosen by the approbation of members of the county who had freehold land valued at forty shillings. This had once been a restrictive franchise, but inflation and the conversion of holdings broadened it considerably. Each county chose two knights of the shire, and in the majority of cases throughout the century only two candidates were nominated on the day of selection. This made choice of knights of the shire a ceremonious and celebratory event – a social rather than a political occasion. When more than two candidates came forward, it was the task of the sheriff to determine which of them would be returned. He could persuade one or another to withdraw, or he could use a variety of means to assess which candidates had the greatest support. As a last resort, the sheriff could appoint clerks to poll the freeholders and count each candidate's supporters. Electoral contests were rare in the early seventeenth century, and polls rarer still. By the late seventeenth century both increased as the social elements of parliamentary selection gave way to the political ones.

Boroughs were even less likely to choose their representatives in an election contest. They frequently relied upon patrons to nominate suitable candidates – candidates who would serve without recompense. Others assigned one of their places to civic officers or to the head of a neighbouring gentry family. Government officials cultivated the leaders of small boroughs in hope of having their nominations accepted, especially towards the end of the century, when it was necessary for the House of Commons to be managed. Even if there were no candidates from whom to choose, borough electors still expected to be 'treated' in return for their support, and parliamentary selections were a boon to the local economy whenever they were held. They were a civic event of symbolic significance.

Sessions of Parliament were of uncertain duration, and many members of the Commons arrived late and left early. Like justices of the peace, those who viewed parliamentary service as a mark of social distinction took little part in its business. Even in times of crisis – perhaps especially in times of crisis – most members remained anonymous and they made no recorded speeches, were named to no committees, and were absent from all divisions. Indeed, the chamber contained seats for barely two-thirds of the members, and even these were rarely filled. About half of all members of the House of Commons served in one parliament only. This constant turnover in the membership of the Lower House inhibited the development of institutional continuity. In the early seventeenth century a number of standing committees were formed and took hold from session to session. The most important of these were the Committee of Privileges, which resolved disputes over membership, and the Committee of Grievances, which distilled issues for legislative initiative. After the Restoration, when the theory of royal finance was different, the Commons established a Committee of Supply and Ways and Means. It was not until the Civil War that the Commons gained control of their own Speaker and developed organs of internal administration. In the later seventeenth century, groups of active members of the Commons coalesced and after the 1680s formed into parties. The parties polarized the institution, but they also gave it shape by choosing leaders, setting forth programmes, and enforcing discipline.

From the point of view of the crown, the principal business of the House of Commons was to grant extraordinary supply. As the crown's need for finance increased throughout the century, so did the power of the Commons. Nine of Elizabeth's ten parliaments had been summoned to grant money, and after 1572 every parliament was called upon for some kind of financial support. It had long been established that English subjects could not be taxed without their own consent, which was given in bills initiated in the Lower House of Parliament. Though Parliament had the right of consent, it is not clear that it had the right of refusal, for the theory of extraordinary supply was that it was required in time of emergency to ensure the safety of the realm.

At the beginning of the seventeenth century, the main form of parliamentary taxation was a tax on wealth, known as the subsidy. The more frequently parliaments were asked for subsidies, the more often they sought something in return. When James I sought subsidies to pay off his debts, the House of Commons launched an investigation of his fiscal practices. When he desired money to aid his son-in-law's military adventurism in 1621, members of the Commons had the temerity to debate foreign policy. The more money the crown needed, the more liberties the Commons asserted, and, while no early Stuart parliament ever refused supply, they became increasingly adept at delaying passage of the subsidy bill while they prepared legislation to redress grievances. Most of these grievances were to close loopholes in existing statutes and to expand the scope of local authority, but after 1621 another form of grievance was the person of royal counsellors whom Parliament wished to remove by impeachment. Finally, some grievances were matters of public policy that brought the Commons into conflict with the crown – particularly over religion. Nevertheless, conflict between crown and Commons was occasional rather than persistent. It was usually an expression of deeper difficulties, and when it proved irresolvable, as in 1640, 1679 and 1688 (when James II could not re-assemble Parliament), royal government itself was in crisis.

The hierarchical structure of Parliament as well as the social dimensions of magistracy made for a distinct form of politics in Stuart England. As deference was a key to social interaction, so it penetrated political decision-making and participants utilized consensual methods whenever possible. The best political decisions were thought to be those which resulted from unanimity. This could be seen across the board: in decisions made by juries and by the bench of justices; in the methods used to select corporate officials or members of Parliament; in the very nature of Parliament itself, where legislation required the assent of king, Lords and Commons to pass. Consensual politics was a set of attitudes that inclined those of lesser rank, age or experience to defer to their betters and their elders. It was a set of practices that stressed acclamation rather than division, the group rather than the individual. As polls were a last resort in the choice of members of Parliament, so were divisions a last resort in the passage of bills through Parliament. Both expressed disunity, and both shamed the losers, whose personal honour was not yet seen to be separate from their political role.

Consensus politics depended upon a set of circumstances that prevailed in the early seventeenth century, and it eroded quickly once they changed. First, significant political participation was limited to a small élite whose wealth, social standing, education, experiences and aspirations were fundamentally similar. While participation in governance stretched far down the social scale – perhaps one out of every three adult males held some local office, and all fathers regulated their families – those who actually governed the nation were a tightly knit group whose connections ramified in every direction. Justices of the peace, aldermen and freemen of corporations, members of Parliament, officers of state: these men were drawn from very narrow circles – circles dominated by the ethos of the social hierarchy. They competed among each other for honour, power and reward, and they competed viciously. One nobleman ambushed a rival, bit off his ear, and carried it around in his pocket; others duelled to the death over real or imagined slights. One gentleman falsified a commission of the peace so his name would appear higher than a neighbour's; others falsified the return of members to Parliament. None of this competition, however, eroded the consensual values they then brought to the public arena.

What did erode consensual decision-making was the emergence of permanent divisions within the ruling élites over beliefs. Initially these were controversies over religion: whether Catholics should be excluded from the political process when they could not be excluded from the social hierarchy. There were deep divisions over Catholic proscription, but by the 1620s it was common to remove Catholic peers from the lieutenancy and Catholic gentlemen from the commissions of the peace. When Charles I reversed this trend in the 1630s all of the old wounds were reopened. The second dimension of religious controversy had to do with Puritanism. Puritans preached a divisive doctrine of damnation and salvation and, though these reforming Protestants stayed within the official church in order to purify it, they were increasingly incapable of subsuming an urgent religiosity to a circumspect political process. Because consensual methods relied upon unanimity, it was appropriate that efforts were made to exclude both Catholics and Puritans from political participation, though for a variety of reasons these efforts failed. In the early seventeenth century irreconcilable systems of belief inflicted dangerous wounds upon the body politic.

In large part the English Revolution resulted from the inability of the consensual political system to accommodate principled dissension. Personal honour could not be detached from social standing, and social standing could not be confirmed without office. If Catholics and Protestants, Anglicans and Puritans could not sit together on the bench of justices or the benches of Parliament then none of the assumptions about magistracy could operate and opponents had to be either reformed or eradicated. Twenty years of war, constitutional experimentation and the constant narrowing of the base of political participants not only failed to resolve this intractable problem, it intensified it by adding royalists and parliamentarians to the mix. After the Restoration, it took another thirty years for consensual assumptions gradually to be subsumed by adversarial ones. Efforts by Charles II and the Cavalier Parliament to recreate a unified political world by purging corporations and imposing loyalty oaths were doomed to failure and did fail. The purgers of one episode became the purged of another. Efforts to eradicate dissent through Conventicle Acts, or Catholicism through the hysteria of the Popish Plot, were no more successful. Rather it was necessary to draw the limits. There would be civil and political disabilities associated with both dissent and Catholicism, but after the revolution of 1688 repression was no longer seen as a viable alternative. There were permanent divisions within the élites: divisions between the court and the country, between the landed and the monied, between the social élite and the political élite, between the Whigs and the Tories. Interests and majorities were the new language of politics.

All of this, however, was in the future on 24 March 1603, when the seventy-year-old Elizabeth Tudor breathed her last. She had taken to bed several weeks before, and, as she would neither eat nor receive medicine, her doctors concluded that she had lost the will to live. Two days before she died, Secretary Cecil, Lord Chancellor Egerton and the Earl of Nottingham hovered over her bed and begged her to say unambiguously who should succeed her. 'I told you my seat had been the seat of kings, and I will have no rascal to succeed me,' she is reported to have replied almost inaudibly. 'Who should succeed me but a king?' This was taken as nomination of her cousin, James VI of Scotland, with whom Cecil had already entered into correspondence, but it was an equivocal reply. On the following day her ministers tried again, but during the night Elizabeth had suffered a stroke. They would get no answer now, and, as Archbishop Whitgift reminded them, it was time for the Queen to turn her thoughts towards God. Two days later James I was proclaimed in London, and the following day Sir Robert Carey, who had set post-horses along the Great North Road, arrived in Edinburgh with the news. The Queen was dead; long live the King.

3

The Scottish Accession
1603–1618

Guy Fawkes sat in the dark. Cruelly, the room reeked of coal, but he lit no fire on this cold November night for fear it would attract attention. He warmed himself with thoughts of what he would accomplish. Next to him were thirty-six barrels of gunpowder; above him was the floor of the Palace of Westminster. In the morning, James I, the Prince of Wales, and the Lords and Commons of England – over 500 of the most important men in the kingdom – would assemble in Parliament and Guy Fawkes would light bundles of dry kindling that would ignite the powder and blow them all sky high. The wood was necessary to give him time to escape, but it had proved even more valuable that afternoon when the Lord Chamberlain made a surprise inspection. Disguised as a servant, Fawkes explained that the room was used to store fuel for the winter and pointed to the stacks against the wall. Now there were just eight hours to wait. The only sign of his impatience was the spurs already strapped to his boots.

Catholics had waited nearly half a century to return England to the religion of its forefathers. Since the reign of Elizabeth, Roman Catholicism had been officially proscribed. It survived through the support of English élites who could maintain chapels and priests. Though these laymen followed the Roman religion, they professed loyalty to the English state. Some attended Protestant services to avoid civil penalties; others served the crown in local offices. They distinguished between private devotion and public duty, and achieved limited success in maintaining their religion in the north-west of England. As each decade passed, the numbers of Roman Catholics in England declined. In response, international Catholicism established Continental training centres for English priests, began a Jesuit mission to England, and created an underground ecclesiastical hierarchy. The presence of the Jesuits transformed quiescent Catholicism into activist recusancy and split the English Catholic community into two groups.

At James's accession members of both sprang into action. Catholic gentry petitioned the King in 1604 and offered voluntarily to expel the priests in return for a limited toleration. Before his accession James had expressed a willingness not to 'persecute any that will be quiet and give but an outward obedience to the law', and for a time he remitted collection of fines against recusants. This lenient policy towards Catholics was only a diplomatic bargaining chip, for after James concluded peace with Spain fines were reassessed and the recusancy laws were enforced.

Activist Catholics had an idea more potent than a petition. Throughout the winter and spring of 1604–5 a tiny group of conspirators plotted to assassinate the King. They expected that their co-religionists would rise in support after they then captured James's daughter Princess Elizabeth and received foreign military and financial assistance. Their leader, Robert Catesby, recruited an inner circle of active conspirators, an outer circle of wealthy peers and gentry who could coordinate the rising, and at least three Jesuit priests who might obtain international aid. Within these groups were Thomas Percy, Gentleman Pensioner to the King and kinsman of the Earl of Northumberland; Guy Fawkes, an Englishman living in Flanders who had a reputation for recklessness and bravery; and Catesby's cousin Francis Tresham, a Northamptonshire gentleman who had recently inherited a large fortune.

Percy led the team of assassins. In May 1604 he rented a house that abutted the Palace of Westminster, and, with Fawkes, began excavating the nine-foot-thick wall beneath it. In September, with the tunnel unfinished, they had a stroke of luck. The chamber under which they were digging became vacant and Percy rented it. They ferried casks of gunpowder from a storehouse in Lambeth, and Fawkes was installed to guard them. In the meantime Catesby implored Tresham to organize the subsequent rising. From the beginning Tresham was lukewarm, raising the issue that Catesby had repressed: the fate of the Catholic peers who would be present in Parliament. Catesby had reconciled himself to their sacrifice being for a greater good, but Tresham had not. On 26 October he sent his brother-in-law Lord Monteagle a veiled warning, and Monteagle revealed its contents to members of the Privy Council, who notified the King. On the afternoon of 4 November the *palace was searched, and it was learned that Thomas Percy had recently rented the ground-floor chamber. Monteagle knew that Percy was a Catholic and that he didn't live in Westminster. Near midnight a second search was made. A booted and spurred Guy Fawkes was discovered along with the gunpowder in the woodpile.*

The revelation of the Gunpowder Plot caused a sensation. Members of Parliament wept at their providential deliverance from what one overwrought minister described as 'hyperdiabolical devilishness'. Lord Chancellor Ellesmere spoke for most when he proclaimed, 'I am ashamed they be English; I am ashamed they be Christians; but at least they be but Roman Christians.' The fifth of November was made a day of celebration – as it remains to this day, commemorated with fireworks and straw images of the 'Guy' – and Catholics were driven underground. Such was the jubilation that for a time it was even forgotten that the new king was a Scot with a penchant for spending money and a plan to create an entity that he called Great Britain.

The accession of James I inaugurated the rule of one of the most turbulent dynasties in British history. The Stuarts had been debarred from inheriting the English throne by the will of Henry VIII, but 'wonder working providence' proved stronger than the wishes of even 'great king Harry'. By his six wives Henry had had three children, the last to be sired by a Tudor. His son, Edward VI, died at the age of sixteen in 1553; his eldest daughter, Mary, died childless in 1558. Though the long reign of Elizabeth I had held many blessings, heirs were not among them and from this queen rule by a Welsh family passed to a Scottish one.

James had been nominal ruler of Scotland since he was an infant and had inherited his throne upon the execution of his mother, Mary, Queen of Scots, in 1587. Thus, at his accession he was more experienced than any English king since William the Conqueror. This training was all the more necessary since the beginning of the seventeenth century was a time of social and economic dislocation and demographic crisis. James inherited a country rich beyond his imagination, but poorer than it had been in many decades. The foundations of royal finance were rotten, and the coffers were bare. Religious controversy smouldered just below the surface, political disquiet damped down only by the habit of obedience to a truculent septuagenarian queen who had ruled successfully for over four decades.

James's reign fell neatly into two periods: one of peace and one of war. Until 1618 his principal concerns were domestic, and they presented themselves within months of his accession when he convened a conference of church leaders, appointed a commission for a union of crowns, and began spending his way into a daunting fiscal crisis. The first impression James I made on his new subjects pertained to the church. Elizabeth had pursued a religious policy that alternately tightened and relaxed the church's hold on individual conscience. The definitive statement of liturgy and doctrine, the Thirty-Nine Articles, was forty years old, and while it had worn well it was not without loose threads or need of patches. The Elizabethan controversies confronted James in 1604 when he convened a conference at Hampton Court to judge them. At the same time he attempted to persuade his counsellors, lawyers and Parliament that England and Scotland were now one united kingdom. He appointed commissioners to attempt to resolve differences in law and custom so that bills might be introduced to establish in law what James believed he had already established in person. Among the intractable issues these commissioners debated were economic ones, and perceptions of the King's lavish spending heightened sensitivity about finance. Money matters were all the more worrying because royal indebtedness was considerable and some of James's more ostentatious gifts went to his Scottish favourites. Religion, the union and finance dominated the first decade of James's reign, shaping the new king's relations with his subjects, his parliaments and his church.

James I was blessed with able ministers, and his own easy-going habits of governing left them wide latitude. Though some members of the House of Commons were eager to lecture the new king on the finer points of the English constitution, a monarch served by the Earl of Salisbury, Lord Chancellor Egerton, Sir Francis Bacon and Sir Edward Coke probably had as much advice as he needed. By giving his Council free rein, James eased what might otherwise have been a difficult transition. As it was, one significant and two minor plots against his life were uncovered in the first two years of the reign. Nevertheless, his loose grip on the day-to-day affairs of government had political costs. The first was the growth of faction within the Council. Without clear cues from the monarch, counsellors went off in every direction, especially when they discovered that the King was both accessible and generous. Even when they did not bring governance to a halt, court factions slowed everything down. Secondly, James's aloofness from administrative detail frustrated his legislative desires. Uninterested in procedure, he was impatient of process and interpreted delay as opposition. This resulted in a number of unnecessary confrontations, especially with Parliament, when his frustrations were expressed as anger and his anger was received with consternation. Such misunderstandings later seemed ominous warnings of the coming storm, though while there was peace they were but puffs of cloud in a brilliant blue sky.

*   *   *

James I acceded to the throne of England at the age of thirty-seven. He was already an accomplished Scottish ruler and something of a philosopher prince. He had written tracts on divinity and had held academic disputations with some of the greatest theological minds of his kingdom. His *Basilikon Doron* ('The King's Gift' – 1599) was an advice book to his son Henry in which he discoursed on the obligations of kings with considerable sensitivity, while his celebrated *The True Law of Free Monarchies* (1598) became a classic statement of divine-right theory. James was described by Sir Henry Wotton, who observed him during a trip to Scotland in 1601, as 'of medium stature and of vigorous constitution, his shoulders broad, and the remainder of his person below somewhat slender'. He was athletic and loved to ride, to play golf and tennis, and, above all, to hunt, which he could do for days on end. He doted on his Danish wife, Anne, who had already presented him with three healthy children, and Wotton reported that 'among his good qualities none shines more brightly than the chasteness of his life'. This report of the king of Scots did not square with observations made of James as king of England. Some Englishmen found his accent impenetrable, his table manners execrable, and his attraction to handsome boys loathsome. James was earthier than his predecessor – Elizabeth had suppressed physical desires all of her life – and the contrast was undoubtedly exaggerated against him. If he was prurient, he was not predatory; if crass, not callous. In the early years of his reign, before he was beset by cares of state and chronic ill-health, he enjoyed being monarch and thought each day 'a Christmas time'. No one ever accused Elizabeth I of that.

James's journey from Edinburgh to London was one of the great events of his life. Crowds mobbed him on the roads and showered him with gifts which he returned in kind. He recalled the happy faces of his new subjects, 'their eyes flaming nothing but sparkles of affection, their mouths and tongues uttering nothing but sounds of joy'. He travelled with a large retinue of Scotsmen, including his personal attendants and bodyguard, though when James reached London one of his first acts was to confirm all of Elizabeth's officers in their places. At the same time he appointed only Scots to serve in his bedchamber – a decision that aroused much jealousy. He raised Sir Robert Cecil, with whom he had been in correspondence for several years beforehand, to the peerage, and accepted the advice of the Privy Council in issuing his first proclamations. During the next few years James was to broaden participation in his Council by reincorporating former followers of the Earl of Essex – whose revolt had disfigured the final years of Elizabeth's reign – as well as members of the Catholic family of Howard. By the time of his coronation, in July, he had already agreed to a cessation of hostilities with Spain, with whom England had been at war since the 1580s. Commissioners signed the Treaty of London in 1604.

Besides his kingdoms of Scotland and England, James I also inherited rule over Ireland. Before the reign of Elizabeth, effective English control of Ireland was limited to the fortified town of Dublin and to its environs known as the Pale. The strategy of governance for the rest of the country involved both an alliance with English settlers whose roots in Ireland pre-dated the Tudor conquest and an effort to Anglicize the heads of the great Gaelic families who controlled vast swaths of the country. This policy of alliance with the 'old English' and cooption of the Gaelic Irish aristocracy faced two insurmountable obstacles: the internecine strife within the Irish tribes and the centrifugal force of religion. Pacts struck between Irish clan leaders and English governors continually unravelled, while distrust between factions of Catholics and factions of Protestants increased. As the sixteenth century wore on, however, English administrators became more effective in controlling Ireland militarily, creating counties in imitation of English local government, and regional councils in imitation of English control of its border lands. Elizabethan government of Ireland was characterized by an increasing militarization of all parts of Irish society, and the colonization of Ulster and Munster created the need for more garrisons. The entire reign was typified by sporadic revolts, with no area of Ireland genuinely pacified. The worst came at the end with the Nine Years War (1594–1603), when Irish rebels led by the Earls of Tyrone and

Tyrconnell attempted to depose Elizabeth by inviting Philip III of Spain to become their sovereign. The Nine Years War was bloody, brutal and expensive. The Spanish troops that landed at Kinsale in 1601 were destroyed; Tyrone and Tyrconnell were captured and ultimately dispossessed of their estates; and £2 million were expended to secure political control of Ireland.

James's accession witnessed a profound transformation of English policy towards Ireland. Rather than a gradual process of absorption, English administrators opted for a policy of colonization. Small plantations had already been undertaken in the sixteenth century, the most successful of which was in Munster, but they were difficult to secure and costly to protect. The planters lived among a hostile population and adopted a siege mentality. Irish land was too poor and the Irish economy too underdeveloped to make small plantations attractive to English settlers. Yet they were attractive to Scots, and James's accession lifted the barriers against Scottish immigration to Ireland. Scots settled along the rugged coast of north-eastern Ireland and pushed their way inland. These communities became the foundation of the greatest of all of the colonization schemes, the plantation of Ulster.

The Ulster plantation, which was in large part the proposal of the Irish Attorney-General, Sir John Davies, was designed to clear Irish inhabitants from six counties and replace them entirely with English and Scots. As in Munster, the crown claimed that much of the land had been forfeited after the flight of the Earls of Tyrone and Tyrconnell from custody in 1607, and it simply confiscated the rest. From an English point of view, the scheme had much to recommend it. Estates would be large enough to attract entrepreneurial planters; security would be assured by the eviction of the resident Irish; and the rents paid to the crown would go a long way towards subsidizing the Irish administration. The plan also set aside lands to endow churches and educational institutions in order to build a Protestant, 'new English', community. These 'new English' planters were to be given every possible advantage. Their property was secured by clear title, while the lands of Irish and 'old English' alike were subject to the capriciousness of a hostile judiciary. The imposition of the oath of supremacy on office-holders, local officials and practitioners in the royal courts dispossessed Catholics. Finally, in 1613 James created eighty-four new Irish parliamentary boroughs, all in the areas of Protestant settlement, that gave the 'new English' the prospect of effective control over the

Irish parliament. With a monopoly on office, control of Parliament and the inducement of land, Davies believed new English and Scots settlers would flood into Ulster and complete the Briticization of Ireland that included the establishment of a flourishing Protestant church.

Religion was one of the first issues that James addressed in England. On his trip south from Scotland he had been met in Northamptonshire by a group of clergymen who presented him with a petition said to have been supported by 1,000 ministers. This Millenary Petition was a moderate appeal to a king who had promised to act 'as a good physician' to the soul of the body politic. It called for reforms of the clergy, ceremony and doctrine of the Elizabethan church. Despite advice that he reject the petition, James decided to convene a conference of learned divines to debate its merits. When the bishops protested that the English church had stood for decades, the King replied that 'it was no reason that because a man had been sick of the pox forty years, therefore he should not be cured'. The conference met at Hampton Court on 14 January 1604 and lasted for three days. James liked nothing more than a disputation where he could exercise his wits, display his learning and demonstrate his rhetorical skills. He wanted nothing more than to establish royal control over the church – a battle he had so far waged without success in Scotland.

The first day's meeting was the crucial one. In a closed-door session James met with church leaders in the presence of the Privy Council. The aged Archbishop of Canterbury, John Whitgift, and his heir apparent, Richard Bancroft, Bishop of London, had pleaded with the King not to hold a disputation with the petitioners – the 'Puritans' as they were derisively called – fearing that it would grant them legitimacy. What they saw less clearly was that the conference was an opportunity for the King to impose his authority over the entire ecclesiastical establishment. James acted as prosecutor, judge and jury, and he played each role flamboyantly. He questioned the bishops pointedly on doctrinal issues, frequently interrupting them to have the relevant texts consulted. He quoted from his own stock of biblical examples, and treated the divines to sparkling displays of exegesis. They were disarmed by his learning and flustered by his crudeness. 'A turd for this argument,' he scoffed at the Bishop of Peterborough. He would rather 'his child were baptized by an ape as by a woman' he concluded in dismissing the custom of allowing midwives to baptize dying infants, which many, including the King, believed was a cover for witches to steal babies for satanic rituals. James summarily ordered the bishops to attend to a host of reforms, especially for the development of a learned and well-paid clergy to minister in Ireland, Wales and the Scottish borderlands.

The second day of the conference was more for show than for substance. Four moderate reformers approved by the bishops themselves debated the central points presented in the Millenary Petition. As the bishops had already been instructed to remedy those things the King deemed abuses, James used the debate as an opportunity to reveal his opposition to radical reformation. He was gracious to his opponents and conceded their desire for a godly ministry and for a new translation of the Bible – a decision which ultimately resulted in the publication of the Authorized or King James Bible of 1611. James had two messages to send to the religious reformers. He would accept moderate reforms that were moderately proposed. But he would give no quarter to radical reformers who wished to replace the episcopal hierarchy by a Presbyterian governance. 'No bishop, no king,' he twice proclaimed.

At the final session of the conference the King heard the bishops' response to the issues he had set before them. A number of substantive changes were accepted. The petitioners had witnessed James's determination 'to confirm whatever be found lawfully established and to amend and correct what was corrupted by time'. The King had shown a willingness to listen but an unwillingness to be persuaded.

Indeed, there was to be little change as a result of the Hampton Court conference. After winning his oratorical bouts the King lost interest in the details of reform. Bancroft, who had opposed the meeting, had his revenge in the Canons of 1604, which reneged on a good deal of what had been conceded to the reformers. By the same token, however, James had an Archbishop of Canterbury subservient to the royal will. Hampton Court was calculated to show the King at his best, and for James it was a spectacular triumph. There was no need for flattery in the private account that the Bishop of Durham sent the Archbishop of York: 'a king and priest in one person to propose, discuss, and determine so many important matters so soundly as I never look to see or hear the like again'.

James's success at Hampton Court foreshadowed the success of religious policies throughout his reign. The compromises that created the Elizabethan church satisfied no one, but 'When the best things are not possible, the best may be made of those that are' was the phlegmatic defence of Richard Hooker, the principal theologian of the English church. The Elizabethan church was peculiarly English: its structure Catholic, its doctrine Calvinist, its liturgy, in the words of Lord Burghley, 'a mingle-mangle'. That is, it was governed by bishops, accepted predestination as its core belief, and borrowed its ceremonies promiscuously. Above all it was Erastian, a church created by the state. Henry VIII's Act of Supremacy (1534) made the monarch head of the church, removing England from papal jurisdiction. Edward VI presided over reforms of ceremony and doctrine that brought England in line with the practices of the Continental reformed churches of Germany and Switzerland. The prayer-book of 1552 transformed the mass into the communion, and doctrinal reform stressed God's free gift of salvation through predestination.

After Mary attempted to undo these Protestant reforms, Elizabeth I finally re-established them in the Thirty-Nine Articles (1563), telling a subsequent House of Commons that she 'will be found the protector of true Protestants'. Yet her Protestantism was cut through with concessions. It was the only way to establish faith by statute. She placated both Catholic lords and radical Protestants by leaving crucial matters of doctrine deliberately ambiguous. But once she settled her church she would compromise no longer. Against all agitation the Queen refused to alter her positions on doctrine or ceremony, even when they were exposed as internally contradictory. She supported church decoration, especially crosses; insisted that clergy wear the white surplice; and defended signing of the cross, kneeling and bowing. By the end of her reign it was an open question whether her motto, *Semper Eadem*, meant ever-steadfast or always obdurate. Elizabeth relied upon obedience, expediency and veneration to enforce a church government that allowed Catholics, conformists and committed reformers to coexist.

James's policy was no different, though without veneration it needed to appear more pliant. Catholics on the right and Protestant reformers on the left both hoped that the ecclesiastical policy of the new king would bend in their direction, and each had a slender reed at which to grasp. James's personal life was bound up with Catholics: Catholicism was the religion of his parents, his wife and his first lover, Esmé Stuart, Duke of Lennox. Moreover, the King believed that, despite its manifold errors, the Roman Catholic church was a true church that could still be redeemed. On the other hand, the hotter sort of Protestants were heartened by the King's personal profession of Calvinism, his lifelong instruction by Presbyterian ministers, and his penchant for theological debate. For many English Protestants the Scottish church was a model to be emulated. James, however, determined to steer clear of 'superstitious blindness the one way or turbulent humours the other'.

The hotter Protestants learned first that the new king was as shrewd as the old queen. Protestant reformers ranged from those moderates who had constructed the Millenary Petition to those who believed the English church so corrupt that true saints had to separate to avoid being contaminated. Separatist congregations were a tiny proportion of Protestant reformers, though their extreme views were a brush with which to tar the more moderate majority. Overwhelmingly, these critics of the established church wished to work from within to enact reform. Even most of those who later physically separated and established their own reformed churches in New England hoped to provide a model for the internal regeneration of the English church.

Adversaries made no fine distinctions between moderate and radical reformers, branding them all 'Puritans', a derogatory appellation that carried the stigma of meddlesome severity and the stain of other-worldly impracticality. In fact Puritans were unified only by their critics. The clerical reformers, like those who met James at Hampton Court, were led by learned divines who desired a combination of intel-lectual and professional changes. Influenced by waves of Continental criticism of Roman Catholicism, they wished the English church to be on the cutting edge of doctrinal and ceremonial reform. They had 'painful consciences' from years of studying and discussing biblical injunctions, and desired to be excused from conforming to practices that the official church itself ruled adiaphora – things indifferent. Equally important was reform of the ministry itself. Too many minis-ters took the job without a true vocation, with little proper training and with no commitment to the communities they served. Too many cler-ical appointments were in the hands of laymen who regarded them as pieces of property rather than offices of responsibility. Ministerial compensation was so inadequate that even bishops were forced to accept multiple appointments. At the parish level, ministers could barely subsist and curates were mostly part-time employees. Such con-ditions only worsened as more university graduates chased fewer decent jobs, thus lowering salaries and raising discontent.

Not all Puritans were clergymen. A vigorous lay movement centred on Protestant piety and personal redemption. It was strongest in urban communities and among the 'middling sort', where moral values of self-discipline and single-minded dedication fitted comfortably with acquisitiveness. The godly took themselves seriously because salvation was a serious business. They sought out able preachers and lecturers; they accepted the responsibilities of local office; and they attempted to convert those neighbours whom they could and to control those whom they could not. While divines debated the convolutions of the Calvinist doctrine of double predestination, the godly followed the chillingly simple logic of the saved and the damned.

Nor were these the only or the most important cleavages among the Puritans. While issues of doctrine and ceremony caused daily friction, differing views of the structure of the true church generated the most controversy. The episcopal structure of the English church sat precariously upon its Calvinist doctrine of the equality of all who were saved. Elizabethan bishops varied, and not all were antithetical to reform. Nevertheless, they constituted the visible power structure, and as the decades passed their office came under attack. Most clerical reformers were still not anti-episcopal – indeed, at the upper echelons of the movement most hoped for their own mitres and copes – and at the beginning of the seventeenth century the Presbyterians among the Protestant reformers were a distinct minority. But they were the minority most capable of rousing the ire of the King, and initially James I equated all hot Protestants with Presbyterians and all Presbyterians with rebels. James proclaimed them 'enemies to all men and to me only because I am king', and only gradually realized that most reformers were moderates and that most moderates were loyal and obedient subjects.

So too were most English Catholics. Like the Puritans, they were a monolith only in the eyes of their enemies. As we have seen, there were many English Catholics who saw themselves as loyal subjects of the crown and rejected the activist stance of the Jesuit mission in England. They refused to be drawn into conspiracies like the abortive Bye Plot (1603) and, though they provided succour to priests, they took no part in those of their activities that were orchestrated from Rome. Initially James led these Catholics to believe that they would be treated leniently as long as they kept the peace, and even after the reimposition of civil penalties and harsh fines for their recusancy he allowed them to practise their religion quietly. Like the rest of the nation, they were shocked by the revelation of the Gunpowder Plot.

Against Protestant reformers and Catholics alike, James's strategy was to unify and conquer. 'Unity is the perfection of all things,' he declared, and he strove to encompass moderates of all stripes. Bancroft's Canons of 1604 limited preaching about controversial doctrines like predestination, while royal proclamations banned seditious religious writings. The King and his ministers refused to use the Gunpowder Plot as a licence to hunt down Catholics. The Oath of Allegiance imposed upon them in 1606 allowed obedience to coexist with conscience. Similarly, though James proclaimed his intention to harry Puritans from the land, fewer than ninety clergymen were deprived of their livings – most in the year after Hampton Court. *Beati Pacifici* – Blessed are the Peacemakers – was James's motto. After James unexpectedly appointed George Abbot Archbishop of Canterbury in 1611, the religious calm was almost eerie. Only two ministers were ousted over the next fourteen years, and even the pamphlet wars lost their wind.

In constructing his church, James I sought the ablest and the most committed no matter what the shade of their opinions. Low-church and high-church, 'Anglican' and 'Puritan', all found reward. He took great care with his ecclesiastical appointments and favoured accomplished preachers like Lancelot Andrewes and John Donne. Most of his bishops had been royal chaplains first, and the King himself had tested their mettle. Though he believed that episcopal office was based on scriptural authority, James saw bishops as a means to control a sprawling ecclesiastical establishment whose functions included moral reform, spiritual regeneration and political conformity. In 1610, after years of manœuvring, James even succeeded in reintroducing bishops into the Scottish church.

While James adapted most of his own attitudes and policies to those prevailing in England, there was one development that had no analogue and on which the new king had set his heart: a union of his two states. James VI & I took literally whatever metaphors theorists had constructed about the renaissance ruler. He was the head of the body politic; the husband in a loving marriage; the father of a well-ordered family. Now he had become the monarch of one Great Britain, united in his person and in his heirs perpetual. 'What God hath conjoined, then let no man separate. I am the husband, and the whole isle is my lawful wife; I am the head and it is my body,' the King told the English parliament. If James's Union of Crowns was to be likened to a marriage, it was not a marriage made in heaven.

For centuries the two states had shared nothing more than a 110-mile border. Warfare between England and Scotland had been endemic. Scotland served as a back door to French ambitions against England, England as a safe haven for Scottish rebels. Both sides engaged in persistent terrorism, marauding at will and reinforcing cultural stereotypes and racial animosities. Four of James's six immediate Scottish predecessors had died as a result of these struggles: two in battle, one on the scaffold and one heartbroken after a devastating defeat. Indeed, there was so little respect between sovereigns that the decapitated skull of a Scottish king was used as a flowerpot in the English royal conservatory.

Nor had the comparative peace of the previous half-century erased such deeply etched memories. Not even a shared Protestant confession or the increasing realization that the Scottish king would accede to the English throne had much effect. In Scotland, the English were known as the 'auld inemeis'; in England, as the Earl of Northumberland averred, 'the name of Scots is harsh in the ears of the vulgar'. The hostility was heartfelt. After Elizabeth's death Scottish leaders feared that their state would be annexed or, worse, their king assassinated. The English élites feared 'swarms of tawny Scots' who, locust-like, would devour office and wealth. When one member of Parliament compared James to a man with two pastures and one hedge he neatly summarized English attitudes in the metaphor 'the one pasture bare, the other fertile and good'.

In truth, Scotland was a poor nation whose inhabitants eked subsistence from a grudging soil. Even the comparatively well off made a staple diet of oats, lived in houses of mud and stone, and wore heavy, coarsely woven plaids – poncho-like garments that covered the body from shoulder to toe. The common comforts that eased English daily life – like meat, chimneys for the ventilation of smoke, and clothes made of the light and durable 'new draperies' – were luxuries in Scotland. Urban areas were few – numbered in tens rather than hundreds – and mercantile activity was exiguous. Export was limited to basic raw materials; imports to the few luxuries that could be purchased in return. Edinburgh, with a population exceeding 25,000 only after the sixteenth-century boom, was a tenth the size of London and a provincial capital in all senses of the word.

Social and political contrasts were at least as great as material ones between the two nations. The Scottish social order was dominated by aristocratic clans who controlled vast estates that they governed almost as satrapies. They were small in number, divided between the autonomous Highlanders, who spoke Gaelic and regarded bloodfeud as law, and the Lowlanders, who by the end of the sixteenth century were coming to be integrated into royal government. James VI worked at establishing a service aristocracy to set beside the landed magnates and created a large number of new Scottish peers. Though the lairds existed as a class of independent landowners below the aristocracy, they were neither numerous nor as upwardly mobile as were the English gentry. As a group, the lairds were too poor and too dependent to pose a social or political threat to the magnates, and their own position in the middle of the social order was secured by the lack of any equivalent to the English yeoman. Magnate, laird and peasant made for a stable social universe, since the gaps between levels were all but insurmountable.

Scottish political stability resulted from a different equipoise. Though the history of the Stuart monarchy in Scotland was bloody – 'they have not suffered above two kings to die in their beds these two hundred years' – the institution was sturdy. There was no challenge to the hereditary principle, and the continuous succession of child rulers for over two centuries posed no threat to the existence of the monarchy. Instead, aristocratic factions battled for control of the person of the king, especially during his minority. Kidnapping Scottish kings was almost constitutional practice, and James himself was abducted twice. Paradoxically, this contest for control of the monarch elevated kingship above the rivalries of the clans and enabled the monarch to act as a comparatively independent arbiter. If kingship's power was weak, its prestige was strong. The secret to the success of the Scottish monarchy was that monarchs recognized its limitations and acted within them. Although James treated his great magnates with caution and respect, he also strengthened the royal council and its fledgling departments of state. He also left legal and administrative institutions without clear lines of authority, so that his personal intervention was indispensable in times of conflict. He was good at face-to-face government, and face-to-face government suited the small, poor, decentralized state that he governed without military might. At least it had until he moved south.

These real and imagined differences created daunting obstacles to James's plan for a 'perfect union' between the two states. Worse still was the King's unrealistic belief that union could be easily and quickly achieved. Even before he met his first parliament, James had a signet

struck which united English and Scottish arms. In May 1603 he proclaimed that he regarded 'the two realms as presently united [and] the
subjects of both the realms as one people'.

When Parliament met in 1604 the union was the dominant issue,
though not the only one. Before the session began, Lord Chancellor
Egerton had voided the selection of Sir Francis Goodwin as knight of
the shire for Buckinghamshire on the grounds that he had been outlawed for debt. Egerton ordered a new election at which Sir John
Fortescue, a privy counsellor, was selected. When Parliament assembled, the Commons condemned the Chancellor's actions as a violation
of their right to judge the returns of their own members. This thrust
James into a thicket of conflicting precedents and a jurisdictional dispute between two courts of his realm. Chancery claimed the undoubted
right to examine the return of its own writs (its written commands),
while the Commons claimed the undoubted right of being a court of
record. James proposed several compromises, and the one ultimately
adopted set aside both Goodwin and Fortescue – a solution which
satisfied crown and Parliament at the expense of the county freeholders. It was also a solution that implicitly confirmed the right of the
Commons to adjudicate returns – a right they abused with impunity for
the rest of the century, capriciously overturning franchises, ignoring the
will of local electors, and transforming legal criteria into political ones.

During the course of the Buckinghamshire election case, the
Commons laid claim to privileges unique to their institution. James, no
doubt on the advice of his counsellors, responded with the stock constitutional answer that he held their privileges in high regard because they
had been grants of immunity from the crown. While this might be
strictly true, it was a formulation which inevitably suggested that what
was once granted might be taken away again. Some members recalled
the battles the Commons had fought (and mostly lost) with Elizabeth
over their privileges and recognized that the time to take a stand was at
the beginning of a new reign. This position strengthened the belief held
by many, but articulated by few, that James, as a foreigner, needed
instruction in English government, as 'no human wisdom can pierce
into the rights and particularities of a people but by tract of experience'. A large committee prepared a defence of parliamentary privilege.
Like most documents drafted by a committee, the Apology of the
Commons, as it was later known, scattered its shot widely. Not only
did it defend privileges, but the Apology attempted to dispel rumours

that the Commons were disloyal, dominated by religious zealots, or opposed to the union of England and Scotland. However defensible, the Apology was defensive; it died in committee and was never presented to the King.

That the Commons felt it necessary to justify their proceedings on the union indicated the importance the King attached to it. James wished only two things from his first parliament: that a commission of union be established and that he be recognized as king of Great Britain. The commission was approved; the title was not. There was no Great Britain, common lawyers argued, and it could be created only by the dissolution of its component states. When Great Britain was born, England expired. Its laws, its customs, its treaties and international obligations all ceased to exist. Such arguments baffled James. After the prorogation of Parliament he simply proclaimed himself king of Great Britain and ordered coins struck to reflect his title and to be used in his empire.

The commissioners could not accomplish their work by fiat. If the idea of union was simple, the reality was complex. There were too many ways to make one state out of two. To the English, the solution was to incorporate Scotland in just the way that Henry VIII had incorporated Wales. This would allow the King to achieve his objective – 'one worship to God, one kingdom entirely governed, one uniformity in laws' – without in any way disrupting English practices. The Scottish commissioners were not amused. Moreover, not even absorption solved all problems. The English remained convinced that if all barriers were dropped the Scots would flood south in search of employment and trade. Punitive commercial duties might be lifted, but both sides remained determined protectionists. While the commissioners easily agreed that the border laws which treated denizens of the two nations as enemies were no longer appropriate, they were less able to agree on conceding full rights of citizenship. The compromise of accepting those Scots born after James's accession – the post-nati – as English citizens was easier to make, for as yet these infants were but potential land-owners and office-holders. However, those born before his accession were a real threat as the King, the Queen and the Prince of Wales all established royal households in London replete with Scottish officials.

The logic of a Scottish king having Scottish servants was impeccable if only prejudice could have been swayed by logic. Although James confirmed all of Elizabeth's office-holders in their places and heaped honours upon English aspirants, nothing could erase the image of the Scots who shared the shower of gold. James Hay, Earl of Carlisle, and Robert Carr, Earl of Somerset, were the most conspicuous of the King's Scottish favourites. Both rose to social and economic prominence through James's bounty, and both were the targets of the intense anti-Scots attitudes that prevailed in England. Hay's lavish spending was particularly resented, and later in the reign he was reputed to have spent £3,300 on a single dinner. By 1610 James had granted nearly £250,000 to Scottish suitors. But as early as 1604 the court gossip John Chamberlain was complaining of money given to the Duke of Lennox, and the government found it necessary to issue an order against 'swaggerers', English toughs who assaulted Scots in the streets of London.

Such prejudices made the work of the commissioners of union more difficult even as they hardened the King's resolve. Thus the near-total failure of the union proposals in the parliamentary session of 1606–7 had long-term political consequences. Though the King had moderated his initial demands and now recognized the complexity of establishing legal and religious union in the short term, the only concrete achievement of several years of work was the abolition of the border laws. In order to establish the principle that the post-nati were English citizens, the crown was forced to bring a collusive action at law, *Calvin's Case* (1608), to gain what could not be obtained through Parliament. Indeed discussions over Scottish naturalization had encroached on the king's prerogative just as debate over Anglo-Scottish trade had questioned the king's regulatory powers. James was not used to a parliament independent of royal will, and certainly not used to being politically outmanoeuvred by lawyers and country gentlemen. He subjected the members of the House of Commons to a blistering attack before proroguing their session. The Commons served as a scapegoat for James's disappointment. In truth, leading ministers, the Privy Council and the House of Lords were equally reluctant to support union. The Earl of Salisbury adeptly screened his opposition behind clients in the Lower House and on the commission. Nevertheless, the failure to achieve even the watered-down version of union that the commissioners had proposed soured relations between king and Parliament for the next decade and bred a mutual distrust that enabled misunderstanding to grow into conflict, and conflict into hostility.

Conflict with the House of Commons over union could not have come at a worse time, for James I was in desperate need of something that only the Commons could give him: money. From the beginning of his reign, James had run a deficit that proved impervious to fiscal expedients. He inherited a debt from the tight-fisted Elizabeth I, and his own open-handed munificence aggravated it. The King did have genuine expenses that Elizabeth had not, including households for a spouse and two heirs; the outlay of converting the royal residence, wardrobe and stables to male occupancy; and the costly ceremonies of interring one monarch and crowning another. But James was generous to a fault, spending lavishly on his friends as well as on himself. He had described his first years as monarch as a 'Christmas time', and the presents were gaudy indeed. In Scotland his annual revenue had been something less than £50,000; in England he spent £47,000 on jewels in 1604 alone. He was soon spending £30,000 a year on pensions to courtiers and favourites, many of them Scots. Even the dullest Lord Treasurer realized that the King had the financial acumen of a child in a sweetshop and that the ill-effects of overindulgence afforded only temporary restraint. The Earl of Salisbury once had gold coins stacked in piles so that James could see exactly what he proposed to give away.

James I worsened his financial problems, but he did not cause them. They ran deep to the foundation of seventeenth-century fiscal theory and practice. The doctrine that in time of peace the king should 'live of his own' – that is, from the revenues of the royal estate and the income derived from the granting of privileges – stretched back into the mists of the Middle Ages. It was a principle more honoured in the breach than the observance, but never vanquished. James's great-grandfather, Henry VII, lived of his own by declaring some of his wealthiest subjects traitors and seizing their estates. Henry VIII lived of his own by confiscating the lands of the Catholic church – a granary so great that it nourished his dynasty for six decades. For all her parsimony, Elizabeth alienated crown lands worth over £800,000 and continued the royal assault on aristocratic and episcopal fortunes. By the time it was left for James I to live of his own there was little to be squeezed from lands, peers or bishops.

Royal revenue combined income that the king derived from land, from prerogative rights and from customs. As a landowner the king had rents, leases and fines such as any lord possessed. Annual income from the royal estate was something less than £125,000, and James continued to sell off real estate to meet current expenses. The crown was also owed certain forms of service that were attached to its prerogatives.

Most of these feudal rights were obscure in origin and of limited financial value, but two – purveyance and wardship – were notable both for the money and for the complaints that they generated.

Purveyance was an obligation imposed upon local communities to provide foodstuffs to the court at fixed prices. Originally it ensured both regular supply for the royal household and regular sale for farmers – a primitive futures market. Because prices were set long before the inflation of the sixteenth century, purveyance soon became a one-sided bargain in favour of the crown. Local officials attempted to fix the quantity of food for which they were liable, but these compromises were a constant irritant between royal officials who desired to maximize yields and local communities which desired to minimize them. In one year for meat and dairy produce alone the purveyors took 17,000 beasts (including 900 oxen), 38,000 fowl and 54,000 pounds of butter.

Wardship was the obligation of the crown to protect the minor children of its deceased tenants. It derived from the fact that these tenants owed the crown military service and their minors were thus a royal asset. But military service had fallen into desuetude at the same time as the crown gained a new class of tenants – those who bought the former church lands seized by Henry VIII. Now the crown sold wardships to the highest bidder, mostly to relatives who paid to prevent predations by strangers. Like purveyance, wardship became the equivalent of a tax: this one on the transfer of estates.

By far the largest part of the king's income was derived from trade. Customs revenues were a tangle of duties, rates and imposts that were probably a mystery even to seventeenth-century administrators. There were varying duties for imports and exports; varying rates for natives and aliens; varying imposts on the products of friends and foes. The king's right to take twelve pence in the pound on the value of specified goods for national defence, known as the subsidy of tonnage and poundage, was confirmed by parliamentary grant. Duties on the woollen-cloth trade were known as the great customs, though they were worth less than a hundredth the duties on other commodities, which were known as the petty customs. The value of petty customs was contained in a book of rates, last updated in 1558. In addition, special imposts were placed on goods such as imported French wines and exported English beer. They began in the reign of Queen Mary and were expanded by Elizabeth despite legal challenge and persistent complaint. In 1600 the Queen began collecting a special impost on red currants imported from Turkey. Six years later John Bate, the largest importer, refused to pay the red-currant impost on the grounds that it had not been granted to the crown by Parliament. In deciding for the king in *Bate's Case* (1606), the Exchequer judges held that the king's right to tax trade was part of his prerogative and that it was inalienable and illimitable.

James no sooner arrived in England than he faced financial crisis on every side. Whatever effect the King's liberality would soon have, Lord Treasurer the Earl of Dorset was already in a state of panic in 1604. Various schemes were immediately launched to lower the deficit and to generate the start-up costs of a new reign. Despite the fact that the last Elizabethan 'benevolence', or forced loan, remained unpaid, privy seals were issued for a fresh loan that brought in over £100,000 in ready cash. The most far-reaching plan was to expand the Elizabethan practice of farming the customs. Special deals for small sums were worked out in the first months of the reign, but the significant decision was to bundle the most lucrative duties together into a single 'Great Farm' which was to be put up for bid. Before this could be done, however, new rates had to be set. Plans for a new book of rates had been ongoing for a decade; those for a great farm of the customs had been made since at least 1599. It took the accession of a new monarch to achieve reform. The book of rates was updated in 1604, and the auction of the great farm of the customs was accomplished the following year. The farm yielded £112,000 per annum – a sum that grew steadily at each renewal.

Farming the customs ensured the treasury a stable source of income and narrowed the guesswork involved in projecting revenue and outlay. Position papers which stated the king's income and indebtedness were exercises in political policy rather than accounting: so much royal income resulted from windfall and so much royal indebtedness from whim that it was impossible to know anything other than the crown's comparative position. This frustrated officials charged with supplying the king's needs, and it did little to moderate the king's wants. Thus the farming of customs revenues was part of a larger plan to regularize royal income.

When Parliament met in 1604, Secretary Salisbury and Lord Treasurer Dorset first floated the idea of commuting the prerogative rights of wardship and purveyance into a fixed annual payment. Both were grievances presented in Elizabethan parliaments, but, since the Queen refused even to acknowledge her subjects' complaints against them ministers had made no effort at reform. Beginning in the parliament of 1604, the pent-up anger burst forth, especially because James promised a new broom to clear the cobwebs of Elizabethan inactivity. Taking their lead from the Lords, members of the House of Commons introduced both petitions and bills that would reform the uncertainties and abuses of prerogative rights. An attempt to remove the obligation of wardship was the immediate cause for the drafting of the Apology of the Commons. Little progress was made in 1604 or in the following session in 1606. By then, even guesses about royal debts were so alarming that James came to the Commons to ask for extra-ordinary supply to clear them. After stern lectures about his extrava-gance – one member argued that the royal coffers could not be filled because 'the bottoms be out' – the Commons granted three subsidies: more than could be expected, yet less than was needed.

By the time the Earl of Salisbury became Lord Treasurer, in 1608, the financial situation had gone from bad to worse. Estimates of the King's debts topped £600,000; estimates of his annual deficit exceeded £75,000. Since Salisbury had grown fabulously rich in service of a seem-ingly impoverished king, he approached the problem on the revenue side. As master of the Court of Wards he assiduously increased royal yields and his own fees. In the first decade of James's reign he sold royal lands to the value of £680,000. Moreover, the Treasurer began the first general survey of crown lands to be undertaken in more than half a century, so that rents could be raised to market levels. Salisbury also took the step that Dorset would not. In 1608, following the decision in *Bate's Case* that the king could tax trade at will, Salisbury raised rates and slapped impositions on new goods, which together brought in over £70,000 annually. By 1610 he may have halved the debt and reduced the annual deficit by a third. Yet, other than increasing impositions, Salisbury had done nothing to solve the structural problem.

This could be addressed only in Parliament, and in the final session of the parliament of 1604–10 Salisbury prepared a proposal for a one-time subsidy to pay off the King's debts and a 'contract' to commute some prerogative rights into an annual tax on land worth £200,000. His plan amounted to nothing short of a revolution in royal finance. He could hardly have found a less revolutionary group in which to propose it. The leaders of the Commons immediately revived discussions for the commutation of wardship, purveyance and other prerogative rights to set in opposition to Salisbury's demand for a free gift. They also rehearsed their complaints about impositions. For five months Parliament debated the 'Great Contract', and for five months Commons and Lord Treasurer spoke past each other, because while the King wanted his revenue augmented the Commons wanted it reformed. The leaders of the Lower House were willing to set a high value on the king's prerogatives, but they were not willing to give something for nothing. Thus Salisbury's hope that a gift of £600,000 would be granted for the royal debts was firmly dashed: the Commons granted a subsidy worth only one-sixth of that figure. His desire that royal revenue should be augmented by £200,000 through the Contract fared little better: the Commons would agree to such an annual payment only in exchange for prerogative revenues which were worth at least half that amount. They even attempted to secure a promise that no further impositions would be promulgated without parliamentary concurrence.

Ultimately even this agreement unravelled. At court, opposition to Salisbury was galvanized by the implications of the Contract. Fees would be lost by officers; the rich picking of wardships would no longer be available to courtiers; the King's honour, reflected in his prerogatives, would be lessened by a bargain – his right to command sustenance for his court and men for his armies would be sold like so many chops! In the country, opposition was equally compelling. Those who lived in the north saw no reason to pay for purveyance, which mostly took place in the south. Landowners protested that only they would be liable for the £200,000 annual tax. Everyone agreed that the proposals were unprecedented; that they violated more than the spirit of the doctrine that the king should live of his own. Some feared for the end of parliaments if the king was financially secure. Others, more prescient, feared that, once the principle of annual taxation was established, levels would rise eternally.

The failure of the Great Contract had far-reaching implications. Without an annual subvention, and with debts mounting steadily, Salisbury embarked upon a campaign that would take advantage of what sources of income there were. Reform of procedures in the Court of Wards brought in thousands; titles were sold outright, with earldoms eventually fetching £10,000 and the creation of the new rank of baronet in 1611 bringing in £90,000 in three years. Land revenue was rationalized by selling off uneconomical parcels, converting copyholds to leases, and putting up rents wherever possible. The farmers of the great customs had their contracts renegotiated upwards, and then found themselves touched for large loans. In 1611 another benevolence was launched. All of these measures had political costs. Salisbury argued with great conviction and a clear conscience that everything James did was within his rights – indeed, most of his financial policy was guided by Elizabethan precedents. As the judges made clear in *Bate's Case*, the king had an absolute power, and the 'wisdom and providence of the king is not to be disputed by the subject'. But the constant debates over money in Parliament, in the Council, in London and in local communities made it very difficult not to question this king's 'wisdom and providence'. Worst of all, political expenses did not translate into financial savings. By Salisbury's death in 1612 the royal debt stood at £500,000, and six years later it had risen to £900,000. This was the largest peacetime debt in English history, and in 1618 peacetime was to come to a shattering conclusion.

4

The Duke of Clubs
1618–1628

On 18 September 1628 a torchlight procession made its way to West-minster Abbey. A little more than 100 mourners followed an empty coffin accompanied by soldiers with muskets on their shoulders and tapers held aloft. Though candlelit funeral processions were not un-common on an autumn evening, this one was different. Companies of the London trained bands lined the streets to prevent disorder. The drum beat was more an alarm than a dirge, and the hurried pace of the participants was less than stately. The soldiers kept weapons at the ready rather than trailing their pikes in honour of the corpse. When the empty coffin reached the abbey church the guard did not tarry to fire a salute but 'left him almost to be buried in the dark, everyone running away with his torch'.

Such were the obsequies of George Villiers, Duke of Buckingham, the most hated man in England. His life had ended two weeks earlier when a lone assassin plunged a knife into his side. John Felton, who blamed Buckingham for his personal disappointments, took seriously the political rhetoric that the Duke was 'the grievance of all griev-ances'. He believed he could do himself and his country a singular service. Felton purchased an inexpensive dagger that he hid in his pocket, waited patiently for the Duke to finish breakfast, and then struck the fatal blow so efficiently that it went undetected by all except the victim. He might easily have escaped had he not been so psycho-logically prepared for martyrdom, sewing what amounted to suicide notes in his clothing. 'I am the man, here I am,' he calmly proclaimed as chaos descended upon the hall. Viewing the scene from a balcony, the Duchess and her sister shrieked inconsolably, while it was all officers of state could do to prevent the crowd of suitors who had surrounded the Duke from tearing the assassin to pieces.

The news travelled fast. The King was four miles away and still at

*prayers when he was informed. Charles I did not rise from the service,
but the colour drained from his face. He wept disconsolately for days
afterwards. At court, men put on a visage of sadness whatever they felt.
The Duke's dependants were dumbstruck; his rivals were silently
elated. As one bit of doggerel held, 'This little grave embraces / One
Duke and twenty places.' There was now much office and favour to be
bestowed, for the very centre of power had evaporated. In the streets of
London, subjects rejoiced openly. When Felton marched to prison, onlookers hailed him as a 'little David' and offered prayers for his salvation. 'Live ever Felton: thou hast turn'd to dust / Treason, ambition,
murther, pride, and lust.'*

*The mob hated the Duke viscerally. Two months earlier his physician
(and astrologer), Dr John Lambe, had been beaten to death by a gang
of youths. Broadsheets advertising a similar fate for Buckingham hung
everywhere. He claimed to be unperturbed as he prepared a fleet to
intervene against the slaughter of European Protestants. He had
already survived one attempt on his life, and he refused to take pre-
cautions against another. For nearly a decade he had survived court
factions at home and diplomatic intrigues abroad. For the past three
years he had been the public symbol of all that was wrong in England.
Though his enemies were great, his power was greater. Then, with a
single blow from a ten-penny knife, his power was gone. It was prudence rather than paranoia that led to an armed funeral procession
with an empty coffin in the black of night.*

The ten years between the outbreak of the Thirty Years War in 1618
and the Petition of Right in 1628 might without exaggeration be called
the reign of the Duke of Buckingham. Though his power never rivalled
that attained by Salisbury, his influence far surpassed that of James's
chief minister. The Duke's good looks, force of personality and administrative talents had made him seemingly indispensable. The last
favourite of James I, he rose rapidly under one monarch and then 'by a
kind of wonder, making favour hereditary' retained his position at the
accession of Charles I in 1625. Buckingham charmed James and be-
friended Charles. At the height of the old king's desperate diplomacy,
the Duke had accompanied the then Prince of Wales to Spain in an
effort to conclude a marriage that they believed might have brought
peace to Europe. Though the diplomacy failed, the experiences of the
two young men on that journey bonded them together such that in later

years Charles I read political criticism of the Duke as personal attacks on the monarch. Censure of the Duke was based first on jealousy and then on fear as Buckingham became the conduit of favour and regulated the flow of places and perquisites to his family, friends and clients. Later, critics made the Duke scapegoat for the failures of the Jacobean and Caroline war efforts, damning him first for being too quick to advocate campaigns and then for being too slow to execute them. Like everyone else in this brutal decade, Buckingham was a victim of war.

War tore apart the essential unity of English government. Decisions of war and peace were absolute prerogatives of the monarchy, but the time had long passed when an English monarch could fight an overseas war without the backing of his subjects. When the king's tenants had still owed military service, he could raise his forces by issuing a call to arms. By the seventeenth century, however, the crown raised volunteer armies, and volunteers had to be paid. Thus, to fight a war, the monarch relied upon Parliament for finance. This was unproblematic in 1588, when invasion by the Spanish Armada threatened the nation and Elizabeth I called Parliament to organize defences. It was more complicated for a war of conquest, though visions of glory and national pride stirred more than one generation of Englishmen, and the exploits of Drake, Hawkins and Ralegh lived on in imagination. It was most difficult when war was a tool of diplomacy. James I faced this last circumstance at the outbreak of the Thirty Years War, when Catholic forces dispossessed his son-in-law Frederick, Elector Palatine, from his lands. James hoped to use the threat of war as a lever to have him restored, but a king could only engage in sabre-rattling if he had a sabre to rattle. The House of Commons was understandably reluctant to give subsidies for a war that might never be fought, especially to an improvident king who might spend them anyway. When James I died in 1625 these issues remained unresolved.

The problems Charles I and Buckingham faced were different. They were eager for war against Spain and temporarily joined forces with those hotter Protestants who saw the Thirty Years War as Armageddon. Then they discovered the shocking state of a military that had been allowed to run down for a quarter-century. They found that the navy was antiquated, few arms were manufactured, training was non-existent, and military thinking was still in the Middle Ages. The crash course necessary for survival was going to be expensive and time-consuming. The wars against Spain and France did not go well and, as they found it impossible to blame the system, critics blamed the Duke. The short cuts the King and Buckingham had to take to produce even inadequate expeditions involved the use of royal prerogative powers, the suspension of the common law, the commandeering of ships, the imposition of martial law in civilian communities, forced loans and a continual bullying of Parliament. Throughout the nation, resentment built over the use of emergency powers for war, until the powers, rather than the war, became the emergency.

*　　*　　*

The war that burst upon Europe in 1618 was the most devastating that the continent had ever known. It combined the dynastic conflicts of the first half of the sixteenth century with the confessional struggles of the second half and resulted in thirty years of unrelieved misery. Not even a king who gravitated towards peace could avoid being sucked into the maelstrom. The events in Europe overthrew all of James's policies. Disruption of trade imperilled his fragile finances, confessional slaughter made mockery of his religious moderation, and open warfare disrupted his careful balancing of pro-Spanish and pro-Dutch factions at his court. Worst of all, the war touched his regality. Until his callow son-in-law Frederick, Elector Palatine, accepted the crown of Bohemia, James's credit with Catholics and Protestants, with Habsburgs and Bourbons, made him the arbiter of international peace. Wanting nothing for himself, he could allow others to strike their bargains. He had planned a Catholic Spanish marriage for his eldest son, Prince Henry, who died prematurely in 1612, and a Protestant German marriage for his daughter Elizabeth, which took place in 1613. He both joined the Protestant Union and kept correspondence with the Catholic League. Now, suddenly, events careened out of control.

Frederick had rushed headlong against Ferdinand Habsburg, and he rebounded in a daze. In defiance of the Holy Roman Emperor, he had accepted the kingship offered him by the Protestant nobles of Bohemia. Ferdinand rose to oppose him, gained allies by offering them a share of Frederick's estates, and decisively defeated the pretender at the Battle of White Mountain in 1620. A portion of Frederick's lands was soon occupied by Spaniards, and another portion by Maximilian, Duke of Bavaria, to whom was also transferred Frederick's rights as an Imperial elector. Moreover, the decisive Catholic victory over Protestant forces emboldened Ferdinand to launch a campaign of religious repression, beginning in Bohemia. James I looked upon all of these events with horror. His daughter and son-in-law were exiles; the delicate balance of Catholicism and Protestantism in central Europe was upset; and Spanish and Austrian Habsburgs had acted in military concert to the terror of the rest of Europe.

Though he had opposed Frederick's actions, James had to intervene on his behalf. Except for the fact that there was no solution, the problem was simple. Frederick and the religious map of Europe had to be restored to the *status quo ante bellum*. James might have expected that the Emperor Ferdinand would prove reluctant to pardon a rebel and Maximilian of Bavaria to disgorge the spoils of war, but it came as a shock to learn that Frederick himself would brook no compromise. He toured the Protestant capitals of Europe demanding military support which, though undeserved, could not be refused. The Austrian Habsburgs had strengthened their grip in eastern Europe and the Spanish Habsburgs had secured the crucial passages along the Rhine whereby they could launch their expected invasion against the Dutch. A settlement would take either all of James's diplomatic skill or all of the resources he could muster for war.

Ever since he came to the English throne, James had pursued a policy of peace in a world riven by war. In 1604 he concluded a treaty with Spain that ended nearly two decades of sporadic fighting, and throughout his reign he attempted to avoid renewal of Anglo-Spanish hostilities. This meant neutrality towards France, Spain's great dynastic enemy, and towards the Dutch provinces which struggled to maintain the independence they had won from Spanish control. The assassination in 1610 of Henry IV made the former easier by removing France from international intrigue during the minority of his successor. James achieved his second objective by balancing religious and mercantile interests. The Calvinist Dutch were natural allies of England, especially when both were openly at war with Spain. Otherwise they were natural rivals, naval and commercial powers which competed for trade all around an ever-shrinking globe. The pressure on the King to support his co-religionists eased in 1609 when Spain and Holland signed a twelve-year truce. For the next decade James balanced the factions at his court as adroitly as ever had Elizabeth.

Though the Earl of Salisbury had monopolized office and patronage, he had never had the affection of the King. After his death in 1612, James dispersed his power, assuming the roles of Treasurer and Secretary himself for a time, and encouraging competition at court. He channelled his personal favours through Robert Carr, a dashing Scotsman who caught his attention by breaking a leg in a tournament. James lavished gifts upon him – lands confiscated from Sir Walter Ralegh among them – and promoted him with unseemly rapidity through the ranks of the English nobility, making him Viscount Rochester in 1611 and then Earl of Somerset two years later. Through his office of Lord Chamberlain, Somerset indulged his taste for frivolous entertainment while carefully controlling direct access to the King. He was aptly described as 'the bright sun at whose splendour or glooming all our marigolds of the court open or shut'.

Somerset's power rested on his role as favourite, and he made little effort to expand his influence. He left politics to his factional allies, the Howards, the premier Catholic family in England, whose ramifying lineage included Lord Admiral Charles Howard, Earl of Nottingham, hero of the repulse of the Spanish Armada; Lord Privy Seal Henry Howard, Earl of Northampton, who effectively controlled day-to-day government after Salisbury's death; Thomas Howard, Earl of Suffolk, soon to set new standards of corruption for a Lord Treasurer; and Thomas Howard, Earl of Arundel, who, as a direct descendant of the Duke of Norfolk, was recognized as the premier peer in England. The Howards were neither a party nor a political pressure group. They did not always agree, either personally or on matters of policy. They were identified with the Catholic, pro-Spanish interest, though Nottingham and Suffolk had distinguished themselves against the Armada and Arundel had converted to Protestantism. Yet they formed a clientage network of great potency and they translated their accumulation of office into political control once Somerset fell desperately in love with Suffolk's daughter, Lady Frances Howard, Countess of Essex.

The love affair between Somerset and Lady Frances Howard was the scandal of the age. Under the tutelage of her septuagenarian uncle Northampton, Lady Frances thrust her ample charms upon the favourite. In order to free herself from the Earl of Essex, she had to make good the claim that her five-year-old marriage had never been consummated and that her husband's impotence resulted from demonic possession. Essex's humiliation was only one consequence of these very public proceedings. More spectacular was Lady Frances's complicity in the death of Somerset's erstwhile companion Sir Thomas Overbury, who opposed the marriage and the rise of the Howards with such vehemence that they contrived to imprison him in the Tower. There he was poisoned. But the discovery of the Overbury affair lay two years in the future when in 1613 Somerset and Lady Frances Howard celebrated their marriage in the presence of the King to the accompaniment of masques by Thomas Campion and Ben Jonson.

The marriage secured the rise of the Howards to power. Suffolk resigned his office of Chamberlain to his son-in-law and consoled himself with the Treasurership. Northampton, in the last year of his life, still directed the Privy Council. He was an able administrator, and his long years of service in collaboration with Salisbury had taught him the practical limitations of royal government. Northampton had proposed a Spanish marriage for the Prince of Wales, and the death of the devoutly Protestant Prince Henry in 1612 had given this policy new impetus. A Spanish marriage would balance the German one recently concluded for Princess Elizabeth and provide James with a large dowry to pay off his mounting debts. These were so serious that the King had already issued writs for a parliament to be held in 1614. Northampton opposed the summoning of Parliament, fearful both of revelations that members of government had accepted Spanish pensions and of criticism of the fiscal expedients of the past four years. With the Privy Council divided, the parliament was a disaster, earning its sobriquet the Addled Parliament from the confusion that dominated its six-week existence. After its dissolution, negotiations for a Spanish match with Prince Charles began in earnest.

Though the Howards had increased their power through their connection with the King's favourite, Somerset, they did not alone control British politics. Indeed, the family's pro-Spanish Catholicism spurred the consolidation of a faction against them which identified itself with the cause of international Protestantism. William Herbert, Earl of Pembroke, England's great literary patron to whom Shakespeare's first folio was dedicated, and Henry Wriothesley, Earl of Southampton, one of the Essex conspirators released from prison on James's accession, led this faction. Both Pembroke and Southampton invested in overseas trading companies and supported the policies which had resulted in the raiding parties that Sir Walter Ralegh led against the Spanish. They were joined by George Abbot, Archbishop of Canterbury, who had fallen out with James over the divorce of Lady Frances Howard, and, somewhat reluctantly, by Queen Anne, whose own Catholicism was offset by the diplomatic needs of her brother, Christian IV of Denmark. This group had supported the summoning of Parliament in 1614 in hopes that James could remain independent from Spain by grants of parliamentary finance. This course was urged by the great polymath Sir Francis Bacon, Attorney-General to the King and the most profound political thinker of the day. Bacon believed that the relationship between James and Parliament could be a constructive one, especially if the King used Parliament to reform laws and air grievances. But the addling of the 1614 session confounded Bacon's strategy.

For the anti-Howard faction to succeed, it needed to fight fire with fire. Somerset's influence and his control of access to the King had to be diminished, and this could be done only by finding a substitute for the King's affection. The choice lighted upon George Villiers, the son of a declining Leicestershire gentry family, who was described by all who saw him as 'the handsomest bodied man in England'. Villiers was primped for his part no less industriously than Lady Frances Howard had been for hers. He already had the benefit of a long Continental stay during which he had refined his deportment and acquired a veneer of grace. Villiers was too poor to cut a figure, and it is an indication of both his potential and the operation of favour at the Jacobean court that Sir Arthur Ingram, one of the shrewdest businessmen of the day, invested £100 to help outfit him. It was money well spent. At the plea of the Queen, Villiers was made cupbearer at the royal table, where he immediately attracted James's eye and Somerset's wrath. In 1615 he was knighted and made a gentleman of the bedchamber, and the following year he became the first commoner to hold the office of Master of the Horse. This anomaly was soon rectified when Villiers was created a viscount in 1616 and Earl of Buckingham five months later – 'his rise was like a flight', observed the historian the Earl of Clarendon.

Though Buckingham took the same path to power as had Somerset, the two had very little else in common. Buckingham was astute and hardworking. He was no mere adornment to the offices he held: he learned their tasks and reformed their administration. As Master of the Horse – normally a ceremonial office – Buckingham imported superior Continental horses and cross-bred his purchases to the advantage of English stock. As Lord Admiral he encouraged the appointment of an investigative commission into the state of the navy. Almost immediately he surrounded himself with the ablest minds of the capital. Francis Bacon advised him on legal and political affairs, and Lionel Cranfield, a spectacularly successful City merchant, tutored him on finances. He undertook a crash course on government administration, domestic policy and foreign affairs. Buckingham was not content to be a mere favourite, even after the revelations of the murder of Sir Thomas Overbury removed Somerset from the King's side. His ambition was to become minister of state: to control policy as well as favour.

Buckingham's dedication to the affairs of his state was surpassed only by his dedication to the state of his affairs. His meagre fortune was incapable of supporting the dignity of even his meanest office. To acquire the wealth appropriate to his station, Buckingham had to rely upon the favour of the King and the informal system of fees, gifts and perquisites which were separated by only a narrow line from bribery, kickbacks and corruption. James, as always, was generous and attached lands to Buckingham's titles in ever-increasing abundance. Cash gifts, the emoluments of office, reversions of places, titles to sell: the King heaped them all upon the favourite. With Cranfield's advice, Buckingham bought and sold pieces of customs farms at huge profits. He peddled his influence openly, accepting cash gifts in return for nominating aspirants to office. By 1620 he may have had an annual income of nearly £20,000, though this enormous sum was only a portion of the money that was at his disposal.

Buckingham set out to create a lineage. He arranged marriages for himself and his relations that brought social as well as financial benefits. He took Katherine Manners, daughter of the Earl of Rutland, for his own wife, securing attachment to England's premier Midland family as well as a dowry of £10,000 and lands worth £5,000 a year. His brother married a daughter of Sir Edward Coke, his sister the son of the Earl of Denbigh. Marriage alliances connected Buckingham to a host of leading aristocratic families, including the Cecils, Manners, Fieldings, Herberts and Montagus. Though it would take some doing to rival the Howards, by the 1620s the Villiers could count a duke and duchess, two countesses, an earl and viscount among their numbers – all created in less than a decade. Buckingham's income went to found a country estate and to underwrite a building campaign on a vast scale. He entertained lavishly, both at court and in the country, where resentment and respect were found in equal parts. Like Salisbury and Suffolk, the more Buckingham's income grew, the deeper he fell into debt. His contribution to the conspicuous expenditure of the age was by no means negligible.

Buckingham's ambition and rapaciousness should not obscure his breadth of vision. However he may have started, he was not just another pretty face – as those who underestimated him learned to their cost. With Somerset as a model and Bacon as a tutor, he understood that great advancement secured great enemies. He attempted to apply the brakes to James's generosity, refusing the post of Lord Admiral at its initial offering on the grounds of inexperience, and the dukedom for the hostility it would provoke. Indeed, Buckingham persuaded James to raise the Earl of Lennox to a dukedom first, so that a Villiers would not be the premier nobleman of the realm. All of this was aimed at the future. So too were his shrewd political instincts. He cultivated the Prince of Wales as assiduously as he did the King, and ultimately turned Charles's aloof disdain into an abiding friendship, despite having been his father's lover. His survival from one reign to the next was the marvel of all observers. Above all he strove to build alliances at court. The prediction made by Queen Anne that those who promoted him would live to regret it turned out to be true, though she escaped the ingratitude by succumbing to dropsy in 1619. Yet throughout his career Buckingham moved between the faction led by the Howards and that led by the Earl of Pembroke, allowing each to feed at the trough of favour and pursuing, at different times, their conflicting programmes.

While Buckingham busily gained his fortune, Frederick of Bohemia busily lost his. The fates of favourite and son-in-law were soon entangled. After the defeat of Frederick's forces at the Battle of White Mountain, his enemies began to dismember his estates. Fears for the survival of the Protestant cause swept England; fears for the revival of all--out war swept the Continent. The twelve years' truce had run its course, and Spain's occupation of the lower Palatinate ensured a resumption of its war with the Dutch. James I engaged in fevered diplomacy to restore Frederick's estates and lower the international temperature. To have any hope of success, he needed the support of his subjects. After a seven-year hiatus, he summoned Parliament to meet in 1621.

Ironically, management of Parliament was left to Lord Chancellor Bacon, who was to be impeached during the session. Bacon urged a pre-emptive strike against those grievances that were likeliest to be raised in Parliament – monopolies and patents – but this judicious advice was ultimately ignored. Complaints against monopolists were long a parliamentary grievance, and the economic recession of the past few years intensified the outcry. In truth, schemes like the Cockayne Project, in which a syndicate of London merchants was given the right to export coloured cloth while the export of undyed cloth was inhibited, were unmitigated disasters. Nevertheless, it was also true that patents encouraged inventions and investment, rewarded ingenuity, and provided remedies for a variety of economic abuses ranging from the manufacture of poor-quality goods to tax evasion. Bacon argued that by curtailing notoriously abusive patents James would propitiate his subjects while heading off a potentially destructive debate. Privately he wrote to Buckingham to inform him that the latter's brothers were investors in at least two patents that were likely to undergo scrutiny. Bacon also urged that a legislative programme be prepared so that the work of the House of Commons in particular would be constructively channelled. As no statutes had been passed in over a decade, Parliament had much to do.

For reasons of his own, James decided to give Parliament its head. He had been stung in 1614 by accusations that he had arranged an undertaking in which he bargained money for reform. Suppressing monopolies before Parliament was convened might create similar distrust. Moreover, the regulation of economic activity was a matter of royal prerogative, and, even if he could be induced to give up the income, he would not barter with the privilege. The highest legal officers of the realm vetted the legality of every patent. If there were abuses, they were in the overstepping of rights, not in their granting. As for legislation, that too could be left to the members. A prepared programme would only distract Parliament from its purpose: the provision of money in response to the European emergency.

The initial session of the parliament of 1621 exceeded even the King's optimistic expectations and he prematurely dubbed it 'the happiest parliament that ever was'. The Commons granted two subsidies immediately to enable James to pursue his options for Frederick's restoration. Anti-Spanish feeling ran high, allowing foreign ambassadors to report confidently that England was preparing for war. The Privy Council had estimated that a force of 25,000 men would cost £900,000 a year to maintain, but the King had not yet asked Parliament to raise an army of invasion. Indeed, in his opening speech James hid his intentions behind rousing platitudes. He described the European situation as a 'miserable spectacle that no man can look upon without a weeping eye' and issued a ringing declaration that he was willing to risk 'my crown, my blood and the blood of my son' to restore Frederick's rights. Behind the scenes, however, he was doing everything possible to avoid an open breach with Spain, refusing even to admit that the Marquis de Spinola's occupation of the lower Palatinate constituted an invasion.

As Bacon predicted, the hounds in the Commons quickly raised the cry of patents and monopolies. James sanctioned the hunt, which resulted in the conviction of Sir Giles Mompesson for abuse of power and in the initiation of a bill to strike down monopolies in general. The King cooperated as far as he could, issuing a proclamation between sessions to abolish monopolies for the regulation of inns had alehouses and for the manufacture of gold and silver thread. The first two impinged upon the governing power of local justices; the third was blamed, implausibly, for contributing to the shortage of specie. Yet if Bacon had anticipated the debate on monopolies and patents, he could hardly have anticipated its consequences. With members of the Commons incapable of questioning the King, they began to question his advisers. Who were the legal officers who had approved the patents? This led, in a circuitous route, to Bacon himself, who was impeached not for his role in authorizing patents but for taking bribes in cases that he had judged. James allowed the impeachment of Bacon to go forward. He may have taken some perverse delight in watching the hectoring Bacon hectored himself, knowing that he could mitigate the worst of any sentence. He may have welcomed the shift in emphasis from questioning his prerogatives to punishing misfeasance. For whatever reason, he left Bacon to twist slowly in the wind, and it is a measure of Buckingham's character that he remained outspokenly loyal to his mentor, casting the single vote of dissent against his punishment in the Lords.

The impeachment of Bacon also diverted attention from foreign affairs, which caused a hasty reconvening for a second session in the autumn. James had hoped that the free gift from his people would strengthen his hand in negotiations with Emperor Ferdinand for the restoration of Frederick's rights. While Parliament was in recess, his ambassadors returned with the disagreeable news that not only had his overtures failed but the Habsburgs had taken even more of the Palatinate, despite the threat of English intervention. The Protestant forces, commanded by Sir Horace Vere, who were garrisoning the last of Frederick's cities urgently needed money. Nevertheless, James believed that Spain wanted England as an ally rather than an enemy in its oncoming war with the Dutch. Spanish diplomats in Vienna had urged Ferdinand to find a solution to the Bohemian crisis that would not plunge the Continent into war. Unfortunately, Philip IV was to have no greater control over his cousin Ferdinand than James I had over his son-in-law Frederick.

In these circumstances, James needed to make diligent preparations for war. Though he had promised to resummon Parliament to finish its work on legislation, the issue of the Palatinate dominated the second session of the parliament of 1621. News of the recent events in Europe had spread throughout the nation, carried in broadsides and newsletters copied from hand to hand. These portrayed the plight of Princess Elizabeth pathetically and whipped popular anti-popery, primarily directed at Spain, to a fever pitch. The House of Commons immediately voted James an additional subsidy, and member after member rose to pledge life and fortune for the recovery of the Palatinate. There the unanimity ended, for on the question of how such a recovery was to take place there was little agreement. Though James wanted wages for war, he refused to say what kind of war would be waged.

This left members of the Commons baffled, until Sir George Goring, one of Buckingham's known spokesmen in the Lower House, moved that 'if the King of Spain withdraw not his forces from the Palatinate and come not to [James's] proposition, let us petition for war against him'. Most members of the House wished to take this course, and they now assumed, despite James's own previous caution, that it was royal policy. The House quickly drew up a petition, and, along with the request for war with Spain, it proposed that Prince Charles be married to a Protestant. If a petition for a specific course of foreign policy trod dangerously close to the King's prerogative, discussion of a royal marriage trampled on it. Even if James was contemplating a war for the restoration of the Palatinate, he would need the prospect of a Spanish match as a means of ending it. Nor did Charles relish subjects debating his marriage as if he were breeding-stock: he complained to his father that his private affairs were 'prostituted in the lower House'.

The Commons' petition wrecked the parliament of 1621 and, more importantly, limited James's options. The King's strongly worded censure of the petition even before it was presented led inevitably to a protest over parliamentary privilege. Members who only days before were unabashed mouthpieces for the government now asserted in a formal protestation that free speech in Parliament was 'the ancient and undoubted birthright and inheritance of the subjects of England'. The King, who had invited a discussion of his foreign affairs, now hid behind the screen of national security and royal prerogative. He summarily dissolved Parliament, forfeiting the subsidy that had been voted but not enrolled, and killing dozens of pieces of legislation that had been left from the first session. In an act of supererogation, he personally ripped the Commons' protestation from their journal and after the dissolution imprisoned five of their leaders, including the privy counsellor Sir Edward Coke. The night James dissolved Parliament his horse flung him head first into a river.

James's frustration was complete. He had failed to find a diplomatic solution with the Austrian Habsburgs and he had failed to prevent the seizure of the lower Palatinate by the Spanish. He could no more control his son-in-law Frederick, who was egging the Dutch into war, or his parliament to grant money without restrictions than he could his horse. Despite the fact that Buckingham had been promoted by the anti-Spanish faction at court, he was increasingly hostile to the Dutch, whose raids on English ships and commercial outposts touched the Lord Admiral directly. He moved closer to the Howards – Somerset and Lady Frances were released from prison – and closer to a war with Holland, a war that necessitated the Spanish match. Negotiations were revived with the intention that, once the marriage treaty was concluded, the English would join in attacking the Dutch.

The diplomatic advantages of a Spanish marriage had to be weighed against its domestic liabilities. The Spaniards, especially after the failure of the parliament of 1621, were likely to bargain hard. Philip IV, who now succeeded his father, practised a rigid religion which would not bow to the necessities of state. If Charles was to marry a Spanish infanta, he would have to agree to tolerate his own Catholic subjects, to allow his wife to practise Catholicism and raise their children Catholic, and to take instruction that would lead to his own conversion. Although James suspended the enforcement of the recusancy laws in advance of negotiations, such terms could hardly be made public, let alone accepted. Anti-Catholicism, never far below the surface of English politics, was at another of its cyclical peaks, rising both on news of events in Europe and in expectation of imminent war with Spain. At one level anti-Catholicism was a hysteria which could grip people of all social groups with a physical fear; at another level it was an ideology which held that Catholic conspirators manipulated human history. When the two strains intersected, as they did in the early 1620s, the interpretation of current events became hypercharged and everything was seen as a plot in which even loyal Protestants could be unwitting victims. Thus the dissolution of the parliament of 1621 was attributed to the machinations of the Spanish agent Count Gondomar, and James I, the intended victim of the Gunpowder Plot, was cast in the unlikely role of a Jesuit tool. In the following year Heidelberg fell and the Emperor re-Catholicized Bohemia. As negotiations dragged on inconclusively, fear of the consequences of a Spanish marriage deepened.

Thus a shocked nation learned, in February 1623, that Prince Charles and the Earl of Buckingham had crossed the Channel and made their way to Madrid. It was not only James who wept, fasted and prayed for the safe return of the Prince: for the only time in his life, Charles was the object of the affection of his people. Rumours that he had been kidnapped or bewitched were used to explain the secret journey. Critics blamed Buckingham particularly, and saw his family's Catholicism as part of the plot. In truth, the Prince wanted to go and claim his bride as his father had done before him. Charles had grown restive over the drawn-out negotiations, many of the details of which centred on his future conduct. He believed that his personal arrival in Spain would show his determination to cut to the heart of the matter. James did not approve of the journey, but he did accede to it. He gave his son over to the special care of his favourite, creating an unbreakable bond between them. It was an episode of youthful high jinks that they could have reminisced about in old age, had either of them grown old. Heavily disguised in beards and periwigs and inverting the roles of master and servant, they crossed, seasick, into France and prepared for the long overland journey to Spain. On the road to Paris alone Buckingham's horse fell seven times, and he ended the day battered and besmirched. Calling themselves the Smith brothers, they visited the French court incognito and then sped their way south.

They reached the home of the English ambassador to Madrid, the Earl of Bristol, two weeks after they had set off from London. Their arrival amazed Bristol only less than it did Philip IV and his chief minister, Olivares, who were genuinely perplexed by the news. Charles's appearance meant that Philip could no longer simply stall: negotiations would have to be either concluded or broken off. Philip was not persuaded that an English alliance was worth the return of the Palatinate or that he needed English help to defeat the Dutch. He had therefore asked the papacy to hold back the dispensation necessary for the Infanta to marry a Protestant. The arrival of the Prince in Madrid at the start of Holy Week suggested that Charles was now prepared to convert to Catholicism and that Philip was to have the credit for bringing England back into the fold of the Mother Church.

While Buckingham took over the treaty negotiations from Bristol, Charles fell madly in love with the Infanta, though Spanish convention had kept the two so far apart that in the first weeks the Prince had seen her only twice – from a distance, and in profile. The longer he stayed in Spain the higher his emotions ran, and Charles actually leaped over a wall to surprise the Infanta walking in a garden. She fled in terror. It was all Buckingham could do to keep the lovestruck Charles from accepting the most humiliating conditions for his marriage, including conversion to Catholicism. Meanwhile, sensing the strength of his position, Philip IV raised the stakes. He demanded guarantees for the toleration of English Catholics while insisting that he could do nothing definite about the restoration of Frederick's imperial rights. Month after month he threw new obstacles in the path. He lowered his offer of a dowry, citing his increased military expenditures. It was not lost, even on the emotionally distraught Prince, that a part of those costs resulted from Spanish occupation of the Palatinate. Indeed, despite Charles's willingness to make concessions, nothing was offered for his sister and her husband in return. At the end of six months there were as many difficulties as ever, and the Prince now agreed with Buckingham that they had been duped.

If Charles played the role of the starstruck lover to perfection in Madrid, he played that of the spurned lover equally well in London. No sooner had he set foot on English soil than he began a campaign for war with Spain. If the self-effacing Prince was discomfited, the haughty Buckingham was in high dudgeon. Despite warning from the Earl of Bristol that the Spanish court was extremely formal, Buckingham had plunged into diplomacy, committing one gaffe after another. The Spanish were shocked at the familiarity he showed Charles – Buckingham was once discovered in the presence of the Prince without his breeches on – and did their best to snub him. Olivares treated him as a servant even after James had elevated him to a dukedom in May. Buckingham could hardly restrain himself from challenging the Condeduque to a duel, and he became so frustrated during a debate over religion with a Jesuit that he actually stomped upon his own hat.

Indeed, it was difficult to know which of the infuriated travellers was more eager for revenge.

The outpouring of popular relief at the return of the Prince without a Spanish bride gave Charles and Buckingham leverage in persuading James to call another parliament. The King, now physically decrepit, could think of nothing he wanted less than another troublesome convention of his subjects, unless it was a war. But he could not resist the combined ministrations of his son and his favourite and, against his inclination, he summoned the parliament of 1624. Charles and Buckingham worked assiduously to make the assembly a success. They were now the very champions of parliaments, and they cultivated potential leaders in both Houses, elevating peers, distributing offices, even engaging in hypothetical discussions about policy. Buckingham's shift from a pro- to an anti-Spanish stance created a veritable revolution in political relationships. He took on board clients who after 1621 had despaired of ever guiding the ship of state. He jettisoned his old dependants, like Cranfield, who opposed what promised to be a ruinously expensive policy. Finally, he prevailed upon James to soften his attitudes. Buckingham would relate to Parliament what had passed in Spain, and the Houses would be invited to debate a specific matter of policy: the breaking off of the negotiations for Charles's marriage and the return of the Palatinate. If, after this, Parliament voted to supply the King, then war would follow.

The task of management was an enormous challenge. The 23-year-old Prince took to attending sessions of the House of Lords and learned at first hand the complexities of policy and legislation. Before the opening of Parliament, the Spanish offered to conclude the marriage and to withdraw their troops from the Palatinate. It was a brilliant diplomatic gambit which divided the Privy Council and widened the chasm between father and son. Charles now resolutely opposed a Spanish marriage, and Buckingham made overtures to France in the hope of finding an equally powerful ally and an equally large dowry. But for James even the dimmest prospect for a peaceful conclusion of the Palatinate crisis was a beacon to be followed. With some privy counsellors opposed to war on fiscal grounds, and others opposed to anything other than attacks on Spanish shipping, it was all the Duke and the Prince could do to keep up a drum beat.

Thus the parliament of 1624 faced both a divided court and a divided crown. The Prince and the Duke wanted war, while James wanted money as diplomatic leverage. As ever, leaders of Parliament were concerned with their pocketbooks and their reputations in their local communities. In 1621 they had given two subsidies and passed no bills. They had expected war with Spain and instead had got negotiations for a marriage. This time they would pass legislation and restrict their spending to specific purposes. Members were willing to support war, though they were not enthusiastic. They had more passion for strengthening laws against recusants and for launching raiding-parties against Spanish shipping than for an expeditionary force to Germany.

Thus members of Parliament advised James to break off the treaties with Spain, but they did not provide the money necessary to regain the Palatinate by force. Even the Duke settled for only half of previous estimates of the cost of war, and when James asked for six subsidies the Commons offered three. Trade was still too depressed, the King was still too generous, and fiscal corruption was still too prevalent. James threw Lord Treasurer Cranfield to the wolves – the Commons impeached him for corruption, though his real crime was opposition to Buckingham and the war – but the King could do nothing about the international economy and, after twenty years, precious little about his own liberality. On the surface, the parliament of 1624 was the most successful of James's reign. The Houses gave three subsidies to be paid in a single year, which constituted the largest grant ever made, and nearly three dozen statutes received the King's assent. At every other level, however, it was a catastrophe. Factional feuding again led to the impeachment of a royal minister – a device which James warned Buckingham was a rod for his own back. Restrictions placed by the Commons on the use of subsidies usurped royal prerogatives and created the conditions for future conflict. More importantly, by starving the crown of money, Parliament drove Charles into a disastrous French marriage and Buckingham into the foreign-policy débâcles of the next five years.

After the conclusion of the parliament, Charles gained a wife and lost a father in rapid succession. If there could be no Spanish match, there would have to be a French one. Only France could provide a counterbalance to Spanish power in Europe and a dowry large enough to make a dent in the royal deficit. Charles married Henrietta-Maria, Louis XIII's younger sister, by proxy. There were no dashing escapades, only the cold realities of diplomacy. The French drove a hard bargain, insisting, as had the Spanish, that the Queen be allowed to practise her

religion and raise her children in it – a concession of the greatest consequence for the future of the Stuart monarchy. She brought her own
Catholic entourage to London, including priests to conduct services. In
a separate memorandum James (and Charles after him) promised to
relax the laws against recusants. In return, Buckingham believed that he
had secured French support for war against Spain. Yet while Louis and
his chief minister, Cardinal Richelieu, opposed Spanish expansion,
they favoured a war of attrition between Spain and Holland. When
James I died, in March 1625, French aid failed to materialize.

James's death released the brakes from a full-scale war effort.
Charles quickly initiated treaties with the Dutch and the Danes and
announced to the parliament that assembled for his accession in 1625
that he would lead England on a crusade to recover the Palatinate. He
had directed Buckingham as Lord Admiral to prepare a naval expedition such as parliaments had advised since 1621 – an expedition that
would attack Spanish ports and intercept the treasure fleets from the
Indies. Subsidies would fund a land war in Germany – a less costly
alternative than an English expeditionary force. Supporters talked of
the advantages of the French alliance – critics worried about the concessions that had been made to secure it – and Charles genuinely expected that his subjects would open their hearts to a new king and their
purses to an active war effort.

Such might have been the case had there been any concrete achievement of royal policy. For four years James I had taken money for a war
that he had never waged, while his diplomacy had achieved nothing.
There was little to show for the three subsidies granted the previous
year; indeed part of them had been spent on Protestant mercenary
forces in apparent contravention of the subsidy act. Moreover, the 'blue
water' policy that Parliament had always advocated meant an increased
role for the navy and for Lord Admiral Buckingham, who had survived
the change of monarchs. He had no experience of war or of naval
command, and critics spitefully recalled his acute seasickness during
the journey to Madrid. Nevertheless, the parliament of 1625 voted two
more subsidies for a naval expedition, though it would give no more
until it saw results.

Results were not long in coming. The expedition that Buckingham
directed achieved nothing. Most of the Spanish treasure fleet was already safely harboured before the English force set out, and the attempt
to take the port of Cadiz – to relive the glories of Sir Walter Ralegh –

failed. Buckingham was faulted for everything. The ships were badly outfitted; the provisions were inadequate; the pressed soldiers were a ragtag; the commanders were inexperienced; the strategy was ill-conceived. Buckingham's true fault was failure, and his failures multiplied. English ships that had been lent to France to attack Spanish forces pounded French Protestants in La Rochelle instead. Worse still, Richelieu secretly negotiated a separate peace with Spain. Buckingham was unable to explain the one or the other; in fact he had been betrayed.

The parliament that met in 1626 was determined to rid the nation of the Duke. The lone voices that had been raised against him in 1625 were now a chorus, and they bayed for blood. If the King wanted money, he would first have to address the grievances of his people, and the grievance of all grievances was the Duke. Though Charles had kept Buckingham's most vocal opponents out of Parliament by naming them county sheriffs, this did little to stifle the outcry. The Duke had too many enemies: there were those whom he had leaped over in his flight to power; those whom he had disappointed; those whom he had opposed. They could now combine with others who disagreed with his military strategy or condemned his incompetence. They talked wildly that he had committed treason while in Spain and that he had murdered James I with a potion. The more astute worried about the survival of their institution, for Buckingham had already urged Charles to adopt 'new counsels' and dispense with parliaments. All of this added up to a furious attack upon the Duke. Charles warned the Commons not to proceed against 'such as are of eminent place and near unto me', but the Commons prepared a bill of impeachment. This incensed the King, and he sent among others Sir John Eliot, one of Buckingham's sharpest critics, to the Tower. Predictably, this precipitated a crisis over freedom of speech from which Charles at first backed down in the hope of getting the three subsidies that had been approved but not yet voted. He warned the Commons that their session was in jeopardy: 'as I find the fruits of [parliaments] good or evil they are to continue or not to be'. By now, too many members of both Houses had eaten from the tree of knowledge. Buckingham's impeachment went forward, and Charles expelled Parliament from Westminster.

The premature dissolution of the parliament of 1626 was a calculated risk. It said something for the King's character that he would not abandon his friend, and he believed, as did the Duke, that victory would redeem all. Unfortunately for Charles, the risk became much greater when Imperial forces defeated the Danes at the Battle of Lutter. It was now urgent that Christian IV be resupplied before defeat became disaster. Without parliamentary subsidy, Charles asked his Privy Council to find another source of finance. They hit upon the scheme of a loan to be assessed at the rate of five subsidies for the express purpose of relieving the Protestant forces.

Forced loans had long been part of royal revenue schemes, yet never had one been so closely linked to the failure to receive parliamentary assistance. Given suspicions that went back to the early years of James I, the forced loan roused concerns for the future of Parliament. Proclamations were issued, sermons were preached, and members of the Council and the House of Lords were sent into the country to emphasize the King's need. A Spanish invasion scare and concern over the fate of international Protestantism contributed to the early success of the loan. But gradually resistance emerged – especially after the royal judges refused an unconditional sanction of its legality. The crown imprisoned over seventy gentlemen for nonpayment, and several of them sued for bail which had been denied when they were jailed by special command of the King. The judges refused bail and also refused to examine the question of whether loan resisters should be so incarcerated. The *Five Knights' Case* (1627) raised fundamental legal questions: could the king raise money without parliamentary consent and could he imprison his subjects without showing cause? For the moment both had been answered affirmatively. The forced loan brought in over £240,000, but if it was a fiscal success it was a political catastrophe. The King had to imprison his subjects, dismiss his chief justice, and replace Lord Lieutenants and JPs to enforce compliance. To shut off a debate over Buckingham, he had to open one over English liberties.

Yet for the time being the money was welcome. It stanched the bleeding of Protestant forces in Germany and it enabled Buckingham to prepare another invasion fleet – this one against France. Ever since Richelieu's secret treaty with Spain, Anglo-French relations had deteriorated, until they had sunk to the same level as Charles's relations with his wife. A teenager in a foreign land, Henrietta-Maria proved as troublesome to Charles as a parliament. She pouted and wept by turns, denied the King his marital rights whenever possible, and became the centre for Catholic intrigue against Buckingham. Though Charles had promised leniency to English recusants and a welcome to his wife's attendants, he soon reneged on both. This gave a personal tinge to a continuing controversy over the return of French ships seized for carrying contraband to Spain. When France retaliated by detaining the entire English wine fleet, the two nations were on a course for war.

The English sold confiscated French cargoes to finance a war fleet which the Lord Admiral himself led in relief of the Protestants of La Rochelle. Buckingham hoped to create an alliance of disaffected French noblemen and dissident Protestants to overthrow Richelieu, and the first step was a military expedition. Stung by the failure at Cadiz, the Duke managed the details of the Rhé expedition himself. He ensured that the ships were serviceable, the provisions fresh, and the soldiers stout-hearted. He spent generously from his own coffers, and omitted nothing necessary for success. Once he had landed and secured a beachhead, reinforcements would follow and England would have an outpost from which to seize French and Spanish shipping. But if Cadiz was a débâcle, Rhé was a disaster. Buckingham did his part, but reinforcements never arrived and the French managed to relieve the besieged garrison just before it capitulated. An English attempt at a storm cost hundreds of lives when the scaling-ladders proved too short for the walls. Even the retreat went wrong, and dozens of English officers were captured. The expedition limped home.

The failure of the expedition to Rhé left Charles more desperate for money than ever. While he resorted to the expedients of selling crown lands and borrowing in advance of receipts, his ordinary revenues were insufficient for the needs of ships and soldiers. Many privy counsellors and Lord Lieutenants had appealed to their countrymen in 1626 to loan money to the crown only on an emergency basis. Such an appeal could not be repeated. Those within the Council who urged the calling of Parliament finally gained the upper hand. They tacitly accepted that any attack upon the Duke would result in immediate dissolution and another wave of prerogative finance. Charles wished to be united with his subjects and to proceed in a parliamentary way, though not at the price of his favourite. In truth, all had reason to believe that the parliament of 1628 would succeed where its predecessors had failed. For one thing, Protestant fortunes in Europe were at their lowest ebb and most Englishmen approved of the attacks on both France and Spain. For another, there was a growing realization that English liberties were in danger and that only Parliament could protect them. Leaders of the two Houses clearly understood that the future of their institution hung in the balance. They would spare the Duke, but in return for subsidies Charles would confirm traditional protection of the property and persons of his subjects. The King gave his permission for a bill of grievances to be drawn which would confirm rights without encroaching on his prerogative.

The first session began well when the Commons approved a grant of five subsidies. The King was overjoyed when informed that the motion had carried unanimously. 'Now I see with this I shall have the affection of my people. I love parliaments. I shall rejoice to meet with my people often.' While the five subsidies had been agreed in principle, they had not been formed into a bill and would not be until the completion of the bill of grievances. This focused upon the issues that grew out of the military emergency. In the localities, provost-marshals forcibly billeted soldiers upon housekeepers. Since they could not pay for their keep, the soldiers simply took what they needed. To maintain order, military commanders placed these communities under martial law, suspending the rights of soldiers and civilians alike. More importantly, the crown had compelled subjects to give money that had not been approved by Parliament. When they refused, they were arrested and denied bail. Examination of the *Five Knights' Case* revealed that the common law did not protect undoubted liberties. The Commons focused on two issues: the king's right to compel money from his subjects and his right to imprison them without a specific charge. Both clearly violated the ordinary law of the land, but both were also clearly permitted in special circumstances.

Though the greatest legal minds in the Commons had no difficulty in identifying the statutes that protected subjects from the seizure of their property and from arbitrary imprisonment, they could not sweep away the exceptions to the rules. On one level it was simply a matter of trust, and Charles, desperate to launch his fleet while it would still do some good, promptly gave his word that his subjects could trust him. This threw the Commons into disarray and divided opinion between the Houses. The Lords believed that the King's willingness to reconfirm those statutes that protected subjects' rights settled the issue. The Commons feared that a general reconfirmation would give them nothing to take back to their constituents. Magna Carta was already the law of the land, and they had no need to purchase it with five subsidies. It was not until Sir Edward Coke proposed that they proceed by petition rather than bill that a way was found around the difficulty. A petition of right was drawn up to confirm four liberties: freedom from arbitrary arrest, from non-parliamentary taxation, from the free billeting of troops, and from being governed by martial law. Charles insisted that in granting the Petition of Right he was neither establishing new law nor limiting his prerogative powers. Thus he answered the petition in a specific rather than a general form. This touched off further controversy, which was ended only when the King responded to the petition as if it had been a bill: '*Le Roy le veult.*' In return, the Houses passed the subsidy bill. Buckingham rushed to Portsmouth to ready the fleet to relieve La Rochelle. Less than two months later he was dead.

5

The Reign of Charles I
1629–1637

The second session of the parliament of 1628 ended in pandemonium. The Speaker of the House of Commons was restrained from dissolving Parliament while members usurped his authority and adopted three resolutions in contravention of the King's instructions. In this one tumultuous moment the worst fears of both Charles I and the leaders of the Commons were realized. The King feared that if he held another session of Parliament members of the Commons would encroach on his prerogatives and openly question his authority. Parliamentary leaders feared that the King would not keep the bargain he had made in the Petition of Right and that he would dissolve their session at the first mention of the liberties of the subject. As the King's serjeant pounded on the Commons' door demanding entrance and the Speaker wept in his chair, the fears of both proved correct.

In the months since Buckingham's assassination in September 1628, La Rochelle had fallen and English ambassadors had entered into peace negotiations with both France and Spain. Outwardly Charles I picked up the pieces of his government as if they had never been dashed with the life of his favourite. Peace would restore his shattered finances and end the emergency measures that had characterized every year of his monarchy since 1625. Then he could ease the political tensions. In his four years as king, Charles had met four sessions of Parliament. Managing Parliament disrupted government for months on end. The Commons acted as a magnet for complaints from everywhere: attacks upon ministers, upon local officials, upon churchmen. Parliament's own committees could hardly keep up with them, and enforcing the statutes made in one session created grievances in the next. He could cover the same ground in the Privy Council; he could remedy the same abuses by proclamation or punish them in the courts. The nation needed a cooling-off period, but Charles needed one more session of Parliament.

When he came to the throne in 1625, the Commons had not voted Charles the customary parliamentary grant of tonnage and poundage for life. Leaders of the House saw the grant of customs duties as an opportunity to place limits on impositions. But with plague in London and the consequent second session at Oxford so short, they were unable to accomplish anything. In 1626 a committee began work on the bill, but it died with the sudden dissolution. In 1628, at Charles's prompting, they promised the necessary legislation, but the Petition of Right pre-empted it. All this time the King collected the levy as usual. The Commons assured him they had no intention of depriving him of this revenue, and he assured them that he could not govern without it. After 1628 the issue became more sensitive, because the Petition of Right explicitly barred the collection of non-parliamentary taxation. Indeed, the King prorogued the first session several hours early to avoid receiving an official statement that the taxes thus banned included customs duties. To resolve the matter Charles had to reconvene Parliament.

In the intervening months merchants had refused payment and officials had confiscated their goods. Hard words had been exchanged, and hotheads had been imprisoned. When Parliament reassembled, members complained that the ink had hardly dried on the Petition of Right before it had become a dead letter. Moreover, not only liberties were in danger. The church was being undermined. Upon advice from the bishops, the King had outlawed discussion of controversial points of doctrine, including predestination. To make the decision seem even-handed, he pardoned those who had recently offended in sermons or tracts. But some of those pardoned had offended Parliament by preaching and writing in favour of Arminianism, a form of Protestantism that some equated with Catholicism. In 1625 the House of Commons had complained bitterly against the writings of Richard Montague, James's chaplain, and his most controversial book was finally banned in 1628. But, to the consternation of the accusers, Charles promoted Montague and other reputed Arminians to bishoprics.

It soon became apparent to the King that the Commons would hold the bill for tonnage and poundage hostage for a remonstrance on religion. In London, some merchants continued their tax resistance, which led to more confrontations over the seizure of goods. One of these even involved a member of Parliament, and raised the thorny issue of privilege. Charles hoped to cool things down by a brief adjournment. *During that time he believed that meetings of privy counsellors and parliamentary leaders might head off an impasse.*

But on 2 March when Speaker Sir John Finch attempted to adjourn the session for another week he was forcibly prevented from doing so. Instead Sir John Eliot insisted that the House take into consideration three resolutions that he and a number of others had prepared. Finch remonstrated that he could not entertain the motion; that the Commons must adjourn. Eliot and others retorted that he was their Speaker and must do what the House directed. When Finch rose to leave, the dissidents thrust him back into his chair. Dozens of ordinary members headed for the exit, only to discover that someone had locked the doors. Finch was assailed from all sides until he broke down and wept. The King had commanded him to adjourn the session, the members to continue it. He did not know what to do: 'I am not the less the King's servant for being yours. I will not say I will not put it to the question, but I must say I dare not.' By now the King's serjeant had come demanding the mace which symbolized the King's presence in Parliament, and the House was in total confusion. Eliot held the floor and made a passionate speech attacking innovations in religion and those who would counsel the King to collect revenues not granted by Parliament. Finally, Denzil Holles, the member for Dorchester, read out the three resolutions against Arminianism and the collection or payment of tonnage and poundage. Shouts of 'Aye! Aye!' echoed in the chamber – the last sounds to be heard there for eleven years.

For four years the government of Charles I had endured one crisis after another, and nearly everything that could go wrong had gone wrong. Support for intervention in the Thirty Years War melted away like the armies that were sent abroad. The English campaigns at Cadiz, the plan to relieve La Rochelle and the landing at Isle de Rhé were progressively catastrophic. The disaster at Rhé was long remembered as the low point in Britain's martial history, the simultaneous wars with Spain and France as the low point in diplomacy. Failure bred conflict. The governing élites were divided over the cost of war and the unrelenting demands of taxation. Peers of the realm and members of the greater gentry had refused the forced loan. Some sincerely pledged to give in a parliamentary way if subsidies were voted; others knew that no Parliament would offer so much. The Privy Council was divided both in the advice it proffered the King and in its attitude towards the war and the measures taken to finance it. The judges were divided over the legality of royal expedients. Parliament was divided over its obligation to support the court and its desire to represent the country.

The sessions of 1626 and 1628 were painful for everyone, and after each Charles imprisoned court critics for encroaching on his prerogatives. He threatened publicly to govern without these unruly assemblies of his subjects, and he bemoaned privately the way Parliament had treated him. Eliot, Wentworth and Coke had created as many obstacles to the successful prosecution of the war as had Richelieu and Olivares. Whatever foresight those who plotted against Buckingham may have exhibited, it was lost after the assassination. In his heart, Charles blamed the Duke's critics for Felton's action, and when Sir John Eliot, who was imprisoned at the end of the 1629 session, died in the Tower in 1632 the King would not allow his family to bring his body home to Cornwall for burial. It was a petty, spiteful act of revenge that symbolized all of his frustrations.

Charles resolved to make the 1630s better. Peace was the key to restoring government to a semblance of normality, and the terms of disengagement could hardly be more humiliating than the results of combat. Slowly he rebuilt his government, choosing officers who shared his penchant for order and who were capable administrators. He issued Council orders to regulate the poor and revive the economy, though these were problems of a previous generation that were gradually being ameliorated by a revival of trade and a slowing of population growth. He ordered studies made of finance which both resulted in efficiencies and discovered precedents for revenues that had been allowed to lapse. These, like fines for refusing a knighthood, forest fines and the search for concealed lands, were exploited to the full, for they were the king's undoubted prerogatives. Charles asserted his regal rights and royal dignities because he felt that they had been trespassed upon in the crises brought on by war. He did not simply institute any money-making scheme to fill his coffers – indeed he put an end to the sale of titles as unseemly – but he intended to have the full measure of what was rightfully his. At the same time he planned a reform of the administration of his two other kingdoms, Scotland and Ireland. These had been haphazardly governed by his father – Scotland less so than Ireland, because James could rely upon ministers personally known to him to enforce his authority. Ireland had been seriously destabilized by continued English and Scots plantations that brought more Irish land under the ownership of Protestants. Ireland needed a strong hand to maintain order, and Charles found it in the Earl of Strafford.

Charles I was a king uncomfortable with ambiguities who inherited a government rife with them. He was not given to the constitutional ruminations of his father, whose taste for platitudes was larger than his stomach for business. Charles's appetites were just the opposite: he spoke infrequently and governed incessantly. Whatever his attitude to critics of royal policy – more than one of them found their way into government – he learned from the criticisms. His court was decorous, his Council orderly; his financial house was put in order. He chose servants who shared his views, and he backed their programmes when they came under fire. His support for Archbishop Laud and the Earl of Strafford was unremitting, and it was one of the great tragedies of his life that they both had to be sacrificed. No less than his father, Charles believed in the necessary unity of church and state and he responded aggressively to threats against it, especially those from the hotter sort of Protestants. It was his misfortune to be better able to impose his will through the group of Arminian bishops whom his father had nourished and he had promoted. He did not feel threatened by British Catholics and opposed the wild demands for their extirpation, not realizing how volatile an issue Catholicism had become. Religious controversy, first in England and then in Scotland, was met with sustained suppression. Ultimately, repression met with resistance. In another age, Charles I would have been a great reforming monarch – how much the nation would have preferred him to his father thirty years before or his son thirty years later – but his own time was filled with contradictions that he felt compelled to resolve.

*   *   *

Many contemporaries remembered the 1630s as a golden age. Treaties with France in 1629 and Spain in 1630 removed England from the European war. Shortly thereafter Protestant fortunes brightened. The glories of the Swedish monarch Gustavus Adolphus, the triumphs of the Protestant League, and finally the entrance of France into the struggle against the Habsburgs combined to lift the dark clouds that hung over those who feared for the survival of their Continental co-religionists. At home there was a comfortable prosperity. English ships could now travel to any port and, as England was the major non-belligerent, they did much transshipping. Merchants forgot their quarrel with the crown over tonnage and poundage once it became clear how profitable peace would be. Even nature cooperated by providing a run of bounteous harvests and blessing the King and Queen with two sons, Charles, born in 1630, and James in 1633. Peace abroad and prosperity at home – considering what came before and after, it was indeed a golden age.

Others remembered the 1630s as anything but bright and hopeful. In their view this was the decade in which the slide towards chaos began. 'The dissolution of this government caused the war, not the war the dissolution of this government,' the political theorist James Harrington later reflected. The calamitous parliamentary sessions in 1626 and 1628–9 caused some to doubt the lawfulness of Charles's government; the preferment of Arminian bishops and the elevation of William Laud to Archbishop of Canterbury in 1628 made them fear for the holiness of the church. The suspension of parliamentary sessions while the King followed the new counsels with which he had threatened his subjects during the controversy over the forced loan heightened the sense that liberties were in danger. An increasing oversight of local religious practice and the imposition of a questionable conformity heightened the sense that religion was threatened. The 'Great Migration' to Massachusetts Bay began in 1630 with the emigration of 2,000 settlers who intended to create 'a city on a hill', a godly commonwealth that would serve as example to their homeland. In little more than a decade 16,000 men and women abandoned England on this errand into the wilderness. Some fled actual persecution, though most fled the threat of it, believing that something was seriously wrong – a fear that increased under the pressures of what they believed was arbitrary government.

Charles I had little in common with his father, and at first glance the comparison was all to his favour. He was an orderly man: fastidious in his personal life and methodical in his government. After a stormy beginning, his relationship with Henrietta-Maria deepened into a lifelong devotion, and his affection for his family provided the perfect antidote to his cold public persona. Where James lived upon a stage, Charles lived behind a curtain and maintained a separation between the public and the private. Deeply impressed by the formality of the Spanish court, he issued orders that clearly defined his private quarters and those who had access to them. He transformed a raucous court into a decorous one, and, if there was no lack of masques, balls and state dinners, a refined sensibility now characterized them: 'the fools and bawds, mimics and catamites of the former court grew out of fashion'. His art collection was distinguished, expensive and much admired. Charles was an aesthete, and around him gathered the shining lights of European high culture.

Though no ruler could imprint himself upon his age, monarchy was a form of personal rule in which the king set the tenor. Thus it is not surprising that Charles I attempted to reorder government in the same way that he reordered his court. After the death of the Duke of Buckingham he did not rely upon a single favourite but made use of a variety of officers and courtiers who shared his penchant for efficiency and probity. The Privy Council became an organ of government with the King in regular attendance and with separate committees established for Ireland, overseas colonies and trade. Just as he issued new regulations for the court, so he issued them for the country. In 1631 a Book of Orders drafted by the Lord Chief Justice attempted to bring the work of county justices under the direct supervision of the Council, especially on matters relating to poor-relief and economic affairs. It was an effort at centralizing local government in a time of crisis. So too was the mostly unsuccessful attempt to create an 'exact militia'. New regulations defined the responsibilities of the Lord Lieutenants and their deputies with a precision markedly in contrast to the slovenly state of the institution they governed. Rules for drill, assembly and equipage were intended to establish the county militia as a viable military force. Similarly, Charles strengthened the powers of administrative bodies such as those that ruled in the North and in Ireland and Scotland. Though the King's love of order was ultimately unrequited, there could be no doubt of the passion.

Charles's most serious concerns, however, were monetary. The war years had left the crown in severe financial distress; indeed the deficit may have reached £2 million by 1629. Thus the most important of his servants was Sir Richard Weston, Earl of Portland, who held the office of Lord Treasurer during the revival of royal finances. Though Charles I was not extravagant in the manner of his father, neither did he take to domestic economy. Besides his art collection and a penchant for building, Charles's five children were the largest surviving royal brood in centuries. His household expenses were considerable. He spent over £130,000 to refurbish the Queen's palace, and he even converted a tennis court to a private chapel. He provided a large annual subsidy for his sister and her son, Charles Lewis, who was now the deposed Elector Palatine. Portland swam against this tide.

The Treasurer's own genius was to make small budgetary gains mount up year after year. He reduced pensions by over a third while increasing fines on Catholics fivefold. Cranfield's campaign to eliminate waste in the royal household was revived, though with less zeal. Commissions of investigation and audits of accounts had a chilling effect even if they did not lead to an overhaul of the system. Portland was a manager rather than a reformer, even though he presided over the creation of new or enhanced revenue measures. Charles had already created a commission to investigate how best to exploit crown rights, and its report recommended the revival of several ancient sources. The first was fines against gentlemen who had not presented themselves to be knighted at Charles's coronation or at the births of his sons. It was customary that men possessed of forty pounds in freehold land be knighted or pay a fine for refusing the honour. No penalties had been exacted in living memory – and, given James's profligate dubbing, the kingdom had far too many knights already – but the legal obligation remained, and the King was determined to enforce it. By 1635 distraints of knighthood had raised as much as £170,000. Similarly, encroachers on royal forests, possessors of concealed crown lands and builders of new homes in London all technically violated laws, and many found themselves mulcted.

The crown exploited ordinary revenues with equal vigour. To stay afloat, Charles had sold over £600,000 of crown lands in the first five years of his reign. This could not be repeated without disastrous long-term consequences. Thus feudal revenues were exacted to the fullest. Yields in the Court of Wards rose; the Treasurer ended compromises for purveyance, raising their real value. The crown sold special licences for projects ranging from the sale of American tobacco to the draining of the fens. The crown issued patents that looked suspiciously like monopolies, with the same mixture of motives as before. The infamous 'popish soap' patent was a genuine attempt to create a better-quality product which used domestic labour and raw materials. Its unpopularity owed more to the failure of the soap to meet its advertising claims – that it 'did wash both whiter and sweeter' – than to the Catholics who were among the projectors. In the end, the crown received a higher royalty from the traditional soap-makers than before the rival company was licensed. Though much of the profits from licensing and patents went into the pockets of courtiers, they were pockets from which the crown borrowed shamelessly.

With the increase in customs revenues that resulted from the trade revival as well as the ratcheting up of rates, royal finances solidified. By the mid-1630s the accumulated debt decreased to approximately £1 million while annual income actually exceeded expenditure. Whatever else might be said of Caroline fiscal policy, Charles I had fulfilled the outmoded obligation of the king to live of his own in times of peace.

But, while England remained on the sidelines, the Continental wars continued. It was only to be expected that the most active maritime nation would become the target of belligerents in search of contraband and of pirates in search of plunder. Throughout the early 1630s there were incidents on the seas that derogated royal honour. The French refused to salute English warships; the Dutch attacked a Spanish flotilla along the English coastline. In 1633 pirates were especially active in the Channel, leading to demands from merchants for protection. Charles ordered that two new ships be built each year to restock the navy. Moreover, the King had never abandoned his commitment to restore the Elector Palatine, though for the past five years he had pursued the objective diplomatically. The Spanish, French and Dutch were all willing to make promises, though each sought the support of the English fleet in return. It was therefore imperative that Charles maintain his naval strength, but the cost could not be borne by his ordinary revenues alone.

In 1634 the King revived a traditional levy for naval support, known as ship money. Ship money had been suggested to Charles in the mid-1620s as a way to finance wartime expeditions, though in its customary form it was too restrictive to serve those purposes. The levy required port towns to provide a ship of a certain size or compound at a fixed cost so that one could be hired. They made their payments to the naval commissioners, and thus the money was suited for emergencies rather than campaigns. When Charles decided to sweep pirates from the Channel, his Council recommended that ship money be used to finance the policy. In 1635 the levy was extended to inland communities, on the principle that the whole realm benefited from safe seas. The decision to raise ship money was carefully formulated and demonstrated royal concern to avoid the appearance of illegality. It was a traditional assessment, justified by the king's emergency power to provide for the safety of the realm, and thus it avoided the prohibition on non-parliamentary taxation expressed in the Petition of Right. All of the money was paid to naval commissioners and used for its designated purpose. Charles even went to the trouble of gaining a judicial opinion of its legality. Each county was assessed a lump sum, the apportionment left to local authorities, and the county sheriff who collected it was personally responsible for the whole. Thus, unlike the subsidy, ship money was fairly assessed and far greater numbers contributed to it. Whatever uneasiness people had about its legality, until the levy was tested in the courts they confined their criticisms to disputes over ratings – which could be ugly enough – and paid their assessments promptly. In the context of seventeenth-century taxation, ship money was a remarkably effective levy. The naval commissioners collected well over 90 per cent of all the money required, and in six years the crown raised nearly £800,000.

The need to find traditional sources of revenue to undertake quasi-military operations was nowhere greater than in Ireland. Ever since the end of the reign of Elizabeth, English government of Ireland required an expensive standing army as well as emergency forces during times of rebellion. Schemes to have the cost of Irish administration borne by Irish revenues continually foundered on the weakness of English government there. This weakness had led James I to his policy of plantation, which, if it had the advantage of establishing more English taxpayers and a larger population from which to create defence forces, had obvious drawbacks as well. It subjugated a proud and courageous people by the manipulation of law and the force of arms. The exile of Irish chieftains, the diaspora of Irish tenants, the merciless depopulation of towns left a bitter legacy: 'The gentry of Ireland on their side did think much that the scum of England should be here to overtop them.' Brutal race warfare flared intermittently, with the savagery of one side surpassed by the savagery of the other. Plantation also had the undesirable effect of driving the 'old English' into the arms of their Catholic co-religionists rather than their English countrymen. The 'old English' had been a crucial bridge in the Elizabethan policy of absorption: they intermarried with the Irish, arbitrated Gaelic disputes with the Dublin government, and, through their dominance of Parliament and localities, legitimated English authority. The decision to supplant them by the 'new English' was not only callous, it was short-sighted. The success of plantation was only a gleam in an administrator's eye; the wrath of the 'old English' was there for every-one to see.

Most importantly, the success of the policy of plantation depended upon it being carried out to the letter, especially as regarded the segregation of Irish and 'new English'. Irish farmers had to be cleared from their land to make way for English and Scottish colonists who ultimately failed to materialize. The City of London was awarded the entire county of Derry in the vain hope that some of the capital's surplus population could be settled in Ireland. The great planters arrived – those upon whom thousands of acres of Irish land had been bestowed – yet it proved difficult to attract the lesser holders. In 1635 the Londonderry patent of the City of London was revoked because the patentees had failed to fulfil the terms of their grant. Indeed, the native Irish who had not actively supported the revolt of Tyrone and Tyrconnell at the end of the sixteenth century quickly re-established their presence in Ulster, gaining control of more land than either the English or the Scots. Even the estates that passed from Catholic ownership largely remained in Catholic hands, for after some disruption many Irish farmers were permitted to squat on their own land. This meant that the Irish were not dispossessed, the English planters did not have to plant anyone, and the Dublin government increased its revenues. But a policy of segregation that did not segregate was a powder keg with a lit fuse.

The slow burn began when Charles I declared war on Spain in 1625. Ireland was a dangerous back door, open to Spanish invaders who could be succoured by the Catholic population. The English government had to increase its military presence and thus its administrative outlay. Forces and fortifications would cost nearly £40,000 a year, and to raise this much revenue the King had to reverse much of his father's policy. In negotiation with a committee dominated by the 'old English', Charles agreed to a series of concessions known as the Graces in return for £120,000 paid over three years. The core of the Graces involved the suspension of the disabilities against Catholics and security of tenure for 'old English' landholders. Though the Graces also made concessions to the 'new English', they drove a wedge between the administration and the recent Protestant planters. Church leaders denounced them as 'religion for sale', while the planters feared a revival of Catholic influence in Dublin. Thus the packing of the Irish parliament in favour of the 'new English' by James I now worked against his son, who could not obtain support for the most important Graces, which failed to be confirmed. The money was paid, but the 'old English' received nothing of value in return.

The Graces alienated everyone. The 'new English' opposed the offer on both religious and political grounds, while Charles's failure to implement them cost him the support of the 'old English'. The government was distrusted on all sides, as successive Lord Lieutenants learned to their cost. If English administration was to succeed, it would need a strong hand to guide it. This is presumably what the King had in mind in 1632 when he sent Thomas Wentworth, ultimately Earl of Strafford, to Ireland.

Strafford was a Yorkshireman who viewed the world through the prism of his county. His greatest desire was to rise higher than his factional rival, Sir John Saville; his greatest ambition to be president of the Council of the North. Both had been frustrated in the 1620s when Saville was a client of Buckingham, and Wentworth was forced to become a vocal critic of royal military policy. Strafford believed that foreign wars weakened domestic government. Better the King should be loved in Yorkshire than feared in Madrid. Congenitally abrasive, he opposed the emergency measures adopted in the 1620s and was one of the organizers of the Petition of Right. But when royal policy turned towards peace Strafford was easily coopted into the King's service. He saw no contradiction in his behaviour and was perplexed when others did. He was a man who could justify feathering his own nest because it benefited his master who owned the tree. Strafford was blessed by an obtuseness that made single-mindedness his only choice.

During four years in Ireland Strafford accomplished two seemingly impossible tasks: he generated a revenue surplus which enriched royal coffers in Westminster and he united antagonists who were otherwise divided by both race and religion. His rule was dedicated and efficient. He immersed himself in a study of the problems of governing a land that was partially conquered and partially colonized. He came to appreciate the policy of plantation, but also realized that the interests of the crown and of the planters were not identical. The Lord Lieutenant had to rule as a sovereign, not an arbiter. The King promised Strafford that he would not allow appeals over his head to London, and with this assurance the Earl went about increasing the power of his office. He dubbed his policy 'Thorough', and set out to 'govern the native by the planter and the planter by the native'. He used the prerogative Court of

Castle Chamber to chasten overweening planters, used the central courts to intimidate local juries, and created a High Commission to eliminate lay patronage in the church, a device that had placed much ecclesiastical land in the hands of 'new English' planters. He farmed the Irish customs at favourable terms and effectively doubled revenues from the Court of Wards, which he used both to remove Catholic minors from the influence of their relatives and as a source of rewards and punishments. Strafford proved adept at managing Parliament, gaining his subsidies first and responding to grievances afterwards. There was much to recommend 'Thorough' to a king bent on good government, though it is a nice question whether Strafford's rule in Ireland was more thoroughly efficient than it was thoroughly detested.

Initially he formed an alliance with the 'old English' for the purpose of controlling Parliament. Since, unlike previous Lord Lieutenants, Strafford had no tie to the 'new English' community, it was hoped that he would back the granting of the Graces. But this marriage of convenience was short-lived. Strafford was willing to suspend the enforcement of disabilities against Catholics, but not to grant security of tenure. He believed in further colonization, which could take place only by the confiscation of 'old English' land. Indeed, to further his scheme to plant Connacht he set commissions to work to prove royal ownership of land that had been occupied by 'old English' for centuries. At the same time he enforced the crown's interests against encroachments of 'new English' planters. His principal target was Richard Boyle, Earl of Cork, who had amassed a fortune through speculating in Irish land. Strafford viewed Cork as a vulture stuffed with carrion stolen from the crown and the church. He harried him everywhere, even spitefully removing the tomb of Cork's wife from St Patrick's Cathedral in Dublin. Strafford brought prosecutions against titles which Cork had done everything possible to legitimize and, with the courts at his disposal, Strafford won a huge judgement against the Earl. Combined with the severe economic downturn of the early 1630s, which threatened their livelihoods, the ferocity of Strafford's attack upon Cork was terrifying to the 'new English'. Title to land obtained during the Jacobean plantations had always been open to dispute, because few Jacobean holders had actually met the conditions of plantation on which their titles were granted. Catholic and Protestant, Irish and English, all now suffered the same insecurities and all now shared a common enemy.

Though Strafford exacerbated the problems of English rule in Ireland, he did not create them. Charles I ruled three kingdoms, and each was dominated by a different religion. Accommodation of Catholics in Ireland – especially English Catholics – was more prudence than policy. An attempt to apply the full rigour of the laws against recusants could only result in warfare and could only be successful through genocide. Offering the Graces to the 'old English' in exchange for money to prevent a Spanish invasion was simply choosing the lesser of two evils. But, to the King's Puritan critics, evil did not come in degrees. Charles's willingness to sell religion, as Judas had sold Jesus, was yet one more example of the strength of the Catholic conspiracy that they believed gripped Britain. In Ireland a flood of priests drawn from the scions of 'old English' families reinvigorated Catholicism. In England the Queen practised her religion ostentatiously, and hundreds flocked to the Catholic chapels of the foreign ambassadors in London. When Charles sent his wife's French entourage packing, they were replaced by English Catholics led by Buckingham's mother. Henrietta-Maria's household became a refuge for Catholic office-holders, whose influence increased with her own. Throughout the 1630s there was a series of well-publicized conversions at court which the King was unable to prevent and unwilling to punish. Over 750 Catholic priests were now resident in England, most in or around London, and after a half-century of decline the Catholic population as a whole grew by 50 per cent between 1603 and 1640. To those susceptible to anti-Catholic paranoia, evidence of conspiracy was everywhere – a plot by the Pope and his agents to sap the strength of English Calvinism; a plot that reached the highest levels of the church itself.

The Elizabethan church had been built on a series of ambiguities that the Jacobean church did little to clarify. It was Protestant to be sure, more Calvinist than Lutheran, but mostly it was an inclusive church. James had supported a learned, preaching ministry and improved the universities where ministers were trained, and he advanced men of ability. As a serious student of theology, he was not ignorant of the doctrinal disputes that kept the presses and pulpits buzzing, but neither did he see them as posing a fundamental threat to religious order. It was fanaticism not flexibility that was the problem. For those who viewed the world in apocalyptic terms, only an apocalypse was sufficient. To them the struggle between Catholics and Protestants was the final battle that would end with a final solution. The blood of Europeans nourished these dreams. But James's dream had been different. Perhaps there was still time to reconcile religious differences, to find a path towards a church shorn of the extremities of pristine Protestantism and complaisant Catholicism. James's own faith had prevented him from travelling that doctrinal road, yet, as his reign wore on, the same impulse in others led to an amalgamation of ideas that was ultimately branded Arminianism.

Arminianism possessed a theological core, but it was not theology that made it so appealing to some and so repellent to others. Jacob Arminius was a Dutchman who wrote against Calvin's doctrine of predestination. He argued that predestination was not an irrevocable divine judgement in which some were saved and most were damned; rather it was a tendency that could be affected by human free will. By their conduct, individuals could extinguish an innate spark of salvation. This meant that good works were a testimony to true faith – a principle that orthodox Calvinists strenuously denied. This seemingly minor modification to theory had enormous consequences for practice. In the first place it broadened the base of those who were potentially saved. This renewed the importance of the sacraments, which had declined in favour of sermons. It also increased the efficacy of prayer. All of this enhanced the importance of the church in the life of the community, for it was in the church that the sacraments were administered, prayers were offered, and moral conduct was expounded. Arminianism split the Dutch Calvinist church asunder, and in 1618 at the Synod of Dort its principles had been rejected in favour of the Calvinist doctrine of absolute predestination. The English representatives to the Synod had all concurred in the majority decision.

But in Oxford and Cambridge small groups of theologians began both to espouse Arminian ideas and to attack Calvinist ones. The doctrine of absolute predestination had two unhappy implications: it consigned the great mass of the damned to a life of hopeless despair and it left the small minority of the saved free from all social constraints. Moreover, it diminished the importance of the official church, the preserve of university clergymen, by stripping it of the central role in aiding Christians to attain salvation. What began as an academic dispute soon developed into a power struggle within the hierarchy of the English church. Many of the ablest scholars and preachers adhered either to the new doctrines or, more importantly, to the attitudes that they fostered. In their turn they became bishops, and in their dioceses they revivified the role of the church. If sacraments mattered, if prayers were answered, then the church was the centre of spiritual life, 'the house of God and the gate of heaven'. After decades of neglect, the Arminians repaired and beautified buildings as a witness to the worship of the congregation and God's presence among them. Discreet statuary and pictorial representations of religious life reappeared in cathedrals, and some stained-glass windows were reinstalled. Since the weekly service now carried greater meaning, it had to be conducted with greater solemnity. The clergy were ordered to wear the surplice and to cover the communion table with a decorative cloth. The table itself might be removed from the centre aisle to the east end, to avoid its casual use. In any event, it should be railed so that children would not sit on it or dogs abuse it.

It was this side of Arminianism that appealed so much to Charles I, because it mirrored his own obsessions with order and beauty. Buckingham had patronized a number of Arminian bishops, and when Charles became king he elevated others. To lead this wing of the Church he made William Laud Bishop of London in 1628 and Archbishop of Canterbury in 1633. Laud was already fifty-five years old when he was translated to London, and had spent most of his career infighting at Oxford, where he never forgot either a friend or a foe. Diminutive and dyspeptic, Laud clothed his lowly origins in the raiment of the high church. He identified himself early as an opponent of the Calvinism that dominated Oxford, and he set about creating a party of Arminians through the shrewd use of patronage and power. He became a royal chaplain in 1611, but the opposition of Archbishop Abbot among others kept him from the cope for another decade. By then he had come to the notice of Buckingham. If he could not replace the Duke in the King's affection, Laud ultimately replaced him in power. He exercised near-total control of the church; placed his ally Bishop Juxon in the Treasurership; was the principal link with Strafford in Ireland; and himself sat on the Scottish privy council.

Where others built bridges, Laud built dams. He did all he could to shore up the Arminian party and protect it from the polluting tide of Puritanism. Laud launched a campaign against the lay impropriation of the rents that supported parish ministries and persuaded the King to shut down the London trust known as the Feoffees for Impropriations which sponsored a kind of Puritan preachers bureau. In this he had two aims: to strengthen the church by increasing its control of income and appointments and to limit the amount of preaching done by non-beneficed clergy. Through control of licensing, Laud exercised a strict censorship over the press, and through control of the Court of High Commission a strict discipline over the conduct of the ministry.

Laud would neither brook opposition nor shrink from a challenge. He increased visitations to ensure that vestments were being worn and that altars were being railed. He punished ministers who defied his orders, and reported the opposition of influential laymen to the Privy Council. When his authority was questioned by the illegal publication of tracts by William Prynne, John Bastwick and Henry Burton, Laud had them hauled before Star Chamber, convicted after trial, and then subjected to the humiliation – unbefitting their social status – of being pilloried, mutilated and branded. More of his critics accepted voluntary exile abroad than compulsory incarceration at home. The first great wave of emigration to New England took place during the Laudian ascendancy. Laud's programme was opposed for both the rapidity with which it was introduced and for the thoroughness with which it was carried out. He had much in common with Strafford, especially the vigour with which he rooted out opponents.

If Laud was willing to trample on those who got in the way, it was because he believed in the positive aspects of the programme he pursued. It was Laud who pressed the policy of restoring the fabric of English churches and who led the appeal for the restoration of St Paul's Cathedral in London. It was Laud who poured money into the universities for the enhancement of scholarship – founding a professorship in Arabic at Oxford, funding the purchase of books and manuscripts, and financing an ambitious building campaign. It was Laud who insisted upon a better-educated and better-paid ministry and who challenged both the crown and the governing élite to pay their share. After decades of slovenly management, he attempted to bring order to religion. There was so much to do and so little time to do it. Archbishop William Laud was an old man in a hurry.

In 1633 he accompanied Charles I on the King's coronation visit to Scotland. Laud saw little improvement in the Scottish church since his trip there in 1617 as one of James I's chaplains. Ministers were still poor and undereducated; church lands were still mostly in the hands of laymen; and the Presbyterian kirk still professed independence from the episcopal hierarchy that James had established. Moreover, ceremonial varied from church to church according to the practice of the minister. There was not even a standard prayer-book. Some places conducted services on the basis of the Edwardian prayer-book of 1552, some on the basis of the Genevan Book of Common Order, and many others on unique combinations of the two. The physical state of the Scottish church was no better than the spiritual. Churchyards teemed with animals, muck heaps adorned the grounds, and even the best-kept buildings were dilapidated. Though the King stayed in Scotland only a month, it was long enough to shock Laud's sensibilities.

Reform of the Scottish church, however, had long been on the royal agenda. James I had been determined to gain control over the Presbyterian kirk, and he made three important inroads during his reign. In 1613 he completed the process of re-establishing bishops in Scotland, giving them a supervisory role over their diocesan ministry through Scottish Courts of High Commission. The bishops had no formal place in the Presbyterian structure of the kirk and no special role in the Scottish General Assembly, which continued to claim autonomous authority over the nation's religious life. James struggled against these claims, establishing the right to control meetings of general assemblies and, through the political pressure of his bishops, to control their decisions. In 1618, by a narrow margin, James forced through an assembly held in Perth five changes that would bring Scottish religious practice more in line with English. The most controversial of the Five Articles of Perth was that communicants should kneel while taking the sacrament. Opposition to the Five Articles persuaded James to abandon further attempts to converge the practices of the two churches. He left his son much unfinished business.

The problems that faced Charles I in governing Scotland were different from those of his father. James I liked to boast that, while it had been all his ancestors could do to govern Scotland by the sword, he governed it by the pen. In fact an absentee monarch could only govern Scotland by sufferance. Throughout the early seventeenth century the nobility and gentry expanded their political power at the expense of the crown. James's efforts to introduce local justices of the peace, for example, foundered on the near-feudal autonomy of local nobles who held administrative and judicial offices by birth. The advantage of a strong nobility was that it acted as a counterweight to the Presbyterian kirk, and for James this was advantage enough. After all, he could still command the personal loyalty of his most potent subjects. But Charles could not. He wished to continue his father's policy of strengthening the episcopal church, and this could be done only by reclaiming its wealth.

Thus his first royal act, in 1625, was to revoke grants of land that had been made to noblemen during the minorities of all of his predecessors since the sixteenth century. Acts of Revocation were not unusual in Scotland, but Charles's violated the spirit, if not the letter, of the practice. The act itself was draconian, though its force was mitigated through the use of Scottish commissioners who assessed both the extent of lands revoked and their value. In many cases compromises were accepted and compensation was paid for voluntary surrenders. The beneficial effects of the revocation were to enhance the value of church livings, raise ministerial stipends, and re-endow the bishoprics. But there were dangerous side-effects. Characteristically, the politically connected escaped lightly while those out of favour were hard hit, contributing to the factionalization of the Scottish nobility. The dubious legality of the act cost Charles much goodwill, as did his subsequent decision to bar hereditary justices from the Privy Council. Perhaps most damaging of all, the compulsory transfer of wealth from the nobility to the episcopacy drove a wedge between two groups that had been drawing closer together. The last thing Charles needed was an alliance between nobility and the leaders of the Presbyterian kirk, yet this was the result of policies which isolated the bishops, who were blamed by the nobility for attacks upon their wealth and by the clergy for attacks upon their doctrine.

The Act of Revocation was an open wound which pained the Scottish nobility for the next decade. One Scottish gentleman, Sir James Balfour, called it 'the groundstone of all the mischief that followed'. It created a series of grievances that complicated the work of the royal administration in Edinburgh. Many members of the King's own Privy Council were involved in suits against the commissioners, and each session of the Scottish Estates scraped at the scab. When the King came for his coronation in 1633 a group of noblemen attempted to present a petition to him that combined economic and religious grievances. Charles refused to receive it, and when its contents became public he lashed out at one of its organizers, Lord Balmerino, by prosecuting him for treason. Balmerino's trial, in 1635, was a fiasco for the crown. Even a carefully picked and instructed jury could convict on only one of three charges, and that by a vote of 8 to 7. The trial provided publicity for the grievances of the nobility; anti-episcopal sentiment increased when the bishops were implicated in the prosecution; and in the end Balmerino was lightly punished – indeed Laud interceded on his behalf.

Laud's role in Scottish affairs was steadily increasing. He had been made a member of the Scottish privy council, had presided over the creation of a new bishopric in Edinburgh, and was working to find a way to impose uniformity on the practices of the Scottish church. As early as 1629 Laud been involved in discussions to create a prayer-book which would institute a single form of service in Scotland and bring it in line with English practice. Laud's inclination was simply to impose the English service, though even the strongest supporters of episcopacy counselled against this. Traditional Scottish practices were different, and the imposition of the English service would be opposed on racial grounds as well. The project stalled until Laud revived it after he returned from Scotland. What he had seen there was not encouraging, and he made known his intention – which was the intention of the King – to institute reform. A committee of bishops, most of them Laudian appointees, was chosen to help formulate both a set of canons and a comprehensive prayer-book. The task took almost three years.

The publication of the Canons of 1636 met with an eerie silence. They affirmed the royal supremacy over religion and episcopal supremacy over the church. The Canons included no mention of the role of general assemblies and they stripped the presbyteries of their disciplinary powers. Nevertheless, they were designed for a Scottish and not an English church and they did not mandate in principle anything that was not already occurring in practice. The reaffirmation of the Five Articles of Perth was not likely to cause anyone else to kneel at communion. But the prayer-book was a different matter. The Canons proclaimed that services would be conducted in conformity to its rules, though it was another six months before it was published. During that time ordinary people were whipped into a frenzy by mostly false rumours of what it contained. It was attacked as 'popish, atheistical and English': the Scots tongue knew no greater imprecations. Copies were leaked before the publication date, and in Edinburgh spoiled sheets were accidentally used to wrap merchandise. Thus opposition to its official introduction on 23 July 1637 had plenty of time to organize. Ministers prepared petitions, leaders of the kirk wrote tracts, and a walk-out was organized for St Giles's Cathedral, where the Bishop of Edinburgh was to preside during its initial use. But the orchestrated opposition to the new prayer-book paled before the spontaneous reaction of members of the congregation. The Bishop's cathedral-trained voice was drowned by wailing cries of 'Woe, woe' and shouts of 'Sorrow, sorrow for this doleful day, that they are bringing in popery among us.' The next thing anyone knew, a three-legged stool was flying through the air and narrowly missed crowning the Dean of the chapel. The Bishop barely escaped with his life.

6

Rebellion and Civil War
1637–1644

The atmosphere in London was supercharged on the night of 4 January 1642. Bonfires that had been lit in the early-afternoon darkness were fed until dawn. Thousands of men roamed the streets with whatever weapons were at hand, racing from one gate to another on rumours that 'The cavaliers are coming to fire the city.' There had never been a night like this. For over a week tension had been mounting as mobs gathered around the Palace of Westminster screaming for the exclusion of the bishops from the House of Lords. On 27 December there was a fracas when the Archbishop of York struck an insolent youth who shouted in his face, 'No bishops, no bishops, no popish lords.' About thirty guards vigorously drove a crowd out of the palace yard, wounding some and killing Sir Richard Wiseman. The next day boys ran amok in Westminster Abbey, damaging 'popish' relics. On the night of the 29th only the cool head of Alderman John Venn prevented a massacre when he persuaded most of a crowd of 2,000 to disperse peaceably. Royal officers bloodied the hundred or so who refused. The confrontations of 27–29 December made clear that the King would no longer sit idly by and allow the mob to win by intimidation what they could not gain by persuasion.

Indeed, after a year of concession and humiliation, Charles I had finally decided to seize the initiative from the House of Commons. In September he returned from a trip to Scotland and cheering crowds flocked along his route to see him, an invigorating contrast to the hostile London mobs. He began to clean house, dismissing from service those who had betrayed their trust and promoting those who had proven steadfast. He remained calm at the news of a rebellion of Catholics in Ireland. He had heard enough about popish plots and had himself been too often accused of papist designs to take much notice. The rumour that he had sanctioned the rebellion was ludicrous –

another political tactic of his opponents, whose goal now was to remove the bishops from the House of Lords in order to pass their radical legislation. A monster petition to unseat the bishops was presented to Parliament in mid-December, reputedly signed by 30,000 Londoners. It had no effect on the Upper House. Daily demonstrations began, each one larger and more threatening than the last. It was no longer a question of nipping the movement in the bud. The garden was all but overrun; the time had come to yank by the roots.

This weeding was especially necessary now that talk had begun of impeaching the Queen. Charles may have sacrificed his ministers, but he would not betray his wife. He calculated the odds carefully. He knew that the nation was weary of political crisis, that he had strong support in the House of Lords, and that the House of Commons was divided. The King chose a bold counterstroke. On 3 January, after secret consultations with only a handful of his confidants, Charles sent the Attorney-General to the House of Lords with articles of impeachment against five commoners and one peer. He demanded that they be immediately imprisoned on a charge of high treason, and took the precaution of sealing up their studies to prevent the destruction of criminal evidence. The Lords were dumbfounded by this request and appointed a committee to consider its legality. In the meantime, Charles had sent a serjeant to the Commons to arrest the five members of the Lower House even before the Lords had agreed to it. The Commons, too, refused the order, returning the answer that an attempt to arrest any of its members was a breach of privilege. Neither the Attorney-General nor the serjeant was prepared for refusal. They could do nothing other than return to Whitehall empty-handed.

Charles received the news in a mood of defiance. The next day he collected a small guard and went himself to Westminster Hall. Word of his coming electrified the crowds that swarmed in the palace yard. By the time the King reached the doors of the lower chamber, his entourage had swelled to almost 400 – many of them the swaggering officers who had battled the apprentices the previous week. No king of England had ever interrupted a session of the House of Commons, and at first the members sat stunned when Charles swept down the centre aisle. Then they remembered their duty and stood bareheaded as the King demanded that Speaker William Lenthall point out the five members he had come to arrest. Lenthall answered, 'I have neither eyes to see, nor tongue to speak but as this House is pleased to direct me.'

Rebuffed, the King gazed along the serried rows of members. 'Well,' he concluded, 'I see all the birds are flown. I cannot do what I came for.' With that Charles strode out of the House as the cry of 'Privilege, privilege' rose up behind him. The five members were ensconced in the City, and all that night citizens were paralysed with fear that the King would come to remove them by force and that civil war would ensue.

For eleven years Charles had ruled effectively without Parliament. Whether by chance or design, his policies had spread the pain of royal necessities to every level of English society. Great noblemen were caught in the net of forest fines, the prosperous gentry were entangled in the Court of Wards, the lesser gentry were entrapped for refusing knighthoods. Sturdy yeomen were subject to increases in militia rates, commission fees, church rates and poor-relief. Merchants paid higher duties on trade, and better enforcement made these more difficult to evade. Ship money reached to places where the subsidy had never gone, as rural leaseholders and tenants and urban tradesmen and artisans were forced to pay a share. Only the destitute escaped, and there were fewer of them as the economy improved.

Similarly, political and religious reform affected governors as well as governed. The Book of Orders and the Exact Militia demanded more from the élite. For the first time the crown politicized commissions of the peace and the lieutenancy, as Charles removed critics of royal policy from both. Religious reforms affected everyone. Laud's emphasis upon repair of the fabric of the church and his insistence that rails be built around communion tables increased local assessments. Campaigns to restore York Minster and St Paul's Cathedral were voluntary only in name.

Charles's efforts at centralizing his monarchies were successful within the constraints of seventeenth-century inefficiencies, though they did not come without cost. He placed the implicit partnership between the crown and the social and political élites under severe stress. There was a widespread malaise towards the end of the 1630s that Charles, or those who advised him, could not be trusted. This lack of confidence was shared by local magistrates, by peers of the realm, even by central office-holders. It had not yet developed into a set of grievances, and certainly not into an opposition: it was rather a concern that the actions of royal government had to be scrutinized; that obedience came no longer by reflex but by reflection. This sense of distrust was reciprocated by Charles and his principal advisers. They too believed that loyalty was strained and that men busied themselves too much in the affairs of government. This was one reason why no thought was given to calling another parliament, which Charles correctly assumed would create more problems than it would solve. Rather, the King relied upon peace and prosperity to undo the ill effects of war and misery.

Thus royal government was unprepared for the consequences of rebellion and civil war. First in Scotland, then in Ireland, and finally in England Charles I opposed armed subjects by appeals to duty and loyalty that were only partially effective. He was incapable of preventing an invasion of England – the first obligation of a sovereign – both through the incompetence of his inexperienced military commanders and through the treachery of members of his parliament. He was equally incapable of suppressing a rebellion in Ireland when Parliament would not trust him to raise the necessary armed forces. Beginning in 1638, his government lurched from crisis to crisis without the capacity to mobilize the resources necessary to resolve them. By 1642 he was faced with the equally unpalatable choices of abandoning his royal prerogatives or making war upon his own subjects.

*   *   *

There was no ground swell of opposition to Caroline government during the 1630s, though there were signs of apprehension that penetrated social groups that had every reason to be content. Ministers and jurists should have been natural allies of the crown – the one defending 'the divinity that doth hedge a king', the other the ancient constitution. Laud intended his reforms to provide better-educated and better-compensated clerics, but at the price of a rigid uniformity. Archie, the King's fool, punned for many when at a royal dinner he uttered the benediction 'All praise to God and little laud to the Devil.' From John Williams, Bishop of Lincoln, who was stripped of his powers, to the members of the growing Puritan underground who wore their painful consciences like a hair shirt, the evidence of clerical alienation was plain to see. So was the evidence of estrangement among the lawyers. Beginning with the crisis over the forced loan, jurists began to dwell upon the limits of the royal prerogative and judges began to split constitutional hairs uncomfortably close to the royal scalp. As it was, Charles had already dismissed three of his own judges – in twenty-two years his father had only dismissed one – and had gained the narrowest of victories in the most important constitutional case of his reign when in 1637 by a 7–5 majority the bench upheld the legality of ship money.

The ship-money case indicated deep-rooted problems. John Hampden of Buckinghamshire brought suit against the crown in the name of the property-holders of England. There were many grounds for the dispute. Hampden resided in a land-locked county traditionally exempt from the levy of ship money. He brought the suit after writs were issued for the second consecutive year and seven years after the last parliament. This allowed his lawyers to argue that ship money could not be defended on the grounds of a temporary emergency and that funds for the navy should be raised by parliamentary subsidy. The legal issues were thorny, and more was at stake than revenue. Yet, for all of its constitutional importance, the deeper significance of the ship-money case was political: it revealed the growing estrangement of the country gentry. Clarendon claimed that Hampden's 'reputation of honesty was universal, and his affections seemed so publicly guided that no corrupt or private ends could bias them'. Hampden was no firebrand; he was moderate in his politics and in his religion. He was connected by birth to the leading families of the Chiltern counties; by association to the Providence Island investors who included noblemen like the Earl of Warwick, Viscount Saye and Sele, and Lord Brooke; and by inclination to those who opposed prerogative taxation. He was imprisoned for refusing the forced loan and was an intimate of Sir John Eliot, who had died in the Tower in 1632. Without the tacit loyalty of men like Hampden, Charles I might govern but he could not rule. Nor could he withstand a crisis.

That crisis began in Scotland. After the riots in Edinburgh in February 1637, the Scottish privy council suspended enforcement of both the Canons and the prayer-book. It was reported to the King that his religious reforms 'will not settle here without much blood'. In Edinburgh, representatives of the nobility, the lairds, the burghs and the kirk formed themselves into a committee known as the Tables and produced a National Covenant that bound its signatories to resist innovations in religion. Initially, the Covenanting movement was conservative in its aims and divided in its tactics. The cleavage between nobles and ministers was as sharp in the movement as it was in local society. Indeed, it was Charles's policy of revocation that turned many Scottish noblemen into Covenanters, and then it was his declaration that all Covenanters were traitors which held the movement together at the beginning.

Charles's difficulties in Scotland were twofold: he did not have the influence to induce his programme and he did not have the power to enforce it. Both he and his principal advisers were out of touch with Scottish affairs. He rarely saw his Scottish counsellors, having made only one visit and held but one parliament in Scotland since his accession. His advisers at Westminster were all 'amphibian' Scots – those who sought power and preferment in London to strengthen their reputations in Edinburgh. Charles relied most upon James, Marquis of Hamilton, heir of the premier family of Scotland. Hamilton had spent his teenage years in England, had attended Oxford, and was a favourite of both James and Charles. After Buckingham's assassination he became Master of the Horse; and his attachment to the British crown was symbolized by his naming his children Charles, James and Henrietta Mary. Charles's other important Scottish adviser was John Stewart, Earl of Traquair. Traquair had risen by his ability to mediate surrenders of land demanded by the Act of Revocation. Haughty and ambitious, he knew how to give with one hand and take with the other. As Treasurer in Scotland from 1631, Traquair defended Scottish economic interests while increasing the flow of taxes southward. In Scotland he dominated the council; in England he had the ear of the King. But nowhere was he trusted. Neither Hamilton nor Traquair was capable of building a Scottish coalition.

More damaging than the King's lack of influence was his lack of power. Charles viewed opposition to his religious reforms as rebellion. The Covenanters obliged him in this view by continuing their banned subscription campaign and by asserting the independence of the general assembly that met in Glasgow in the autumn of 1638. Not only did the assembly vote to abolish episcopacy, it also challenged royal authority to summon and dissolve its meetings.

Though Charles ordered Traquair to Edinburgh in September to negotiate with the Covenanters, he had already asked his English privy council to place the nation on a war footing and to raise an invasion force of 30,000. The council revived border law, mustered the trained bands, and commandeered merchant ships. Hamilton was given command of the seaborne expedition into Scotland. Although the King succeeded in raising an army, he failed to prevent the Covenanters from capturing nearly every defensible position in the south of Scotland.

What had been rebellion in word had become rebellion in deed. Hamilton's own mother threatened to shoot her son if he invaded Scotland with an English army. She had no need to load a gun: the English landings were aborted and the advance ground forces under the command of the Earl of Holland withdrew without a shot being fired.

No sooner had the First Bishops' War ended than both sides began preparing for the second. Charles sent Traquair to negotiate a settlement, though he regarded it as no more than a cease-fire. So too did the Covenanters. Through a series of parliamentary manœuvres they gained control of the essentials of Scottish government, and by the beginning of 1640 they were buying arms from Holland and soliciting troops from France. A national tax was imposed to equip a standing army. For his part, Charles attempted to arm Irish Catholics under the leadership of the Marquis of Antrim for an invasion of Scotland from the west. This came to little, both because of Strafford's opposition to arming his enemies in Ireland and because of the practical difficulties of raising forces there.

More significantly, Charles decided that the time was ripe to summon a parliament in England. In the face of open rebellion and with the possibility of invasion, the King believed that he could rely upon the loyalty of his subjects. In this belief he was mistaken. Although his case for supply was a powerful one, it could not overcome either the hostility generated by ten years of extra-parliamentary taxation or the suspicion that once Parliament granted money the grievances of the kingdom would go unredressed. It was better to follow the old ways, when grievance and supply went 'as twins . . . hand in hand'. Yet, unlike the parliaments of the 1620s, when military demands were pressing but not urgent, the situation in the spring of 1640 was a genuine emergency. There was no time for the ritual delays that slowed subsidies and speeded reforms. Though the Commons dangled ten subsidies in front of the King, when the first speech made after the session opened asserted that the invasion of England was not as great a threat as attacks upon the liberties of the subject, there was little doubt that the crown would pay dearly for them. Charles made one attempt at compromise, agreeing to allow an appeal of the ship-money case to the House of Lords, in return for an immediate grant of subsidies. When this failed he dissolved after three weeks what came to be known as the Short Parliament.

Not even a compliant parliament could have prevented the military catastrophe that followed. In one swift movement, the army of the Covenanters swept south, routed an English force of 3,000 at Newburn in August 1640, and occupied Newcastle, the source of London's coal. After another week the Covenanters had command of the counties of Northumberland and Durham, and could have marched on York were they so inclined. But, for all of its aggressiveness, the Covenanters' campaign was essentially defensive. They maintained a strict discipline, especially in regard to looting; they issued persuasive manifestos defending their actions; and they collaborated secretly with a group of English peers whose religious sympathies leaned more towards the Scots than to the King and Laud.

After the Scottish victory, the clamour for another parliament intensified. The Scots suggested it, the 'Twelve Peers' who corresponded with them petitioned for it, and London mobs demanded it. Out of money and out of options, Charles I summoned a parliament to convene in London on 3 November 1640. It sat for the rest of his life.

From the moment it met, the Long Parliament had a sense of its destiny. With the autumn selections following so quickly those of the spring, there was a political continuity to the choice of members. The conventional leaders of the county communities – justices of the peace and royal administrators – met to compile lists of grievances, beginning with the drain on local purses that resulted from six years of ship money and two years of militia levies. Shire officials could not keep up with the demands placed upon them, and for once their complaints that the localities were overburdened rang true. Nor were the county gentry alone in cataloguing grievances. Godly ministers met in conclaves to protest at Arminian innovations and 'popish' practices; merchants renewed their opposition to tariffs; craftsmen protested at monopolies. Nearly half of the English counties sent formal lists of grievances to Westminster with their knights of the shire, and scores of petitions flooded in.

At the beginning, the desire for reform united members of the Long Parliament. There was as yet no inkling that the nation was on the brink of civil war or that Parliament and crown would become separate institutions in opposition to each other. Though its role in representing grievances had expanded, Parliament was still one of the king's councils, and this accounts for the confusion that characterized the Long Parliament's first six months. There was quite simply a vacuum of power. Charles called Parliament to provide extraordinary supply to repel the Scots, either by negotiating a settlement or by renewing the fighting. Yet, as he discovered in the spring, he could not press for supply before Parliament presented its grievances. Indeed, once the session began, the Privy Council nearly ceased to function. Everything awaited the initiative of Parliament.

But Parliament was not an institution designed to initiate. Its conventional leaders were the king's servants who presented the crown's fiscal and legislative desires and steered them through the two Houses. The Long Parliament would have to develop its own leadership. During these first months, small groups coalesced in both Houses that eventually became an informal parliamentary leadership. Those close to Charles were not excluded from this process – indeed they were a vital conduit to the King – yet those who came to be most trusted were those who were most independent. In the Lords they were the Earls of Essex and Warwick, who had refused to support the forced loan; Viscount Saye and Sele and Lord Brooke, who were lay Puritans; and the Earl of Bedford, the organizer of the Petition of the Twelve Peers. In the larger House of Commons, leadership was dispersed. Hampden and his counsel, Oliver St John, were identified with opposition to ship money; a group of northern MPs led by the two Sir Henry Vanes was identified with the Scottish war. There were orators like Sir Benjamin Rudyerd, whose polished scripts were published within days of being delivered on the floor, and Sir John Culpepper and George Digby, whose ardour for reform slowly eroded.

The least likely of the parliamentary leaders, but ultimately the most powerful, was John Pym. A man of mean estate and modest station, he brought his social self-effacement into the political arena. Pym's greatest talent was to lead by seeming to follow. A client of the Earl of Bedford and a confidant of his aristocratic circle, Pym had led these lords into treasonable communications with the Scots. For the next two years his attempts to extricate them from complicity in one war led inexorably to their participation in another. If Pym had political principles they were that popery had eroded the fabric of the English church and fiscal mismanagement the fabric of the English state. But he was perfectly capable of holding tenaciously to contradictory positions which he would compromise without hesitation. An opponent of arbitrary taxation, it was Pym who demanded that Londoners be compelled to loan money. A defender of due process of law, it was Pym who quickly agreed to proceed against Strafford by a bill of attainder rather than trial. Indeed, in the early months of 1641 it looked as if Pym would follow in Strafford's footsteps from parliamentary leader to royal adviser. If he did, he would have to ensure that he stopped one step short.

The Long Parliament was hardly a week old when the attack upon Strafford began. By 25 November he was imprisoned in the Tower of London while a committee prepared articles of impeachment. The impeachments of Laud, of Lord Keeper Finch who had prosecuted the ship-money case, and of the judges who had found against Hampden followed in quick succession. The object of attacking crown ministers was twofold: to disable them as parliamentary leaders and to assail royal policy without impugning the King. As petitions of grievances poured in, demands for redress swamped the Houses of Parliament. On 11 December a delegation – some said a mob – of 1,500 Londoners accompanied a petition for the abolition of episcopacy, 'roots and branches'. This forcefully connected English grievances to Scottish ones. To some parliamentary leaders the continued presence of the Scottish army in the North was the lever with which they envisaged moving the world. But to others, especially the northern MPs, its presence was both an irritant and an affront. By Christmas the Commons had agreed in principle to raise four subsidies to pay the arrears of the Scottish and English armies.

As the first flush of euphoria faded, attention focused on the impeachment of Strafford. At the end of January 1641 the articles were ready, but the managers already realized that the case for treason was weak. That Strafford had counselled a hard line, especially against the Scots, was unquestionable. He had advocated bringing Irish troops into England, and after the failure of the Short Parliament he had declared that the King could rule by his prerogative in repelling the Scottish invasion. Strafford had no difficulty parrying the charges of treason and no hesitation in hinting that the real traitors were those who had brought the Scottish army into England: 'Should I die upon this evidence, I had much rather be the sufferer than the judge.'

If Parliament intended to remove Strafford, it would have to proceed by a bill of attainder rather than a judicial trial. Charles had promised to preserve his minister, and throughout the proceedings he attempted to negotiate a compromise with parliamentary leaders that would deprive the Earl of his offices though not of his life. When negotiation failed he resorted to threat, plotting with army officers to rescue Strafford by force, yet letting his machinations be known. This failed even more decisively. His troops were denied entrance to the Tower of London and, at the crucial moment, Pym revealed the details of this Army Plot in order to push through the bill of attainder.

Indeed, by the end of April 1641 there was near-hysteria in London. Mobs screamed for Strafford's blood, while shopkeepers boarded their stores – afraid of invasion by Irish, or papists, or the King's own army. The terror that incited the mobs infected the peers and the monarch. Strafford's allies in the Lords feared for their lives. When the vote for attainder came, most absented themselves. The Queen cringed inside Whitehall Palace in dread that she too would be a victim. With the bill of attainder waiting his signature, Charles could find no way out. Visceral demands for punishment met his reasoned pleas for mercy. As an obdurate Earl of Essex declared, 'Stone dead hath no fellow.' On 12 May Strafford wondered aloud on the scaffold 'whether the beginning of the people's happiness shall be written in letters of blood'.

The death of Strafford was one of two concessions that a panicked Charles granted. In February, when MPs feared that the King might dissolve Parliament rather than allow Strafford's trial, they passed a bill that stripped the crown of its control over sessions. It provided that parliaments would be held every three years; that they would sit for a minimum of fifty days; and that the Houses could select their own Speakers. Reluctantly, Charles signed what came to be called the Triennial Act, yielding, as he said, 'one of the fairest flowers in my garland'. Now the Army Plot again raised alarm of a sudden dissolution, and the Commons prepared a bill so that the Long Parliament could be dissolved only by its own consent. Again the King capitulated.

By the middle of May, Charles realized that he faced a greater crisis at Westminster than he did at Newcastle. As long as the Scots remained in England, Parliament held the reins of government. Throughout the summer its course became clear. The Commons prepared bills to end the prerogative courts of Star Chamber and High Commission, to exclude the bishops from sitting in the House of Lords, and, most ominously, to abolish episcopacy in England. It was time for the King to regain the initiative. At the end of May he announced that he would travel to Edinburgh to conclude a treaty with the Scots. At the beginning of August he set off, prepared to concede and conciliate, to pray with Presbyterians, and to treat with traitors in order to neutralize the Scots.

Charles's decisive action undercut his parliamentary opponents. They too had been negotiating with the Scots, and it was hardly an edifying experience. Scottish occupation of the North drove a deep wedge among the reformers, as did Scottish insistence that the two churches be brought to a Presbyterian conformity. But it was also plain that much of what the Scots wanted could be more easily granted by the King than by Parliament: security of land tenures, the abolition of tariffs on trade, and a greater role for Edinburgh in civil and ecclesiastical governance. Now Commons leaders suspected that the King might make his own deal – a deal that obviated the need for Parliament. To those who had leaped to the conclusion that Strafford had counselled the King to rule England with an Irish army, it was a small step to imagine that Charles might attempt to govern with a Scottish one.

The mistrust that members of Parliament felt towards their king, their paranoia about plots and their delusions about Charles's intentions were crucial components in the origins of the Civil War. It was not just that these fears could be manipulated – and at this Pym was a master – they also became the prism through which all events were viewed. In these months, people constantly feared for their lives. There were sudden unexplained panics in London. Milling mobs and gangs of youths presented the terror of class warfare. Tears streamed from the eyes of parliamentary orators. Swords were drawn at the slightest provocation. Parliament begged Charles not to go to Scotland, even holding a Sabbath-day session to prepare one more plea. Once he left, there was nothing to do but wait and worry. Parliament adjourned for six weeks, leaving a committee to oversee its affairs.

When the Houses reconvened in late October 1641, it was to further revelations about the Army Plot and of a shadowy conspiracy against the Scottish leaders Hamilton and the Marquis of Argyll in Edinburgh. Though Charles denied all involvement in what came to be called The Incident, Pym beat the rumours like a tocsin. The King and his supporters were desperate; they would even countenance assassination. Such allegations gained credence when a package containing a rag from a plague victim was sent to Pym with a note threatening his life. It was in this context of plots and conspiracies that on 1 November the first hysterical reports arrived of a rebellion in Ireland. The Catholic conspiracy, so long imagined and so exquisitely dreaded, had finally occurred. Initial accounts claimed that Catholics had slaughtered tens of thousands of Protestants in their beds. The atrocities would have been unspeakable were not the details so fascinating. The wombs of pregnant women ripped open; babies tossed on to pikes: the same hideous cruelties that it was imagined were perpetrated by Catholics in Germany or 'Turks to Christians – no quarter is given, no faith kept, all houses burnt and demolished, man, wife and child put to the sword' – were now ascribed to the rebels in Ireland. As refugees poured into Chester, they embellished all of these horrors and added one more to it: the Irish chieftains claimed to be acting in the name of the King.

Reports of the rebellion in Ireland were only slightly more confused than the event itself. Though the Earl of Strafford had been despised by all groups of Ireland's political structure, his lieutenancy had been effective in checking the worst tendencies of each. This was appreciated only when he was removed. 'Old' and 'new English' joined together to orchestrate his downfall, and there were few tears shed in Ireland at his demise. But without Strafford's strong hand the delicate balance of Ireland's irreconcilable divisions tipped in favour of 'new English' administrators who supported both the Scots and the Puritan parliamentarians. Well-armed Scottish forces camped a short boat ride from Ulster, and the Dublin government made clear its intention of enforcing the letter of the law against Catholic worship. The King, who had contemplated raising a Catholic army in Ulster under the Marquis of Antrim, was increasingly overwhelmed by crises in Scotland and England. The Ulster economy, barely recovered from the crisis of the early 1630s, took another turn for the worse beginning in 1640, exacerbating personal relationships between debtors and creditors and creating a sense of despair. Throughout 1641, Ulster Catholics grew restive; grumbling developed into discontent, discontent into conspiracy. The Irish rebellion was born of fear but nourished by hope – hope that Dublin was weak, that the English and Scots would remain divided, that the King was willing to make concessions; hope that the moment had finally come for Irish Catholics to take back the rule of their homeland.

The rebellion began with two separate objectives: a rising in Ulster and the seizure of Dublin Castle. The first was plotted by the descendants of dispossessed Gaelic families – 'men of broken fortune' – the second (if indeed it was plotted at all) by officers recently returned from the Spanish wars. The Ulster rising began on 22 October 1641 with a well-planned attack on Protestant settlers who occupied the estates of ancient Catholic families. Though it was the rebels' intention to leave the recently arrived Scots settlers in peace and thereby forestall an invasion from Scotland, once the rising began it quickly spiralled beyond the control of its leaders. It was a sudden, unexpected blow, and a considerable number of Protestants were murdered in the initial days of the rebellion, and a far larger number were driven from their homes and abused as they fled. Hard times had created hard edges. The rebels, led by Sir Phelim O'Neill, issued a declaration that they had risen to defend their liberties and were not in arms against the King. At the same time, efforts to seize Dublin Castle and thus the centre of royal government in Ireland came to nothing. The plot was betrayed, and a number of conspirators were arrested.

Initially, the heads of 'old English' families, who had been using Charles's difficulties with the Scots as a lever to push for the adoption of the Graces, remained aloof from the rebellion and criticized the rash behaviour of the Gaelic chieftains and their allies. But ultimately the rising spread. In an effort to save Strafford, Charles had disbanded the forces under the Lord Lieutenant's command, and this made it impossible for the Dublin government to launch an effective military response. A force sent to relieve Drogheda at the end of November 1641 was defeated by the rebels – a psychological victory of great importance in persuading the 'old English' to abandon their neutrality. By the following spring, Ireland had erupted into civil war.

What really happened in Ireland was of less significance than what people in Scotland and England believed had happened. The royal commission that rebel leaders waved was an outright forgery. The massacre that horrified the English, though brutal enough, was actually a controlled rising by the native Irish and 'old English' to curtail the power of the 'new English' planters that had grown since the execution of Strafford. Taking their cue from the Scots, the Catholic Irish believed that a limited rebellion might force the King to concessions, including legislative confirmation of the Graces. But at Westminster the massacre transformed the political situation. During the recess of Parliament in the autumn, Pym and his allies had begun to lose control of events. Resentment over their leadership swung the balance towards the King and a return to normality. Peace with the Scots removed one barrier, and Charles's reluctant agreement to the abolition of Star

Chamber and High Commission another. With the certainty of another session three years hence, perhaps the Long Parliament would agree to its own dissolution.

The Irish rebellion ended any such hopes. Not only did the parliamentary leaders have to manage a new crisis, it was a crisis that required putting the King in command of another army. Desperately Pym attempted to apply the brakes to motions in the Commons to supply arms, raise loans and enlist the aid of the Scots to suppress the Irish rebels. If Charles was to be supplied, Pym argued, he should be counselled only by those trusted in Parliament. Such caution was thrown to the winds of anti-Catholic hysteria. Pym revealed himself as more afraid of the King than of the Pope. While a committee pressed forward with preparations for a military expedition, Pym revived the subject of grievances. To lists that had been compiled throughout the year, Pym added the recent plots in England, Scotland and Ireland. As Charles returned home from Edinburgh through cheering crowds who flooded the highways to greet him, the Commons spent long, dark afternoons debating the Grand Remonstrance.

Uncertainty over the situation in Ireland, fears of Charles's intentions after his success in Scotland, and the bitter memories of the past decade all fed into the debates over the Grand Remonstrance. At one level the Remonstrance revealed the continued mistrust of the King by parliamentary leaders. There could be no doubt that Charles had considered using force against the parliamentary leadership. There was little reason to believe that he would not consider it again. But at another level the Grand Remonstrance revealed the weakness of the reform movement. The issues that now confronted the reformers – stripping the King of his military powers and reforming religion – were divisive in themselves. More than anything else, the Remonstrance was a history lesson that reflected the excesses of Charles's rule. When it was first proposed, nearly a year before, it had been likened to a mirror by which the King might better see himself as his subjects saw him. But now it was only broken shards, as dangerous to the members as to the monarch.

The Grand Remonstrance set out in voluminous detail a history of the baneful rule of Charles I and the beneficent reforms of the Long Parliament. Its tone was at once angry and defensive, and so too was the debate about its passage. Since the death of Strafford, royal supporters in Parliament were more vigorous. To them, the Remonstrance served no purpose other than to open old wounds. Why complain of prerogative courts when the King had already agreed to their abolition? The King's evil counsellors were dead, in prison or fled abroad. What purpose could be served by vilifying their memory? But for its supporters the Remonstrance justified Parliament's aggressive stance and provided a rationale for further reform. It was not only necessary to remove evil counsellors, it was necessary to put trustworthy ones in their places. The Remonstrance insisted on the appointment of those who had the confidence of Parliament. It was not only necessary to repudiate innovations in religion, it was also necessary that an Assembly of Divines restore pure Calvinist practices.

With the lines drawn between those who wished to step back and those who wished to plunge forward, the battle over the Remonstrance divided Parliament into royalists and parliamentarians. The royalists protested that, instead of bringing the complaints of the people to the King, the Grand Remonstrance brought 'complaint[s] of the King to the people'. The parliamentarians argued that without further reform there could be no security for the future. At 2 a.m. on the morning of 23 November the Remonstrance passed the House of Commons by a vote of 159 to 148. The unified reform movement of the first year of the Long Parliament had collapsed.

The presentation on 1 December of what Charles I called 'a declaration of a very unusual nature' stiffened the King's resolve. On 10 December he issued a proclamation requiring conformity to the rituals of the Church of England as established by the 'laws and statutes of the land', and on 23 December he answered the Remonstrance by denying its assumptions and refusing its demands. By then he had decided to reclaim his government. Rather than appointing counsellors trusted by Parliament, the King dismissed the elder Sir Henry Vane from office and, as we have seen, set in motion the events that led to the attempt to impeach five leading members of the Commons and one of the Lords. It was hard to see what else he could do. There was no doubt that Parliament's demands to approve counsellors, reform religion and oversee the military expedition to Ireland all encroached upon royal sovereignty. 'By God!' Charles exclaimed, 'you have asked that of me never asked of a king.'

Had Charles succeeded in arresting the parliamentary leaders, he might have defused the political crisis. His failure ignited it. After hustling the Queen and his children safely out of Westminster, the King abandoned his capital. Cheering throngs of Londoners returned Pym and his allies to their seats, while the newly elected leaders of the City made known their support of Parliament. There was now no question of trusting the King with an army, and step by step the two Houses inched towards military power. First they gained control over the Tower of London. Then they prepared a bill for Parliament to appoint all Lord Lieutenants and leaders of the trained bands. Sir John Hotham was sent to Hull, where the largest magazine of war supplies was stored, with orders to protect the fortress in the name of Parliament. This he did at the end of April, when Charles appeared at the city gates. Hotham kept the drawbridges raised and refused the King entrance, and Charles declared him a traitor for his pains. At Westminster the King's arrival at Hull could only signal war. On 5 May 1642, after Charles refused to surrender his power of military appointments, the two Houses simply expropriated it through a Militia Ordinance that they did not submit for the King's approval. It was hard to see what else they could do. Intercepted letters from the Queen revealed plans to enlist foreign allies. Three weeks later, Charles condemned the Militia Ordinance and branded as traitors those who accepted parliamentary commissions.

King and Parliament were now on a collision course. Charles was gathering forces in the North while Parliament was vigorously recruiting under the guise of sending an expedition to Ireland. This was made necessary by the creation of the Catholic Confederacy of Ireland, which transformed the rebellion in Ulster into a national movement, with a parliament – an executive known as the Supreme Council – and an effective military led by Owen Roe O'Neill, a veteran Spanish commander and an heir to the great Tyrone estates of Ulster.

At the beginning of June 1642 the Houses made an attempt to avoid bloodshed in England, by presenting Charles with the Nineteen Propositions, which were essentially terms for the King's unconditional surrender. Parliamentary desires had hardened into demands, and they left no aspect of the royal prerogative untouched. Parliament would endorse all future royal counsellors and judges. It would oversee the education of the King's children and approve royal marriages. It would advise on matters of war and peace and have full control over the militia. Finally, it would share responsibility for church reform.

The Nineteen Propositions left little room for compromise, and Charles rejected them. The royal response lectured the Houses on the prerogatives of the monarchy and the functions of Parliament. 'The House of Commons [was] never intended for any share of government'; if the King yielded to these demands he would turn monarchy into anarchy and 'the long line of our many noble ancestors in[to] a Jack Cade'. On 12 July Parliament voted to raise an army, and a little more than a month later, on 22 August, Charles unfurled the royal standard at Nottingham. It read, 'Give Caesar his Due.'

Still, the nation hardly plunged into civil war. In most counties the leading gentry avoided choosing sides. Some went so far as to adopt formal neutrality pacts; others simply refused to have either the Militia Ordinance or the royal Commission of Array read out. Their first object was to keep strangers out of their counties and their own militias in them. The peripatetic royal court forced the issue in Yorkshire and the Midlands, where Charles began his recruitment. London made Parliament supreme in the East, where its well-equipped militia helped disarm potential royalists and convert neutralists. The first months of jockeying were a time more for the settling of local scores than for the clash of principles that lay behind the rupture.

But it was principle that made compromise impossible and bloodshed inevitable. 'Every man almost in this generation durst fight for what either was or pretended to be truth,' the historian John Rushworth concluded. Royalists fought for the traditions of religion and monarchy that their ancestors had preserved and passed on to them as a sacred inheritance. They believed in bishops and the divine right of kings not so much as intellectual propositions than as the moorings of a hierarchy in church and state. Their fundamental principle was loyalty – an instinct deeply etched in the patriarchal nature of their society. Disloyalty was base – a violation of a code that made oaths as strong as contracts, voluntary obedience more dependable than law, and self-sacrifice a welcomed duty. Devotion was the emotive force behind the King's cause. Parliamentarians fought for true religion and liberty. They too defended an ancient inheritance – a church purified of recent innovations and a government that respected the inviolability of property. They feared for their souls, and felt that salvation was too important an individual matter to be left in the hands of the church. Their fundamental principle was consent – an ingrained belief in the cooperation between subject and sovereign that maintained the delicate balance between prerogatives and liberties. Without consent, monarchy became tyranny and free men became slaves. Their principal emotion was fear: dread at what would happen if they did not make a stand; terror at what would happen if they failed.

The crisis that began with the Scottish rebellion segregated principles and emotions that in calmer moments had been united. It was not that those who defended the prerogatives of the monarch did not also uphold the liberties of the people. It was not that those who feared popery did not also feel loyalty. There was not a member of the Long Parliament who questioned the hierarchical nature of English government or that monarchy was divinely ordained. There was not a royalist alive who disputed the inviolability of private property. The Civil War forced people to choose one set of values over another. Was popery more dreadful than anarchy? Were the rights of the sovereign to be preferred to those of the subject? The Civil War turned a stable marriage of beliefs into irreconcilable differences.

As the war ground on, these positions hardened into the bedrock of two ideological causes. Those who found it easiest to gravitate to one pole or the other took the lead in forcing moderates to choose. Small groups of extremists on each side wielded disproportionate influence. Propagandists waged a war of words that appealed to high principle and base emotion. Thousands of tracts poured from the presses to debate matters of the moment. Printed speeches brought national prominence to Pym and his allies; yet in sheer popularity there was no competing with the King. Whenever possible, booksellers placed a royal portrait on the cover of their products, despite the fact that most presses were located in London and most pamphlets were pro-parliamentarian. Propaganda helped shape opinion, but it was experience that determined commitment. Counties divided along their conventional fault-lines. Familial disputes, or hostilities between town and countryside, took shape as people had to choose sides. In general the North and the West were strongly royalist, the South and the East predominantly parliamentarian. But when fathers divided from sons and brothers fought each other there were few patterns. Moreover, the struggle took on its own logic. Victims sought revenge; outrages demanded retaliation. The price of blood constantly escalated: armies enlarged, battles intensified, treasure was expended in unimaginable quantities. Soon the war was being fought to justify the war.

Once war was declared, both sides raised armies of over 20,000 men. The largesse of the aristocracy supplied the King; the Marquis of Worcester alone lent £100,000. Parliament relied on the deep pockets of

London for men and material. Veterans of the European conflicts led both armies. The King's ablest commander was his German nephew Prince Rupert, whose dark good looks and youthful enthusiasm camouflaged a callous brutality. The parliamentarians appointed the ill-fated Earl of Essex Lord General of their forces. Essex was more haughty than he was rich, though he was one of the wealthiest men in England. His childhood was scarred by the execution of his father; his manhood by the failure of his two marriages – the first by his alleged impotence and the second by his wife's adultery.

Both generals believed that they would quickly win the war: Rupert because of the superiority of his cavalry; Essex because he possessed a better-equipped infantry – 'the most resolute foot in Christendom'. As both correctly assessed their strengths, the first campaign was indecisive. After some weeks of manœuvring, the armies engaged at Edgehill in Warwickshire on 23 October 1642. Rupert's cavalry swept its opponents from the field and chased them to the parliamentarians' headquarters. The royalists based their claim to victory on this rout and their plunder of the parliamentarian baggage train. Yet the inability of Rupert to regroup his horse meant that the King's infantry was left without protection on its flanks. It was broken by the stout fighting of the parliamentarian foot, and only the early darkness prevented a massacre.

If Edgehill proved that the King could not simply crush his opponents, it also proved that the parliamentarians could not stop a royalist advance. After regrouping, Charles moved south, occupying the towns of Banbury, Oxford – where he set up headquarters – and Reading. He aimed to re-enter London before the onset of winter. Essex chased the King along a parallel path and would not have caught him except for Charles's caution. Instead of racing to the capital, the royalists methodically took Brentford on London's western outskirts. Thus they faced a massed force of 24,000 at Turnham Green on 13 November, and the King decided to pull back into winter quarters. It was a typical decision: to bring the crisis to within an inch of resolution and then to withdraw. Charles would never get a better opportunity.

The English Civil War heeded the rhythms of the agricultural year. In the spring new armies were planted; in the summer they fed off the land; and in the autumn they reaped victories or defeats. In the winter they rested and peace was proposed. Thus, as 1643 began, Parliament presented Charles with the Oxford Proposals. They were the result of a struggle within the Houses that revealed a deep fissure between those who sought a negotiated settlement and those who sought a military one. Denzil Holles, who had read out the Three Resolutions in 1629 and was one of the five members Charles attempted to impeach in 1642, headed the 'peace group'. Second son of the royalist Earl of Clare, Holles knew personally the bitterness of 'this war without an enemy', and believed no one would wish to prolong it. He had seen the killing first-hand at Edgehill, where he stared death in the face and blinked. The peace group was opposed by those who wanted the King forced to terms. They were led by 'the fiery spirits', as one diarist labelled them – particularly the younger Sir Henry Vane and Henry Marten, the renegade son of a judge of the Court of Arches. They supported grim administrative expedients, including a weekly assessment modelled on ship money and an excise modelled on impositions. Between war and peace groups stood Pym and his allies, who held the parliamentary cause together by compromising the extremes.

Initially Pym found it easy to occupy the centre. The peace group's Oxford Proposals were too radical for the King; the war group's military expedients were too radical for the people. Indeed, both sides found it necessary to organize their armies around local leaders who could command respect and resources. The King consolidated his hold in Wales, the Midlands and the North through the efforts of aristocratic commanders like Lord Herbert and the Earls of Derby and Newcastle. Parliament governed through a committee system and gave military commands to its own members. To counter the reluctance of local militias to leave their counties, Parliament created regional forces of which the army of the Eastern Association under the command of the Earl of Manchester was the most important. One of Manchester's cavalry colonels was Oliver Cromwell, a natural military genius who was also an awe-inspiring field commander. Sir William Waller, a seasoned soldier in the European conflict, commanded the army of the South-Western Association.

These regional forces dominated the campaign of 1643. In the spring and early summer the King held sway. Parliamentary forces were decisively beaten at Chalgrove Field (18 June), where John Hampden was killed; at Lansdown (5 July); and at Roundway Down (13 July), where Waller's army was annihilated. Two weeks later Prince Rupert concluded a successful siege of Bristol (26 July), England's second city and a vital port of entry for weapons and reinforcements. At the same time, most of Yorkshire came under the control of the Earl of Newcastle.

While royalist forces pressed forward, the Earl of Essex sat still. His army, ringed about Oxford and wasted by disease and desertion, failed to take the royalist capital. At the beginning of September, Parliament reinforced Essex's army and ordered it to raise the siege of Gloucester. This it did, though at the cost of leaving the main royalist force with a clear path to London. Having quick-marched to the West, Essex now had to quick-march back through foul weather and darkening days. The paths of the two armies intersected at Newbury, where another of the indecisive pitched battles of the war took place. The King could not take advantage of the higher ground nor Essex the advantage of superior artillery. But, like Turnham Green, Newbury reversed royalist momentum and left the sides stalemated as they headed for winter quarters.

The winter of 1643–4 was one of grim determination. Both sides licked their wounds, though for those who had perished there could be no balm. Charles lost Lord Falkland, his closest adviser and one of the few men who might have persuaded him to come to terms. Parliament lost John Pym, whose wasting illness in the final months of the year seemed a commentary on the failing war effort.

Even while cancer consumed him, Pym laboured tirelessly to complete a military alliance with the Scots – the Solemn League and Covenant. In return for a commitment to religious reform 'according to the word of God and the example of the best reformed churches', the Scots would bring an army into England. The Solemn League and Covenant was mostly the work of the younger Sir Henry Vane and his war-group allies, though it also found support among Presbyterian members of the peace group. The entry of the Scots into the war necessitated structures for joint decision-making. The Scots sent representatives to the Westminster Assembly of Divines, which had been established to debate proposals for church reform, and they took places on a new executive, the Committee of Both Kingdoms, which was to be the strategic centre of the war effort.

Charles, too, beefed up his forces, negotiating a cessation of the war in Ireland that enabled him to bring over most of the royalist army that had been recruited to suppress the rebellion. They were led by James Butler, Duke of Ormond, who succeeded Strafford as Lord Lieutenant of Ireland and faced the challenge of controlling the Catholic rebellion that had spread to all parts of the kingdom. Catholic victories once again reduced effective control of Ireland to Dublin and the Pale, and the division between royalist and parliamentary Protestants sapped Ormond's strength. The Ulster Scots effectively carried on their own reprisals and refused to accept the cessation. Catholic counsels were equally divided between those who wished to force Charles to concessions and those who wished to make Ireland independent of Stuart rule. At the end of 1643 Ormond established a tentative peace.

But Parliament tasted the first fruits of these various alliances. The arrival in the North of a Scottish army under the command of the Earl of Leven made possible a concerted attempt on York in the summer of 1644. Local levies under the command of Sir Thomas Fairfax joined the Scots and the forces of the Eastern Association under the Earl of Manchester in an army of nearly 28,000 men. To repulse them, the King ordered two of his most successful generals, Prince Rupert and George, Lord Goring, to combine with the Earl of Newcastle into an army of nearly 21,000. Both forces were heterogeneously composed and used to fighting under their own commanders. Unexpectedly, at the moment of battle the parliamentarians were better able to coordinate their forces than were the royalists.

The engagement took place on 2 July at Marston Moor, and was one of the great set battles of the war. For the first time a parliamentary cavalry assault, under the command of Oliver Cromwell, turned back a royalist wing. This proved decisive as Cromwell regrouped his horse and deployed them against the royalist infantry that, despite its numerical inferiority, had held the first charge of the Scots. Marston Moor was a clear-cut parliamentarian victory. York was taken the following week, and the North was secured for Parliament. The royalists lost 4,000 dead, including many able officers. They also lost their sense that they were the inherently superior force that must ultimately triumph.

Yet the Battle of Marston Moor and the occupation of York were to be the high points of the parliamentary campaign of 1644. In the South, bickering between Essex and Waller as to who would be given pre-eminence in defeating the King threatened the strategy set out by the Committee of Both Kingdoms in London. This was to trap Charles between the two armies and bring him to a decisive battle. While Essex moved from Plymouth into Cornwall, Waller was in London airing complaints about the Lord General. Though the Commons ordered him back to his army, it was already too late. Reinforced by Goring, the

King's army was overwhelmingly superior and Essex retreated ever deeper into Cornwall. Finally there was no place to go. The entire parliamentary infantry ignominiously surrendered at Lostwithiel (2 September) while the Earl fled in a small boat.

Worse was yet to come. The royal army, freshly resupplied by what they confiscated in the surrender, wheeled east and headed for London, gathering strength along the way. Parliament ordered its three main armies into action, to be governed by a fractious Council of War in which Essex, Waller and Manchester all refused to defer to one another. Thus they frittered away numerical superiority at the second Battle of Newbury (27 October), when Manchester failed to support a successful parliamentary attack and then watched helplessly as Charles relieved Donnington Castle (7 November) and retrieved most of his heavy artillery.

Three years of fighting and still there was stalemate. The exhaustion of the armies, evident as both sides headed for winter quarters, was no greater than the exhaustion of the nation.

7

Civil War and Revolution
1645–1649

On 30 January 1649 Charles Stuart mounted the scaffold where his life would end. He gazed upon a sea of faces, talked briefly with the hooded executioner, who waited with axe upright, and then stared steadily ahead. The minister who accompanied him recited a short prayer, and then Charles addressed the small crowd that had gathered within the yard of the Palace of Westminster, kept well back from the raised platform by armed soldiers. But few could hear his words in the wind. He spoke in a steady voice: 'I go from a corruptible to an incorruptible crown; where no disturbance can be; no disturbance in the world.' Charles tucked his hair beneath his white satin cap, knelt, and lowered his head.

Towards the end of January 1649 a High Court of Justice established by the rump of the Long Parliament had been convened to hear charges of treason against Charles Stuart, king of England. The court was composed of members of Parliament, civilians and Army officers nominated in the name of the 'free born people of England'. There was little enthusiasm for the work that had to be done. No more senior judge than John Bradshaw – a minor circuit justice – could be found to preside, and throughout the proceedings he wore a hat ringed with iron in fear of assassination. The charges against the King had little legal basis: 'all which wicked designs, wars, and evil practices of him, the said Charles Stuart, have been and are carried on for the advancement and upholding of a personal interest against the liberty, justice and peace of the people of this nation, by and from whom he was entrusted'. Charles was to be sacrificed to the law of necessity, not the law of England. At the trial, Charles deftly exposed the charade: 'For the charge, I value it not a rush; it is the liberty of the people of England that I stand for. For me to acknowledge a new court that I never heard of before, I that am your king, that should be an example to all the people of England for to uphold justice, to maintain the old laws; indeed I do not know how to do it.' When he would not answer the charge against him, he was taken to have pleaded guilty. It was left to Bradshaw to catalogue his great crimes and pronounce sentence: 'That the said Charles Stuart, as a tyrant, traitor, murderer, and a public enemy shall be put to death, by the severing his head from his body.'

There were three days left to the King. On Sunday he sat in prayer with William Juxon, Bishop of London, who stayed with him throughout the final ordeal. On Monday 29 January Charles was allowed to see his two youngest children. To the ten-year-old Henry, Duke of Gloucester, the King had a special plea: 'Now they will cut off thy father's head and perhaps make thee a king. You must not be a king so long as your brothers Charles and James doth live. For they will cut off your brothers' heads when they can catch them and cut off yours too at the last. And therefore I charge you not be made a king by them.' To this the boy replied, 'I would rather be torn in pieces first.'

The King's judges were busy on those last days too. For one thing a death-warrant had to be signed, and at the last moment there were defections. Pleas for Charles's life came flooding in, many from parliamentary supporters. His eldest son, the Prince of Wales, sent in a blank commission offering to agree to any terms that Parliament would impose if only his father might be spared. In the Painted Chamber of the Palace of Westminster the warrant was spread on a table. Fifty-nine signatures and seals were ultimately obtained, though many would later recount stories that Oliver Cromwell, who had now convinced himself that the King's death was the only solution, had forced them to sign. Meanwhile workmen erected a scaffold against the second-storey windows of the royal banqueting-house, an edifice on which Charles had lavished so much money and which contained Rubens's exquisite ceiling panels. The King could hear the workmen cutting planks and driving nails throughout his final day.

Tuesday 30 January dawned clear and bitterly cold. Charles determined to fast during his last day on earth, but Bishop Juxon coaxed him to a small meal of bread and wine, a final communion among the living. After that the King spent the morning in prayer.

Thou, O God, art both the just afflicter of death upon us and the merciful Saviour of us in it and from it.

Yea, it is better for us to be dead to ourselves and live in Thee than by living in
  ourselves to be deprived of Thee.
Though my destroyers forget their duty to Thee and me, yet do not Thou, O
  Lord, forget to be merciful to them.
For what profit is there in my blood or in their gaining my kingdoms, if they
  lose their own souls?
Lord, let Thy servant depart in peace, for my eyes have seen Thy salvation.

Charles wore two shirts, for fear that he might shiver in the cold and
be thought afraid to meet his fate. He placed his head on the low block
and then spread out his arms, the signal for the executioner to do his
work. The axe fell true, and the King's head tumbled into the basket.
The executioner plucked it up and uttered the ritual words, 'Behold the
head of a traitor.'

The Wars of the Three Kingdoms were a devastating experience that
marked generations of Britons. The combat that began with the
Scottish invasion of England in 1640 quickly spread throughout the
archipelago. There were permanent military establishments in Ireland
and Scotland and near-continuous warfare in England for four years
beginning in 1642. Perhaps as many as one out of every eight adult
males participated directly in the fighting; perhaps twice that number
were involved in sieges. Civilians frequently fared worse than combat-
ants, as private property was commandeered, casual violence grew, and
taxes increased to as much as ten times pre-war levels. Though atrocity
stories were stock-in-trade of the propaganda distributed by both sides,
there can be no doubt that some of the outrages described took place
and that many which took place were never described. The number of
casualties remains speculative, though the proportion was probably
higher than in any British military engagement until the First World
War. But neither death nor destruction is sufficient measure of the chaos
created by civil war. The bonds that held society together were everywhere strained, and often broken. Families divided; communities were
rent asunder. Tenants refused to follow their lords; apprentices defied
their masters. The King was called tyrant, the parliamentarians traitors. Obedience, deference, order and civility were the unmeasurable
casualties of war.

The parliamentarian victory in the First Civil War was by no means
inevitable and, indeed, would hardly have been predicted until after the

Battle of Naseby. Parliament's internal divisions vitiated the advantage of its superior resources, and the longer the war ground on the more people longed for a return to normality. The bitter experience of the fighting made this increasingly unlikely, yet, while the war continued, Parliament did not develop any alternative other than to bring Charles I to terms. For his part, the King believed that he must ultimately triumph. He knew his cause to be just, his generals superior, his forces adequate to the task. More importantly, he was certain that only he could dictate the terms of settlement, whatever the outcome on the field of battle. Thus the series of defeats which Parliament inflicted upon his armies did nothing to soften his political stance. There could be no government without him, and sooner or later his enemies would have to trust him to rule.

Parliament was victorious, yet it did not prosper. Its cause was unified only in opposition to the King, and once this gravitational force was removed the components broke apart in every direction. The Scots demanded concessions that the English would not abide. The City of London threatened a tax revolt. Political groups within the House of Commons vied for power in anticipation of a restoration and royal munificence. Soldiers demanded arrears of pay and fretted over their futures. And religion reared its many heads. Episcopal reformers were branded backsliders by Presbyterian zealots. Presbyterians were derided as 'new forcers of conscience' by Independents. Fissiparous sects proliferated, gaining strength from Parliament's inability to conclude a religious settlement without the King or to enforce discipline in the interim. The war created radicalism; radicalism did not create the war.

As the fighting had taken on a life of its own, so now did political activism. The limited claims of Parliament to act on behalf of the people in bringing a recalcitrant monarch to heel were extended into contractual arguments about the nature of government and democratic arguments about the liberties of the people. These were heady days for Utopian plans to create a new Jerusalem through fundamental political reform that limited the power of kings and parliaments and made both responsible to the will of the nation. As royal and parliamentary commissioners debated arcane clauses of proposals for peace, new statesmen adopted the slogan *Salus Populi est Suprema Lex* – 'The Safety of the People is the Highest Law'. The deadlock was finally broken by the Army, first in 1647, when it resisted disbandment and directly challenged the authority of Parliament, and then after the Second Civil

War, when it simply swept king and Parliament aside and turned civil war into revolution.

*   *   *

The campaign of 1644 was a disaster for both sides. The losses in the North deprived the King of both men and money. The able Earl of Newcastle, the leader of the Presbyterians, chose exile in France rather than humiliation at the royalist court, where his disagreements with Prince Rupert were being publicly aired. Lord Wilmot was another of Charles's distinguished soldiers who resisted Rupert's ascendancy. Discovered communicating secretly with the Earl of Essex, Wilmot was arrested, stripped of his command, and sent into exile. His regiment nearly mutinied at the news. Parliamentary failure was just as deep-seated. The inability to build upon the victory at Marston Moor and the increasing tension between Essex and Sir William Waller had already caused concern at Westminster when a bitter dispute broke out in the Eastern Association army between the Earl of Manchester and Oliver Cromwell. Cromwell had roused the ire of the Scottish officers in Manchester's army by his opposition to their Presbyterianism, which he thought as rigid a yoke as the King's Arminianism. He favoured religious freedom for individual congregations in a loosely organized system known as Independency. For their part, the Scots lumped Independents together with the most extreme separatists. The quarrel between Manchester and Cromwell was tinged by these religious differences, though at its centre it was a dispute about prosecuting the war. At both Newbury and Donnington, Cromwell advocated aggression and Manchester defended inaction: 'If we beat the King ninety and nine times yet he is king still; but if the King beat us once we shall all be hanged,' the Earl reasoned. After these fiascos, Cromwell brought the controversy into the open, charging Manchester with incompetence.

The disputes among the parliamentary commanders no less than the inconclusive results of their efforts steeled members of Parliament for a thorough reform of their military. While the peace group again pushed forward with proposals for a settlement – what became the unsuccessful Uxbridge Propositions (January 1645) – war-group leaders and those who were saddled with military administration sketched out a plan for a New Model Army. This would combine the three major forces of Essex, Waller and Manchester into one national army of

22,000 men. It would be funded by a monthly assessment levied on each county, and it would be administered centrally in London.

There was little new in the 'New Model'. The remnants of the existing armies were simply combined and their overlapping commissaries and treasuries were unified. What was new was Parliament's decision to impose a self-denying ordinance upon all of its members, stripping them of military and civil office. Self-denial not only disabled the senior military commanders but all members of the House of Lords. This was less an attack upon the aristocracy, however, than it was upon the local basis of military organization. As Lord Lieutenants and regional commanders, many peers had raised their own regiments and defended or attacked local strongholds. The Committee of Both Kingdoms found it impossible to coordinate these forces with the efforts of their large armies. By stripping all peers of their military commands, local forces were necessarily brought under central authority and local commanders under the subordination of Parliament's new general, Sir Thomas Fairfax.

Fairfax was one of the few senior commanders who held neither a title nor a seat in Parliament. A scion of an established Yorkshire family, he was a perfect choice to bridge the divisions in the parliamentary cause. As a teenager he had served under Sir Horace Vere in the Netherlands, and subsequently he married Vere's daughter, Anne, a staunch Presbyterian. Yet he had raised a troop of dragoons for the royal service against the Scottish rebellion in 1639. A religious and political moderate, Sir Thomas threw in his lot with Parliament and successfully commanded the Yorkshire horse throughout the war. He compelled loyalty in his men by sharing the rigours of the field and the dangers of battle. But he was otherwise self-effacing – a welcome contrast to the trio of egotists he was replacing. He had collaborated successfully with the Scots – as it was hoped the New Model would do in the coming campaign – and had consistently supported aggressive military action. He had shown himself willing to take orders, willing to fight and willing to fade into the political background: 'For he did, with his utmost skill, /Ambition weed, but Conscience till.'

Fairfax's second in command, Sir Philip Skippon, was nearly his carbon copy. A professional soldier without strong religious or political affiliations, Skippon had led the London trained bands and commanded Essex's infantry before he was compelled to surrender at Lostwithiel. He was given the task of reorganizing the New Model foot-soldiers. The task of leading the New Model's cavalry ultimately fell to Cromwell. Although barred from command by the self-denying ordinance, Cromwell's abilities were too valuable to relinquish. He was given a number of limited exemptions until Parliament ordered him to join the Army permanently in June 1645.

The creation of the New Model Army took place within an atmosphere of crisis and tension. War weariness sapped the parliamentarians more than it did the King. Their use of emergency powers, martial law and fiscal exactions mocked their abstract defence of liberties. Royalist propaganda, published in Oxford, shifted blame for the war on to Parliament and effectively exposed corruption and peculation among its members. This was one reason for self-denial: the self-denying ordinance ostensibly stripped members of their civil offices and the fees attached to them. In fact it was proving necessary to provide even more members with income to enable them to remain at Westminster rather than to return to their estates. But the charges of gorging at the public trough weighed heavily and created personal animosities which added to divisions over religion and the conduct of the war. Moreover, the ordinance exacerbated the conflict between the Houses that had been growing throughout the war. The Lords twice rejected self-denial, obstructed the enabling bills for the Army, and held up approval of the list of officers for the New Model in the hope of restoring both Essex and Manchester to command. Despite the fact that these peers would play a prominent role in directing the war as members of the Committee of Both Kingdoms, the Lords viewed their removal as both an attack upon their accomplishments and a derogation of the powers of the aristocracy. A single proxy vote prevented an impasse between the Houses and a constitutional crisis. In April, as royal forces took the field, Fairfax hastily mustered his army and began training, 'from seeds and small beginnings'. No one expected a bounteous harvest.

Cautious strategists dominated the Committee of Both Kingdoms, which was given charge of directing the war. Though the peace negotiations at Uxbridge had failed, they had revealed that there were as many leading royal counsellors willing to find a settlement as there were members of Parliament. Secret meetings and private negotiations encouraged some to believe that peace was at hand. At the same time, it was recognized that the New Model was too weak to risk a showdown battle. Thus the Committee ordered Fairfax to lay siege to Oxford while it called the Scots south to protect the counties of the Eastern

Association. This defensive posture encouraged Charles and Rupert to believe that the parliamentarians were even weaker than the reorganization of their armies suggested. 'My affairs were never in so hopeful a way,' Charles wrote to his wife. Indeed optimism pervaded the royalist camp. It was still not clear to either side whether the campaign of 1645 would assume the pattern of past years, with small regional armies besieging strongholds and occasionally challenging each other, or if the main royalist and parliamentary armies would engage in a single pitched battle. Throughout May the King detached brigades into the North and West while Fairfax hived off a piece of his army to relieve the siege of Taunton. But by early June both sides had decided separately to fight. Rupert lured the New Model from its siege of Oxford by capturing and sacking Leicester. This opened the North and the East to royalist depredations and forced the Committee of Both Kingdoms to order Fairfax to action. Cromwell was given command over the cavalry and Fairfax tactical authority over the army. Battle was at hand.

The two armies met at Naseby on 14 June 1645. The parliamentarians were the larger force; the royalists were better organized and more experienced. Cromwell and the brigade he had raised in the Isle of Ely joined the main army only two nights before the battle. He was to command the right wing of cavalry. The left wing was unexpectedly put in charge of Cromwell's son-in-law, Henry Ireton, who had been elevated to commissary-general the previous day and who now undertook his first significant command. The troops he led were an amalgam from the older armies; several of the companies were under new commanders, and they had never before fought as a brigade. The centre of the field was commanded by Fairfax and contained over 6,000 infantry. The parliamentary infantry had been reconstituted after the surrender at Lostwithiel, but its backbone remained the London militia which had been drilled by Sir Philip Skippon. Opposite Cromwell, on the royalist left flank, was the brigade of northern cavalry commanded by Sir Marmaduke Langdale. For three years he had successfully controlled the North for the King, commanding a flying brigade that inflicted defeat after defeat upon Fairfax's regional forces. Rupert commanded the right and set the battle in motion. He had argued against giving fight, and now had to defend the judgement of others with his own sword. Sir Jacob Astley, newly made Lord Astley, Charles's veteran infantry commander, controlled the centre of the royalist lines. Sixty-six years old, he had been a professional soldier all of his life, serving in the Dutch wars as well as the German ones. It was Astley who had tutored Rupert in the arts of war. He had been major-general of foot in the Scottish campaign, at Edgehill, and in both engagements at Newbury. In contrast to the New Model, the royal forces were led by proven commanders.

The battle itself resembled Edgehill and Marston Moor. Rupert's cavalry charged through Ireton's wing and routed it. They continued in pursuit until they reached the parliamentarian baggage train, which they turned upon to plunder. Though heavily outnumbered, Fairfax's lifeguard regiment refused to surrender the baggage, and the ensuing fight kept Rupert's horse from returning to the field. In the centre the two masses of infantry came to push of pike, though the field was initially too crowded for the parliamentarians to make use of their numerical superiority or the royalists the horse regiment that they had stationed in the centre of the field. The hand-to-hand combat was strenuous but indecisive. Cromwell charged last. His troops occupied unfavourable ground and he hoped that Langdale would advance towards him. But at last the parliamentary cavalry cantered forward crying 'God is our strength!' and after a fierce charge overwhelmed Langdale's forces. Cromwell's brigade was numerically superior and he was thus able to have the fleeing royalist cavalry pursued by one part while he returned to the infantry battle with the other. This was the decisive turn of events. With Cromwell's horse attacking from the left side and parliamentarian dragoons from the right, the royalist infantry cracked. They had held their ground for nearly three hours, and at one point threatened to break through. But once the cavalry arrived the odds were against them. To prevent a slaughter, Astley surrendered his forces *en masse* – over 4,000 soldiers and 500 hundred officers. In addition Charles lost his entire artillery train and 8,000 weapons, the plunder that the royalists had garnered from Leicester, and his private correspondence with his wife.

The Battle of Naseby did not bring the Civil War to an end, though it made a parliamentarian victory all but inevitable. Charles could not recover from so massive a loss of men and material at the beginning of the campaigning season. The western counties that the royalists dominated were already overtaxed, and the defeat at Naseby meant that the King was cut off from the resources of the Midlands as well as of the North. Charles pinned his hopes on recruiting Catholics from Ireland and mercenaries from France, though these were soon dashed. His captured correspondence with the Queen, which Parliament callously ordered to be printed, revealed these machinations as well as Charles's duplicity at the Uxbridge negotiations. This was a political catastrophe to match the military one.

After the victory at Naseby, Parliament's primary objective was the West Country, where most of the remaining royalist strongholds lay. The campaign was brutal and bloody. Royal forces were entrenched in the largest towns, and royal armies fought with a savage desperation. The first confrontation was with the forces of George, Lord Goring, whose army had terrorized friend and foe to earn the sobriquet 'Goring's crew'. The New Model, now divided into several fighting brigades, broke Goring's siege of the parliamentarian garrison at Taunton and met his main army at Langport (10 July). A frontal assault up a steep hill not only broke the royalist ranks, it broke their spirit as well. Despite a shortage of men, money and *matériel*, the brigade commanded by Fairfax fired the town of Bridgwater (22 July) and accepted the immediate surrender of Bath (30 July).

Sherborne in Dorset proved more challenging, both because the castle was well defended and because mobs of peasants who took the name of Clubmen confronted the Army. The Clubmen insisted upon their neutrality and claimed to oppose whichever side they believed to be the aggressor in their county. In Somerset, the Clubmen held their grudge against Goring and thus aided Fairfax with carts, horses and fodder. Their programme echoed a parliamentary Protestation of 1641. In Dorset they viewed the New Model as interlopers and hindered their operations wherever possible. Led by minor gentry and local clergymen, the Dorset Clubmen defended the traditional values of their tightly knit communities against fears of Puritan innovations. But they defended themselves with no stouter weapons than clubs – hence their name – and they were no match for Cromwell's seasoned troops once attempts at persuasion failed. Sherborne fell on 15 August, and Fairfax turned west towards Bristol.

Bristol was all that now remained of Charles's western fortifications. The castle was believed to be impregnable, as its seventeen-foot-thick walls were situated on a high hill and girded by deep moats. When Parliament had lost Bristol in 1643, its commander was immediately court-martialled for incompetence. It was now defended by Prince Rupert, who expected Charles and the remnants of his armies to relieve him in just three weeks. The city was well supplied, and the recent outbreak of plague within the walls was as likely to deter attackers as to deplete defenders. But Fairfax was determined. Bristol would be stormed, not starved. On 4 September he summoned the town, and for nearly a week Rupert stalled the negotiations. Finally the assault began, and in less than a day, to the astonishment of Charles no less than Fairfax, the Prince surrendered.

The Civil War continued for another eight months, but it consisted mainly of mopping-up activities by the parliamentarians. During the winter of 1645–6, attention focused on peace rather than war. The coalition of interests that supported Parliament now had to construct the terms upon which the King would be restored. There was much disagreement. Since Pym's death at the end of 1643, parliamentary politics had oscillated between the alternatives of war and peace. There remained much common ground among all parliamentarians, as well as a preference for finding policies that did not widen philosophical differences. They had all been branded traitors and rebels, and they would all hang together if the King prevailed. Nevertheless, the divisions among parliamentary leaders did grow, and the wedge that prised them apart was religion.

As long as Charles was the focus of parliamentarian thinking about religion, there was general agreement: all were opposed to Laudian innovations. But, as Parliament began to develop its own programme for religious reform, its members broke into three groups: reforming episcopalians, Presbyterians and Independents. The episcopalians were the majority. Though they wanted significant change, they wanted it within the context of the Elizabethan settlement. The minority, divided into Presbyterians and Independents, supported the abolition of bishops. Ultimately the minority dominated both the Westminster Assembly of Divines and Parliament's committees on religion. As Lord Falkland remarked about attendance at debates on episcopacy, 'those that hated bishops hated them worse than the devil and those that loved them loved them not so well as their dinner'.

The anti-episcopalians were overwhelmingly Presbyterians. A phalanx of London ministers, heirs to the underground traditions of Elizabethan Puritanism, supported them. They desired a national church with strict doctrinal conformity, but a church organized upwards from the congregations rather than downwards from a supreme governor. Lay elders were to have a significant role alongside ordained ministers. These English Presbyterians were also supported by the

Scots, whose system they emulated, if they did not adopt it entirely. The Independents were the much smaller group of anti-episcopalians. They opposed the hierarchy of Presbyterian organization as well as their insistence upon national doctrinal conformity: 'New Presbyter is but old Priest writ large.' They wished to have each congregation govern itself within the context of an essential uniformity, to allow for the practices of 'tender consciences that differ not in fundamentals'. Presbyterians and Independents held much in common, and it was temperament more than theology that divided them. Presbyterians were willing to sacrifice liberty to prevent licence; Independents were willing to tolerate licence to protect liberty.

With the prospect of victory came the necessity of preparing the terms on which the King would be restored to power. The Scots insisted that the Solemn League and Covenant had promised a Presbyterian conformity along the lines of their kirk. The Independents pleaded for toleration. Though they were a distinct minority, their cause was boosted by the success of Oliver Cromwell. With the litter of corpses around him, he wrote from Naseby field imploring Parliament to protect liberty of conscience. During the course of the next year the debate over church government intensified. With the Presbyterians in control of pulpit and press, they aimed a steady barrage against the proliferation of what they described as 'all manner of heresies, errors, sects, destructive opinions, libertinism and lawlessness'. They indiscriminately lumped the Independents together with radical sects like the Baptists, who denied the efficacy of infant baptism, or the Antinomians, who preached that the saved could not sin.

The influence of the London Presbyterian ministers reached beyond their congregations. They colluded as co-religionists with the Scottish commissioners to Parliament and were strongly linked to the governors of the City of London. The Scots and the City of London had been Parliament's staunchest allies. The Scottish army had re-entered England at the behest of Parliament in 1644, though it ultimately had contributed little to the war effort. As the Army of the Covenant moved south, royalist forces under the Marquis of Montrose gathered in the Highlands. Montrose's success, in what was a brutal clan war, eviscerated the Scottish commitment in England. Nevertheless, the commissioners insisted upon the fulfilment of the terms of the Solemn League and Covenant, which included Scottish ratification of any peace proposals. London had also made its sacrifices. Its trained bands had been the backbone of the parliamentary armies, its treasure the sinews of war. Loans had been made on weak security, taxes had risen, and business had been interrupted. With the war over, London demanded its due: an expansion of the City's privileges, repayment of loans with interest, and the disbandment of the expensive military establishment.

The power of these pressure groups increased immeasurably in May 1646 when Charles I, disguised as a servant, slipped out of Oxford and presented himself at the headquarters of the Scottish army at Newark. There he hoped to play divide and conquer as he had in 1641. The King entered into negotiations directly with the Scots, straining relations between the two kingdoms and raising the fear of another war. This placed a sharper edge on Parliament's own peace proposals, which on 30 July 1646 were presented to the King on neutral ground at Newcastle as terms to be acceded to rather than negotiated. Foremost among them was the establishment of a Presbyterian church, parliamentary control of the military for twenty years, and the exclusion from pardon of over fifty of Charles's most prominent supporters. Asked to abandon 'his church, his crown, and his friends', Charles took the low road and stalled. He had already rejected the Scottish demand for the abolition of English episcopacy, despite pleas from his wife, the agents of his foreign allies, and all of his political advisers. If he would not accept the lenient terms offered by the Scots, surely he would not accept harsher ones offered by Parliament. But if the King would not compromise religion it was difficult to see what the Scots had to gain by sheltering him. Thus, while Charles deceived himself into believing that he was a guest, the Scots forthrightly regarded him as a captive. They negotiated the withdrawal of their army from England and the return of the King for a payment of £400,000.

These negotiations marked the political high-water mark of the Presbyterians in Parliament. They had long been allied to the Scots and to the financial leaders of London, and both groups were now vital to secure the King. Denzil Holles, Sir Philip Stapleton and the Earl of Essex (until his untimely death in September 1646) were the parliamentarians who had backed the legislation for the Presbyterian church settlement, had calmed Scottish outcries over religious diversity, and had supported the fiscal schemes of the City government. Now only they could negotiate the release of the King and raise the money necessary to effect it. They ramrodded bills through Parliament for the sale of bishops' lands, negotiated favourable terms for loans, and supported petitions from the City of London to expand its jurisdiction. These political alliances quickly paid off. On 30 January 1647 English gold was exchanged for King Charles I. In the company of parliamentary commissioners, he was brought by stages to Holmby House in Leicestershire.

Control of the King was part of a coordinated plan that the Presbyterian leadership now put into effect. Charles's declarations at Newcastle had made clear that he would never willingly bargain away his bishops or his military prerogatives. Thus the only possible settlement was one in which the King did not participate in dismantling the episcopal church or in constructing an invasion force to suppress the Catholic rebellion in Ireland. From his commanding position as leader of the Presbyterians in the House of Commons, Denzil Holles devised a brilliantly simple plan to remove these obstacles to peace. The exclusively Presbyterian church that Parliament established in March 1646 would be fortified from within and from without. Parliament directed the Assembly of Divines to conclude the Confession of Faith and encouraged the growth of the fledgling London Presbyterian classes. Bills were introduced to prevent the growth of heresy and to prohibit laymen from preaching. Most significantly, the decision to sell bishops' estates led finally to the abolition of bishops. Five years of theological dispute over root and branch was resolved by a few weeks of fiscal realism. No bishops, no lawsuits reasoned the London money men. If bishops were abolished, so were their titles to land – as Henry VIII had proved with the monks. Secondly, Holles laid plans to pacify Ireland. Major-General Edward Massey's brigade, already stationed in the west of England, would be joined by a detachment of the New Model Army to make a sizeable invasion force. In England, strategic garrisons would be manned by parliamentary appointees while other strongholds would be demolished. Then the remainder of the parliamentary forces could be disbanded. All of this would be accomplished before the King was invited to resume his government. Charles would have to concede nothing: he would simply return to Westminster and rule.

In all of this Holles reckoned without the Army. Throughout the years of fighting, the New Model Army had remained apolitical. The rank and file were largely pressed men, kept in place both by the draconian penalties for desertion and by the steady build-up of unpaid wages. The officers were parliamentarians by choice, but they comprised a spectrum of religious and political viewpoints. 'Presbyterians, Independents, all agree here [and] know no name of difference,' Cromwell wrote of the New Model. Thus Holles's plan to break up the Army and send a part to Ireland struck a personal rather than a political note. In March 1647 troops in scattered regiments began to voice concerns about arrears of pay, indemnity for acts committed during wartime, and impressment to serve in Ireland. They initiated a petition to Fairfax and the Council of War, but before it made much headway rumours of its existence reached Holles in London. He was horrified. Resistance in the Army would undermine the entire settlement; even delay might be fatal. Committees were already at work to provide security for material concerns, and nothing could be allowed to compromise the relief of Ireland. On 30 March he propounded a savage parliamentary declaration branding the petitioners 'enemies to the state'. Parliament sent commissioners to Army headquarters in Saffron Walden, Essex, to investigate the origins of the petition, and there they arrested some of its promoters.

The declaration of 30 March led to a near-mutiny in the army. Though the petition was abandoned, the rank and file began to organize. They selected regimental 'agitators', or agents, to represent their grievances to the Council of War. These agitators became so vital a conduit between soldiers and officers that eventually they were incorporated into a newly created Council of the Army. Regiments held rendezvous to instruct their agitators and to discuss complaints. Grievances multiplied, and now included both the original material concerns and a vindication of the honour of the Army from charges that it was obstructing the service in Ireland.

The demand for a vindication of the Army's honour played into the hands of Holles's political opponents at Westminster, including Cromwell and Henry Ireton. They were MPs as well as senior Army officers, and they believed that the New Model should be kept intact until the Irish rebellion was suppressed. But the agitation in the Army increased the pressure for disbandment. The money to fund the Irish invasion and pay the arrears owed the soldiers could only be raised in London. London leaders insisted on disbandment, to lower both taxes and the political temperature. Thus Holles pressed on. He continued to recruit New Model volunteers for Ireland, placing them under the command of politically reliable officers, and he continued with his plans for demobilization. In May he introduced legislation to provide indemnity as well as a cash payment and paper securities for arrears. But nothing was done to vindicate the Army's honour.

In the Army, the pressures against disbandment were equally intense. The Army's radicalization was all the more potent for being spontaneous. The soldiers believed that their service had been touched by the finger of God and they expected a hero's reception at war's end. Instead of accolades they were rewarded with accusations: that they obstructed the service in Ireland, that they hindered peace, that they were led by royalist infiltrators. Nor was it clear how they could be vindicated. Parliament had closed off the avenue of petitioning. Many junior officers shared the concerns of the rank and file, and in April they had met to declare solidarity with the soldiery. But the senior officers were in a more difficult position. For one thing, they were responsible for discipline, which was threatened by continued political agitation. Cromwell, Ireton and Skippon were all members of Parliament who had to mask their personal preferences. While Fairfax was sympathetic to his soldiers' concerns, he was the dutiful servant of Parliament. As instructed, he encouraged his officers to join the Irish expedition, and a number of Presbyterian colonels took up the offer, destroying the possibility of unified resistance. Those who accepted Irish service drove a dagger into the heart of those left to be disbanded.

By May the agitators were in a frenzy about their security and believed that the Presbyterians in Parliament were engaged in a conspiracy to destroy the Army. Once they were ordered to disband, their options were obedience or mutiny. On 1 June they chose mutiny. Soldiers intercepted the treasure caravan destined for the mustering out, and the agitators held a rendezvous of their own on 5 June where they took a Solemn Engagement not to disband until all of their just grievances had been redressed. They denied that their actions constituted a revolt and dismissed accusations that they were politically motivated. But chests of gold were not all that the soldiers hijacked. On 3 June, Cornet George Joyce with two troops of New Model cavalry appeared at Holmby House. With the knowledge of senior officers – though not their approval – he insisted that the King accompany the troopers to Army headquarters – an invitation that Charles, ever alert to divide his enemies, accepted with alacrity.

The seizure of the King wrecked Holles's plans. Charles could now use the Army Independents as a counterweight to the parliamentary Presbyterians, and throughout the summer he dangled the prospect of a tolerant religious settlement in front of them. Moreover, the Army was more insistent than ever that its just grievances be redressed, and these now included the impeachment of Holles and ten of his allies on a variety of charges. In the Commons, moderates began moving away from Holles and his party. But the Presbyterians still held a majority, and throughout July they resisted Army demands that their eleven leaders be impeached and that all of the funds raised for the disbandment be paid to the New Model troops.

Indeed, throughout July disbanded soldiers from Parliament's former armies flocked into London to claim their own arrears. These soldiers, called reformadoes, organized monster petitions which they presented at huge rallies outside the Palace of Westminster. They too had served Parliament faithfully and, unlike the New Model, when ordered to disband they had returned to their homes peaceably. The time had come to settle their accounts too. With soldiers massing inside London – both reformadoes and troops waiting to be dispatched to Ireland – and the New Model massing outside it, fear of military confrontation grew. Holles and his allies refused to withdraw from the House while the Army's charges against them were adjudicated, and they did nothing to discourage talk of resistance.

The deadlock was broken when Parliament was invaded by London apprentices and reformadoes who demanded that their grievances rather than the New Model's be redressed. On 26 July the Houses of Parliament were held hostage by mobs who forced votes against the Army at sword point. Both Speakers and nearly 100 members of the two Houses fled London that night and appealed to Fairfax for protection. For the next five days London armed in anticipation of war. Parliament sent commissioners to the Army to prevent an invasion, but Fairfax and the Council of War never hesitated. They brought the Army to a rendezvous and began an orderly march towards London. When commissioners from the City government arrived at headquarters, they were informed that if the gates were not kept open London would be stormed. On the night of 2 August opposition to the Army melted away. The following day thousands of New Model troops marched into the capital to restore the Speakers and members of Parliament, to oust Holles and his supporters, and to assert the Army's role as a political participant.

The entry of the Army into politics dramatically transformed the conditions necessary for the settlement of the English Civil War. All along, the war had been fought to restrain the abuses of government, but until now they had been the abuses of the monarch. During the course of the summer the Army discovered that parliamentary tyranny was equally dangerous. The charges of impeachment against the eleven Presbyterian leaders included corruption, electoral irregularities and the systematic misuse of power. The Army's declaration of 14 June proclaimed, 'We were not a mere mercenary army hired to serve any arbitrary power of a state.' The terms for settlement that the Army presented to Charles in August – the *Heads of the Proposals* – began with reforms of Parliament, including a fixed date for the dissolution of the Long Parliament, and reform of representation and of the franchise.

The Army's attack upon parliamentary tyranny also made it a refuge for other marginalized groups. The creation of a Presbyterian church and the attacks upon religious diversity posed a direct threat to the Independent congregations in London. In the spring of 1647 they allied themselves with a coalition of radicals known derisively as the Levellers and petitioned Parliament for civil liberties and religious toleration. Like the soldiers' petition, Parliament declared the Levellers' Large Petition seditious and arrested some of its supporters. This led to pleas for the right to petition and for freedom from arbitrary arrest – issues which again paralleled the Army's own demands. Throughout the summer Leveller leaders like John Lilburne appealed to the army to support their cause. Lilburne was an uncompromising firebrand. He had been imprisoned by the bishops in 1638, by the royalists in 1643, by the House of Lords in 1645, and by the House of Commons in 1647. Each confrontation was of his own making, for he had the rare capacity to see a nettle whenever an olive branch was offered him. His charisma was based on a talent for elevating the personal to the universal. If John Lilburne were imprisoned then all Englishmen must be slaves.

Leveller entreaties to the Army leadership were unsuccessful throughout the summer, and in the autumn of 1647 they focused instead upon the rank and file. Cromwell and Ireton were accused of selling the soldiers' blood for their own aggrandizement in negotiations with the King and with the corrupt Parliament. With Lilburne still in prison, his fellow radical John Wildman pressed the Levellers' attack, calling for the election of new agitators and a mass meeting to prevent the Army's disbandment. Leveller agitation played upon the apprehensions of soldiers and junior officers who were distanced from the decisions made by the Council of Officers. The attack upon the 'Grandees', as Wildman opprobriously labelled the senior officers in his scathing pamphlet *The Case of the Army Truly Stated*, led to a meeting of officers, agitators and Levellers at Putney Church at the end of October.

There the Levellers presented their first *Agreement of the People*, a political compact which asserted popular sovereignty and parliamentary supremacy. The *Agreement* set aside the monarchy, invested Parliament with executive and administrative authority – though no coercive power over religion – and advocated electoral reforms based on the principle of manhood suffrage. In the autumnal gloom the *Agreement* was debated inconclusively. The argument over the franchise generated more heat than light. Ireton and Cromwell insisted that only property-holders – those with 'a permanent fixed interest' – should vote, while Colonel Thomas Rainsborough, the only senior officer to side with the Levellers, averred that 'the poorest he in England hath a life to live as the greatest he'. Though the Levellers were willing to exclude paupers and servants, and the Grandees to include all parliamentary soldiers, this did little to narrow the philosophical differences. Nor could there be much compromise between the Army's engagement to restore Charles I and the Levellers' determination to exclude him. When the Levellers saw that they could make no headway in debate, they called for action. But the senior officers were determined to reassert military discipline. The agitatators were returned to their regiments, an incipient mutiny was quickly quelled, and the concentration of troops around London was dispersed into winter quarters.

The agitation over radical franchise reform, however prescient for the future, heightened anxiety over the Army's intentions in the present. Viewed from the nave of Putney Church, there was a world of difference between the Army's intentions and the Levellers' desires. But, seen from the countryside, the accusation that the Army 'was one Lilburne throughout' rang true. The Army's intervention in parliamentary politics, first as a pressure group and then as a protector, even frightened moderates in the House of Commons. Throughout the autumn, attendance declined and disputes became more acrimonious. All of this played directly into the hands of the King. Though he was under the nominal control of the army, first at Hampton Court and then at Carisbrooke Castle, to which he escaped on rumours that the Levellers were planning an assassination, Charles happily treated with everyone.

He was too astute to agree to anything while his enemies were divided. Thus he prolonged negotiations and allowed pebbles of disagreement to become stumbling-blocks. The King's agents reported widespread revulsion from military rule and overtures of support from former parliamentarians. Ensconced on the Isle of Wight, Charles continued to behave as if he were on top of the world rather than at the end of it.

No one was more threatened by the Army's rise to power than the Scots. They had surrendered the King and withdrawn their forces from England on the understanding that Holles and his allies would conclude a settlement that would protect Presbyterianism. Negotiations between Army leaders and the King not only undermined the newly created Presbyterian church, they also threatened the security of the kirk. Throughout the winter of 1647–8 the Scots renewed their overtures to the King, promising to use their army to restore him to power if he would guarantee Scottish Presbyterianism, extirpate English Independency, and provide a role for Scots nobles in his government. This position, known as the Engagement, further split the Covenanting movement, which was already severely strained by issues arising from the war. Charles agreed only to allow the practice of Presbyterianism in England for three years, while the radical clergy remained committed to a unified Presbyterian church.

Charles's negotiations with the New Model and the Scots left Parliament a frustrated observer. In September the Houses revived the Newcastle Propositions, though they were so obviously less attractive to the King than the *Heads of the Proposals* that the Army simply used them as intimidation. Parliamentary radicals twice introduced measures to break off all negotiations with Charles, but these were rejected in a triumph of hope over experience. Rumours of the Scots, proposals increased the urgency of a parliamentary initiative. By December 1647 the Army leaders realized that they would not reach an accord with the King and feared that, if the Scots did, war would resume. Thus the Independents and moderates in Parliament appealed to the Presbyterians to form a united front to propose one more set of terms: the Four Bills. These granted Parliament control of the militia for twenty years and required that the King accept the recent parliamentary church legislation, including the abolition of bishops. The Four Bills were presented to Charles on 24 December. Two days later he signed the Engagement with the Scots.

For the members of Parliament this was the final turn of the screw.

Not only had they set aside their political differences at enormous cost – the eleven Presbyterian leaders were invited to return to Parliament, which led to calls in the Army for the impeachment of Cromwell and Ireton – but they had diluted their conditions far beyond prudence. On 3 January 1648, by a majority of fifty, the House of Commons passed the Vote of No Addresses. They would offer no more terms to a king so bent on self-destruction. In the Army, alongside the clamour for the ousting of the Grandees, came cries for the deposition of the King. Even Cromwell began exploring the possibility of placing the sixteen-year-old James, Duke of York, on the throne, before the Duke, hearing the rumours, made a sudden escape and joined his brother, the Prince of Wales, in France. Stories that the King would be assassinated or that he would flee to the Continent spread like wildfire in London. In the country there was a swelling of loyalty to Charles I.

The Vote of No Addresses was a logical response to the King's intransigence, but it was a response that created despair. How would the war end; how would the ceaseless turmoil be resolved? Throughout the nation, resentment grew against the apparatus of parliamentary and military government: the county committees that had assumed administrative control in the localities and the garrison commanders who employed martial law. Both exercised forms of rough justice that were barely tolerable during the exigencies of war. But their continued existence was necessary to ensure that taxes were collected and order was maintained. The committees became a special target of attack – the symbol of arbitrary government and parliamentary tyranny that increasingly alienated the gentry from the men at Westminster. They were the focus of hostility against the excise, the military assessments and the continued disruption of settled life. Committeemen and commanders became beleaguered as justices of the peace and governors of towns attempted to circumvent their authority, to restore a semblance of normality in the localities. Clashes between civilians and military became increasingly common in the winter of 1647–8. Committees dealt with tax resisters by quartering soldiers in their villages, and the soldiers became the targets of provocation. Some provocations were simply the revival of festivities associated with traditional society, like the football match that led to a riot in Kent. Others were more deliberately challenging, like the celebration of Charles I's coronation day in Norwich. In either case, they set centre against locality, Parliament against people.

Throughout the winter, communities seethed under these tensions. Fairfax had managed to reduce the size of the parliamentary militia by almost half, disbanding provincial forces in Wales and the North and trimming the New Model by 4,000, though at the price of increased taxation to pay for demobilization. Moreover, the disbandment in Wales was resented by officers and soldiers alike, and it was there that the sporadic local riots that flared throughout the nation burst into conflagration. The troopers took the disbandment money and then joined a renegade force that declared for King and prayer-book. By the end of April 1648 South Wales was in revolt and a contingent of New Model troops was in danger of being overrun. Cromwell was immediately dispatched south. The rising in Wales may have been spontaneous, but, ever since Charles signed the Engagement with the Scots, plans had been laid for a general royalist rebellion in England to coincide with a Scottish invasion. Thus, as Cromwell mustered at Gloucester, news came of trouble in the North, while at the same time a petition from the county of Essex called for the end of extraordinary taxation, the disbandment of the Army and a personal treaty with the King.

Charles had now managed to join together his English supporters with discontented Scots who opposed the Army's intervention in politics. The result was the Second Civil War – a combination of local risings and an invasion from Scotland. It demonstrated only that Parliament had lost its grip in its strongholds of power and that the Army was thoroughly detested everywhere. For all of that, Parliament had better resources and organization than its opponents. Despite the best efforts of the royalist Scots, led by the Marquis of Hamilton, several months elapsed between the risings in Wales and the Scottish invasion. Hamilton had to overcome the active resistance of the kirk and the passive resistance of the Covenanters in order to win support for war. The churchmen thundered against the Engagement in pulpit and press, adding to the difficulties of recruitment. The Marquis of Argyll, who had dominated Scottish government since the Bishops' Wars, secretly corresponded with Cromwell and placed what obstacles he could in the way of his political rival. Hamilton's army comprised former Covenanters and former royalists, enemies as likely to fight each other as the English. By July 1648 he had amassed over 10,000 men, crossed into England, and raised a standard for the King.

By July, however, the Welsh had been crushed; Fairfax had taken

Maidstone, scattering the Kentish royalists; and Colchester was under siege. The well-timed risings that would have left the North unprotected had badly misfired. As Hamilton marched south, Cromwell and his Ironsides headed to meet him. There was still an opportunity for a rapid Scottish victory such as had been achieved in the Second Bishops' War, for the royalist forces vastly outnumbered those of Parliament under John Lambert. But the Scots, disorganized and undersupplied, failed to engage them. This allowed Cromwell time to arrive and assume command of a potent brigade. When battle was finally joined, outside Preston on 17 August 1648, the fate of the Scots was sealed. The seasoned New Model troopers cut the Scottish cavalry to pieces and, through a drenching rain, pursued Hamilton's fleeing army until they could run no more. In three days' fighting Cromwell took 10,000 prisoners and Hamilton was forced to surrender to save the remainder of his troops. He was taken to London, tried, and executed. The fearsome Scottish invasion proved a damp squib.

Only Colchester now held out, and Fairfax commanded the siege, which began uncharacteristically with the repulse of a New Model regiment on 13 June. For eleven weeks a force of 9,000, many of them crack New Model regiments, tightened a noose around the Essex town. They cut off trade, food, water and all means of escape. A steady artillery barrage reduced much of the town to rubble and terrorized the civilian population. The 4,000 defenders could take only grim pleasure from the occasional success of their snipers and commando raids. They were simply starved into submission. The surrender was signed at the end of August. Two of the royalist commanders were summarily executed, and the townspeople were forced to pay for the privilege of not being plundered. If the Second Civil War had been generated by resentment of Parliament and hostility towards the Army, the treatment meted out to Colchester did little to lessen either.

The Second Civil War produced two entirely different reactions among parliamentarians: it softened the stance of the politicians and hardened the hearts of the military. The ground swell of loyalty to the King that was evident in so much heroic sacrifice against such great odds chastened those who had taken the hard line after Charles rejected the Four Bills. Too many moderates in the countryside were willing to restore the King unconditionally for them to adhere to the Vote of No Addresses. On 28 April 1648 the Commons voted that they would not alter the 'fundamental government of the kingdom by King, Lords, and

Commons', and revived discussion of the Four Bills. In the following month petitions flooded the two Houses for a personal treaty, including one from the City of London which urged that Charles be brought to the capital to negotiate. This was received favourably by the House of Lords, which increasingly saw its own fate bound with that of the monarchy. But the Commons rightly feared that if the King were brought to London he would be swiftly restored. Their compromise was to accept another round of negotiations on the Isle of Wight.

The moderates and Presbyterians who combined to propose the Treaty of Newport sought peace desperately; however, they did not abandon the principles for which they had fought. They required the King to grant Parliament control over the militia for ten years, to establish Presbyterianism for three years, and to exclude the most prominent royalists from future office. Though these were the major points of the Newcastle Propositions and the Four Bills, they were subtly softened and, most importantly, they were no longer non-negotiable. Parliamentary commissioners were sent to Newport and given forty days to secure agreement with the King. They arrived on 15 September. A month earlier Charles had informed his exiled advisers that he intended to enter into a 'mock treaty' while making plans to escape his captivity. Disingenuous from the start, Charles must have been startled by the intensity of the parliamentarians. They begged and wept and pleaded. Old Viscount Saye and Sele, exhausted from his travels and himself an opponent of Presbyterianism, went down on his knees to implore Charles to accept the treaty. Yet it was easy to see the King's point. Every time he lost a civil war, Parliament reduced its demands. And, he deluded himself into believing, he might get better terms still from the Army.

But a cold resolve swept the soldiery after the Second Civil War. The riots and risings had been directed against them as much as against Parliament. It was this attitude that had made the fighting so bitter. Pembroke had held out for nine weeks, Colchester for eleven without hope of gaining either political or military objectives. There was a bloody-mindedness abroad, and it was contagious. After all the talk of assassinations, it was an Army officer, Colonel Thomas Rainsborough, who was the first victim, murdered by royalists. The introspection of prayer meetings and camp-fires was less of lofty ideals than of basic revenge; biblical texts highlighted the retribution of the Old Testament rather than the mercy of the New. Charles Stuart, 'that man of blood',

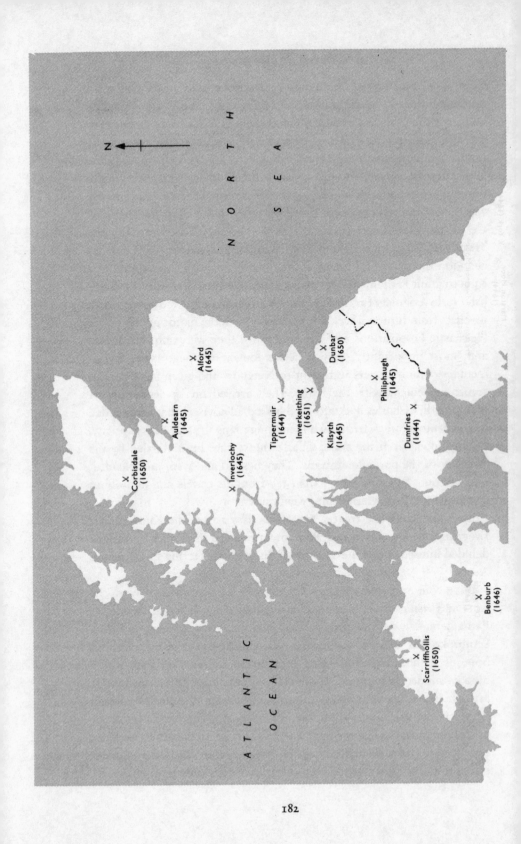

NORTH SEA

ATLANTIC OCEAN

N

Corbisdale (1650) X

Auldearn (1645) X

Alford (1645) X

Inverlochy (1645) X

Tippermuir (1644) X

Inverkeithing (1651) X

Kilsyth (1645) X

Dunbar (1650) X

Philiphaugh (1645) X

Dumfries (1644) X

Benburb (1646) X

Scarriffhollis (1650) X

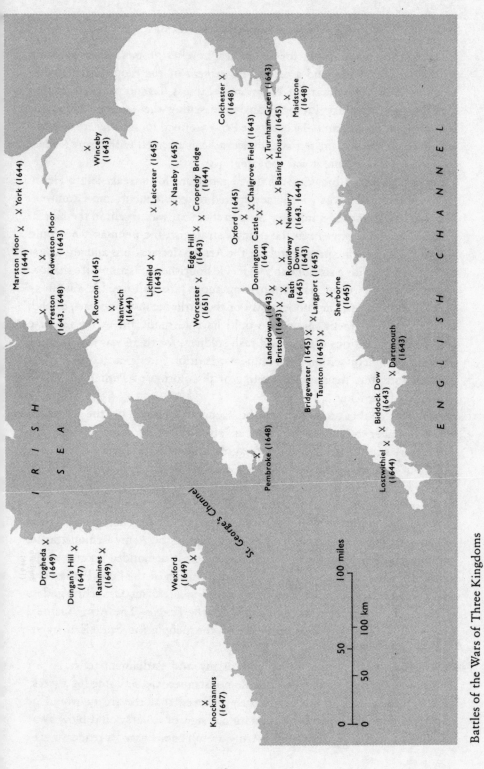

Battles of the Wars of Three Kingdoms

would be made to pay for his crimes. Leveller propagandists gained a new lease of life, and a second *Agreement of the People* circulated in the Army. The Treaty of Newport became a flashpoint. Charges that the parliamentary Presbyterians were selling the soldiers' blood for bishops' estates and places on the Privy Council found a receptive audience. Moreover, the parliamentary radicals pleaded with Army leaders to intervene before it was too late.

The work of breaking off the negotiations for a treaty fell to Henry Ireton. Fairfax was vocally committed to a settlement, and Cromwell, who had opposed a military coup in the past, was absent in the North. Ireton had always been the Army's strategist, the penman who could write the stirring propaganda of the Army's declarations and argue first principles with a schoolman's logic. He flourished in Cromwell's shadow, a cool head to contrast with his impetuous father-in-law. He was surely behind some of the subtle moves of the parliamentary radicals, though he left few tracks. Now he would have to guide the Army's course between cautious officers and rash soldiers, for there was no doubt of the sentiment within the regiments. Petition after petition arrived at headquarters demanding a purge or dissolution of Parliament and a trial of the King.

The deliberations within the General Council of the Army in November 1648 took place in an atmosphere of crisis. Despite the expiry of the forty-day limit for agreement on terms, negotiations continued at Newport. Though the General Council had agreed to abide by the treaty, rumours of even greater concessions being made to the King drove moderate officers to reconsider their commitment. So too did the agitation within the ranks, stirred by the Levellers with all their might. Ireton's programme was contained in the Army Remonstrance, presented to Parliament on 20 November. It demanded an end to the treaty, a trial for the King, and the dissolution of the Long Parliament, the successor to which would be chosen on a reformed franchise and its powers specified in an *Agreement of the People*. The Army justified itself as the true representative of the people, as evidenced by its providential victories.

For the next two weeks both Army and Parliament jockeyed for position. In the Commons, the Remonstrance was set aside for a week, by which time it was confidently believed that the treaty would be concluded and the collective national sigh of relief would blow away the Army's objections. In the Army, Ireton coordinated a rendezvous to bring together the scattered regiments and initiated a new round of political discussion with radical MPs and civilian Levellers. There were still many decisions to be made, for the Remonstrance remained deliberately ambiguous on all of the contentious issues. The most important consideration was also the most practical: should Parliament be dissolved or purged? If it was dissolved, by what authority would a trial take place? A new parliament might be less willing to bring the King to justice. If it was to be purged, how could the Army be assured that even an attenuated Parliament would not be corrupt? In the end, it was decided to purge. Charles – by now secured in Hurst Castle, near Newport, following rumours of a liberation attempt – had conceded nothing, yet still the Commons held a marathon session on 4 December – lasting until the following morning – to debate whether they could go on. Their fears were both palpable and hallucinatory. On 6 December Colonel Thomas Pride stood on the steps of Westminster Hall and forcibly excluded the members who were to be prevented from entering the Commons. Pride's Purge kept nearly half the members from their seats and imprisoned over forty to prevent concerted opposition to the plan to bring the King to trial.

Even the purged Parliament – the Rump, as it would be known to posterity – blanched at the work to be done. The Lords would not co-operate at all, and they were simply excluded from the proceedings as an irrelevance. It took the better part of a month to establish the High Court of Justice. In the immediate aftermath of Pride's Purge it was difficult for the Commons to achieve a quorum, as members stayed away from Westminster. The Army's staunchest supporters resisted becoming a rubber stamp, and in truth it was not at all clear what was to be stamped. Would the trial lead inevitably to a conviction and execution? Did the soldiers literally demand blood for blood?

In the last weeks of December Army officers, including Cromwell, who had now returned to London and assumed a leading role in the proceedings, sought alternatives. But the King's behaviour had become more erratic since his failure to escape from Hurst Castle. His moods swung wildly between a belief that his enemies had no alternative but to restore him and a desire to become a martyr to his church and his monarchy. As late as Christmas he rejected a secret overture that would have restored him to the throne, and throughout January he opposed the scheme that would have placed his youngest son, Henry, Duke of Gloucester, there. Whether his motivation was steadfast principle or stiff-necked stubbornness, he eliminated his opponents' options one by one. Once the trial began there was no turning back. The prosecution's case was narrowly construed: the King had made war against his people. Witnesses deposed that they saw the King in armour on various battlefields. It could hardly be denied. Charles's tactic of challenging the legitimacy of the court got him no further than it ever had John Lilburne. Defendants who refused to enter a plea were guilty, and treason was a capital offence. On 30 January 1649 justice was executed in the name of the people. The English Revolution had begun.

8

Saints and Soldiers
1649–1658

On the morning of 20 April 1653 Oliver Cromwell entered Parliament and sat quietly for a time listening to the debate. When he finally rose to speak he praised all of the efforts of the Rump over its lifetime; but then Cromwell put on his hat and changed his tone. 'The Lord has done with you and has chosen other instruments for the carrying on his work that are more worthy,' he rebuked the astonished members. He strode down the aisle and addressed his remarks more particularly: 'Some of you are whore-masters,' he shouted at Henry Marten, 'some drunkards, and some corrupt and unjust men and scandalous to the profession of the Gospel. You are no parliament, I say you are no parliament; I will put an end to your sitting.' At that he summoned two files of musketeers into the chamber. The Speaker was removed from his chair – 'Fetch him down,' Cromwell directed Major-General Thomas Harrison in a parody of that moment, nearly twenty-five years ago, when the Speaker was forcibly kept in his place. 'Take away these baubles,' Cromwell directed a soldier towards the mace of Parliament, symbol of its authority as representative of the people.

For the previous six months Cromwell had kept the wolves at bay. Sentiment in the Army ran strong for a forcible dissolution of the Rump. The Army had waited nearly six years for the Long Parliament to end its sitting, and it would wait no longer. Demands for franchise reform and new elections had been repeated annually, but the times were never propitious. First there was war in Ireland, then in Scotland, and now with the Dutch. The Rump lurched from crisis to crisis, and each interfered with its plans to dissolve. The bill for a new parliament elected on a new franchise had been in committee for years. Only under intense pressure did the Rump agree that a new parliament would assemble on 3 November 1654. Yet by the end of 1652 no progress had been made to establish franchise and electoral reform. By the end of 1652 patience in the Army had worn thin.

Cromwell struggled against a coalition of senior commanders who agreed only that the Rump had outlived its usefulness. Some were imbued with heightened millenarian expectations and wished to sweep away the artifices of men: 'The interest of God's people is to be preferred to 1,000 parliaments.' Others were opposed to the perpetuation of a body that had ceased to be representative of the people. The Army had debated constituency reform for six years since the impeachment of Holles and franchise reform for six years since Putney. In the meantime members of the Rump had feathered their own nests behind a smokescreen of debate and delay. Cromwell was oblivious neither to the chiliasm of the saints nor to the criticisms of the soldiers. But he was a practical man with practical objections. What would follow a forcible dissolution but greater uncertainty about the future? How could the Army justify seizure of supreme authority?

Rather, Cromwell argued, it was necessary to keep up the pressure for reform. The problems were complex, and progress, however glacial, was being made. Beginning in February 1653 the Rump spent every Wednesday debating the bill for a new representative body. The Army continued its agitation; petitions and remonstrances were circulated among the scattered brigades and then presented to the Rump. The major sticking-point concerned the method of monitoring the new selections. All proposals for franchise reform included clauses excluding 'the disaffected' from both participation and selection. The question was, How would this be enforced if the Rump dissolved? There were several possibilities. The first was that the Army could implement the provisions of the bill, though it possessed no constitutional authority to do so. The second was that the Rump could remain in session until after the elections, to vet the results. This would resemble the work of the Committee of Privileges. Finally, the Rump could simply recruit itself to full strength. This would have the advantage of maintaining both legislative and legal continuity.

It was this third possibility that the Army most feared. Recruitment would effectively keep the Long Parliament in power and prolong the hostility between the members and the Army. It would also allow those members whom the Army believed to be corrupt to escape the judgement of the electors. Paradoxically, the more the officers and soldiers worried that the Rump would recruit itself, the more opposed they *became to the second alternative: that the Rump would continue in existence to monitor elections to its successor. This would also prolong its life and perhaps allow another crisis to prevent new elections. These fears led to meetings at Army headquarters and to a compromise solution proposed by Cromwell to Army officers and leading members of Parliament. The Rump would complete those segments of the bill for a new representative body that redistributed seats and redefined the franchise. Then it would appoint a council composed equally of soldiers and civilians, and finally it would dissolve itself. The council would determine the timing of new elections and judge the results.*

Cromwell made these proposals on the evening of 19 April 1653. Most of the parliamentarians agreed that it was a workable compromise, and they all pledged to put off discussion of clauses of the bill that extended the Rump's existence in one way or another. The next day, as Cromwell held meetings at his lodgings, a messenger hurried into his presence with news that the morning session of the Rump had attracted a large attendance and that motions had been made to pass the unaltered bill for a new representative body. Without pausing to dress, Cromwell crossed New Palace Yard, gathered to him the troops that were stationed outside, and dissolved the Rump.

The English Revolution was born of the axe, an unplanned child of necessity surrounded by angry predators. It survived a decade of external hazards, internal dissension and its own inherent contradictions. The regicide made England an outlaw nation, ostracized by the civilized states of Europe, which declared open season on English shipping. Charles II was proclaimed king of Britain in Scotland, where he raised an army and organized an invasion. He was also proclaimed king in Ireland in whatever cities and towns were controlled by royalists. In England, the greater part of the nation accepted the Commonwealth and then the Protectorate sullenly. Its *de facto* authority, as Hobbes argued in *Leviathan* (1651), was preferable only to the brutal state of nature that was perpetual civil war. Most gentry withdrew from local government, giving way to men lower in the social order and leaving justice and administration in the hands of novices. Even supporters of the Commonwealth fell back upon an intense and literal legalism. Time-serving justices, gentlemen who kept their places on no stronger impulse than inertia, insisted upon the old forms. So too did the parliamentarians who were coaxed back to Westminster after Charles's corpse had settled in its grave. They knew that their power rested on the Army, and that their support in the countryside was dependent upon how quickly they could restore a semblance of normality. They knew too that the Commonwealth and Protectorate were minority governments whose principle of popular sovereignty was theory rather than reality.

Yet for enthusiastic supporters of the Revolution these realizations were untroubling. Weight, not numbers, was the crucial measure, Milton declared. 'More just it is that a less number compel a greater to retain their liberty, than that a greater number compel a less to be their fellow slaves.' What did it matter if less than a fifth of the House of Commons had sanctioned the trial, that less than half of the High Court of Justice had given judgement? It took only one 'to execute, not accidentally but intendedly, the wrath of God upon evil doers'. The Revolution was sustained by a passion for perfection and by a searing vision of the future. Both were products of the intense millenarianism unleashed by the King's execution. For many, dethroning the King and defrocking the bishops fulfilled ancient prophecies. The Revolution would usher in a new Jerusalem; the nation would be governed by the saints, God's own minority through which he would uproot the corruption of this world. At first the Revolution was a springtime of hope when everything seemed possible and great plans were laid. Only gradually did the days darken and damp despair descend.

For at its heart the Revolution comprised contradictory impulses. The force of Puritan enthusiasm propelled it forward; the strength of gentry constitutionalism impeded its progress. The zealous regarded the outward forms as unimportant, and they quickly tired of the bickering over paper constitutions. Their interest in civil government was to end its interference in matters of conscience. Too long had they languished underground, hunted by the bishops, traduced by the Presbyterians, persecuted by both. Now they would bloom in the light of day: 'Methinks I see the kingdom of Jesus Christ begins to flourish, while the wicked do now perish and fade like a blown-off blossom.' The strength of the 'godly' was in the Army, in the London Independent congregations, and in the proliferating sects. On the other hand, the constitutionalists were fixated on government, and their support was in Parliament. Whether republican theorists, common lawyers or ordinary local governors, for them the problem of the Revolution was a problem of order. Did the English state fall with the monarch or could it be put back together again by the substitution of 'Keepers of the Liberties of England' for 'king' in statutes, wills and deeds?

For nearly a decade these contradictions spawned unsuccessful experiments with republican forms of government. Each constitution attempted to recreate the tripartite system of executive, council and parliament, and each foundered on its inability to locate a single fundamental authority. The Rump laid claim to being the purest form of a republic, without a single person at its helm. It suffered from the distrust of Parliament that had built up since 1640. The Nominated Assembly that followed was an attempt at government by the 'saints'. It collapsed through its own internal bickering. The Protectorate, which lasted longest, restored most of the traditional forms of government – ultimately even a House of Lords – but it too was built upon quicksand and avoided being sucked down only by the remarkable personality of Oliver Cromwell. His death sounded the knell of the Revolution itself.

* * *

Nowhere were the conflicting forces which defined the English Revolution so violently yoked together than in the personality of Oliver Cromwell, who rose to national prominence in these years. Cromwell was nearly fifty when he boldly signed the King's death-warrant. For his first forty years he had lived in obscurity, victim of primogeniture, hard times and his own irascible temperament. His grandfather was Sir Henry Cromwell, 'the Golden Knight'. When Sir Henry was done showering his fortune on all that attended his table, the residuum was left to Oliver's spendthrift uncle. Oliver's own inheritance was a small estate near Huntingdon, the town he represented in the parliament of 1628. He lost both face and influence in a local dispute, sold up, and moved to nearby St Ives, where he farmed and lived in the style of a yeoman. At the time of his financial crisis Cromwell experienced a spiritual rebirth accompanied by assurance of salvation. By the early 1630s Oliver Cromwell knew that he had been chosen for more than tribulation.

The war was Cromwell's godsend. Elected MP for the town of Cambridge, he was a notable hawk in 1641 and an active officer even before the King raised his standard. Though he had never been a militia commander, Cromwell at once displayed a military genius, 'guided by faith and matchless fortitude'. Gustavus Adolphus was one of his early heroes, and he imitated the reckless courage that had cost the Swedish king his life. Cromwell possessed two special qualities: he could inspire others to overcome their limitations and he could discipline his own ferocity in the heat of battle. The first made him Parliament's most successful recruiter and commander; the second enabled him to win every engagement he ever entered. Time and again Cromwell's troops held their ground, charged uphill, or attacked when outnumbered. In the crucial battles of the Civil War his ability to regroup his men when they were routing the enemy proved decisive. Despite his average stature and prominent warts he was an imposing figure, with cold blue eyes and a menacing brow. He had 'an exceeding fiery temper', and was given to swift swings of mood which only added to the force of his personality.

Though an original member of the Long Parliament, Cromwell spent little time at Westminster during the wars. Thus his political commitments were less developed than the loyalty he felt for those who risked their lives in what he regarded as the parliamentary cause. This he articulated as a set of liberties: to be secure in person, property and conscience. His preference for the 'honest man that knows what he fights for and loves what he knows' was as near to self-description as he ever came. Cromwell was not a theoretician and had little patience for the legal conundrums that bedevilled government. He believed in necessity as a principle of politics and right reason as a principle of morality. Neither was a prescription for consistency, and he was frequently called hypocrite. But, while his political allegiances oscillated unpredictably, his basic beliefs held steady. His defence of the security of property was absolute and brought him into conflict with the King, the Levellers and those who would abolish tithes. It also led him to support the preservation of the monarchy in 1648 and the establishment of the Protectorate in 1654. His defence of liberty of conscience brought him into conflict with the bishops, the Scots and the English Presbyterians: 'Liberty of conscience was a natural right, and he that would have it ought to give it.' He held firmly to the belief that the nation should not be governed by the sword, and this principle, more than any other, determined the course of English politics for the next decade.

The Commonwealth was established legislatively. The decision to purge rather than dissolve Parliament meant that there would be no interregnum in its role as a representative body. During the first week of February 1649 the Commons propounded bills to abolish the monarchy as 'unnecessary, burdensome and dangerous', and the House of Lords as 'useless'. Characteristically, they took six weeks to become law. The bill declaring England a commonwealth took rather longer, not reaching the statute-book until the middle of May. All the while the leaders of the Rump were reaching out to those members who might be co-opted back into the House. This could be seen in the decision to require restored MPs only to conform to what had been done rather than to affirm it. Nearly eighty members returned to their seats in the first month after the execution – more than the number who had remained after the purge.

Though those who were allowed to return were generally less revolutionary than those who had remained, the conservative character of the Rump was evident even among its most radical members. The decision to abolish the House of Lords was contentious, the language abolishing the monarchy ambiguous. The appointment of the Council of State, which in accordance with the Army Remonstrance was to serve as an executive check upon Parliament, was more conservative still. Only fourteen of the forty-one members nominated by the Rump were regicides, and two of these – Ireton and Major-General Thomas Harrison – were rejected by the Rump for their prominent role in Pride's Purge. The Rumpers chose five peers, including the Presbyterian Earl of Pembroke who had served as temporary Speaker when members fled to the Army in 1647. The councillors, too, were required only to swear to uphold the government of the future.

Nevertheless, this was still a commitment to condone the Revolution, and many would not make it. Half of the Central Court judges resigned their lucrative positions. Several of the nominees for the Council of State refused to sit, and others pre-empted nomination by making their opposition known. In the counties, much local government initially ground to a halt. Mayors of royal boroughs were at a loss to know if their charters remained in force; justices of the peace wondered the same about statutes. Resignations and absenteeism further disrupted the re-establishment of order. As at Westminster, the Rump initially took a soft line. Except for vocal opponents and known royalists, it left local governors in place. Not until 1650 did the Rump require an Engagement to the Commonwealth, and this too was a minimum test of loyalty. The localities were more conservative than the Rump, and this meant that there would be little immediate social reform and that religious radicalism would continue to be suppressed.

In truth, it had never occurred to the leaders of the Army or of the Rump to turn the world upside down, to institute a thoroughgoing social and political revolution. Beyond religion, their quarrel with the King had been to compel him to abide by the settled laws of the nation – those that protected patriarchy, hierarchy and property. To do so they were themselves forced into violations of these fundamental principles, the greatest of which was killing the father of the nation, abolishing his rank, and confiscating his estates. The road they had travelled was all downhill; the momentum unstoppable. Several times events had careened out of control: in 1647 when the Army was radicalized; in 1648 when genuinely popular revolts attempted to restore Charles I. But once they had survived the hairpin turns the path had levelled, and now they proceeded cautiously. The incorporation of practical moderates at Westminster and in the localities could only have a steadying effect. Besides, they needed every ally they could get. From the beginning, the Commonwealth was beset by enemies: royalists and Presbyterians secretly subversive, Levellers and sectaries openly hostile.

One thing was certain: no one could co-opt John Lilburne. He had opposed Pride's Purge and the broken-backed Army *Agreement of the People* and had refused a place on the High Court of Justice. He couldn't see that the government of the Commonwealth was any different from the government of the King – an extreme position even among his own followers. For most of the political radicals the execution was an epiphany; because they had never expected it to come to pass, they had never looked beyond it. Now they drifted away: Wildman to business, and his fellow Leveller leaders William Walwyn to religion and Edward Sexby to his Army career. The impressive Leveller organization with its sea-green colours, its party dues and its newspaper, *The Moderate*, was beginning to dissolve. Only Lilburne and Richard Overton stood firm, bombarding the newly formed government with a thoroughly radical critique. Their programme for social justice was constructive. They stood for poor-relief, redistribution of wealth, legal reform and political empowerment. But their agitation was destructive. They issued a scathing attack upon the Commonwealth.

On 26 February 1649 Lilburne published the first part of *England's New Chains Discovered*. In it he asserted the illegality of the High

Court of Justice, the Council of State and the Council of the Army. His argument, that the Council of State rested on no better authority than the corrupt members of Parliament who appointed it, challenged the Rump's executive and legislative powers. His complaint that the Council of the Army had degenerated into a council of officers was already a grievance among the soldiers. Lilburne and Overton labelled the officers 'the Lords of the Army', and urged the soldiers to cast them aside and seize power in the name of the people. With the survival of the Commonwealth still so precarious, such a direct challenge could not go unanswered. Lilburne, Overton and some others were arrested for treason. This fanned the flames briefly. Elizabeth Lilburne organized a petition demanding her husband's release and was rebuked for activity unsuited to her sex. She returned to Westminster with a petition for women's rights signed by 10,000. The redoubtable Katherine Chidley drafted it. 'Have we not an equal interest with the men of this nation in those liberties and securities contained in the Petition of Right? Are any of our lives, limbs, liberties or goods to be taken from us, no more than from men, but by the due process of law?' But others thought Lilburne had gone too far. The powerful London Baptist congregations withdrew their support, and the Leveller movement as a whole nearly collapsed.

This agitation in London only furthered the unrest already present in the Army. Arrears were mounting; the harvest failure of 1648 – the worst of the century – made the Army a burden; and rumours circulated that soldiers would be forced to fight in Ireland. As before, portions of the Leveller programme spoke directly to Army issues and were openly espoused. At the beginning of March, five soldiers were cashiered for presenting a petition questioning the legitimacy of the Council of the Army and comparing Cromwell and Ireton to Holles and his gang. Indeed, comparisons with 1647 were apt, for the Commonwealth was organizing an Irish invasion force and the soldiers were demanding arrears and immunity from impressment. But the senior officers had learned their lesson. When a London regiment mutinied over pay, a soldier was court-martialled and shot. More serious disturbances followed among the regiments chosen by lot to go to Ireland. The soldiers were unhappy with the terms and demanded the right to elect agitators and debate the Irish service at a general council. Two separate mutinies occurred. In the largest, nearly 900 troopers from three cavalry regiments refused either to serve or to disband, but they were quickly overwhelmed by the presence of Cromwell, Fairfax and five New Model regiments. Some soldiers made a stand at Burford Church, were fired upon, and ultimately surrendered. Three were ceremoniously shot and discipline was reasserted.

While the Levellers challenged the political authority of the Commonwealth, the Diggers challenged its moral authority. The Diggers were the unlikely creation of Gerard Winstanley, a small businessman who began his career wholesaling cloth, ended it wholesaling grain, and in between sandwiched a mid-life crisis of epic proportions. Winstanley was born in Lancashire, apprenticed in London, and began trading there. He was ruined in 1643 when he could not collect debts to pay off his creditors. He sold his London shop and moved to his father-in-law's small estate in Surrey. In 1648 he began to have visions which called him to preach the commonality of goods. He published several pamphlets of a deeply mystical nature which denied predestination, the Holy Trinity and the second coming. In 1649 his visions led him to denounce the buying and selling of goods, wage labour and private property.

Along with a band of twenty-odd followers, he began digging and planting crops on the common wasteland of St George's Hill in Surrey. When challenged by local magistrates and summoned before Sir Thomas Fairfax for disturbing the peace, Winstanley responded with *The True Levellers' Standard Advanced*, a work which preached that the earth was 'a common treasury'. A second experiment, in Cobham, provoked even stronger local hostility until Army troops dispersed the Digger community. Winstanley's plans for larger communes in the spring of 1650 did not materialize, though his ideas spread. He championed the downtrodden agrarian labourers by preaching the eloquent language of 'succour'. Winstanley challenged the members of the Rump to provide for the poor and distressed, to redistribute wealth in accordance with the ideals of a Christian commonwealth, and to protect the masses of 'people' in whose name they ruled.

Coming on the heels of Leveller agitation and Army unrest, the Digger movement appeared more ominous than it actually was. Initially it revived conservative challenges against the Rump's ability to govern. Royalists and erstwhile parliamentarians quickly tarred the Commonwealth with the brush of social and religious radicalism. Leveller attacks on tithes and Digger attacks on private property fed fears and uncertainty. They also fed opposition. Throughout 1649 the

Rump anticipated a new round of royalist risings. The King's coronation day passed quietly, but editions of *Eikon Basilike* – 'The Image of the King' – Charles's supposed scaffold testament, poured from the presses despite the imposition of a Licensing Act in September. New editions expanded to include Charles's prayers, his last speech and a selection of his private correspondence. Each addendum magnified sympathy for the monarch. Thirty-five English editions of *Eikon Basilike* were published within a year of the execution; it was a runaway best-seller. It was also widely distributed in Ireland and Scotland, where royalists openly expressed their sentiments and threatened renewed warfare.

The Rump had decided to pacify Ireland almost immediately. The new regime needed to secure its flanks from invasion, and throughout the winter rumours spread that Charles II would land in Ireland. The Rump also needed to prove its bona fides to parliamentary creditors. Since the beginning of the war, Parliament had borrowed money on the security of Irish land, and the lenders clamoured for repayment. Finally, the memory of the Irish rebellion was seared deeply into Protestant consciousness. Parliament had sworn that the slaughter of innocent thousands would be revenged. The Rump appointed Cromwell to lead an expedition and guaranteed him sufficient manpower, money and *matériel* for the task. His brief was to relieve the parliamentarian forces in Dublin, secure the Protestant ascendancy in Ulster and Munster, and conquer as much of the rest of the island as he could.

Since the rebellion of 1641, the situation in Ireland had become a tangled skein of religion, loyalty and self-interest. Both the rebels and those who opposed them were made up of political and religious misalliances incapable of withstanding the pressures of war. The rebels were a coalition of native Irish and 'old English' known as the Catholic Confederacy of Ireland. Though they continually declared their loyalty to Charles I, the Confederacy assumed sovereignty over the territory they could control. Among the native Irish who fought for the Confederacy were those who envisioned, as their motto held, 'a united Ireland', freed from domination of English and Scottish Protestants. Their Catholicism was infused with the spirit of the Spanish Franciscans, their commitment firmed by military leaders who had fought for the Catholic side in the Thirty Years War. Among the 'old English' who joined were many who believed that the rebellion would lead to a compromise settlement that would secure the property rights of Catholic landowners, and freedom for Catholic lawyers – who comprised nearly a third of the membership of the Confederacy's Supreme Councils – to practise their professions. The Confederates were opposed by an amalgam of 'new English' and Ulster Scots – the new English predominantly royalist, the Scots parliamentarian. Beginning in 1642, these forces were under the leadership of James Butler, Duke of Ormond, scion of an 'old English' family who had been raised as a Protestant in England. He commanded the remnants of Strafford's army and local Protestant troops in the name of the King.

In 1643, in order to bring Ormond's army to England, Charles had negotiated a cessation of the Irish rebellion by granting a temporary toleration to Catholics. Curiously, this cessation split apart both alliances. Predictably, the pro-parliamentarian Protestants refused to abide by its terms. But the Confederates, too, divided. Under guidance from Rome, the native Irish leaders demanded a complete restoration of Catholicism. Their 'old English' allies were less obdurate, for they perceived that Charles I needed support from Ireland to survive.

Despite the cessation of 1643, desultory fighting continued in Ireland until the end of the First Civil War. There were a number of significant Confederate victories – Owen Roe O'Neill's triumph against the army of the Ulster Scots at Benburb in 1646 was the military high point of the rebellion – but divisions among the Confederates prevented co-ordination of their military effort and stymied a Catholic triumph. Ormond's patient diplomacy kept the Confederates politically divided, and both factors allowed the royalist Protestant interest to survive. The situation altered in 1647. With Charles a virtual prisoner, Parliament assumed control in Ireland. Colonel Michael Jones landed with 2,000 troops and garrisoned Dublin Castle. A New Model brigade would have followed were it not for the frenetic events of the summer of 1647. The arrival of parliamentary forces should have ended the bitter conflicts among the Confederates, as Parliament was committed to their suppression as to a holy war. But in fact they only worsened. Ormond offered permanent concessions to the 'old English' in return for support in what became the Second Civil War. But the papal party, under the political control of the Florentine legate, Giovanni Rinuccini, and the military control of Owen Roe O'Neill, refused all compromise. They would not join a coalition that contained 'new English'

Protestants and Ulster Scots Presbyterians, even if it was a coalition certain to drive the English parliamentary forces into the sea.

In the fighting that followed, Ormond and his Scottish allies attempted to reclaim Dublin and Ulster from the parliamentarians. Neither the defeat of the main royalist forces in England and Scotland nor the trial and execution of Charles I halted their advance. By the spring of 1649 Ormond held most of the eastern coastline and was closing a noose around Dublin. It was then that the Rump intervened. At the end of July, Dublin's slow suffocation was relieved with the arrival of over 2,000 English reinforcements. A week later (2 August) Colonel Jones routed Ormond's largest army at Rathmines, and this allowed Cromwell a safe landing on 15 August. With 10,000 battle-scarred veterans and a train of siege artillery, Cromwell marched south and invested the town of Drogheda. When the garrison refused a summons the bombardment began, and within a single day 200 cannonballs were fired, the walls were breached, and the town was taken. No quarter was given, and nearly all of the defenders were killed. As Cromwell informed Speaker Lenthall, he hoped that this show of resolve would discourage the resistance of others. Nevertheless, he made elaborate preparations for the siege of Wexford, where an even more brutal massacre took place when his soldiers broke the leash of military discipline. The garrison at Drogheda had been executed; the act was cold-blooded, within the rules of warfare, and most of the victims were soldiers, many of them English. The population of Wexford was slaughtered. The act was passionate, the result of years of racial and religious propaganda, and the victims were civilians, most of them Irish. Nor did Cromwell's calculated brutality have its desired effect. Catholic propaganda had predicted the slaughter, and by fulfilling the prophecy Cromwell ensured that every inch of Ireland would be defended to the death. Despite superior force, it took three years to subdue the Catholic armies. Part of the price that was paid was the life of the Revolution's theoretician, Henry Ireton, in 1651.

Though all indications were that Charles II would join the Irish wars with whatever aid he could muster from his European allies, in fact his overtures to the Irish had been coldly rejected. Rather, in 1650 he completed a treaty with the Scots in which he agreed to take the Presbyterian Covenant in return for support to claim his English crown. Neither side expected happiness from this marriage of convenience. Charles II's shotgun acceptance of Presbyterianism contrasted

markedly with his support of the Marquis of Montrose, whose predations had only just been ended by his capture and execution. The
Covenanters were equally faithless, forcing Charles to exclude all
former Engagers from the movement. News of this coalition outstripped Charles's arrival in Scotland, and leaders at Westminster
decided to launch the New Model into a pre-emptive attack. When
Sir Thomas Fairfax refused to command the force and resigned his
commission, Cromwell crossed the Tweed at the end of July 1650 as
Parliament's new Lord General.

Cromwell had spent the autumn of 1648 in Scotland, and he knew
that the Scots were politically divided. He appealed to both Argyll and
the leaders of the kirk to repudiate the King and prevent another war.
This might have been easier to achieve if Charles had not already
landed. Everywhere he went he drew adoring crowds, and his appearance at the camp of the Scots army made fighting a certainty. On 3
September Cromwell scored a crushing victory at Dunbar against an
army nearly twice the size of his own. Four thousand Scots were killed
and 10,000 taken prisoner. English troops soon occupied Edinburgh
and Glasgow without bloodshed or much rancour. Instead, Cromwell
visited both and attempted to persuade civic authorities of the
common ground shared by the godly of the two nations. His most
powerful argument was the judgement of battle, and throughout the
winter his propaganda campaign sapped Scottish resolve. Forces led by
Major-General John Lambert won an important victory in the west,
and in 1651 Lambert and Cromwell defeated a large Scottish army near
Stirling. In a last desperate effort, Charles II dashed south into England
hoping that a general rising such as occurred in 1648 would ensue. But
there was little enthusiasm for another civil war and even less for supporting a Scottish invasion. On 3 September 1651 Cromwell obliterated
what was left of the royalist forces at Worcester. Charles II escaped the
battlefield with little more than his life. His dignity was left in the
hollow of an oak tree, where he hid from the victors.

The nature of the Cromwellian conquests of Ireland and Scotland
reflected the nature of the countries' subsequent settlements. Ireland
became a vanquished nation, absorbed into the Commonwealth and
governed by English policy. The war had been financed by promise of
plunder, and nearly 40 per cent of Ireland was confiscated to repay the
loans of English civilians and the wages of English soldiers. In the Act
of Settlement (1652) six Irish counties were cleared of their Catholic

landholders. Though such a massive transfer of wealth might have created a social revolution in Ireland, it mostly created a deflationary land market. The beneficiaries were the 'new English' planters of the Pale, who ultimately enlarged their estates under the protection of an effective army. As Lord Lieutenant of Ireland, Cromwell did experiment with social reform, but the underlying problems created by racial and religious discrimination were impervious to policy adjustments. Scotland, on the other hand, was treated differently. Only the estates of active royalists were confiscated, and the Rump proposed a voluntary union – though the Scots had little choice but to volunteer. The union came into effect in 1654, and a Scottish Council of State was appointed in the following year.

It is not surprising that a regime empowered and sustained by its military should have its greatest success in war. Nevertheless, the scope of the Commonwealth's military achievements were breathtaking – 'a new Rome in the west' Milton dubbed them. In Ireland, the Rump accomplished in three years what English monarchs had failed to do in over a hundred. In Scotland, Cromwell's victories erased the humiliating memories of the Bishops' Wars. The Commonwealth set afoot plans for a comprehensive union of what was once Charles's composite monarchy. At the same time, the government of the Commonwealth enhanced England's traditional naval power, building or refitting seventy-seven ships of the line. Control of the seas was an important element in domestic security and a vital one in international relations, especially with Holland. Since the beginning of the century, English and Dutch maritime interests had clashed. Their merchantmen trawled the same imperial waters, where the Dutch were the indisputable leaders, and competed for the same European carrying trade. Except for their shared Calvinism, the two states were natural enemies, and their diplomatic relations mirrored the struggle in each nation between God and Mammon. In 1651 the Rump passed a Navigation Act designed to cut into the Dutch carrying trade to North America. This strained an already taut situation on the high seas, where confrontations between armed ships escalated. Finally, in 1652, the two nations declared war. Against all expectations the English withstood early setbacks and, under the brilliant command of Admiral Robert Blake, outfought what was thought to be invincible Dutch power.

Military enterprise at home and abroad dominated the first years of the Commonwealth. Survival outweighed reform. But survival was expensive and, as the Rump's commitment to reform receded, so did the enthusiasm of its supporters to foot the bill. Despite years of effort to curtail military costs, the army of the Commonwealth was more expensive than ever. The monthly assessment had risen to £90,000, and the hated excise continued. To pay off its staggering debts to parliamentary soldiers and London moneylenders, the Rump sold the newly acquired estates of the crown and the remnants of its holdings of church land. After the Battle of Worcester, it impounded the property of the few prominent royalists who had joined Charles's cause, and in successive years it passed bills confiscating the wealth of more than 750 former royalists. But these windfalls were simply sucked into a whirlpool of expenditures. The garrisons in Ireland and Scotland were bottomless pits; expenditures on the navy escalated even before the shock of the Dutch war. The rise in commodity prices and the fall in revenue from trade pinched the government as well as the average citizen. Estimates of the annual deficit run to £700,000, excluding the largest part of military arrears.

Acute fiscal distress complicated proposals for radical reform, though this was not the disease from which they died. Efforts to reform the law, the church and the constitution were stymied by a lack of will, by the political process and by self-interested legislators. Law reform was the key to revamping social policy – a fact not lost on the congenitally conservative lawyers who controlled parliamentary procedure. They were excoriated as 'vipers and pettifoggers of the commonwealth' – charges which they self-righteously rejected. Unscrupulousness was supererogatory when punctiliousness made one just as rich. The law's delay was a watchword – suits passed from parents to children as heirlooms – and proceedings were conducted in law French and recorded in court hand. All this was true, yet the lawyers would not yield control of professional matters to amateurs. Thus, despite the assiduity of Sir Matthew Hale, who chaired the commission on reform, the Rump made only a few petty changes in four years of agitation, the most significant of which was making English the language of the law.

Religious reform was a different matter. Clergymen were barred from Parliament and the hierarchy had been abolished. Here the problem was conflicting visions of the future. While some wished to loosen civil control of religion, others desired to tighten it. Progress was made in fits and starts. In 1650 the Rump abolished compulsory attendance in the established church. This was a position that had been advocated by

Independents and resisted by Presbyterians, but now the two groups found themselves increasingly in agreement on substantive issues. The Rump created commissions for the North and for Wales, to help the propagation of true Christian religion in these 'dark corners'; used some of the income from the sale of episcopal and royalist lands to support poor ministers – thus avoiding a great battle over tithes – and passed laws to deal with moral offences in the wake of the dissolution of the church courts. The most famous of these was the Adultery Act of 1650, which made adultery a capital offence. The act was less enforced than was the sexual double standard, as the only executed adulterers were four women.

Further church reform foundered on the rocks of radical religion. Calvinism was disintegrating, and Puritan ideas were being driven to their logical extremes. Sects of separatists proliferated, mocking the idea of a comprehensive church that reformers had worked so hard to achieve. The sects were small – both few in number and few in members – yet they had a powerful impact upon a political regime desperately seeking middle ground. Some sects like the Baptists were willing to accept the rule of the Commonwealth in exchange for the peaceful practice of their beliefs. Though the Baptists were chiefly identified with opposition to infant baptism, by the early 1650s they were beginning to develop a mystical, internal religiosity. But other groups opposed the regime outright. The Fifth Monarchists took the execution of the King as a sign that the final corrupt monarchy of man was at an end. They demanded that the Mosaic code be substituted for the laws of England and that only known saints be members of the government. The Fifth Monarchists were politically aggressive, petitioning the Rump and recruiting successfully in the Army. The most troubling of the radical sects were the Ranters – if they were a sect. Antinomians – they believed that the saints were beyond the power of the law – the Ranters taught that to the pure all things were pure, and demonstrated it by practising free love and swearing the blasphemous oaths from which their opprobrious name derived. It was to prohibit practices such as these that the Rump passed the Blasphemy Act (1650) against 'monstrous opinions and wicked and abominable practices'.

Efforts to control the overzealous, unsuccessful as they were, indicated the underlying problem that bedevilled the Rump: its friends were as dangerous as its enemies. None were more dangerous than the Army. Relations between Parliament and Army had remained precarious since

1647. The soldiers had demonstrated their willingness to enter the political process decisively, the parliamentarians their willingness to remain independent of military control. Their distrust was mutual and well-founded. The situation was always best when the Army engaged in battle and Parliament united in providing supply. It was always worst when the troops were idle. After the victory at Worcester, the Army felt keenly the Rump's disappointing progress in reforming the nation. As the troops dispersed to garrisons and winter quarters, agitation began for the dissolution of the Rump and the calling of new elections.

These demands for constitutional change were born of frustration at the failure of social and religious reform. Year after year the Rump's product diminished. In 1649 125 acts had been passed; in 1652 only 44. Attendance was down; there were fewer committees. Members were more concerned about their own welfare than the nation's. Personal corruption became the focus of Army attacks. Legal officers were accused of blocking law reform; the rich of opposing land reform; the ungodly of refusing to abolish tithes. Pamphlets and broadsides were published detailing the offices and fees accumulated by Rumpers. Yet the demands for the dissolution of the Rump flew in the face of the temper of the nation. The Army might compel new elections, but it could not control their results. Royalists, Presbyterians, the conservative gentry: they represented the will of the people. The debate over a new representative body was desultory for a purpose. If it was evaded the Army would intervene; if it was concluded the people would speak. In either event the Commonwealth would come to an end. For the men at Westminster, Cromwell was preferable to Charles II. As we have seen, on 20 April he expelled the Rump.

Cromwell's decision to dissolve the Rump had been taken in anger and resulted in what he regarded as untenable military rule. Two alternatives to the Rump had been actively debated within the Army councils. The first, proposed by Major-General John Lambert, was for the institution of a single ruler with a council that would be checked by mandatory parliaments. Lambert, son of a Yorkshire gentleman, had done his military service in the North, a companion of Sir Thomas Fairfax, who brought him into the New Model. He may have been Fairfax's protégé in the Army councils, as Ireton was Cromwell's, for his hand was seen in the *Heads of the Proposals*. Lambert was given command of the northern forces in the Second Civil War, and his military service in Scotland in 1648 earned him the respect of

Cromwell. The second scheme, advocated by Major-General Thomas Harrison, was for a nominated assembly, a body modelled on the Sanhedrin of the ancient Hebrews. Harrison began as a captain in the Earl of Essex's lifeguard and rose to command all the New Model forces in England. Imbued by a sense of righteousness and closely associated with the Fifth Monarchists, Harrison was always for cutting the Gordian knot. He wanted to march on London in the spring of 1647, to depose the King after the Putney debates, and to expel the Long Parliament. He was a member of the High Court of Justice, and signed the King's death-warrant in a firm hand. Lambert's scheme was more practical, though it was also more like the Rump that had failed. Harrison's plan was visionary, with the focus upon reform. Yet both alternatives were still inchoate when Cromwell impulsively dissolved the Rump. As was later recounted, 'the spirit was so upon him, that he was overruled by it; and he consulted not with flesh and blood at all'.

Once he had acted, Cromwell accepted the idea of an assembly of the godly as also being 'of the spirit'. The decision fell in with Harrison's general outline. The Army asked the gathered churches to send in names, though the Council of Officers took charge of decisions. The Nominated Parliament was composed of 140 members, including six from Scotland and five from Ireland. Critics contemptuously labelled it the Barebones Parliament, after Praise-God Barebones, one of its more obscure members. In reality its composition was much like the Rump's, although there were more religious enthusiasts – though only thirteen known Fifth Monarchists – and fewer lawyers and officers. While few had parliamentary experience, a very high proportion had served as local justices of the peace. Efforts were again made to co-opt former political leaders like the younger Sir Henry Vane and Sir Thomas Fairfax. Vane, a committed republican, challenged the authority of the Nominated Parliament; Fairfax simply refused to participate. Yet the attempt again demonstrated the determination of the leaders of the Revolution to have the broadest possible base, even within the context of a solution as novel as an assembly of saints.

Despite Cromwell's insistence that the assembly had been called to consult with the Army, among its first acts were to declare itself a parliament and to appoint a mostly civilian Council of State to govern with it. It set a symbolic concluding date of 3 November 1654, and then turned to the same issues that had bedevilled the Rump: legal and religious reform. It made some progress on law reform – though moves to abolish lawyers and institute the Mosaic code were repulsed – and passed thirty ordinances during its five-month existence.

Even the nominated saints were divided over questions of religion. The radicals in the assembly wanted to abolish all semblance of the national church, including tithes, uniformity in doctrine, and predefined 'scandalous sins'. The moderates wanted a comprehensive Protestant church. The most vexing issue was over tithes. Tithes raised complex religious and civil problems. The sects argued that they should not be forced to contribute to a church to which they did not belong, but they proposed no alternative for maintaining ministers in the large national church. Moreover, tithes were property. Landowners had bought them, and to abolish tithes would be to confiscate private wealth. The tithe debate drove a wedge between the small knots of radicals and moderates who dominated the five months of sittings.

Attendance in both Parliament and Council was sparse, and majorities fortuitous. After the opening ceremony Cromwell never appeared, and even Harrison ultimately drifted away. Patience with the Nominated Parliament shortened with the autumn days. In December the radicals unexpectedly had the numbers to push through several bills on church reform. This frightened the moderates sufficiently for them to plan a counterstroke. On 12 December they arrived *en bloc* early in the morning to be assured of a majority and then simply voted to resign their power. They collected the mace and the Parliament rolls and delivered them to an astonished Cromwell. 'Whither it came, thither it went,' was Sir Arthur Haselrig's sarcastic post-mortem.

For a second time in less than a year, civil authority returned into the hands of the Army, and for a second time Cromwell refused to lead a military government. Instead he turned to the plan proposed by Lambert for a written constitution, the *Instrument of Government* (1654). The *Instrument* established a government composed of a Lord Protector, a Parliament and a Council. Originally Lambert and other officers hoped that Cromwell would accept the title of king, but he steadfastly refused and thus the expedient of the Protectorship was introduced. The *Instrument* began with no statement of sovereignty, though it was based on classical principles of mixed government. The failure of monarchy under Charles, of a form of aristocracy under Barebones, and of a form of democracy under the Rump weighed heavily in the thinking behind the *Instrument*. Power was divided among Protector, Council and Parliament in ways that checked the potential abuses of each. In addition, the *Instrument* specifically protected religious rights. All 'peaceful' Christians, except Catholics and episcopalians, would have freedom of worship which neither Protector nor Parliament could abrogate.

The Protector embodied executive power. All legal matters ran in his name, he controlled the military, and he superintended diplomacy. Parliament was a single chamber composed of 460 members, including thirty each from Scotland and Ireland. County seats predominated, and borough representation was sharply constricted. All adult males with property worth £200 could give voices in county selections – a compromise which both expanded participation and confined it to men of substance. Members chosen were to be 'of known integrity, fearing God, and of good conversation'. The *Instrument* provided for triennial parliaments of at least five months' duration. It charged Parliament with the power to make and change law and to introduce all revenue measures except the annual maintenance of the standing army. Bills passed by Parliament but not signed by the Protector became law after twenty days, though the *Instrument* could not be amended without the Protector's consent. The Council was small, composed of between thirteen and twenty-one members who served for life. It was charged with advising the Protector on civil and military matters and legislating with him until the first parliament came into session. Its chief responsibilities were to judge elections and to choose successive Lord Protectors. The *Instrument* also provided for a standing army of 30,000 men, a sufficient navy, and a paltry annual income for government of £200,000.

The *Instrument* combined elements of proposals for constitutional reform that had surfaced since 1647. It borrowed from the Army's platforms, from the Leveller *Agreements of the People*, and from the writings of republicans. But to its opponents it was nothing other than 'monarchy bottomed by the sword'. Cromwell attempted to refute this judgement immediately. At his installation the Protector wore a plain black outfit with grey worsted stockings, and the Council he and the officers appointed contained only four Army commanders. Viscount Lisle and the Earl of Mulgrave gave the body some social cachet, and five of its members had long-standing connections with Cromwell, including its President, Henry Lawrence, who had once been Cromwell's landlord. The choices were both uninspired and undistinguished: a support staff for a strong man.

In the months before the first Protectoral Parliament met, Cromwell and his Council ruled England effectively. Judges, military commissioners, justices of the peace, myriad assessors and collectors were appointed to serve the new government. The plums were given to the Barebones moderates, though the Cromwellian regime was as eager as its predecessors to bring the traditional governing class to the table. Ordinances established long-delayed legal and religious reforms, and over twenty financial measures were passed.

The Protector's first parliament met on 3 September 1654 – the anniversary of the great victories of Dunbar and Worcester. As he told the assembled members, he hoped the session would be one of 'healing and settling'. The electors had returned a group heavily Presbyterian, with a sprinkling of known opponents to the regime like the republicans Vane and Haselrig. Together they were likely to open old religious and political wounds. Presbyterians were eager to re-establish the boundaries of the national church and to control the growth of the sects. The republicans were eager to challenge the powers of the Protector and the authority of the *Instrument of Government*. Indeed the first action of the session referred the *Instrument* to a committee to dissect it clause by clause. Immediately Cromwell intervened. He demanded that all members take an 'oath of recognition' that government was in the hands of a single person and Parliament before they could return to their seats.

Over seventy members – mainly republicans – refused. They argued that only a parliament had the authority to constitute government and that the *Instrument* was the work of a clique of Army officers. Their exclusion poisoned the session from the start, and they continued to denounce the Protector and the Army. Even those members who remained had serious reservations about critical elements in the *Instrument*. In debates over a new government bill, the Presbyterians attempted to narrow the parameters of freedom of worship. Other members questioned the need for so large a military establishment and the right of the Protector to control it. Criticisms built to a climax as the five-month term of the parliament neared its close and bills were readied for presentation. Cleverly, Cromwell avoided the confrontation by calculating the months by the moon rather than the calendar and dissolved the session twelve days early.

With Parliament concluded, the Protector ruled with his Council and attempted to repair the damage of the addled session. The regime itself had little support. In the West Country known royalists had been returned to Parliament and close supporters of the government had been spitefully rejected. The godly were rancorously divided between church and sect. The older sects like the Fifth Monarchists blasted the regime in a barrage of pamphlets and sermons. Cromwell was the little horn of the devil, they revealed, a warrior of the Antichrist. Newer sects challenged the very foundations of Protestantism. The Quakers, led by George Fox, grew from a few itinerant preachers and scattered congregations in the north of England into a potent movement. They attracted the middling sort in rural communities and were genuine democrats – the only sect that for a time accepted women as absolute equals. They practised a form of social levelling that included a refusal to doff caps, to take oaths, and to address social superiors formally. The Quakers preached universal redemption through the power of the inner light of the Holy Spirit. They rejected the existence of heaven, of hell and of a personal God. Most controversially, they denied that the Bible was the word of God. Rather they were ecstatic believers, and their doctrine of perfectibility led them to provocative demonstrations of purity such as going naked, fasting near to death, and attempting to perform miracles. In one of their most sensational acts, John Naylor, a Quaker leader, rode into Bristol on a Sunday in 1656 in imitation of the entry of Christ into Jerusalem. He was savagely punished for his blasphemy.

Few were waving palms in the Army. Throughout the sitting of Parliament there had been steady pressure to disband a portion of the bloated military establishment. The *Instrument* had provided for an army of 30,000, though there were nearly twice that many on the muster rolls. Cromwell adopted the popular expedient of lowering military taxation, but he was not prepared to slice the Army in half. Indeed, the cuts he made were for other purposes. Not all of the Army commanders accepted Cromwell's pre-eminence, and some, like the parliamentary republicans, were dismayed by his assumption of regal airs. He had already had a falling out with Harrison, and the Leveller John Wildman had resurfaced with his charges of Cromwellian perfidy. When opposition came out in the open, the Protector dealt with it firmly. Cromwell cashiered several senior officers, including John Okey and Robert Overton, both original New Model colonels, for publicly opposing the Protectorate. The soldiers were nervous as well. Local communities were hostile both to their presence and to the practice of radical religion within their ranks. Arrears mounted, and as always the pressure for disbandment turned soldiers' thoughts to grievances.

In this context the regime faced the first serious royalist conspiracy in England since the Second Civil War, Penruddock's Rising in Wiltshire. Though Cromwell was targeted for assassination, his secretary, John Thurloe, ran such an effective security operation that there were never serious threats. Rumours of coordinated royalist plans reached Thurloe at the beginning of 1655. A general rising was set for the beginning of March, but failed to come off when the government arrested several of the key figures. In Wiltshire, however, a force led by Colonel John Penruddock managed to seize control of Salisbury and capture two assize judges and the county sheriff. They proclaimed Charles II and terrorized the countryside for several days before a detachment of New Model regulars and local forces hunted them down. To ensure the pacification of the West Country, Cromwell placed Major-General John Desborough in command of the militia and charged him with meting out retribution. The rebels were convicted of treason and a small number were hanged. Desborough remained as a regional military governor, and over the next several months Cromwell appointed major-generals to oversee all of the localities.

The major-generals were part of a plan to reduce the overall size and structure of the military and thereby to effect economies. But they quickly became a means in which a reforming centre gained control over recalcitrant localities. The nation was ultimately divided into a dozen administrative districts, with the cost borne by 'the decimation' – a tax of 10 per cent on the value of royalist estates. Cromwell ordered the major-generals to keep the peace by disarming the disaffected, patrolling the highways, and warding off beggars. He also enjoined them to 'encourage godliness and virtue' – an open-ended commission that led some to suppress alehouses, Sunday sports and popular festivities. In Wales Major-General Berry found 'vices abounding and magistrates fast asleep'. Few were more zealous than Major-General Pride, whose territory included Southwark, the red-light district to the south of London. It was said that he prohibited the popular pastime of bear-baiting 'not because it gave pain to the bears, but because it gave pleasure to the spectators'.

Though their tenure lasted barely a year, the major-generals were detested in the localities. They were outsiders who imposed alien values without regard to the fabric of local society. They imprisoned former royalists and dealt sternly with uncooperative gentry. They displaced the commissions of the peace in which local men, even the new men of the Cromwellian regime, filtered the rigour of the law through the prism of familial and communal relations that they knew so well. The major-generals enforced a moral reformation whether the localities wanted one or not. Some deluded themselves into believing that they were popular; others, like Major-General Whalley, that they were effective: 'it's the best way that ever was devised for the peace and safety of the nation'. Like the Nominated Parliament, the experiment was an attempt to establish godly rule over an unregenerate nation. Like the Nominated Parliament, it failed. It was a product of Cromwell's belief that government was 'for the people's good, not what pleases them'.

But Cromwell was not beyond pleasing the people when godly zeal and popular prejudice intersected. Shortly after the conclusion of the hostilities with the Dutch in 1654, he laid plans for a war with Spain. For Cromwell's generation, Spain was the nation of Antichrist, the most potent Catholic power on earth. In the Parliaments of the 1620s members had advocated war with Spain on the open seas, a 'blue water' policy that was now put into effect in Cromwell's Western Design to seize a large island in the West Indies, disrupt Spanish trade, and, if possible, capture a treasure fleet. Eventually, naval forces achieved all three goals, though the initial assault on the island of Hispaniola was a failure and the commanders had to settle with taking Jamaica. But the great dream of financing the war by capturing the silver fleet proved chimerical. The game turned out to be more expensive than the prize, and Cromwell was forced to summon his second parliament in 1656 to pay for the war.

To avoid a repetition of the fiasco in 1654, when members had had to be expelled, the Council used its power of judging elections to exclude republicans and other opponents of the regime at the beginning. Though the uproar on the left was predictable, in fact the members who sat in the parliament of 1656 were representative of the conservative mainstream that supported the regime. They urged Cromwell again to accept the crown. Monarchy was a known form of government, they argued, and the erection of the house of Cromwell would settle the endless constitutional experiments. Along with the offer of the crown, the members prepared the *Humble Petition and Advice* which made significant modifications to the *Instrument of Government*. It created a bicameral legislature, adding an Other House of life peers appointed by the Protector and Council which would be able to check the excesses of the single-chamber assembly established in the *Instrument*.

To ensure that Cromwell would accept the crown, it was tied to the new constitution in a single bill. At first, Cromwell hesitated. Though he had no desire to be king in name, he knew that he would be king in fact. He had apparently set his mind to agreeing when a number of senior Army officers informed him that they would not serve a monarch. In the end he chose loyalty to his comrades-in-arms. He averted a crisis by persuading Parliament to decouple the crown from the constitutional reforms. Cromwell accepted the *Humble Petition and Advice* in May 1657 and appointed Army cronies, relatives and some of the more socially distinguished supporters of the regime to the Other House. But the *Humble Petition and Advice* did not provide for vetting the elected members of the Commons, and when Parliament reconvened in 1658 many of those who had been excluded in the first session took their seats and attacked the new settlement. Frustrated and disgusted, Cromwell dissolved Parliament.

By now it was apparent that the regime was held together by Cromwell alone. Within his personality resided the contradictions of the Revolution. Like the gentry, he desired a fixed and stable constitution; like the zealous, he was infused with a millenarian vision of a more glorious world to come. As an MP from 1640, he respected the fundamental authority that Parliament represented; as a member of the Army, he understood power and the decisive demands of necessity. In the 1650s many wished him to become king; yet, like Caesar, he refused the crown, preferring the authority of the people to the authority of the sword. He was now fifty-nine years old, and the hardships of an active life weighed upon him. The failure to establish a settled form of government and the failure to resolve the vexing questions of religious freedom absorbed his diminishing energies. In August 1658 his favourite daughter died, and thereafter his will to live seemed visibly to weaken. When George Fox, the Quaker leader, came to visit him at the end of the month he 'saw and felt a waft of death go forth against him; and when I came to him he looked like a dead man'. His health deteriorated rapidly. He named his eldest son, Richard, to succeed him and died on 3 September 1658, the anniversary of his greatest military triumphs.

9

The Restoration Settlements
1659–1667

No one will ever know how it started. At 2 a.m. on Sunday 2 September 1666 Thomas Farrinor awoke to the smell of smoke in the rooms above his bakery in Pudding Lane. His investigation discovered a fire consuming the shop, and in shock he led his family to safety and raised the alarm. It was heard in the inn whose stable was behind his garden, and guests in nightdress peered through their windows to see flames licking away at the wooden structure. It had been a hot summer, London was bone dry, and for the past week warm breezes had blown from the east. They now caught the flames, and embers landed among the inn's haystacks. As the onlookers rubbed sleep from their eyes, three more buildings were struck by shards of burning wood and a serious fire had begun. Within an hour City authorities were on the scene and water-pumping machines were being wheeled into action. The Mayor, Sir Thomas Bloodworth, had seen many fires that seemed more threatening than this and he was peeved to have been roused from sleep to view it. Before returning to bed he judged dismissively, 'A woman might piss it out.' It would become his epitaph.

The east wind first carried the blaze on to London Bridge, where it rapidly destroyed a third of the buildings on the main thoroughfare between the City and Southwark on the other side of the Thames. The bridge acted as a fire-break to the south, but the flames destroyed the largest of the City's pumping mechanisms and made battling it with water more difficult. The conventional means of fire-fighting was to clear a path too wide for the flames to jump and then to extinguish the sparks that blew across. But in London it was law that anyone who pulled down another man's dwelling must pay for it to be erected again, and, with the fire only a few hours old, the Mayor was reluctant to act without authority. By the time it came – delivered by Samuel Pepys from the mouth of King Charles II – the sun was up and the whipping winds were carrying 'whirlwinds of tempestuous fire'. Panic had set in as churches and warehouses along the river erupted. Pepys saw an arch of flame a mile long that night, and the diarist John Evelyn witnessed it consuming 'churches, public halls, exchange, hospitals, monuments and ornaments, leaping after a prodigious manner from house to house and street to street'. The good news that day was that the conflagration had been halted in the north at the great Leadenhall, which simply resisted the flames. The bad news was that there was now only one direction in which it could move: west towards the Guildhall, Cheapside and St Paul's Cathedral.

Tuesday 4 September was a day every Londoner would always re-member. Finally the effort to halt the fire's spread was coordinated. Trained bands from the surrounding counties arrived to maintain order. They established camps at Moor Fields and Spitalfields and on the Artillery grounds for the tens of thousands of refugees. They helped unclog the roads to the north that teemed with families fleeing with their possessions on their backs. Most importantly, they freed the City's own levies for fire-fighting. From five in the morning till midnight the Duke of York rode from site to site encouraging and directing the efforts. The King, against the advice of his counsellors, was in the thick of the smoke, grimy and bespattered, handing out gold coins to work-men who were now demolishing everything that stood in the direct path of the oncoming inferno. It was all to no avail. Across Cheap Street it flew, aided by the debris of the houses the workers had demol-ished, consuming St Mary-le-Bow and sending the Bow bells to the ground, where they melted from the heat. On to Goldsmiths Row the fire roared, 'before it pleasant and stately homes, behind it ruinous and desolate heaps'. Grocers' Hall, Merchant Taylors' Hall, Drapers' Hall and then the great Guildhall itself: all were consumed in huge balls of flame whose vacuum imploded towers and walls as if they were made of papier mâché. There was now no hope to break the fire at St Paul's Churchyard. It consumed the Stationers' Hall and the shops of dozens of booksellers as an appetizer to the meal ahead. At 8 p.m. the massive timbers that supported the cathedral's roof were alight, and soon rivu-lets and then streams of lead were pouring down Ludgate Hill as the largest church in Britain burned. 'All the sky was of a fiery aspect, like the top of a burning oven.'

When it was over, two days later, the toll was incomprehensible: over 13,000 buildings, 87 churches, 44 company halls, 4 bridges and, with few exceptions, all of the great landmarks of an ancient and proud city were gone. One hundred thousand people were homeless, and the cost of rebuilding was reckoned at over £10 million, or eight times the annual revenue of the monarch. How had it happened, who was to blame? It was the work of enemies – Dutch or French, with whom England was currently at war. It was the work of Catholics. There was so much xenophobic hysteria that during the initial frenzy a number of foreigners were spontaneously lynched. But, as ministers of all stripes were quick to proclaim from pulpit and press, a catastrophe this extensive could have only one source. It had begun on a Sunday, it followed by less than a year the most devastating outbreak of plague in the nation's history. Plague and fire, war and destruction: these were God's weapons. It was the persecution of the godly, claimed the dissenters; it was the toleration of the Catholics, moaned the Anglicans. It was the King's mistresses; it was the nation's sins. The reign of Charles II had begun so well, but now there was a judgement upon the land.

The death of Oliver Cromwell in 1658 was a moment of re-evaluation of the Revolution's achievements and failures. Support had been intense though shallow; opposition ran silent and deep. Cromwell's personality, his grip over the military, and the realization that he could provide order to an exhausted nation all propped up the regime. No one else could provide the same benefits without much greater costs. Thus the political chaos of 1659 was not unexpected by those who contemplated the future. To the committed revolutionaries it was only one more challenge which God would provide the means of meeting. Many were still in positions of power or influence, although many more had decamped, defected or died. In truth the Revolution was awash in contradiction, and the second generation of revolutionaries had neither the vision nor the experience of their predecessors. They had not suffered monarchical tyranny nor felt the threat to lives and property that had propelled the Civil War forward. Their grievances were different: the lack of moral discipline that years of reformation had still not overcome; the failure to settle a single form of government that would put an end to the bickering of politicians; the arrears of pay that mounted despite legislative provision for the military. Their loyalties were divided, their support ripe to be plucked by any leader who could yoke together vision and power.

To those who for years had sought a restoration of the monarchy, the death of Cromwell was also a godsend, though of a wholly different kind. They welcomed the disorder, played upon it, and did their best to manipulate public opinion against every expedient. Agents crossed the narrow channel from the Spanish Netherlands with instructions to shore up secret supporters and to suborn discontented government officials. They still planned for a military rising, despite the years of catastrophe and the hopelessness of confronting veteran regiments with untrained countrymen. The most they could hope for was anarchy in London, a tax revolt which led to the breakdown of the military command. Not in their wildest dreams did they imagine that the restoration was so close or that it would be achieved with such ease.

The Restoration of Charles II was both an event and a process. The King's peaceful accession to the throne of England in 1660 put an end to twenty years of internecine war. What were left were the intractable problems that had created the conflict and the bitter legacy it had engendered. If he had had his way, Charles would have put an end to them as well. Unlike his father, he was capable of living with contradiction and was more than willing to absorb those, like the Presbyterians, who could be absorbed. He wished his reign to be a time of healing, just as he wished his life to be one of pleasure. The first Restoration settlement bore his stamp. The second settlement bore the stamp of the country: bitter, divided, attempting to make sense out of what to so many now seemed sheer madness. The motivation of Lord Lieutenants, justices of the peace and members of the Cavalier Parliament, elected in 1661, was to ensure that it would never happen again. They would impose oaths on the conscientious and disabilities upon the ambitious; there would be penalties for those who persisted in dissenting from the church or published in their defence. Their restoration, unlike the King's, would not admit of ambiguities.

*   *   *

The peaceful accession of Richard Cromwell, the new Lord Protector, in 1658 had been a hopeful sign. The regime's enemies waited expectantly for a collapse that did not come. Oliver's funeral procession rivalled that of Queen Elizabeth I, and his son succeeded him without incident. European heads of state recognized the transition – indeed the French court went into mourning. Addresses of loyalty flowed in from the localities, and the Army pledged support to the new head of state.

But Richard Cromwell was not born to rule. A thoroughly decent man who had been deliberately kept out of the fray of war and politics, Richard had married into a Hampshire landed family and briefly lived as a local gentleman. He became Lord Protector at the age of thirty-one and possessed neither the ambition nor the ruthlessness necessary to hold the government together. His Council was riven by factions that Oliver had self-consciously manipulated but which were beyond Richard's grasp. More ominously, the Army was divided and restless.

The Protectorate contained three separate armies. The army in England, militarily idle though politically active, was under the command of Richard's brother-in-law, General Charles Fleetwood. It was a crucial if precarious position – Major-Generals Harrison and Lambert were cashiered while holding it – for the army in England was the sentinel against royalism. Richard's younger brother, Henry, commanded the second army, in Ireland. Had ability been more respected than birth, Henry would have succeeded his father. He possessed Oliver's self-assurance and impetuousness, though in Henry it was un-mixed with periodic bouts of introspection. In Scotland, General George Monck led the third army. A veteran of the Continental wars, Monck had served the King, Parliament and the Protectorate in turn. Taciturn and able, Monck's career had the consistency of the professional soldier: he preferred the winning side.

These distinct commands were no problem while Oliver was Lord General, but Richard lacked military experience. Moreover, the English army was no longer the well-muscled New Model. It had been thinned of veterans by natural wastage and constant purges, and weakened by divisions between the senior and junior officers. Fleetwood and Major-General John Desborough were the main military props of Richard's government. They conducted their business from Wallingford House in Whitehall and maintained the loyalty of the highest-ranking officers. The junior commanders held their own meetings at St James's Palace. Their men pressured them for arrears of pay – nearly forty weeks overdue – and for political and religious reforms. The soldiers' loyalty to Fleetwood was not welded in the forge of battle, for few had seen an engagement.

Agitation for arrears was only one of the government's financial problems. The Spanish war persisted, as did the deficit spending that kept it going. Government indebtedness approached £2 million and necessitated the summoning of Parliament. The Council decided to revert to the traditional franchise for the selections, in the hope of attracting gentry support. Although this led to accusations of packing, the parliament of 1659 was no different in political composition from its immediate predecessors. The Presbyterians controlled it, and the Commons contained the same small knot of republicans determined to ensnarl this Parliament as they had the last. Sir Arthur Haselrig, who had opposed every regime since the dissolution of the Rump, led them. Truculent and self-regarding – liveried servants attended his coach – Haselrig had spent nearly two decades mastering the techniques of obstruction. He was unrivalled at impeding debate, stalling committees and thwarting bills. Though it might be said of his public life that he had prevented some evil, it could not be said that he had done any good. Now he determined to make mischief, to bring down the parliament and if possible the Protectorate. To these ends, Haselrig seconded every expression of opposition from those who represented what was coming to be called 'the good old cause'. He organized a filibuster against the recognition of Richard Cromwell. He backed parliamentary attacks upon the Army, and then he supported military grievances against Parliament. He opposed the elevation of Fleetwood to Lord General while he entered into negotiations with the Wallingford House leaders to bring Richard down. Month after month he stymied the Council's efforts to govern, until the Army precipitated a crisis. At the end of April 1659 Fleetwood and Desborough forced Richard to dissolve Parliament, and by July Richard and his brother Henry had been ousted and the Army was purged of their supporters. After intense negotiations, military leaders, including the reinstated Lambert, decided to recall the Rump.

The year that followed made instability a byword, with governments coming and going in dizzying succession – a total of seven in less than twelve months. It was a year of high anxiety: paranoid, bewildered, chaotic. 'My fears are greater than my hopes,' wrote the normally optimistic Secretary Thurloe. The summer was long remembered as the 'great fear'. Once the Protectorate fell, the gloom that had descended upon royalists at Richard's accession briefly lifted. The Sealed Knot, their secret conspiratorial society, resumed activities and a national rising was planned for August. Though it failed to come off, Sir George Booth, a former parliamentary Presbyterian, raised a force of 6,000 and occupied most of Cheshire before being routed by Lambert. As royalist hopes revived, radical fortunes diminished. Baptists and Quakers were persecuted in the localities, and the resumption of power by the Rump revived fears of further religious backtracking. Even republicans despaired. The Rump might lay claim to the original authority of the Long Parliament, but it was no republican government. Theorists like James Harrington, whose *Oceana* (1656) had outlined a republican government based upon the redistribution of wealth, opposed the Rump's unchecked single-chamber rule. Ideologues like John Milton saw republicanism as a force for moral reformation and feared that the rapid transitions in government would lead to the return of a king.

Though Haselrig and his faction claimed that the Rump was the legitimate representative of the people, when it reassembled in July it contained only forty-two members. It had been brought back to power through an alliance with the Army, though it was not an alliance of mutual interest. The soldiers demanded their pay and protection for religious radicals; the officers demanded the appointment of a select senate and the election of a new parliament. Haselrig's efforts to purge the Army high command and recruit members rather than hold new elections – the only practical way to avoid a rejection of the republic at the poll – had predictable results. In October, Lambert forcibly dissolved the Rump and instituted government by a Committee of Safety.

Military rule was now unadorned and unabashed. It was also uncontrolled. Generals who could barely govern their own regiments struggled for power. By virtue of his action against Booth, Lambert emerged as a potential leader, but he had limited influence over his junior officers and no support in London. Moreover, he was opposed by the army in Scotland. Monck and his officers viewed the mounting chaos in England uneasily. Both the Rump and Wallingford House had attempted to infiltrate his regiments, and Monck did all he could do to isolate newly arrived officers from the core of his loyal commanders. When news reached Edinburgh of the dissolution of Parliament, Monck declared against it. Shorn of support from even the military, the Committee of Safety collapsed and for the third time the Rump occupied Westminster Hall. With 7,000 soldiers, Monck began a march to London on 1 January 1660 as cries for a free parliament echoed round the nation.

The Rump's third incarnation was brief. While Haselrig initiated a thoroughgoing purge of the Army, the taxpayers of London revolted. They refused to sanction rule by the Rump and demanded new elections to a free parliament. Incredibly, the Rump again voted to recruit new members. By the time Monck arrived in London, civil government was in total confusion. Rumours were rife that there would be a new parliament, that Monck would be declared Lord Protector, or that Charles II would be recalled. But Monck was reluctant to enter the fray. He knew that if he supported the Rump in its confrontation with the City he jeopardized the soldiers' pay. He knew that if he enforced the City's call for a 'free parliament' those elected would vote to restore monarchy. 'Obedience is my great principle,' he once proclaimed – only it was no longer clear to whom it was owed. After a day of agonizing uncertainty, on 11 February Monck threw in his lot with the City and dissolved the Rump Parliament. That night lived in memory as 'the roasting of rumps', when exuberant celebrations made 'all the night as light as day'. Standing on Strand Bridge, the diarist Samuel Pepys counted thirty-one bonfires, and his journey home was accompanied by the rich smell of seared meat. Two weeks later the secluded members of the Long Parliament were readmitted to their seats. They made Monck Lord General; appointed a Council of State that included Sir Thomas Fairfax and the old Presbyterian leader Denzil Holles; set a date for new elections; and, thus exhausted, dissolved.

The Convention Parliament opened on 25 April 1660. Although former royalists had been barred, over a hundred were chosen to sit in the Commons, while the House of Lords, with the exception of the bishops, was restored entirely. Early test cases before the Committee of Privileges demonstrated the strength of sentiment for a royal restoration. The Revolution had collapsed. Despite the coordinated efforts of the Presbyterians to control the pace of reaction, they were overwhelmed by royalist and back-bencher gentry who wished to rush headlong. The experience of the previous year had taught them that there was no time to lose. The House of Lords declared that government consisted of king, Lords and Commons, and passed a motion that Charles should be invited home. On 1 May the two Houses voted to restore the King. The only significant question that remained was, On what terms would he be restored?

Governments had changed so quickly at the end of 1659 that it was impossible for royalist agents to know whom to approach. They trawled indiscriminately in all waters except those of the republicans and the English army, netting moderate Presbyterians and, after the revival of the Rump, hooking some prominent Cromwellians. Negotiations between royalist go-betweens and Monck, however, were tentative and inconclusive. The general's support was vital, for, however strong was sentiment, it was no match for force. As ever, Monck's views were difficult to fathom, his principles hard to ascertain. He said little, and nearly all of it was contradictory. Having assured Haselrig that he would defend the Commonwealth, Monck then restored the purged royalist parliamentarians. Having promised his soldiers that he would hold firm against monarchy, he dismissed republicans from his ranks. The situation was too fluid for someone with such strong instincts for survival. He urged Charles to renounce retribution and requested justice for his soldiers and toleration for his religion. But his terms were not specific. In the Army, the soldiers clamoured for indemnity, secure possession of the royal and episcopal lands they had purchased, and safety from subsequent prosecution. Presbyterian preachers and propagandists agitated for a comprehensive church and security of tenure for their ministers. In the end, Monck settled for a dukedom.

If Monck was naturally cautious, Charles II kept his own counsel from experience. As he sat idly by in the Spanish Netherlands, ending up at Breda, the situation in England rapidly deteriorated. Yet Charles developed no plan to regain his throne. He had no military options, and few political ones. His counsellors were divided over the terms that could be accepted. One group, led by Henry Jermyn and the Queen Mother, Henrietta-Maria, urged Charles to agree to anything. The possession of his kingdoms was all that mattered; unpalatable conditions could be repudiated later. Another group, led by Sir Edward Hyde, soon to be Earl of Clarendon, cautioned Charles to negotiate every detail carefully. The success of his reign depended upon the terms by which he was restored. The division of opinion was conducted with all of the intrigue that passes for power at the court of an exiled king. The opportunists appealed to Charles's taste for dissimulation; the legalists to his habit of indolence. As he waited, the two positions converged. One after another the conditions for restoration evaporated: 'The nation runneth unto the King as Israel to bring back David.' On 4 April, in accord with Monck's wishes, Charles issued the Declaration of Breda, which offered a general pardon, liberty of conscience, and security of property as to be established by Parliament. Once the Convention met, even these concessions seemed superfluous. The biggest obstacle to an immediate restoration was adverse winds.

Thousands of onlookers accompanied Charles to his place of departure. He boarded the *Naseby*, flagship of what was now his navy, and rechristened it *Royal Charles*. Two days later the King knelt on English soil, his every move cheered by tens of thousands of his subjects. General Monck was the first to be received, embraced for his loyalty at the crucial moment. The town of Dover celebrated all night with bonfires and a clamour that dizzied the King. This was no staged reception orchestrated by the Master of Revels but the genuine enthusiasm of ordinary people who thronged simply for sight of him. The way to Canterbury, where Charles prayed at the cathedral, was lined with cottagers, freeholders and gentry alike. Flowers were strewn in his path, and traditional Sabbath entertainments sanctioned by the Book of Sports, though long officially proscribed, were enjoyed again in his honour.

The trip to London, fortuitously timed to the royal birthday, occurred in the same atmosphere of joy. Women cast posies of sweet herbs at the royal carriage; shouts of 'God save King Charles' cascaded from village to village. At Blackheath the King reviewed Monck's troops, drawn up for the occasion in 'splendid and glorious equipage'. He paraded through them on horseback, and gave no indication of the mixed feelings that he must have felt at seeing the backbone of the Cromwellian regime so arrayed. On Tuesday 29 May he entered the capital. All that day the streets ran with wine and open house was kept in the palaces along the Thames and in the apartments of diplomats and men of influence. At night the sky glowed orange with bonfires in which rumps of meat were roasted in scorn and effigies of Cromwell were burned in derision. 'I stood in the Strand and beheld it and blessed God,' John Evelyn confided to his diary.

Charles II arrived in London on his thirtieth birthday. All his life he had been buffeted by fortune. Heir to the throne, he achieved adolescence and exile at once. He came of age in Europe, a child of diplomatic intrigue, broken promises and unfulfilled hopes. A king in name only, he was governed first by his overbearing mother, and then by the foreign hosts off whom he sponged and the English exiles who used him for their own advancement. Most of all he was haunted by the ghost of his father and the contradictory conclusions to be drawn from his death: either that no sacrifice was too great or that no compromise was. Of necessity, Charles II had developed a thick skin and a cynical political realism. He believed he could read character from a person's face, and that was usually all of the effort he put into his judgements. His insouciance was more apparent than real – a seeming distance from things that had once been taken away – though there is no doubt that he was inattentive to government. He worked hardest at earning the sobriquet 'merry monarch'. His thick lips, arched eyebrows and sparkling black eyes proclaimed his sensuous nature. Charles acknowledged fourteen illegitimate children and dallied openly with his mistresses. Like his interest in science, his affairs were diversions that allowed him to avoid political confrontation: the first gave birth to the Royal Society; the second to the Duke of Monmouth.

Charles's desire for settlement was immediately apparent in his choice of counsellors and officers of state. These were divided nearly evenly between former supporters and opponents. The core of the Privy Council was those ministers who had been with him in exile: Clarendon as Chancellor, the Earl of Southampton as Treasurer, and Sir Edward Nicholas as Secretary. But important posts were given to former Cromwellians, including the appointment of Monck as captain-general of the army and Edward Montagu as vice-admiral, under Charles's brother, James, Duke of York. Former parliamentarians like Holles and the Earl of Manchester were also accommodated. The King showed himself equally catholic in showering earldoms and baronies upon those who had sustained his exile and those who made possible his return. Monck leapt from commoner to Duke of Albemarle in a single bound.

Nor did Charles wish to wreak vengeance on those most responsible for what was being called 'the usurpation'. He urged the Convention to pass the Act of Indemnity and Oblivion which excepted less than a hundred persons or estates from complete pardon. The savagery felt by those royalists aching for revenge was done to the corpses of Cromwell, Ireton and Bradshaw, which were disinterred, dismembered and disgraced. Cromwell's head, set on a pole outside Westminster Hall, was on view for a quarter-century. Those who escaped into exile were hunted by assassins. There were eleven public executions, including those of the millenarian General Thomas Harrison and the republican Thomas Scot, who wished his epitaph to be 'Here lies Thomas Scot who adjudged to death the late king.' Sated or not, the blood lust was at an end.

The Restoration took place in stages. It involved negotiation and compromise among a variety of groups and interests whose power was unequal and unstable. The Convention Parliament worked rapidly and efficiently to complete the first settlement. It was carried along on a tide of euphoria too strong for either parliamentary or royal pressure groups to resist. It made pragmatic decisions designed to deal in a direct way with large and obvious problems. The first was the law. All acts signed by Charles I were reconfirmed, and all legal proceedings of the past twenty years were declared valid. Anything less would have resulted in chaos – civil plaintiffs and criminals demanding that their cases be reopened. But this meant the end of prerogative jurisdictions such as Star Chamber and the regional councils. It also meant that Charles would be required to abide by the Triennial Act and summon regular parliaments. The second obvious problem was the military. Not even the staunchest royalists contemplated providing Charles with a standing army. Yet members of the Convention knew that every previous disbandment scheme had resulted in revolt. Before ordering demobilization they passed an Indemnity Ordinance and levied a special assessment to pay the soldiers full arrears in return for swearing oaths of loyalty to the new regime. Miraculously, the Army disappeared. Regiments melted into town and countryside as if England had not just experienced the longest period of military occupation since the Norman Conquest. The invincible parliamentary armies left two incompatible legacies: pride at the accomplishments that made England an international power and prejudice against the demands of a professional army. For the next century, prejudice would hold sway.

With good reason, Charles had assigned the difficult decisions on indemnity, land-holding and religion to the Convention Parliament in the Declaration of Breda. Each held its own hornets' nest, and even the wary could not approach them without being stung.

There was much wrangling over the individuals to be excepted from the Act of Pardon, as the King demanded justice only for his father's death. But many other fathers had died, and the royalist peers had particular scores to settle. To the regicides proper were added central figures of the revolutionary regimes – Lambert, Haselrig and Vane were the most prominent – though the military escaped lightly, thanks to the intervention of Monck. The act also contained clauses mandating a collective national amnesia, forbidding the provocative slanders and opprobrious labels which nevertheless became such a feature of local life for the next thirty years.

The land settlement was too complex to be solved by act of Parliament. Not since the dissolution of the monasteries had so much land passed through so many hands in so brief a period. It was easy to restore the crown estates and the lands of the church, though hard to evict tenants and to void leases. It was equally simple to return land awarded to prominent parliamentarians and Cromwellians that had been confiscated from royalists. The problem was what to do about land that had been sold under duress or repurchased on mortgage. The finances of many families had been ruined by their loyalty to the King. They had sold bits of ancestral estates on the open market to pay composition fines, decimation taxes or just their quarterly bills. They would receive no relief and were to become the backbone of the sullen former royalists who vented their frustrations in petty acts of revenge.

The religious settlement proved most difficult of all, and the Convention contributed very little to it. The commitment to toleration of tender consciences that Charles had conceded to Monck dissolved when placed in the hands of acidulous Anglicans and Presbyterians. It was hard for anyone to describe the nature of the church as it existed in 1660, except that it was neither national nor episcopal. It was about to become both. Yet there were genuine questions as to the form and content of such a church. These were not the pragmatic issues at which the Convention excelled, and there was probably a parliamentary sigh of relief when the theological issues were shunted to a conclave of learned divines. In October they proposed an interim arrangement – the Worcester House Declaration – which created a mixed episcopal and Presbyterian structure. The Convention's one contribution to the religious settlement was Solomonic. Throughout the 1640s and '50s Anglican ministers had been dispossessed of their livings for a variety of functional, political and moral lapses. They now petitioned to be reinstated as vigorously as did their replacements to be confirmed. By act of Parliament, the ejected ministers were reinstituted provided that they paid compensation to those whom they replaced. A few high-profile personalities were deprived of their places altogether, yet less than 10 per cent of parish clergy were affected. A lasting religious settlement was left to the parliament that was to be convened in the following year.

The initial Restoration settlement eased the resumption of monarchical government in England. In less than five months of work the Convention reinstituted king, lords and bishops and disbanded the Army. Charles II reclaimed his crown without condition, but it was a different crown from the one that had tumbled into the basket in 1649. Parliament, church and king were now inextricably tied together. By withstanding attacks from monarch and army, Parliament had made good its claim to be the representative of the people, even if the concept of representation and the definition of the people remained elusive. If it had ever been an event, Parliament was now an institution. By enduring assaults upon its structure and doctrine, the episcopal church proved an essential part of the spiritual life of the nation. Its place as the mean between extremes of papists and Puritans gave Anglicanism, as it would soon be called, the essential identity it had lacked. By surviving overthrow and exile, the monarchy laid claim to the hearts of the people. Though it retained its trappings of divinity – Charles II enthusiastically provided the miracle cure of the king's touch – monarchy was revealed as a system of government rather than the reign of a king. It was a system of government that the English people had selfconsciously chosen when they had the choice: a system best able to provide security, stability and prosperity.

The settlements in Ireland and Scotland were at once more simple and more complex. In Ireland, the Cromwellian regime had pursued the same policy of plantation as had the Stuarts, but with greater success. Lord Lieutenants ruled as viceroys, their deputies oversaw government of the Protestant communities, and the Catholics were controlled by the sword. Charles II was proclaimed in Dublin two weeks after he was in England, and at first he chose to leave most of the Cromwellian personnel in place. Land, not personnel, proved the main issue in Ireland. The Cromwellian conquest had been effected by hiving off huge areas, clearing them of Catholic landowners, and awarding possession to soldiers who risked their lives and 'adventurers' who risked their money. Some of this land had been owned by Protestant families dispossessed during the rebellion – those refugees whose baleful tales so heated the blood of the conquerors – some of it by Catholics who had not joined the Confederacy. Moreover, the same lands were the subject of dispute between 'old' and 'new English' the resolution of which Charles I had promised in the Graces. After several frustrating years of judging claims, the Duke of Ormond concluded that there would be insufficient land to satisfy rightful claimants if there were two Irelands. The original plan was to confirm the holdings of the soldiers and adventurers and to try to satisfy others through compensation. This had the advantage of keeping owner-occupiers in place and enhancing the prospect of a permanent Protestant plantation. It had the disadvantage of rewarding parliamentarians and

Cromwellians at the expense of former royalists. Even after modifica-tion, the Irish land settlement left a bitter legacy for Catholics and Protestants alike.

The problems in Scotland were different. There Charles II had been king since he had taken the Presbyterian Covenant in 1650. None of his three kingdoms had proved more devoted to the Stuarts than Scotland, from which the Second Civil War and the attack on the Commonwealth in 1650 had been launched. But it could not be for-gotten that it was in Scotland that the civil wars had begun. Moreover, the King had his own experiences to draw upon – two years of doleful domination by flinty lairds and hectoring ministers that had ended in ignominy. Like his grandfather, James I, his opposi-tion to the Presbyterian kirk was visceral. Charles exacted revenge by imprisoning leaders of the Cromwellian regime and ordering the exe-cution of Argyll. He also reimposed 'the government as it is settled by law'. The *status quo ante bellum* in Scotland meant conciliar control of a subservient parliament, royal control of an all-powerful privy council, and the restoration of episcopacy. In this Charles could draw upon the divisive nature of Scottish politics, in which rivalries of region and clan were generally stronger than those of ideology. In 1662 the Scots repudiated the Covenant and readmitted the bishops without a lead from London. The Recissory Act (1661), which ob-literated the work of every Scottish parliament since 1633, was passed against the wishes of the English privy council for fear that it went too far too fast.

These initial settlements more closely represented the interests of the King than what came later. Following the condign punishment of the ringleaders, Charles genuinely wished to start anew, to banish all memory of the recent past. He was willing to govern with the coopera-tion of his subjects and to leave critical decisions about the future of church and state to Parliament. He favoured an inclusive episcopal church as long as the censorious Presbyterians were kept under control. If anything, he showed less interest in Ireland and Scotland than had his father. The governments of the periphery were useful dumping-grounds for unwanted politicians – Monck refused to take the bait of the lieutenancy of Ireland – and training-grounds for the young and ambitious, but the King made no effort at integration. Even the ready-made opportunity to include Scots and Irish representatives in the Commons was fumbled away. Ireland was too tainted by Roman

Catholicism, Scotland by Genevan Calvinism for either to become part of a unified kingdom.

The second phase of settlement was more divisive than the first. The artificial unity maintained by the Convention Parliament as long as the security of the monarchy was in doubt quickly disappeared. In its place came contentions that revealed the weak hand of the King. The full Privy Council was too unwieldy to set policy. The balanced factions cancelled each other's views and the body grew to over fifty members. This led to the creation of a very small 'cabinet council' of principal advisers led by the Earl of Clarendon.

Clarendon's aspiration had been to serve Charles I – a task for which he was eminently suited. His was the acceptable face of 'Thorough', that of a pragmatist who revered the common law. He supported both the king's prerogatives and the subjects' liberties and broke ranks with the reformers in the Long Parliament only when he determined that they were more concerned with fixing blame than abuses. From the mid-1640s Clarendon effectively became Charles II's guardian and assumed a solemnity that was in comic contrast to his libertine ward. Charles treated him like an overbearing though indispensable governess. Doggedly loyal, Clarendon upheld the Stuart cause during the long and dismal exile and had his reward in 1660. Both his religious and his political views were frozen in the attitudes of 1641. Thus he was more accepting of Presbyterians than Catholics and more optimistic that the House of Commons would accept royal policies. He immediately became the focal point for criticism: from the bishops for supporting toleration too strongly and from the Presbyterians for not supporting it strongly enough. Young royalists thought he was too soft on the old revolutionaries, Cromwellians that he was too uncompromising. His reputation for integrity was shaken first by the revelation that his daughter had secretly married the Duke of York and then by the realization that the Portuguese queen he had sponsored was barren. He survived one impeachment in 1663 but not a second four years later, and he ended his days in exile completing his *History of the Civil Wars and Great Rebellion in England*.

The second Restoration settlement began with the Cavalier Parliament (1661–78). Charles summoned Parliament to affirm the coronation and provide for his financial security. The elections took place at the confluence of a rushing tide of royalism and a receding one of Presbyterianism. Winning candidates in electoral contests campaigned upon their record of loyalty. The greater gentry returned to the hustings, and borough patrons were aggressive in controlling corporate seats. The result was a young and inexperienced House of Commons and a House of Lords dominated by the elevations of Charles II and his father. More than half of the House of Commons had impeccable royalist credentials; nearly a quarter had been punished for their loyalty. As a group they were embittered by the experiences of the past two decades. The years out of favour, when they had been deprived of places, dignities and worth, may have scarred their psyches but had taught them invaluable lessons. Time had not so much healed their wounds as made plain why they had received them. Thus the legislative programme they favoured, which brought them into conflict with the King and earned them a reputation for vindictiveness, was designed more to cauterize than to poison.

The first acts of the Cavalier Parliament provided a history lesson in the causes of the Civil War. To repudiate the influence of the mob, they made it a crime to gather more than twenty signatures to a petition or have a delegation larger than ten deliver it. The House of Lords restored the bishops to their seats and reversed the attainder of Strafford. Next, it was essential to reassert loyalty to church and king, because religion and politics were inseparable. Thus all MPs were required to take the sacrament according to the rites of the Church of England. Parliament ordered the Solemn League and Covenant burned by the common hangman in every town of the realm. The two Houses passed statutes making it treason to derogate royal authority or link the king's name with Catholicism. There were even proposals brought in to reestablish the prerogative courts of Star Chamber and the Council of the North, though these failed. Parliament then turned the clock back on its own independence by modifying the Triennial Act which had received Charles I's signature and whose principles were embodied in every constitutional experiment of the Interregnum. The new act (1664) dropped the clauses which mandated that writs be issued in the absence of a royal directive and made advisory the requirements that parliaments be triennial and of a set minimum duration. Finally, a new Licensing Act (1662) regulated printing and censored works. Licensing was assigned to the church, and enforcement to the watchful eye of the Surveyor of the Press, Sir Roger L'Estrange, a rancorous controversialist with a financial interest in restricting printing.

While this legislation represented a rather tardy closing of the barn door, the Houses also worked industriously to provide stronger locks for the future. The great structural weakness of the Stuart monarchy was fiscal. The theory that the king should finance government from his ordinary revenues smacked hard against the realities of the seventeenth-century state. The resistance of the English governing classes to a level of taxation appropriate to support their monarchy had created the constitutional crises of the 1620s and '30s. The civil wars, however, demonstrated that the economy could absorb rates un-imagined in the past. Beginning in 1642 the armies alone were costing the equivalent of nearly three subsidies *a month*, and Oliver Cromwell was thought to have eased the burden when he reduced it to the equivalent of two. The operational costs of government were met by consumption taxes, especially through the introduction of the excise, which, like customs, was easy to regulate and collect. Though the governments of Commonwealth and Protectorate engaged in near-constant warfare, supported a standing army of over 50,000 and garrisoned Ireland and Scotland, their fiscal situation was no worse than that of James I.

When the Convention Parliament sought to restore the monarchy, it intended to do so on a sound financial footing. It also intended to take advantage of reforms such as the abolition of feudal tenures and the Court of Wards and of innovations such as the land tax and the excise. The theory of crown finance underwent a subtle shift. While parliamentarians continued to believe that royal government was to be funded out of ordinary revenues, the concept that the king should 'live of his own' was rendered archaic. Fiscal prerogatives gave way to direct grants of taxation, and Parliament, willy-nilly, became responsible for granting a sufficient ordinary income. In 1660 a parliamentary committee investigated anticipated revenue and expenses with the intention of putting them into balance. It concluded that the King needed an annual income of £1.2 million and that this could be provided through enhanced customs, continuation of the excise at lower rates, and a special land tax to make up the loss of revenue from the Court of Wards. There can be little doubt that the Convention intended to provide Charles II with an adequate revenue and no question that it failed to do so. Ledger entries were little more than guesses – most of them uneducated – and members of the committee proved worse mathematicians than prognosticators when they double-counted the income from the excise on wine.

Thus Charles II fell into debt almost immediately and turned to the Cavalier Parliament for relief. As in 1660, there was sympathy for the King's plight, but now there was also resistance to the likeliest means of relieving it. Many country members were themselves in straitened circumstances, while borough members reported that the towns would not endure another increase in the excise. Initial expedients included a benevolence – an extraordinary grant of a year's revenue – and finally the introduction in 1662 of the Hearth Tax. In theory, taxing chimneys was more progressive than raising the excise on beer. The number of hearths correlated to the size of houses, which in turn correlated to wealth. The urban poor would be exempt and the rural poor would be taxed at the lowest rate. But no tax which allowed the gentry to assess each other was likely to be progressive. The Hearth Tax yielded less than a third of the most conservative estimates and was as unpopular as the excise. The King's government continued to run at a deficit.

The most difficult problems faced by the Cavalier Parliament concerned security. The want of an army had made Charles I vulnerable to attack from Scotland and dependent upon Parliament for his survival. The want of clear statutory authority had made possible the Militia Ordinance by which the Long Parliament had raised forces against the King. The Cavalier Parliament wished to remedy these defects. Nevertheless, there was nothing more feared and hated in English society than the army. Too many members of Parliament had had first-hand experience with swaggering soldiers and crippling military taxation to be willing to support a permanent standing militia of the kind that Charles II craved. Every abortive revolt – like Thomas Venner's rising of thirty-five Fifth Monarchists in January 1661 – every farcical plot reported to the Secretaries of State was magnified to prove the need for a royal militia. Especially in 1661, the government gauged the mood of the people exactly. Pathetic as it was, Venner's rising led to a vicious crackdown on religious dissenters, especially Quakers and Baptists, who were imprisoned by the thousands without due process. But demands for a royal army were still resisted. The militia was the purview of the peerage and the local gentry through the structure of the lieutenancy. Attempts to convert it to a centralized force smacked too much of Cromwell. Thus the Militia Act of 1662 vested all military authority in the king through the county militias, although Charles was given money to maintain the lifeguard that had protected him since 1660, for another three years.

Issues of security were also behind decisions taken to regulate corporations. Urban areas – the 'seminaries of faction' – had offered crucial support to Parliament against the King. They had also undergone much change under the Protectorate, which granted new charters and allowed the replacement of corporate officers. As with the militia, the government's inclination was for centralized control, especially over key personnel. A plan which emanated from the House of Lords would have required the reconfirmation of all charters, given the king the right to select town officers, and eliminated boroughs' exemption from the jurisdiction of county JPs. But the Commons balked at such an extension of royal power. They were more concerned with restoring those who had lost their places and assuring the loyalty of corporate members. The Corporation Act of 1661 was a victory for the Commons. For a period of thirteen months, commissions made up of county élites regulated corporations by imposing the oaths of supremacy, allegiance and non-resistance and by requiring abjuration of the Solemn League and Covenant. Some did their work thoroughly and exacted revenge; other visitations were perfunctory, and the declaration against the Covenant accounted for most of the exclusions of old Cromwellians from town government.

The acts to settle the militia and to regulate corporations demonstrated the limits of royal control over Parliament. Even the strongest predisposition towards cooperation did not ensure passage of the government's programme, especially when central and local interests conflicted. In no area was this conflict greater than in religion, and in no area were the phases of restoration so different. In the Declaration of Breda, Charles II had offered to accept a tolerant religious policy as determined by Parliament. His own inclination was for leniency in matters of conscience and severity in matters of obedience. Even a broad church would not encompass those who 'disturbed the public peace' – groups defined either by their own actions or by others' reactions. This category included Catholics, Independents and all sectarian Protestants. Whether it also included Presbyterians was the crucial question. Initially, the King and his leading ministers favoured comprehending Presbyterians within the established church. Their motives were political rather than theological. They believed that Presbyterian support was crucial for a successful restoration. The Presbyterians were the largest group in the Convention and a key constituency among London financiers, and General Monck was of their ilk. Charles offered bishoprics to three Presbyterians and appointed a number of them royal chaplains. He also signalled his favour towards moderate Presbyterians in the Worcester House Declaration of October 1660, which promised a review of the structure and doctrine of the re-established church.

When the Cavalier Parliament met six months later the political situation had radically altered. The Convention had not placed religious conditions upon the crown, and Presbyterian support had not been vital in the initial Restoration settlement. The parliamentary selections of 1661 further diminished the Presbyterians' strength, while all but one of their clerical leaders had abstained from accepting church office. The conference on reforming the Book of Common Prayer convened at Savoy House in April proved a tower of Babel. Most decisively, the episcopacy had been restored and the bishops had their own ideas about the shape of an Anglican church. William Juxon, who had comforted Charles I on the scaffold, was Primate, but Gilbert Sheldon, Bishop of London, was the power behind Convocation. Sheldon was a tough-minded, practical man who had worked tirelessly to sustain traditional religion during its period in the wilderness. His tombstone would read 'Protector of the Church'. He was an administrator rather than a scholar, and had kept out of the dispute over Arminianism. This made him an ideal choice as Bishop of London and as Juxon's successor in 1663. Though no ideologue, Sheldon did not view doctrine as an object of political compromise. The church had its own martyrs, had suffered its own privations, and had not had the luxury of exile. Pastors had stayed with their congregations and had provided the stability and comfort of traditional ceremonies and festivities. When the test of loyalty came, the vast majority of incumbents had upheld the practices of the established church. Despite the Puritan ascendancy, the old religion endured. Upon the solid rock of such churchmen, not the malleable clay of the politicians, would Sheldon build Anglicanism. Thus the revisions to the prayer-book made following the Savoy Conference offered little to even moderate Presbyterians, and Sheldon refused all compromise when they were debated in Parliament.

The independence of Sheldon and the hierarchy of the church was matched by the independence of members of Parliament. There was no consensus on questions of religion. Both Houses included a spectrum of religious adherents, and almost all of the critical decisions were made by a minority of members for a variety of reasons. But it was quickly apparent that the tolerant policy of 1660 did not fit the intolerant mood of 1661. After the passage of a rigorously Anglican prayer-book, the two Houses agreed to a rigidly conservative Act of Uniformity (1662). Like the officers of corporations, all clerics and teachers were to abjure the Solemn League and Covenant, renounce the right of resistance, and conform to the established practices of the Church of England. Those who did not would be ejected. Though the intention of the act was to exclude dissenters from the ministry, it trapped many others as well. Over 1,000 clergymen in England and Wales were now deprived of their places. Sheldon turned a deaf ear to every plea for leniency and vetoed every exception to the rule. He steeled the courage of Charles II and, with the enthusiastic support of Parliament, beat down the objections of Clarendon to such intolerance. The bulk of exclusions in 1660 had satisfied the demands of equity; those of 1662 satisfied the rigours of law.

King and Chancellor opposed the Act of Uniformity for different reasons. Though both had expressed support for a tolerant church settlement, Charles had done so for the sake of Catholics, Clarendon for the sake of order. Half the King's family were Catholics – he would soon marry a Catholic queen – and he wished to soften the impact of the recusancy laws. Comprehension of Presbyterians might lead to tolerance – though not toleration – of Catholics. Clarendon opposed the Act of Uniformity because he feared the creation of a permanent fifth column, especially in urban areas. By treating moderate Presbyterians the same as radical Baptists and Quakers, Parliament was creating a movement out of splinter groups. Reluctantly, Clarendon supported Sheldon's hard-line approach, and the ejections were accomplished without great difficulty. But the King did not achieve his objectives, and towards the end of 1662 he issued a Declaration of Indulgence which announced his desire to soften the rigours of the law. He requested that Parliament prepare a bill which would allow him to suspend enforcement of the act on an individual basis. A policy of indulgence had the advantage of maintaining the unity of the established church while allowing the crown room for political manœuvre. It had the disadvantage of establishing the precedent that the king could dispense with the law. On these grounds even Clarendon opposed it.

In fact, the temper of Parliament in 1663 was more obdurate than indulgent. Despite the rigours of the Act of Uniformity, dissenting ministers thundered from their pulpits. Despite the vigilance of L'Estrange and the censors, Presbyterian polemic poured from the presses. It was scathing and embittered, the wail of an ensnared animal forced to desperate acts of self-preservation. Every cry brought the hunter closer. The royalists had never forgiven the Presbyterians their part in the origins of the Civil War. It was they who had eroded the authority of the church, who had made the pact with the devilish Scots that brought all to ruin. It was they who had incited the Commons to take up arms against their lawful sovereign. Without the prodding of learned divines, wealthy citizens and comfortable gentry there would have been no stampede of mobs and mad prophets. It mattered little that the Presbyterians had recanted: indeed this only confirmed the royalist judgement that Presbyterian conscience was not so much 'painful' as 'prideful'. In the Commons, members introduced bills to extirpate dissent.

These had little chance of passage until government spies and provocateurs revealed the details of a plot in Yorkshire to overthrow the regime. The accounts were such a tangle of misinformation, rumour and lies that it took several months for authorities to believe in the existence of a northern conspiracy. Pre-emptive arrests of suspects and the mustering of Yorkshire trained bands effectively ended the threat, though subsequent investigation revealed that the motley collection of former republicans, Cromwellians, Baptists and Quakers included a substantial group of Presbyterians. This was all the excuse that the leaders of the Cavalier Parliament needed. They revived the bill against Protestant dissent and intensified its penalties. The resulting Conventicle Act (1664) banned religious services other than those of the Church of England. Anyone caught attending a conventicle was subject successively to fine, imprisonment and transportation as an indentured labourer. For the purposes of the act, Presbyterians were to be treated the same as Quakers, and there was to be no leniency afforded those who occasionally attended Anglican services. In the following year Parliament passed the Five Mile Act, which prevented dissenting clergymen from living within five miles of a corporate town, effectively excluding them from their urban bases of support, especially London. The punitive nature of this legislation was justified by Sheldon: 'Those who will not be governed as men, by reason and persuasion, shall be governed as beasts, by power and force.' The only saving grace for dissenters was that all of these acts, which were collectively misnamed the Clarendon Code, were difficult to enforce.

The fractiousness of the second Restoration settlement was a better indicator of the future of Charles's government than the unity of the first. The Cavalier House of Commons had demonstrated its independence, royal government its ineptitude. The King's legislative programme was haphazard, his parliamentary management non-existent. The government's greatest failure was not to secure an adequate revenue when Parliament was inclined to provide one. This meant that every session began with a begging-bowl outstretched to the House of Commons, whose control of the purse weakened the House of Lords as well as the King. The Lords suffered from their own divisions. Court factionalism intensified as government stabilized and the spoils of power increased. Clarendon remained the lightning-rod for opposition, especially as his health began to fail. His hold over the King was based on his strengths as a politician: the grasp of detail, the manipulation of underlings, the ability to know when to stroke and when to squeeze. But the two had no emotional ties, and Charles despised his chancellor's priggishness as much as Clarendon disapproved of his king's debauchery. It was easy for Clarendon's opponents to gain the King's ear. Finally, the religious legislation that separated Protestants into conformists and dissenters masked the far greater hostility of both to Catholics. If the Declaration of Indulgence was a trial balloon, it had burst with a resounding pop.

So too had the protective bubble that surrounded the King. Not only was the court divided, by 1662 public criticism of royal policy was on the rise. Charles's marriage to Catherine of Braganza was initially disliked on the grounds of her Catholicism and subsequently on the grounds that she was barren. There could be no doubt of the King's potency. Though a diplomatic blow aimed at alluring France and repelling Spain, the marriage was a match made for money. The King of Portugal's daughter brought a seemingly large dowry and the strategically significant port of Tangier. Those who marry for money usually earn it, and Charles II was no exception. Much of the dowry went unpaid, Tangier was abandoned in 1684, and England's financial support of Portugal's war with Spain offset trading concessions in the East. Fiscal considerations were also behind the decision to sell the Cromwellian prize of Dunkirk to France. Its capture from Spain represented England's first toehold on the Continent since Queen Mary had lost Calais in 1558. The town had long been a staging-point for privateers, and its capture meant they could no longer target English shipping. Thus Charles's determination to offload Dunkirk offended both the nation's sense of honour and the merchants' sense of security. At court the disposition was a triumph of foreign policy. The town was too expensive to be maintained indefinitely – it could only be sold or abandoned – and the sale to France further harmed Spain. But in the country the decision was uniformly unpopular.

Charles's ties to Portugal were directed against the crumbling might of the Spanish empire. The Spanish Habsburgs had never recovered from their near-capture of Paris in 1643. The ensuing years had been one long retreat. France was now the great European power, and her robust king, Louis XIV, made plans to acquire territory and *gloire*. To achieve his aims he needed only to prevent all of his potential enemies from uniting against him – a task made easier by their inability to perceive the French menace. England had fought a brief war against Holland and a longer one against Spain, and in both conflicts it sought French aid. The Dutch opposed Spain more naturally than even the British, their hostility the result of eighty years of near-unremitting warfare. They too courted Louis, and successfully concluded an alliance in 1662.

By the 1660s international politics had lost its predominantly confessional motivation. A Europe that had once been starkly divided into Catholic and Protestant had evolved into one dominated by a *realpolitik* so cynical as to make Machiavelli blush. Foreign policy was conducted on few principles other than opportunism. French and Spanish ambassadors were little more than bagmen for their princes, deputed to put as many leading ministers as possible on the payroll. Royal navies were indistinguishable from pirates; the fleets of trading companies behaved no differently from invasion forces. The European powers formed and broke alliances with such regularity that the diplomatic marriages they made were as worthless as counterfeit coin. Monarchs lived openly with their mistresses as if to traduce the kings and princes whose daughters they married. The world was like a playground filled with bullies spoiling for a fight. Every imagined slight was interpreted as a provocation – a matter of personal dignity for the monarch and of national pride for his people.

Such a setting provides an understanding of the Anglo-Dutch war of 1665–7. Its causes were obscure, its objectives illusive. Only its greedy motives were clear, as there was no need to cover them with a shroud of decency. Each nation savoured the possibility of carving a larger share of world trade out of the flank of the other. The English wished to inherit the Portuguese interest in the East, the Dutch to replace Spanish dominion in the West. Moreover, both sides had their justifications for war: claims for compensation on illegal seizures had not been paid; the conditions of settlement after the war of 1652–4 had not been met. There was new provocation as well. The Dutch would not share the lucrative West African trade, ruining the overseas company set up by the Duke of York and other powerful English courtiers. New Amsterdam smugglers wreaked havoc on North American customs collections, and the presence of the Dutch in the middle of the English settlements was more than a fiscal nuisance.

Nearly everyone but Clarendon supported the war. The naturally cautious Chancellor had no financial stake in the rivalry with the Dutch and he continued to fret over the demands of domestic policies and the budget. He didn't believe that England could afford a war. Against Clarendon stood his son-in-law, James, Duke of York, who was itching for a military engagement in which he could distinguish himself as he had during his European exile. As Lord Admiral, James would lead a war against the Dutch, and he bullied his brother into the aggressive acts that led to the conflict. In 1664 a raiding-party seized New Amsterdam – subsequently renamed New York – and warships sailed to West Africa. Charles summoned Parliament to provide funds to outfit ships of the line, and to everyone's consternation the Commons voted £2.5 million. This allowed James to assemble the largest armada in England's history and to win one of its greatest naval triumphs – off Lowestoft in early 1665. War fever swept the nation, and the King regained the popularity of the Restoration.

The victory off Lowestoft swelled English pride, though it did nothing to resolve the military situation. The Dutch recouped their strength and settled in for the long haul. Their alliance with Louis XIV meant that the English would have to defend Atlantic shipping from French privateers and thus dilute their energies. It also meant that Charles would have to raise even larger sums of money to keep his fleet in action. The campaigns of 1666 ended in nothing better than a draw, war weariness replaced euphoria, and public support turned to criticism. Plague raged in London; rebellion flared in Scotland. Worse was to come the following year. While the Privy Council discovered that it was easier to begin a war than to end one, the Dutch made preparations for an aggressive campaign. In June their admiral De Ruyter broke the boom that prevented ships entering the Medway and made his way to the shipyards at Chatham. There he bombarded a stationary fleet – kept in dock for lack of funds – setting fire to three large warships and towing away the *Royal Charles*, the King's flagship built by Cromwell and originally named *Naseby*. Had the old Protector had a grave, he would surely have been spinning in it.

De Ruyter's romp up the Medway disastrously concluded the second Anglo-Dutch war. Everyone connected with government was tainted by the result, the King and his brother coming in for humiliating personal criticism. The war nearly bankrupted the crown and placed the King at the absolute mercy of Parliament. Politicians took the opportunity to settle old scores. In the Lords, the Catholic Earl of Bristol and the dissenter Duke of Buckingham not only reclaimed royal favour, they combined to ruin their common enemy Clarendon. In truth the war needed a scapegoat and Clarendon had outlived his political usefulness. He was unpopular in Parliament and unpopular with the people. On the night that Chatham Docks burned, a crowd attacked his home. Thus the Chancellor was the easy sacrifice, even though he had opposed the war, and it was all his friends could do to prevent capital charges of treason being brought. Two decades before, Clarendon had promised Charles I that he would protect his son. Now he had to be impeached to do so.

IO

For Church and King
1668–1685

On 17 October 1678 the body of Sir Edmund Berry Godfrey was found face down in a ditch. It had been run through with a sword, though that was only the most obvious wound. The discovery ended an extensive manhunt and began an even more extensive witch-hunt.

Even in the vast metropolis that was late-seventeenth-century London, Sir Edmund Berry Godfrey was a notable figure. A successful wood and coal merchant and a staunch Protestant who served in his parish vestry, Godfrey represented that class of prosperous citizens who governed England. A justice of the peace for London and the county of Middlesex for nearly twenty years, he exercised his office firmly and fairly. He warded sturdy beggars out of his parish yet gave from his own pocket to aid the truly needy. His fame was based on his heroic behaviour during the Great Plague of 1665. As King, court and anyone who could hire a coach fled the capital, Edmund Berry Godfrey remained at his post, overseeing mass burials and prosecuting grave-robbers. The worst that anyone could say of him was that he stayed to protect his coal trade and took small risk in that he had neither wife nor children. But his efforts were recognized by the King in a gift of 800 ounces of gold plate and by the reputation he secured as a man of worth. He was often seen walking the City streets, his long-drawn face tilted downwards to accommodate his stooping gait. He wore a distinctive black wig and adorned his hat with a bright gold band. His presence was unmistakable.

So, it transpired, was his absence. On 12 October 1678 Sir Edmund Berry Godfrey disappeared. For several weeks he had intimated to all who knew him that he feared for his life. Withdrawn and distracted, he took to his bed for several days, and then wandered the streets as if in a daze. He was certain that he was being followed. The melancholy that came upon him – so it was subsequently described – resulted from his knowledge of an explosive secret. Twice in September he had taken depositions from Titus Oates, who revealed an astounding conspiracy to murder the King and a number of other prominent Protestant leaders. Teams of assassins hired by French Jesuits were already in London completing their preparations. The plot was about to be hatched. Oates laced his story with his own paranoia – how he and his colleague Israel Tonge were in peril for revealing what they knew of the plot, as was anyone else who did not act immediately to prevent it. Godfrey took extensive notes the second time he interviewed Oates, and these he turned over to the Lord Chief Justice. The story troubled Godfrey deeply. For over a month rumours of a Catholic conspiracy circulated in London and bits of Oates's evidence, which had already been given to the Privy Council, began to leak out. Godfrey kept his own counsel and carried his sword wherever he travelled.

When Sir Edmund Berry Godfrey failed to keep a lunch appointment, his servants raised the alarm. Witnesses claimed to have sighted him in St Martin's Lane, in St Giles-in-the-Fields, in Paddington and Marylebone, and then in the Strand. When the justice did not return home that night and could not be found all the next day, worry turned to panic. The third day was a Monday, and Godfrey's brothers brought the disappearance to the attention of the Lord Chancellor. By then, all London knew that he had vanished, and most believed him murdered by papists. Misinformation came flooding in to the authorities, sending search parties hither and yon. The brothers made a public appeal for information, yet Tuesday and Wednesday passed and the mystery deepened. On Thursday it rained much of the day, and in mid-afternoon two men took a short cut through the fields of Primrose Hill on their way to the shelter of an inn. There they discovered a cane and gloves and, returning with the landlord, found a body face down in a ditch. They roused a magistrate, and Sir Edmund Berry Godfrey was soon identified.

The populace was stunned by the news. All fears had been confirmed, and it did not take some wag long to turn the seventeenth-century spelling of 'Edmund Burie Godfrey' into the anagram 'I find murdered by rogues.' The coroner's inquest only fuelled the fires. Godfrey had not been killed on Primrose Hill, but had been transported there on the day his body was discovered. Nor was it clear that he had died by the sword that was found in his body. His head and chest revealed the discoloration of a severe beating, and his neck gave

*evidence that he had been strangled. The five days of mystery contrib-
uted to the outrage at the murder of a Protestant justice. Suspicion
turned to certainty. Sir Edmund Berry Godfrey was the first victim of
the Popish Plot.*

In the first decade of his reign Charles II had been constrained by the
need to re-establish and consolidate monarchical power. This meant
compromises over policy and sacrifices over religion. After the early
purges of Commonwealthsmen, he allowed local government to find its
own level and demonstrated none of the centralizing ambitions of his
father. He had a strong working relationship with the aristocracy,
many of whom had sacrificed blood and treasure for the Stuart cause.
He followed the family tradition of being generous with honours, creating more dukes during his reign than the total that had lived in the
previous century. Through the House of Lords he had firm control of
Parliament, and Charles preferred to raise his chief ministers to peerages rather than leave them to manage the Commons. The Lower
House was as unruly as ever, yet, as the expedient of adjourning the
same parliament year after year continued, more of its members depended upon government posts and perquisites, and soon the body had
earned the popular sobriquet of the 'Pensionary Parliament'. Charles II
managed his parliaments better than had either of his predecessors,
even after the end of his Restoration honeymoon.

By 1668 he was ready to flex his royal muscles. The Dutch war may
have been a failure, but monarchs made their marks through war.
Charles was dazzled by the aura of power that surrounded Louis XIV,
who was now entering the full vigour of manhood. Though Charles
was soon to become entangled in Louis's ambitions, he was never
blinded by them. Increasingly he conducted his own foreign policy and
set his own course on matters of religion. Freed from dependence on
Clarendon, he never again allowed himself to be controlled by a minister. Indeed, in succeeding years he shuffled ambitious politicians from
the top to the bottom of the deck with careless ease. Not until he
embarked upon the unpopular religious policy of indulgence was
Charles in need of skilled political managers, and then the Earl of
Danby emerged with such timeliness in 1674 that it could be thought
the King had been keeping aces up his sleeve.

Charles II possessed unshakeable convictions of what constituted the
core of his monarchy which led him to clash with Parliament and with

public opinion. The first had to do with foreign affairs: the ways in which monarchs dealt with each other. Charles believed that, as king, he was free absolutely to make war and peace and to arrange and approve the marriages of members of his family. The second had to do with his patrimony: royal prerogatives passed through the generations and re-established after the irruption of civil war. These included his office of supreme governor of the church, which he took seriously enough to quarrel with each of his Primates; his political position as the greatest of the three parliamentary estates – it was made a crime to assert that the estates were co-equal – and his obligation as head of his family to control the hereditary succession in the absence of a direct male heir.

This combination of values, derived in the King's mind from divine injunction, immemorial custom and the laws of nature and nations, led to the only significant crisis of his reign when, in 1678, anti-Catholic hysteria found a political outlet in a movement to exclude the Duke of York from succession to the throne. The Popish Plot was fuelled by the King's pro-French foreign policy, and the demands for Exclusion by the Duke's public conversion to Catholicism in 1673. That Charles rode out these storms testified to the strength of both his monarchy and his convictions. He let the plot take its course, but used every political tactic at his disposal to prevent parliamentary passage of an Exclusion bill. He emerged from the crisis with his power invigorated, and he marked the last years of his reign by a campaign to ensure that the crown could maintain political order in time of crisis. Charles II undertook the most ambitious scheme of centralization known in England before the nineteenth century. Corporations were reconstituted, the lieutenancy was purged, and the commissions of the peace were rigorously scrutinized. But he died too soon to complete the consolidation of his power or to build a base sufficiently secure to survive the advent of an openly Catholic king.

*   *   *

The fall of Clarendon in 1667 removed a weight from the King that he had borne all of his adult life. While the Chancellor was mocked by Charles's mistress the Duchess of Portsmouth for prudishness and ridiculed by the King's boon companions for pomposity, Clarendon's constant presence in the chamber and at the Council board exercised a restraint upon the King. The Earl's political Anglicanism bolstered the bishops and checked the King's preference for an indulgent religious policy. Clarendon's desire for a partnership with Parliament curbed Charles's absolutist tendencies. If there was little he could do to suppress the monarch's sexual appetites, his unrelenting disapproval made the King self-conscious about his manners. It is no coincidence that Charles's all-too-public liaisons with actresses came after Clarendon's dismissal. Whatever the Chancellor's faults – he had outlived his age and was too cautious and too sanctimonious for the new one – he had served the best interests of the kingdom. Callously, his successors would serve the best interests of the King.

Beginning in 1667 Charles II took the direction of government into his own hands. He left vital offices vacant or gave them to be run by several commissioners and he capriciously raised one minister to power by overtipping another. His chief servants in this period were attacked as a cabal – ministers carrying out secret and self-interested designs. The charge mostly stuck because CABAL was an acronym of some of their initials. In fact they had little in common and vied with each other for power and favour. Charles had been raised with the dissolute Duke of Buckingham, and the two shared the personal tragedy of a slain father. They sowed acres of wild oats together, but their relationship was tempestuous and the Duke became as familiar with the inside of the Tower of London as the throne room. Though Buckingham had been instrumental in Clarendon's fall, he was unpredictable and unreliable. Because he publicly championed the cause of dissent, he was a useful foil for Charles's religious policy. Opposite in almost every way to the Duke was Henry Bennet, Earl of Arlington. He inherited Clarendon's role as royal workhorse in the more suitable position of Principal Secretary. There he guided Charles's foreign policy and quickly became the most powerful of the King's ministers. He was infinitely flexible, bending to the direction of royal winds and working assiduously to build a personal interest at court. He displayed his lifetime loyalty to the Stuarts in the disfiguring scar on his nose that he had received in the Civil War, and his eternal devotion by his emulative deathbed conversion to Catholicism.

Sir Thomas Clifford, another crypto-Catholic, had been brought into service by Arlington to help reorganize the royal finances. A tireless administrator of great capacities, Clifford was indispensable in managing the House of Commons. The Cavalier Parliament was ageing none too gracefully, and the numerous by-elections to fill its vacancies changed its character. Two different types could be seen entering its ranks: the would-be courtier and the would-be patriot. The former wished for nothing more than a share of the booty: a piece of a loan syndicate, a receiver's post, a lucrative brief. They were grist for Clifford's mill. The latter became part of an inchoate 'country' disposition: an attitude of devotion to the King and the established church and of suspicion towards everything else. The 'country' disliked ministers, distrusted courtiers, and detested bankers. It had a sharp eye for graft and a keen nose for corruption, though neither was necessary to expose the fiasco of the Dutch war concluded the previous year. The 'country' was neither a party nor an opposition: it was simply a tendency to raise awkward questions and prevent government from confusing its interests with the nation's.

The 'country' was no more fixated on finance than was the court. Not only had the Dutch war absorbed millions in extraordinary grants, it had contributed to a fall of one-third in the crown's ordinary revenue. This resulted mostly from loss of customs during the interruption of trade. Charles's deficit was so serious – over £2 million in 1670 – that he had to allow the House of Commons to launch a humiliating inquiry into the administration of the monies laid out for the war. The King also made concessions to London financiers in the form of 'in-course' repayments of debt that ensured that old loans would be retired before new ones. In return, Charles received enhanced customs and excise duties, though even these did not make the crown solvent. In 1672 £1 million of debt came due and Exchequer officials had no choice other than to defer payments of principal or face bankruptcy. Needless to say, this Stop of the Exchequer further eroded royal credit.

It was while trapped in these murky fiscal waters that Charles took the bait of a French alliance. England had sought French support before the Dutch war, but now Louis XIV was in need. He had determined to swallow up the Spanish Netherlands and invade Holland. Louis lured his English cousin by casting as negotiator Charles's beloved sister Minette, wife of the duc d'Orleans, and by offering a shiny annual subsidy and the promise of a share in the dismemberment of the Dutch empire. In return, by the Treaty of Dover (1670), Charles committed England to a naval attack at Louis's direction and, in two secret clauses, to suspension of the penal laws against Catholics and his own public conversion at a propitious moment. These concessions were so potentially damaging that they were revealed only to his Catholic ministers: Arlington, Clifford and his brother, the Duke of York. To protect the secret, Charles perfidiously appointed two dissenters, Buckingham and the Earl of Shaftesbury, to negotiate a second pact which did not contain the religious clauses. This treaty too was kept secret, for there was as yet little enthusiasm for another war with the Dutch and much hostility to any alliance with France. Both treaties gave hostages to fortune, though Charles seemed unaware that he had now made Louis XIV master of his fate.

However shrewdly the King had calculated the stakes – forcing Louis to accept a smaller English military commitment and a larger English share of the spoils – he never pondered the odds. Charles's strategy was that of the gambler who doubles his bets to make back his losses. If he defeated the Dutch, national pride would swell, trade would burgeon, and the royal coffers would be filled. The English were enthralled by military victories: they had propped up Cromwell, and had even given Charles a temporary boost. Triumph over the Dutch would damp down part of the inevitable fire-storm which would result from a policy of Catholic relief. Dissenters would draw the logical connection between a pro-French foreign policy and popery, and would raise the spectre of absolutism when the crown became financially independent. But they too would benefit by suspension of the penal laws – especially the recently promulgated second Conventicle Act (1670). The King seems not to have considered the consequences of defeat. The French subsidy of £225,000 would only finance a knockout blow; indeed, it would hardly cover the customs losses from the disruption of trade. A prolonged war would be ruinous in itself, whatever the eventual outcome. Moreover, without the protective coating of victory, the outcry over the change in religious policy would corrode the King's ability to govern even if the secret clauses of the Treaty of Dover remained secret. None of this mattered to Charles or his ministers, because the Dutch were ascribed no chance of surviving the combined might of the English navy and the French army.

Two days before he sent his fleet into action, Charles fulfilled the first of his private obligations. He issued a Declaration of Indulgence (1672) that defended the church established by law but licensed dissenters and permitted Catholics to worship privately. English and French ships joined together in a powerful armada, and Louis XIV propelled his soldiers across the Rhine. As so often happens, a smaller force fighting for survival was a match for a larger one fighting for plunder. Abandoning first their republican principles by making William of Orange stadtholder – or ruling prince – and then their rich farmlands by accepting his decision to breach their own dikes, the Dutch repelled the French invasion. On the seas, the battles were ferocious and inconclusive. The Duke of York commanded the first encounter off Sole Bay (1672), where two English flagships sank and the Earl of Sandwich drowned. Both sides inflicted heavy damage, though the Dutch achieved their objective of preventing an English landing. The naval campaign of 1673, commanded by Prince Rupert, fared no better. The two sides fought to a grudging standstill, their heroisms mutually acknowledged. The Dutch fleet limped into port, but again it had safeguarded its coast. However admirably they had acquitted themselves, the English forces had not secured the decisive victory that was the only useful result.

The King and his counsellors were now at the mercy of an angry Parliament and a wary nation. Francophobia – never far below the surface – was stirred masterfully by the Dutch, who portrayed the war as a Catholic conspiracy organized by Louis XIV and English ministers on the French payroll. They stopped just short of accusing Charles II of taking bribes, for even the paranoid fantasies of propagandists were too tame when compared to the truth. In return for an annual pension, Charles had given France control over his foreign policy; in return for an additional supplement he ceded domestic policy as well. Louis XIV did not wish an English Parliament to meet until he had launched the war, and Charles obliged by extending the adjournment of the Cavalier Parliament for nearly two years. When it met in 1673 it was as resolute as ever had been the Long Parliament. Debate on the Declaration of Indulgence loosed two virulent strains of argument. The first was the predictable bigotry of the Anglican majority, though it was now more sharply focused on the Catholic menace. Rumours that the treaty with France was tied to Catholic toleration were pervasive. The second was expressed in the potent language of liberty. If the crown could suspend the law, then lives and property were in danger. Thus the Commons voted that only Parliament had the authority to revoke religious legislation and that Charles must withdraw the Declaration of Indulgence. The King's repudiation of absolutist intentions, his invocation of precedent and prerogative, his appeal to loyalty and obedience all failed. He had to rescind the Declaration.

Indeed, Charles had little choice. He might fool himself into believing that one more naval campaign would turn the tide, but without parliamentary grants his fleet was as useless as ships in a bottle. The Treasurer of the Navy, Sir Thomas Osborne, worked miracles to keep the government solvent, especially after the Commons declared that as they had not been asked to support the war they had no intention of paying its debts. The price of parliamentary grants was to be an Anglican government. All civilian office-holders and all military officers were to take Anglican communion publicly, and all were to swear an additional oath denying transubstantiation. It was this oath that gave teeth to the Test Act (1673). The reservations of conscience that enabled attendance and even participation at Anglican services – what was known as occasional conformity – could not sanction the repudiation of so central a doctrine of Catholic faith. In acts of incomprehensible self-contradiction, Lord Treasurer Clifford gave up his office – he was replaced by Osborne – and then took his own life. More importantly, James, Duke of York, resigned the admiralty.

As the Dutch war of 1665–7 had ended Clarendon's career, so the war of 1672–4 put paid to Arlington and Buckingham, who became targets of the nation's wrath. The Earl of Shaftesbury followed them into the wilderness, dismissed by the King for supporting the Test Act and opposing the Catholic marriage of the Duke of York. No one would have guessed by looking at them in 1674 that James was as old as forty-one or Charles as young as forty-four. Office, if not pleasure, had gouged deep lines into the King's face and removed the sparkle from his eye. He had no legitimate heir, and no hope of one after the Queen's miscarriage in 1678. Most likely James, and most certainly his children, would inherit the throne. In 1672 James's first wife, Anne Hyde, had died having delivered two daughters, Mary and Anne, both of whom were raised Protestant. James quickly decided to remarry and chose as his wife a Catholic princess, Mary of Modena. This revitalized schemes to alter the succession, though Charles refused both of the obvious courses open to him: to divorce his barren wife or to legitimize his eldest son, the Protestant Duke of Monmouth. He would not even prevent James's hasty Catholic marriage, which took place between parliamentary sessions to avoid protests in the Commons.

But the reality of a Catholic brother and the spectre of a Catholic heir further narrowed Charles's options. When the second naval campaign failed to crush Holland, the King was once again thrown back upon Parliament and in desperate need of a minister in whom both he and the Houses might have confidence. The obvious choice was Lord Treasurer Osborne (soon to be Earl of Danby), who had salvaged royal finance, opposed the Dutch war and was a staunch Anglican. Danby quickly ended hostilities by concluding a separate treaty with Holland that abrogated Charles's commitments to Louis XIV.

Paradoxically, peace rehabilitated royal revenue. Neutral English ships captured business from both belligerents, and customs receipts soared. Spending still outstripped income, yet the gap had narrowed. Danby hoped to close it entirely through parliamentary grants which he believed would be the reward for his popular Anglican and anti-French policies. These were the attitudes of the 'country' back-benchers, and Danby pandered to them shamelessly. He had some success in 1677 when over £600,000 was voted for the navy, and some in 1678 when another £600,000 was given to disband the army he had earlier sought to raise against France. But Danby could not rule by the 'country' alone. His Anglican policies alienated urban dissenters; his clientage network outraged governmental reformers. His attempt to build a parliamentary majority by use of jobs and pensions was more resented than it was effective and formed the basis of attempts to impeach him in 1675. He faced powerful opposition in the Lords, where Buckingham and Shaftesbury opposed him at every step, even contemplating a rapprochement with the Duke of York to unite the Catholic and dissenting interests against high Anglicanism.

Yet the greatest obstacle to Danby's success was Charles II. It was not entirely true that Danby had been forced on the King, but they continually worked at cross-purposes. Danby was a parliamentary manager who could not prevent the King from proroguing Parliament; a cost-cutting treasurer who could not get the monarch to economize; a pro-Dutch Anglican who could not wean Charles from his French Catholic foreign policy. Still, Danby had the perfect temperament to serve a faithless master: his principles were untainted by idealism. Thus what he could not compromise he could ignore. This was especially true of foreign policy. Forced to cash his chips, Charles still yearned for a seat at the table. When Louis XIV offered a subsidy if Charles would dissolve the Cavalier Parliament, he collected by adjourning it for fifteen months. The King entered into more secret treaties with France, though Danby refused to countersign them. Instead, he pursued his public pro-Dutch policy and in 1677 persuaded both Charles and James to offer the Duke's eldest daughter, Mary, in marriage to William of Orange. This move was prelude to the revival of a Protestant foreign policy. Parliament passed bills in 1678 to ensure the Protestant upbringing of all potential heirs to the throne, and Danby proposed that preparations be made for a joint military venture with Holland. That these failed in Parliament was a signal of how low the reputation of government had fallen. With £100,000 and a handful of specious arguments, French agents turned the Commons' Francophobia into fear of 'Popery and Arbitrary Government' (as Andrew Marvell entitled his famous pamphlet) at home.

Discontent with Charles's religious and foreign policies had been building from 1672. But opposition was scattered and inconsistent. Its sole unifying element was that it was anti-Catholic and thus largely anti-French. Anglicans feared the growing power of Catholics at court and opposed foreign influences in general. Anglicanism was a distinctive brand of Protestantism practised only in Britain, and it needed to be nourished by its British monarchs. Thus, while most Anglicans were anti-French, they were not pro-Dutch. In Holland, both religion and politics were motley: the one a jumble of competing Protestant sects that practised peaceful coexistence with each other and with their Catholic and Jewish neighbours; the other an unstable amalgam of republic, oligarchy and monarchy, each vying for fundamental power. English dissenters were viscerally anti-Catholic – their passions stirred by the worsening condition of the French Huguenots – but only some were pro-Dutch. Many successful London merchants were dissenters, and their consciences struggled with their pocketbooks because war with the Dutch was good business. The populace, especially in large urban areas and particularly in London, was rabidly anti-Catholic, its prejudices brilliantly stoked by Dutch propaganda and firebrand preachers. Before 1678, however, anti-Catholicism could not join together what opposing confessions of faith had rent asunder. To Anglicans, Charles's policy of indulgence yoked dissenters and Catholics together and made both targets. The Conventicle and Test Acts were designed to exclude dissenters from public life as much as to disable Catholics.

What gave Anglicans and dissenters common cause was not royal policy but public hysteria: the uncovering of a Popish Plot to destroy the nation by murdering Charles II. Though the plot itself was specific enough – hundreds of pamphlets would expose its most minute details

– it seized upon hidden rather than overt fears. After all, as we have seen, Titus Oates revealed the conspiracy before it had been hatched, and the King was in no danger of being assassinated. Yet the terror that gripped the nation for nearly two years could not have been greater had the plot succeeded. The sophisticated and the simple genuinely believed that Britons were in imminent danger of being enslaved, that their lands would be occupied by the French, their treasure shipped off to Rome. This apprehension of danger necessitated political rather than legal remedies. No number of executions could save the nation from the international Catholic conspiracy – a conspiracy which could succeed only if a Catholic monarch ruled the nations of Britain. This was the underlying dynamic of the Exclusion Crisis as popular hysteria gave way to political manœuvrings so intense and complex that they changed permanently the structure of parliamentary politics.

The years between 1678 and 1681 were frenzied in the same way as were the opening years of the 1640s. For all of his institutional power, his growing financial security and the stability that came from nearly two decades of rule, Charles II was helpless to prevent the crisis that descended upon him. But he was not incapable of facing it down once it was clearly defined. His support in the House of Lords, his power to dissolve parliaments and his influence within the governing class were all brought to bear. He tapped well-springs of loyalty that he might not have imagined existed, especially in London, where Tory mobs contested supremacy with the Whigs. Shrewdly, Charles played up the association of church and king. He co-opted members of the opposition when he could and punished others when he couldn't. As the crisis progressed, he continually raised the stakes so that his opponents had to risk first the future of parliaments and then the future of the monarchy. Throughout he was flexible as to means and implacable as to ends. Thus he emerged from the crisis with the principle of hereditary monarchy intact and with his political power enhanced – though it was a close-run thing.

'Popery' was a familiar trope of English political life. It invoked the enemy within – all the more dangerous in that it was largely unseen. By the 1670s the Catholic population of England and Wales was probably no more than 2 per cent of the whole, but anti-popery was only tangentially related to English Catholicism. At one level, popery was an essential element in the making of Protestant England, serving the purpose of the evil god in a creation myth. The papists had burned the hundreds of martyrs canonized by Foxe; the papists had sent the greatest armada ever assembled to conquer England in 1588. The Jesuits, the Pope's own warriors, had incited English Catholics to the Gunpowder Plot in 1605, the Irish rebellion of 1641 and the setting of the Great Fire of London in 1666. This litany of events, always connected one to another, was known to every man, woman and child. The fifth of November was a national holiday on which effigies of the Gunpowder Plotters were defiled; 17 November, Queen Elizabeth's Day, was an occasion for burning elaborate replicas of the Pope. At another level, popery was the enemy without. Popery was in the thrall of foreign masters whose object was the total subjugation of England. It worked by stealth and conspiracy, by infiltration and corruption. Popery was abominably cruel, and its agents committed the most heinous barbarities. Fear of foreign invasion, especially staged from Catholic Ireland, recurrently gripped government ministers and ordinary people alike.

Popery was everyone's worst nightmare; thus anti-popery was omnipresent. But anti-popish hysteria waxed and waned. Every rational seventeenth-century Protestant believed that Jesuits plotted to subvert English laws and liberties, that 'popery and slavery, like two sisters, go hand in hand'. Yet this belief did not ordinarily lead to witch-hunts which accepted mere accusation as proof and abandoned the protections afforded by the common law and the jury system. It did not usually lead to panic in the streets and paralysis in the government. Only an extraordinary concatenation of events could convince the greater part of a nation that its fears had come true. Such a conjunction took place in 1678. The heir to the throne and his recently pregnant second wife were openly Catholic. Like the Queen, the Duke and Duchess of York maintained an entourage of Catholic priests, including a number of Jesuits. The King's mistress Louise de Kéroualle, Duchess of Portsmouth, a French Catholic, was increasingly influential in public affairs. In Europe, Louis XIV wore down his Dutch opponents and captured strongholds in the Spanish Netherlands. Efforts in Parliament to provide military aid to William of Orange were stymied by Charles and James, who remained pro-French, and by Danby, who, as Treasurer, knew that it could not be afforded.

Ever since James's conversion had become public, people feared for the King's life. There was an immediate fright in 1673, and thereafter every drought, flood and eclipse was taken as a portent. Anxiety heightened in the brutally hot summer of 1678, when a plot was finally hatched in the feverish brains of Israel Tonge and Titus Oates. Tonge, an Anglican clergyman, was a delusional paranoiac who stoked his obsession by translating Catholic tracts and compiling a history of the Jesuits. For several years he had warned anyone who would listen of an active papist conspiracy in London. One of those who did listen was Titus Oates, who had been sent down from his preparatory school and two Cambridge colleges, though these indignities did not disqualify him from taking Anglican orders. He was then ousted from his first parish living (in England) for drunkenness, and from his second (in Tangiers) for sodomy. Along the way he was indicted for perjury, and this entire record was compiled before he reached the age of thirty. Yet none of this seems to have blighted his career. Oates had the knack of ensconcing himself in the graces of older men just long enough to benefit from their patronage. In 1677 he seemingly converted to Catholicism, travelled to the Continent, and spent brief periods in two Jesuit training schools which, characteristically, expelled him. Tonge had helped finance one of these expeditions, and when Oates returned to London he re-established the relationship by spinning a story of Jesuit intrigue that involved the assassination of Charles II, the Duke of Ormond and Tonge himself. These fabrications were set before the King, who, doubting their veracity, passed them on to Danby, who, sensing their political value, decided to investigate. Danby found an unlikely ally in the Duke of York, who also believed that he could ride the tiger without being clawed.

Titus Oates was that rare character, the genuine charlatan. He concocted a story that people were disposed to believe, and embellished it whenever challenged. His most potent weapons were an ability to tell a brazen lie and near-total recall of the details he invented. When a letter he claimed incriminating was proved innocent, he simply asserted there were two. He testified to meetings that never took place between people who couldn't have been there, and he was eventually hoist on his own canard. Each time he told his story the list of charges grew and the number of conspirators multiplied. Still, he might not have succeeded in securing the conviction and execution of twenty-four innocent people, provoking the most serious political crisis since 1640, and dooming the reign of James II before it began had he not also had luck. His first bit came when, among the people he accused, one James Coleman, then secretary to the Duchess of York, was found to have letters in his possession that referred to a French triumph over England

and its eventual reconversion to Catholicism. None of these letters referred to the plot fabricated by Oates, but they were revealed within the context of hysteria created by a second stroke of fortune. One of Oates's sure-fire tactics was to insist upon being sworn before testifying. A clergyman with a Bible in his hand was as much an icon of truth as a mother with a babe in her arms was one of comfort. Thus Oates twice visited the Middlesex justice Edmund Berry Godfrey to swear his evidence, which was duly recorded for investigation. But, as we have seen, before Godfrey could investigate he disappeared, and he was eventually discovered dead in most suspicious circumstances. His death seemingly confirmed the Popish Plot.

Details of the plot electrified the populace, especially in London. Shops were boarded, chains were stretched across major thoroughfares, and ferry passengers were detained for questioning. Informers crawled from tenement cellars to betray their neighbours who were undoubtedly involved in the plot or the murder of Justice Godfrey. The King issued proclamations to enforce the recusancy laws – over 1,200 Catholics were prosecuted in London in 1679 alone – and priests were ordered out of the capital. The first trials resulted in convictions and executions accompanied by mass demonstrations. It became a crime to deny the existence of the plot, and this made it difficult for those caught in the ever-widening web to defend themselves. Suspicion of being a Jesuit became sufficient proof of involvement.

As the blood-lust vented itself, Parliament reassembled and immediately the plot took on a new dimension. Catholic peers were sequestered, a second Test Act (1678) was passed, which excluded all Catholics except the Duke of York from either House of Parliament, and Oates, testifying under oath at the bar of the Commons, accused the Queen of complicity in the conspiracy to assassinate her husband. All of this was serious enough for the government, but worse was to come. Ralph Montagu, who blamed Danby for the loss of his post as ambassador to France, revealed secret communications of negotiations for a French subsidy at precisely the same time in 1678 that Danby had induced Parliament to raise an army against France. The Commons impeached the Treasurer, and Charles had no choice but to dissolve the Cavalier Parliament rather than risk further revelations of his secret treaties.

Thus did the Popish Plot meld into the Exclusion Crisis and popery give way to arbitrary government as the national bugbear. Dissenters

first raised fear of arbitrary government after they were refused comprehension into the established church. Arbitrary government posed a
threat to English liberty that could be seen in the denial of religious
freedom, the ever-increasing burden of taxation, French domination of
foreign policy, and, most recently, the raising and maintaining of a
standing army. Andrew Marvell best summarized the case: 'for divers
years a design [has] been carried on to change the lawful government of
England into an absolute tyranny and to convert the established
Protestant religion into downright Popery'. Evidence was found in
Charles's attempts to suspend religious legislation and in his refusal to
enforce recusancy laws or impose oaths on office-holders. It was seen in
what was known and what was suspected about the King's pro-French
foreign policy. It was forcefully revealed in the accumulation of troops
in Scotland and Ireland as well as in the maintenance of the army that
Parliament had paid to disband. In this version, arbitrary government
was a deliberate design by the King to rule in the French style and
become as absolute as Louis XIV. The spectre of arbitrary government did not only unsettle dissenters: it haunted the largely Anglican
'country' opposition to Arlington and Clifford in the 1660s. To the
'country', arbitrary government was a code for corruption and mismanagement, for government by cabal. It was the attempt to build a
court party by bribery, and to sell foreign policy to the highest bidder.
It was undertaken not by the crown but by self-serving ministers who
sold liberty for their own aggrandizement. These two meanings of
arbitrary government were at once reinforcing and contradictory. So
were the components in the movement for Exclusion.

Initially the stories of Catholic conspiracy played into the hands of
the government's opponents like the Earl of Shaftesbury, who had long
urged Charles to alter the succession. Shaftesbury was the most enig-
matic of the King's ministers. He survived his Cromwellian past long
after the Restoration, and was raised to Lord Chancellor in 1672 and
to the rank of earl the next year. Although favoured by the King,
Shaftesbury 'disdained the golden fruit to gather free'. He supported
the first Test Act, urged Charles to divorce his wife, and earned the
implacable hostility of the Duke of York. Shaftesbury was more astute
than he was able. Widely read, he patronized advanced thinkers like
John Locke, whose *Two Treatises of Government* were inspired by the
debate over Exclusion. But Shaftesbury's interventions in constitutional
matters left much to be desired, and he was publicly rebuked by the

House of Commons for issuing electoral writs when Lord Chancellor in 1673 and was imprisoned in the Tower by the King in 1677 for insisting that a parliament adjourned for longer than a year was legally dissolved. Though Shaftesbury publicly championed dissent, he had no difficulty in taking the Anglican oaths after the passage of both Test Acts. Nor was his conscience troubled by the support he gave to the Popish Plot perjurers. His uncompromising stance on Exclusion over the next three years confirms Dryden's judgement: 'In power unpleased, impatient of disgrace.'

The dissolution of the Cavalier Parliament was followed immediately by new elections. The nation was still in the grip of the plot after the trials and executions of the first victims. Though the opposition had little time to organize, they also had little need. The revelations of Danby's conduct discredited the government, while anti-Catholic fever united Anglicans and dissenters. The parliament that assembled in March 1679 was thus a perfect tool for Shaftesbury's plans. It spent several weeks attacking Danby – who was subsequently imprisoned in the Tower – and listening to further revelations from Oates about the plot. All the while it worked up sufficient courage to pass a bill altering the succession by excluding the Duke of York. This was the most serious challenge to royal prerogative since the Militia Ordinance of 1641 attempted to strip the king's military power. Even an optimistic Duke of Ormond would only predict, 'I think monarchy will not be struck at the root, but I fear it will be very close cropped.'

Whatever Charles thought about his brother, there could be no question of allowing Parliament to dictate the succession. The King had many options: he could attempt to circumvent the bill in the Commons; use his considerable influence to prevent its passage in the Lords; or veto it himself. Nevertheless, he could be neither certain of success nor ignorant of the similarities to the crisis that had overwhelmed his father. Charles had learned those lessons well. He attempted a two-pronged attack against the Commons. To deflate charges of arbitrary government he dismissed his Privy Council and replaced it by co-opting a number of opposition leaders, including Shaftesbury himself, whom he made Lord President. To derail Exclusion, he sent the Duke of York out of the kingdom and offered to sign any reasonable legislation that would limit the powers of a non-Protestant monarch. This pre-emptive strategy initially failed. The Commons read the Exclusion Bill for a second time and Charles dissolved the parliament. But, over the long term, a policy of co-option and compromise split the opposition.

The elections to the second parliament of 1679 took place in an atmosphere of political frenzy. Shaftesbury and his supporters had co-alesced into a political movement soon to be called the Whigs. At the Privy Council, the Earl opposed the dissolution and the Whigs deter-mined to return an even larger Commons majority in favour of Exclusion. Lists were compiled of the 'vile' and the 'worthy', election tactics were formulated, and strategy was coordinated. The Whigs met in London coffee-houses and in the Green Ribbon Club to combine politics and sociability. They orchestrated a lurid press campaign – made possible after the Licensing Act lapsed – to keep up interest in the Popish Plot long enough to influence the October elections. Their reward was a House of Commons solidly behind their programme of Exclusion of the Duke of York, limitation of the royal prerogative, and relief for dissenters.

They faced a resolute King. For one frightening week in August Charles fell deathly ill, and this may have concentrated his mind. He dismissed Shaftesbury from the Privy Council and stripped the Duke of Monmouth of his offices. Though he accepted the inevitability of the Whig electoral victory, the King deprived the parliamentary party of its lifeblood by refusing to allow Parliament to meet, playing a game of cat and mouse through seven prorogations that lasted for a year. The prorogations were unpopular, but their purpose was to frustrate the Whigs. Shaftesbury organized monster petitions demanding a parlia-mentary session; one was a hundred yards in length, with subscriptions taken door to door in London. They had no effect. The Earl even attempted to have the Duke of York indicted as a recusant and the King's mistress as a prostitute, though the judges would not hear the cases.

In the meantime, Charles recouped some strength. He brought pres-sure to bear to achieve the acquittal of the Queen's physician, Sir George Wakeman, on charges that he had plotted to poison the King. Wakeman's trial was the first in which the judges scrutinized the testi-mony of Oates and his confederates, and they easily shredded the tissue of lies. The acquittal was unpopular, especially in London, but the momentum built up by the Popish Plot had finally diminished. More-over, the novel political organization developed by the Whigs came to be imitated by the King's supporters, who were soon labelled Tories.

They too met in London clubs, organized a vigorous press campaign, led by the redoubtable Sir Roger L'Estrange, and solicited support among the masses. Their efforts were mostly reactive, parrying Whig thrusts and then quickly disengaging. Thus the 'petitioners' who demanded that Parliament be allowed to assemble were opposed by the 'abhorrers' whose loyal addresses denounced these efforts to restrict royal prerogative. While Whig propagandists harped upon the dangers from the plot, Tory polemicists revived fears of 'forty-one'.

Parliament finally convened in October 1680, and the large Whig majority in the Commons quickly passed the Exclusion Bill and sent it to the Lords. This was the moment that Shaftesbury was waiting for. Charles II had never yet withstood a confrontation: he had been forced to rescind the Declaration of Indulgence and to accept the two Test Acts and the marriage of William and Mary; he had abandoned Clarendon, Arlington and Louis XIV. His Council pressured him to relent, and even his mistress urged the path of least resistance. Thus Shaftesbury had reason to believe that the King would accept Exclusion and reject his brother. Ever since 1673 Charles had viewed his brother as a political liability. He now sent James into exile in Scotland and urged him to abandon his religion for the sake of the crown.

But the year of prorogations had hardened attitudes all around. The relentless attack on the Duke had given way to an examination of the hereditary right of kings and the power of parliaments. The doctrine of *Salus Populi* was again espoused; the language of liberty was again revived in opposition to the crown. Such arguments relied upon a contract theory of government – a theory which allowed the people to set aside a king. In response, the Tories reburnished the divine right of kings and preached passive obedience to an indefeasible hereditary succession. Sir Robert Filmer's *Patriarcha* (1680), which argued that hereditary monarchy descended from Adam, was published a half-century after it was written. Charles could see it was the monarchy rather than his brother that was at stake. In the Lords, with the King in attendance, a majority of two to one threw out the Exclusion Bill. Infuriated, the Commons attempted to impeach royal officials, judges, even provincial magistrates who opposed Exclusion. They refused to vote any supply, and thus made themselves superfluous. Charles dissolved the second Exclusion Parliament and summoned a third to meet in Oxford two months later.

The governing class was now irredeemably divided. Charles made no secret of his hostility to the Whigs, dismissing all of his counsellors who had voted for the bill and purging the lieutenancies and commissions of the peace of opponents. In the country, sentiment for Exclusion remained strong and many counties returned their sitting MP without even the pretence of selection. The ideological argument had sharpened too, and crown propagandists discovered that people feared rebellion more than popery. Anglican ministers, fearful of anarchy, labelled Exclusion a ploy of the dissenters to destroy church and king, and finally broke down Protestant solidarity against the Plot. In the spring of 1681 Tory mobs replaced Whig ones as the dominant force in London. Histories of the Civil War drew alarming parallels to current events, with Shaftesbury cast in the role of Pym and the Duke of Monmouth in that of Cromwell. Charles twice issued proclamations reasserting Monmouth's illegitimacy. The Protestant Duke would sit on the throne only if he could seize it. Politics increasingly polarized around two choices: loyalty or rebellion. In this atmosphere, the parliament of 1681 assembled in Oxford. Charles was adamant: 'Let there be no delusion, I will not yield, nor will I be bullied.' So too was the Commons, where a motion against Exclusion could not find a second. The King dissolved Parliament within a week.

For the next four years royal government reverted to a style not seen since the 1630s. Every aspect of administration was subjected to a political test. The King cleansed the judiciary of all except loyal judges, making possible capital convictions for sedition and ruinous judgements for slander. Among the victims was Titus Oates, whose lies were no longer convenient and who was fined £100,000 for his attacks on the Duke of York. After a decent period in exile, James was retrieved from Scotland, where he had hammered the Presbyterians and scourged the Whigs. He took Exclusion personally, and savoured his revenge. In contravention of the Triennial Act, Charles summoned no parliaments, purchasing this respite by financial stringencies. He was back on the French payroll, having negotiated an annual subsidy of £125,000 for vague foreign-policy concessions, and rode the crest of the rising tide of European and North American commerce which increased customs. Given the circumstances, he adhered to the advice of his treasurers concerning domestic economies, and the Earl of Rochester, Clarendon's second son, realized the solvency of which Danby had only dreamed.

Most importantly, Charles finally abandoned his expensive dabbling in European affairs, and turned his attention to those he now viewed as enemies at home. The first, of course, was Shaftesbury, whom he had arrested for treason and who escaped with his life only because the grand jury empanelled by the Whig sheriffs of London refused to return an indictment. Shaftesbury's punishment was to be so savagely lampooned by John Dryden in *Absalom and Achitophel* (1682) that his reputation lay in ruins for over two centuries. The Earl fled to Holland and died there of natural causes in 1683. Some of his closest allies were not so lucky. In 1683 perjured testimony was obtained to implicate a number of prominent Whigs in the Rye House Plot, which was an attempt either to assassinate the King and the Duke or to lead an insurrection to bring down the monarchy. Utilizing the dubious precedents established in the Popish Plot, Charles and James took their revenge. William, Lord Russell, who had carried the Commons' Exclusion Bill to the Lords, and Algernon Sidney, a republican theorist, were among those executed, while the Earl of Essex died under mysterious circumstances in the Tower. Others formed the core of a group of Whig exiles in Holland. Rye House provided impetus for the ongoing assault on dissent. Tory propagandists treated its discovery as if it were the Gunpowder Plot. As Anglican addresses of loyalty poured in from the countryside, justices enforced the statutes against dissenters with the utmost rigour. Over 1,300 Quakers were imprisoned during the following year.

Persecution of dissenters struck hardest in London, where the crown felt most vulnerable. As long as Charles pursued an active foreign policy he had to tread carefully around City privileges, for he depended upon London financiers for loans. London had been the headquarters of Shaftesbury and the Exclusionists, and the Green Ribbon Club met openly in the King's Head Tavern in Chancery Lane. Their mobilization of Whig crowds in 1679–80 and again in 1681, whether to burn effigies or to support petitions, demonstrated both the unwillingness and the inability of the London governors to maintain order. The failure to indict Shaftesbury demonstrated their hostility to the court. The crown began its counterattack in 1682 in an election dispute over the London sheriffs. Then the Attorney-General, Sir Robert Sawyer, trumped up charges to be levelled against the Corporation itself, and this ultimately resulted in a *quo warranto* proceeding to confiscate London's charter. Corporate government was a privilege granted by kings, and Charles now declared his willingness to revoke it. Not only were the London livery companies made to pay massive fines to gain reincorporation, their new charter gave the crown the right to veto the election of executive officers.

The attack upon the London charter was a prelude to a widespread campaign to regulate corporations. Despite the Corporation Act of 1661, dissenters had regained urban offices and the oaths of loyalty and non-resistance had become ineffective. While the countryside proved supportive of the crown, urban centres seethed with discontent. The return of so many Whigs to the parliament of 1681 with instructions from their constituencies to support Exclusion demanded action. From 1683 to 1685 the crown reissued charters to fifty-one boroughs. They extended royal control over executive and legal officers, but more importantly they demonstrated that self-government was a tenuous privilege. Indeed, most of the reincorporations resulted from voluntary surrenders and complex negotiations in which the boroughs acquired economic rights in return for surrendering political ones. Though the policy of reincorporation inevitably affected parliamentary representation – some Whigs were purged from closed corporations – its aim was not to pack Parliament with Tories: rather it was to allow the King to exercise control over the localities.

By 1685 Charles II had reacquired the powers that a war-weary nation had freely given him in 1660. His ordinary income had finally reached the level projected for it twenty-five years earlier and was in balance with expenditure for the first time in the seventeenth century. His throne was safe, as was the succession of either his brother or James's children, both of whom, after the marriage of Anne to George of Denmark, had Protestant husbands. The Anglican church was securely established as a bulwark against dissent and Catholicism. It was inseparable from the crown, and preached a doctrine of passive obedience that made church and state one. If England could not be reckoned a military power – Tangiers had been abandoned as indefensible in 1684 – it was certainly a commercial one. Its share of the European carrying trade increased, it challenged the Dutch for supremacy in the East, and it dominated the lucrative North American routes.

But, like his father, Charles II had purchased his power dearly. The governing classes in local communities were ideologically divided over religion and politics. No amount of persecution in London had been able to crush dissent; no amount of favouritism had been able to advance any but a few Catholics. The King could not summon his parliament, and this meant he could pursue no foreign policy other than as a client of Louis XIV. He died in February 1685 with his power intact and his options limited. If he could not have said 'After me, the deluge', he must have known that his brother would not see much sunshine.

11

A Protestant Succession
1685–1689

Westminster Hall had never witnessed a scene like this. On 29 June 1688 the Archbishop of Canterbury and six of his brethren were brought from the Tower of London to answer a criminal complaint of seditious libel made against them by the King of England. They were charged with writing a petition to explain their refusal to obey an order from the King that the Declaration of Indulgence be read in every pulpit. The petition brought the King's government into disrepute and touched James II directly. The case seemed open and shut, even before an English jury. Conventionally the question of whether a petition was seditious was one of law, to be decided by the judges. All the jury would determine was whether the bishops had published it. That they had could hardly be denied. A copy was nailed to every post in London, and their petition had made the bishops instant celebrities.

The crisis had begun in 1687, when James II decided that he could achieve toleration for Catholics only by allying with dissenters. During the first two years of his reign he had supported Tory Anglicans in the hope that they would support his co-religionists. Initially the Anglican hierarchy was willing to withhold the rod from Catholic backs in order to beat more strongly on those of dissenters. But ultimately the Anglicans could not reconcile their principles with those of Rome, and the Tories were unwilling to share power with the King's Catholic confederates. In April 1687 James issued a Declaration of Indulgence which set aside the penal code against Catholics and Protestant dissenters. This reversal of alliances had some effect, but it also drove the Anglican hierarchy into active opposition. The King had already suspended Henry Compton, Bishop of London, in 1686 for failing to suppress anti-Catholic sermons and chose to banish William Sancroft, Archbishop of Canterbury, from court for his refusal to support toleration. A year later James reissued the Declaration with a twist. On

4 May 1688 the Privy Council ordered the diocesan clergy to read the Declaration in their churches, beginning in London two weeks later.

The order was a snare for the clergy in more ways than one. If they obeyed, they would add their moral authority to the King's controversial assertion that he could dispense with the law. If they refused, the Commission for Ecclesiastical Causes could suspend them from their duties as it had Bishop Compton. This left them little choice, and less time to make it. Hurried meetings of clergymen revealed strong opposition to reading the Declaration. Impromptu gatherings of the bishops currently in London uncovered the same sentiment, but the bishops were more cautious. In the first place, they realized that to be successful they would have to be united. They sent letters to those bishops not in London urging their attendance in the capital. In the second place, they could not let their opposition to reading the Declaration drive a wedge between themselves and the Protestant dissenters. Thus they framed their protest around the issue of the king's power to suspend laws made in Parliament. Twice in the reign of Charles II Parliament had declared such a power illegal, and the bishops decided to stand on this ground. Finally, rather than refuse a direct command from the supreme governor of their church, the bishops decided to petition the King to withdraw his order rather than to force the churchmen to disobey it.

They presented their petition in a private interview with James, who had not anticipated this reaction and realized immediately that he had been outflanked. The bishops reasonably requested that they not be ordered to read the Declaration until its legality could be determined in the upcoming parliament. By petitioning the King to withdraw the order, the bishops had effectively expressed their opposition without actually refusing to obey. Moreover, once the petition became public, pressure shifted from the clerics to the monarch. In all of London, only seven clergymen read the Declaration at the appointed time.

On 8 June the bishops were brought before the Council, where they were informed that they would be charged with sedition for publicly disputing the King's commands. But when they were requested to enter a bond for their appearance in court they all refused. If the King wished to treat his loyal clergy as criminals, he would have to imprison them. The sight of seven bishops being marched to the Tower was a public-relations calamity, and even James's closest advisers urged him to find a way to avoid a trial. When the Prince of Wales was born two days later, *it was suggested that a general pardon would do the trick, but the King was obdurate.*

The trial surprised everyone. Immediately it became apparent that the royal judges were divided in their opinion of the case. Against nearly all precedent, they allowed the jury to hear evidence, first on the technical question of whether a petition to the king was a publication within the scope of the Libel Act, and then on the more controversial question of whether this particular petition was libellous. Thus the jury was presented with parliamentary declarations made against the dispensing power in 1673, as well as statements from two of the judges that it was illegal. Despite the fact that the Attorney-General had left nothing to chance – the royal brewer was one of the jurymen – the verdict was not guilty. London erupted in celebration so exultant that the King was disturbed by the noise of exploding cannon. When informed that the bishops had been acquitted, James bristled: 'So much the worse for them.' In fact he had written his own epitaph.

The rule of James II created a crisis for the British monarchy. It revealed the bedrock of commitment to the Protestant religion and the faultlines along which belief in an indefeasible hereditary succession would crack. James's accession was accepted because he promised to rule by the established laws and maintain the independence of the Anglican church. The rebellions against him in Scotland and England that were organized by small groups of extremists were easily crushed. The nation had already returned a conservative, Anglican parliament in 1685 that allowed the King to continue the Tory reaction that had begun at the end of the Exclusion Crisis. As long as James followed in the paths marked out by his brother, he had broad-based support in court and country. The memory of the chaos of the Civil War and Revolution, though now a quarter-century old, still burned bright, and few wished to live through such times again. This was another form of conservatism from which the monarchy benefited.

James II's difficulties were twofold: he was a Catholic zealot and a political reformer. He had the misfortune to rule when neither the élites nor the public would tolerate either. James could not help but push to the limit his desire to remove civil disabilities from his co-religionists or make possible the open practice of Catholicism. He held to his religious principles passionately, and had suffered for them when he was ousted from his offices and exiled to Scotland. Moreover, the agitation for toleration of dissent provided an open door through which he hoped Catholic emancipation might also march. As a political reformer, James did not shrink from centralizing power. He utilized his unlimited patronage to reward and punish on the basis of the narrowest tests of loyalty. At the beginning of his reign, when he believed that he could make an alliance with the Tories, he filled local and central positions with their stalwarts. When the Tories demurred, he purged them ruthlessly in favour of Whigs, dissenters and Catholics. His efforts to control the counties, the towns and ultimately the parliament demonstrated the potential power of the crown – a power that no previous monarch had ever fathomed.

James's policies succeeded in alienating nearly every segment of the political nation, but alienation was not revolution. His downfall came because he allowed himself to become a pawn in the power politics of Europe. His brother had played the same dangerous game, taking subsidies from Louis XIV mostly in return for neutrality, and James had greater personal reasons to be attached to Catholic France. This made it all the more necessary for William of Orange, who led the mostly Protestant coalition against France, to neutralize English sea power before Louis was ready to strike. William's plans for an invasion of England were in the making before either the pregnancy of the Queen was known or the birth of the male heir had occurred, but the prospect of a permanent Catholic dynasty quickened his pace. It also accelerated James's plans to end discrimination against Catholics. In well-publicized assaults upon corporations and colleges the King crystallized his intentions and the opposition to them. When the struggle came, he was deserted on every side.

* * *

James II was fifty-two years old when he came to the throne – an advanced age, which imparted urgency to the King and patience to everyone else. His accession had been dreaded by all but the nation's tiny minority of Catholics, and even they were divided between the English country Catholics, who wanted a quiet life, and the London-based, foreign-bred Catholics trained by the Jesuits, who wanted a national conversion. The Popish Plot and the Exclusion Crisis cast a long shadow across the reign. Rumours that James had poisoned his brother were widespread, while the prosecution of Titus Oates for libel gave his tale of Catholic conspiracy greater credibility. Nevertheless, the change of monarchs was peaceful. Bonfires and bells greeted the new king, and men kept their own counsel when the Anglican portions of the coronation ceremony were deleted. James was the head of a church that preached passive obedience and non-resistance, thus the Anglican establishment necessarily supported him. He was the head of a state that for four years had vigorously persecuted dissenters and Whigs and had reduced their active support to a small hard core. They could expect little favour from the new regime, and that would have to be earned. Their deliverance lay in the fact that James's daughter Mary was heir to the throne, and her Dutch husband, William, was a Calvinist.

In many ways James II was the most capable of all the Stuarts. Decisive and resolute, James had a clear vision of the monarchy and of the state. Though his intellectual gifts were modest and his education haphazard, James pondered problems tirelessly. His conversion to Catholicism resulted from his own conclusion that there was no sufficient justification for the Reformation. He had an unshakeable loyalty to his lineage and his descent. He suffered silently his brother's harsh criticisms and never encouraged the reversionary interest of supporters awaiting his brother's death. Fears that he would set aside his Protestant daughters had no basis in fact and were so alien to his character as to dispel any subsequent notion that the heir he eventually fathered was supposititious. James had a long schooling in English politics and a varied apprenticeship during his brother's reign. In his youth he had mastered the arts of war, and he was a dauntless, if not an effective, general on land and sea. He so willingly hazarded his life that Charles forbade him active command after the Battle of Lowestoft. As Lord Admiral, his administrative abilities earned even Pepys's admiration, and his exclusion from office after the 1673 Test Act deprived Charles of a valuable asset. In 1679 he was sent to Scotland with quasi-regal powers as Commissioner to the Estates, and gained his first experience of personal rule.

Because of its long tradition of Presbyterianism, Scotland found the reign of Charles II especially traumatic. The Scottish Act of Settlement (1662) had re-established episcopacy, but in Scotland episcopacy had simply overlaid the kirk. The decision in England to exclude Presbyterians from the established church created a crisis in the northern kingdom. A small group of privy counsellors headed by the Duke of Lauderdale directed Scottish affairs from London. An original Covenanter, Lauderdale became a leader of the Engagers who had proclaimed Charles II King of Scotland in 1650. He fought at the King's side at Worcester, and was taken captive when Charles escaped. One of the inner circle of ministers from the Restoration, Lauderdale uniquely survived every change of government for twenty years. His power was based on his relationship with the King, who, oddly, never betrayed him.

Lauderdale ruled Scotland according to the precepts set down by English policy, but with a careful eye to punishing his enemies. He drove kirk leaders and former Covenanters from Edinburgh into the western shires, and he enforced the stringent laws against dissent upon them. Nearly a quarter of Scottish ministers were deprived of their livings at the Restoration, and many were subjected to debilitating fines. This led in 1666 to a pathetic revolt whose suppression not only increased the suffering of Presbyterians but allowed the crown to establish a permanent militia to harry them.

In 1677 further penal statutes were passed against Scottish Presbyterians, depriving them of offices and civil rights and forcing landlords to give bond for the behaviour of their tenants. In the next year, the government brought Highland troops to subdue the Lowland population, with predictable results. In 1679 the annual celebration of Charles's coronation became an opportunity for riots in favour of Exclusion, and these developed into rebellion. Charles sent the Duke of Monmouth north to suppress the insurgents, which he promptly accomplished at Bothwell Brid (1679). His efforts to treat the vanquished with mercy were stymied by the Scottish privy council. In this context, James arrived in Edinburgh and achieved passage of bills securing his own succession to the Scottish throne and imposing a Test Act upon Presbyterians every bit as strenuous as the one the English parliament had imposed upon Catholics. There followed a brief reign of terror in which those who scrupled to swear the oaths were treated savagely. The Earl of Argyll was sentenced to death on trumped-up charges of treason – he escaped to Holland – and James watched others undergo the torture of having their legs crushed in a mechanical device known as the boot. He believed that Presbyterianism could be eradicated from his northern kingdom, and one of the first acts of his reign in 1685 made religious dissent a capital crime in Scotland.

Once on the throne, James's principal objective was to alter permanently the disabilities suffered by his co-religionists. In this he was un-likely to receive much help from his ministers. His brothers-in-law, Lord Treasurer Rochester and the Earl of Clarendon, Lord Lieutenant of Ireland, followed their father in a devotion to the Anglican church as a political bulwark to the monarchy. They were capable men who had served the Stuarts faithfully, but neither was strong enough to attempt to guide a headstrong monarch. Clarendon's flaw was greed, Rochester's pride, and both could be satisfied only by the emoluments of high office. Thus to high office they clung. The Marquis of Halifax was an equally staunch Anglican without the redeeming grace of being a Tory. He defined himself as a Trimmer – one who sails between the two parties – and he had survived the last years of Charles's reign by his brilliant abilities and the debt he was owed for the defeat of the Exclusion Bill in the Lords. James could not stand his trenchant wit, and had as much use for a gadfly at his court as his brother had had for a virtuous woman. He soon drove Halifax from the presidency of the Council. Ironically, the King's closest official adviser was the Earl of Sunderland, who had supported Exclusion and who had been turned out of his place as a result. He had wheedled his way back in through the graces of the Queen, and as Principal Secretary he proved a willing tool for all of James's policies. Even in an age renowned for un-principled politicians, Sunderland's career was worthy of study. He had an uncanny ability to change course too soon and still survive the ad-verse winds. He was an Exclusionist who served James II and a Roman Catholic convert who supported William III. He claimed no religious sentiment whatsoever – which diminished the King's feat in converting him – and in politics he favoured unadulterated absolutism.

Sunderland undertook to return a Tory House of Commons to the parliament of 1685. To JPs, Lord Lieutenants and their deputies, and the newly installed officials of the remodelled boroughs he circulated instructions to select loyal Tory members. In fact the campaign was superfluous. The Exclusionists who had dominated the last three parliaments wished to avoid the steely gaze of the King and kept out of sight during the selection process. There were relatively few contested elections, and the House of Commons was composed of nearly 400 first-time members. James declared it as good a parliament as he him-self could have nominated, and his fears that the Commons might withhold revenues until it knew the direction of policy were groundless. He was voted the same supply that his brother had enjoyed, as well as a supplement for the navy. James II became the wealthiest English monarch since Henry VIII, with an average annual income of over £2 million. This was supplemented almost immediately on the news of insurrections in Scotland and the west of England.

The Whig exiles in Holland were a diverse group of republican ideologues, dissenting ministers and outlawed noblemen. A core, including Charles's illegitimate son the Duke of Monmouth, were the remnants of the Rye House plotters. Others were in exile from the Tory persecution that followed. They were a community with neither leadership nor common principle, but they all shared the hope of overthrowing the Stuarts and returning to their homeland. No moment seemed more propitious than the accession of a Catholic king, though it was a measure of their capacities that it took six months to organize an expedition. It was also an omen of the outcome.

The rebellion was to have two prongs. The Earl of Argyll led a landing in Scotland, though he was hamstrung by a divided council of war which vetoed the only sensible strategy of raising an army among Argyll's Highland tenants. This invasion was a short-lived fiasco. The Duke of Monmouth led the second force. For years Monmouth had resisted overtures that he establish himself as a Protestant rival to the Duke of York. If he had any ambitions, they were to supplant York's daughters if James predeceased his brother. Thus he served Charles II capably and unobtrusively, and was himself a victim of the Exclusion Crisis. His personal popularity, based on striking good looks and a crude joviality, became a political liability in 1679. Shaftesbury had never been comfortable with Monmouth and suggested that he be legitimized only after Charles had rejected every other alternative. The crisis created animosity between York and Monmouth that resulted in the latter being stripped of his offices and led to his knowing just too much about the Rye House Plot for his own good. With a father's broken heart, Charles II sent him into exile, where he lived off his wealthy mistress and a state pension. Why Monmouth abandoned this comfort for the rigours of an uncertain military campaign was a question he later came to ponder, and neither he nor anyone else has answered it satisfactorily.

Monmouth represented the Protestant cause, and he could count upon the support of the nation's dissenters. As a direct assault on London was impractical, the West Country, with its tradition of Puritanism in the clothing towns of Dorset, Somerset and

Gloucestershire, was the best option. Monmouth landed at Lyme on 11 June 1685, raised a standard, and recruited over 4,000 men on a platform of annual parliaments, toleration for dissenters and the abolition of the standing army. Some days later he declared himself King. Monmouth's support came from the middling sort of artisans and yeomen. The gentry were staunchly Tory Anglicans, and the local militia raised a better-equipped force of nearly equal number to oppose him – though they were conscripts and Monmouth's men were volunteers. The Duke marched his followers aimlessly through three counties until he offered a daring night-time battle on 6 July at Sedgemoor. The opposing commander slept through his own victory.

Monmouth was led to London for execution, where he disgraced himself by vainly begging James's pardon while his followers were left to the less than tender mercies of Chief Justice George Jeffreys, soon to become James's Chancellor. Jeffreys was brutal and vindictive – traits not entirely appropriate in a legal system which conferred large powers of discretion on judges. He threatened witnesses, bullied jurors, and even browbeat his brother justices. He took pleasure in describing the savage rigours that the law would inflict and delight in pronouncing sentence. He had over 300 supporters of Monmouth executed, and transported hundreds more to almost certain death in the West Indies; and it was said that the blood from quartered bodies ran ankle-deep at Somerset assizes. James applauded Jeffreys's resolve. No Stuart could take armed rebellion lightly – especially not one whose accession was so contested. While a nobler monarch might have tempered justice with mercy, and a gentler one might have sooner slaked his thirst for blood, Monmouth's rebels were traitors and were executed for treason.

The effective suppression of Monmouth's rebellion strengthened the King's hand. There had been no general rising against his government, he had received the complete support of the Anglican hierarchy, and his son-in-law, William of Orange, had even offered to repatriate the British regiments that served in Holland should they be needed. James now resumed the parliamentary session in hope of gaining repeal of the Test Acts which debarred Catholics from office.

If James sufficiently understood his constitutional position to propose these changes to Parliament, he sufficiently misunderstood his political position to think he could get them. Not even 'the most devoted [parliament] that ever was chosen' would re-enfranchise Catholics. Indeed, rather than repeal the Test Acts, Parliament demanded their enforcement. At news of Monmouth's rebellion, James, with parliamentary approval, had commissioned a number of Catholic officers to command the regiments sent west. Parliament insisted they now be dismissed, despite James's argument that he had the right to dispense with the penal laws in individual circumstances. Instead, James prorogued Parliament and spent the next year pressuring individual members to support repeal. This 'closeting' demonstrated that only the most venal would succumb, and that venality was in unexpectedly short supply.

If the King could not achieve toleration of Catholics through Parliament, he still had considerable powers to improve their plight. He sincerely believed that were Catholicism allowed to flourish the nation would gradually be reconverted. In this he was at one with his Anglican opponents, though their analogy was of weeds in a garden. James behaved with the blinkered zeal of a proselyte. Ministers and bishops were horrified when the King allowed the establishment of seminaries in London, sent an envoy to the Pope, and patronized Catholic presses in London and Oxford. He also undertook the redemption of his leading ministers and his daughter Anne, and went so far as to dispatch a priest to Holland for Mary's edification. His singular lack of success – even the Earl of Rochester found something that meant more to him than office – did not deter him, but it proved that he would not be able to convert his government to Catholicism. Thus James fell back upon the dispensing power. He replaced half of the royal judges and then colluded in a case designed to test his prerogative. In *Godden* v. *Hales* (1686) the court decided in favour of the monarch's power to dispense with laws, with the Chief Justice citing as precedent God's commandment that Abraham kill his son.

Armed with impunity, James transformed his government with celerity. In the next month he appointed four Catholics to the Privy Council and created an inner cabinet composed of his Jesuit confessor Edward Petre, Sunderland and Jeffreys. They instituted a purge of recalcitrant MPs from government office and began the formidable task of intruding Catholics into the local magistracy. The commissions of the peace issued for 1686 replaced over 250 JPs with Catholics. Catholics were commissioned into the county militia, and more Catholic officers were appointed to posts in the standing army. The universities – training-ground for the Anglican church – had Catholics imposed upon them, beginning with a head of chapel at Oxford and a master of a college at

Cambridge. When in 1687 James insisted upon the election of a Catholic master at Magdalen College, Oxford, he encountered such stiff resistance that it was necessary to dismiss the entire body of fellows to impose his will. Magdalen became a Catholic college. Finally, in January 1687, James dismissed his brothers-in-law, Rochester and Clarendon, appointing commissioners to run the Treasury and making the Catholic Earl of Tyrconnell deputy Lord Lieutenant of Ireland.

No one greeted James's reign with greater trepidation than the Protestants of Ireland. They had achieved their wealth and power through the subjugation of the Catholic majority and maintained it by military might. Though Charles II had attempted to mitigate the worst excesses of the confiscation of Catholic estates and urged lax enforcement of the penal laws, the Duke of Ormond ruled Ireland with an iron hand. He bought his longevity and autonomy by running the country at a profit and remitting the surplus to London. Tyrconnell had long been a thorn in the side of the Irish government. He complained bitterly of Ormond's administration and the repression suffered by Catholic landowners. A companion of the Duke of York, he was known none too affectionately as 'lying Dick Talbot'. His brother, a Catholic archbishop, had perished in a Protestant prison; Tyrconnell vowed revenge, and kept his word. At his accession James made him lieutenant-general of the Irish army, and Tyrconnell began immediately to purge the ranks of Protestants. In less than a year he had replaced 3,500 soldiers. After Clarendon was dismissed in 1687, Tyrconnell lobbied for his post, though it was unthinkable to appoint a Catholic Lord Lieutenant. James compromised by leaving the lieutenancy vacant and naming Tyrconnell deputy. The ship that brought him to Dublin returned to England filled with wealthy Protestants fleeing his regime. In the next year he replaced every Protestant sheriff and confiscated the charter of every Irish borough. Fewer than 500 Protestants remained in the army.

James's policy in Ireland belied his oft-repeated claim that he had no intention of establishing Catholicism at the expense of the Anglican church but simply aimed to remove the disabilities from which Catholics suffered. The new Irish refugees told lurid tales of a Catholic ascendancy. Protestant sensibilities were already heightened by Louis XIV's revocation of the Edict of Nantes, which for nearly a century had limited Protestant persecution in France. Once James began dispensing with the penal laws, the pulpits of London quaked with denunciations of popery and the presses emitted an avalanche of anti-Catholic tracts. Though the King did not seek a confrontation with the leadership of the church, he would not shrink from one. He issued orders that the bishops restrain anti-Catholic preaching, and when these proved ineffective he created a Commission for Ecclesiastical Causes which appeared suspiciously similar to the outlawed Court of High Commission. William Sancroft, Archbishop of Canterbury, was appointed its head, but he refused to participate and Sunderland served as stalking-horse for the King. The Commission's first work was to suspend Henry Compton, Bishop of London, from office for his refusal to remove a rabidly anti-Catholic minister from his London pulpit.

By the end of 1686 James realized that the greatest obstacle to his programme of Catholic emancipation was the established church itself. With the exception of Jeffreys and a few others, the Tories had proven more Anglican than absolutist and blocked his manœuvring for parliamentary repeal of the Test Acts at every turn. Already he had struck up an unlikely friendship with William Penn, who in 1682 had founded a Quaker colony in North America, and their relationship led to the release of over 1,000 Quakers from imprisonment. Now he declared himself willing to license dissent as long as it was practised peaceably. Penn's influence on the King was all the more remarkable in that he had supported Exclusion and was the acknowledged leader of the most obdurate of all dissenters. But Penn's charisma was universally acknowledged, the two had endured personal persecution, and they were both simple idealists who believed in the potency of religious conviction. Thus Penn persuaded James to adopt the discarded programme of the early 1670s and issue a Declaration of Indulgence. This James did in 1687, based on his dispensing authority confirmed by the judges and with the knowledge that he would dissolve the parliament of 1685 without bringing it back into session.

James based his decision to build an alliance upon a combination of Catholicism and dissent on two fatal misunderstandings. The first was that the Anglican majority was hoist on its own petard of passive obedience and posed no threat to this change in policy. The second was that dissent was a large and potent force. James could be excused both miscalculations. The former was informed by his dealings with the time-serving Anglicans in his own administration; the latter on the Utopian aspirations of Penn and the exaggerated propaganda of polemicists. Moreover, his own experiences confirmed his assumptions.

He had found Anglican judges to uphold his powers, bishops to cast a blind eye on Catholic worship, and magistrates to prosecute his foes. When he dismissed loyal servants like Halifax, Rochester and Clarendon they went quietly home. Now James determined to put out thousands of Anglicans from the military, the commissions of the peace and the urban corporations. London was stripped of prominent Anglican aldermen, militia captains and members of livery companies. A new attack on corporate charters began – this one led by Chancellor Jeffreys. Towns that had recently paid for the privilege of casting out dissenters now paid to have them put back in – many as returning-officers in parliamentary boroughs. Over 2,000 changes took place. Unlike his brother's campaign, which aimed at maintaining local order, James's aimed at packing Parliament. Sunderland circularized the Lord Lieutenants with orders to put three questions to all JPs and members of parliamentary corporations: if elected to Parliament would they support the repeal of the Test Acts, would they support the promulgation of the Declaration of Indulgence, and would they pledge to give their votes only to members who would? The three questions became the litmus test for employment in local government.

Although William Penn had organized petitions of thanks from some dissenting congregations, and others cooperated willingly with James's policies, the majority of dissenters remained aloof. They could hardly refuse freedom of worship, but they looked askance at offers of political appointments. Presbyterian leaders, who only too recently had felt the lash of Jeffreys's tongue, refused all overtures. The case against cooperation was put with devastating effectiveness in *A Letter to a Dissenter* (1687), published anonymously by the Marquis of Halifax. With measured prose, subtle argument and irrefutable logic, Halifax exposed the paradox of an alliance of dissenters and Catholics – 'of Liberty and Infallibility'. Characteristically, he urged inaction, in the belief that Protestant toleration would not have to be purchased at the price of Catholic emancipation in the reign of the next monarch. Indeed, when James attempted to gain the approval of his daughter and son-in-law for a policy of toleration he was strongly rebuked. William of Orange drew the precise distinction between freedom of worship (which he supported) and political empowerment (which he opposed). He would not endorse the Declaration of Indulgence nor what the Anglicans were now labelling the 'suspending' power – the right James claimed not only to dispense with the laws in individual cases but to suspend them entirely. These publicly expressed opinions gave comfort to Anglicans and dissenters alike, until it became known, in November 1687, that Queen Mary Beatrice was pregnant.

There were several potential outcomes to the Queen's pregnancy, and an age which saw the invention of 'political arithmetic' by Sir William Petty and Gregory King might have been comforted that only one was a live male heir. But, though her other children had died in infancy, from the moment the news became public no one considered any other possibility than that she would give birth to a boy who would live and be raised Catholic and so make permanent the temporary aberration of a Catholic monarchy. One Catholic's letter of congratulation prophesied that his 'cradle is the tomb of heresy and schism'. This was certainly how the court viewed the situation where the King's policy of combining the ends against the middle now had the goal of securing a Catholic succession. The campaign to select a compliant parliament was stepped up as commissioners visited every parliamentary borough to compile information on the nature of the franchise, the identity of civic dignitaries and the influence of outside patrons. More Tories were put out of local government and replaced with Whigs, dissenters and Catholics. In April 1688 the King decided to reissue the Declaration of Indulgence and require that it be read in all of the nation's churches. Though Indulgence had been official policy for nearly a year, the reassertion of James's right to dispense with the laws was more ominous in the context of a potential Catholic heir. By mid-May the London clergy had decided to refuse to read the Declaration in their pulpits and, as we have seen, seven bishops petitioned the King to rescind the order. By now it was known that the Queen would not miscarry, and James determined to bring the Anglican church to heel. He hauled the bishops before the Privy Council and threatened them with criminal prosecution. They stood their ground. Parliament had declared the dispensing power illegal, and they could not endorse it. The seven bishops were tried for seditious libel and were acquitted by a London jury. Though the result was a defeat for the King, his mind was elsewhere. After several weeks of hovering between life and death, James Francis Edward Stuart, Prince of Wales, had survived.

The birth of a male heir had impact beyond the confines of English politics. For one thing, it altered the succession and displaced Mary and her Dutch husband, William, who was himself third in line to the English throne through his mother, Mary Stuart. William of Orange was a Protestant prodigy. Through his veins coursed the blood of William the Silent, Henry of Navarre, James of Scotland and Christian of Denmark – all luminaries in the galaxy of reformed princes. At the age of twenty-two he had been thrust into the role of saviour of the United Provinces and had spent his every waking moment combating the menace of Catholic France. William was cold-blooded and ruthless, sombre and haughty – what his friends called determined and aloof. 'The depression of France was the governing passion of his whole life', and he pursued it with every weapon at his disposal but compromise. Until now he had displayed tact in his relations with his father-in-law and cunning in his relations with James's ministers, most of whom cultivated Mary's reversionary interest with titbits of information and hints of support. But the tides were once again shifting, and the birth of the Prince of Wales was only one of the waves crashing against the Dutch shore.

Though thought to be a sated power, Louis XIV was again mobilizing his armies. In the past year he had abrogated the tariff concessions made in the Treaty of Nijmegen, assaulted Dutch shipping, and begun to deploy his forces. In Holland, mercantile interests shifted from opposition to William's claims of monarchical power to support for his military operations, providing him with the funds necessary to prepare for war. All Europe braced itself for the attack that would come in the spring of 1689. Against just this eventuality William had reconstructed the League of Augsburg – the Grand Alliance which had isolated France from all of the major states of Europe but England. Like his brother, James II was on the French payroll. He had begun taking subsidies at his accession, and his dependence grew with the dissolution of Parliament, though his increasing customs revenues should have kept him afloat. An Anglo-French alliance would force William to fight a war on two fronts, and he alone would take the brunt of the English navy.

Thus William and the political leaders of the United Provinces decided to accept an 'invitation' sent to him by seven politicians on 30 June 1688 to come to England and investigate the circumstances of the birth of the Prince of Wales and the condition of English liberties. If he could shackle James with a parliament, he could either bring Britain to his side or keep it out of the war.

The invitation came as no surprise, for the Dutch had already been making preparations for a military invasion of England. Through his agents, William had been organizing an English fifth column for over a year. In June he had requested the invitation from, among others, the Tory Earl of Danby, the Whig Earl of Shrewsbury, Bishop Compton of London, and, most importantly, Henry Sidney, who had been Dutch envoy under Charles II and whose brother Algernon had been executed for his supposed part in the Rye House Plot. 'The immortal seven', as they later came to be called, kept William informed of disaffection in James's military and gained specific pledges of support from commanders in both the army and the navy.

Though the invitation urged haste, another four months passed before William could assemble his force. The last successful naval invasion of England had occurred in 1485, and the logistical problems were still formidable. The seaborne operation had to evade the superior English navy, while the landing-party might face James's large standing army. Moreover, William had to succeed quickly. He could not have his crack regiments in England when Louis XIV invaded the Netherlands.

While William was well informed of England's domestic and international policies, James was unaware of his son-in-law's intentions. Though there had been a dispute between the two over the return of the British regiments lent to the Dutch, James did not seriously entertain the possibility that his own daughter would sanction an unprovoked attack. Dutch envoys played on the King's credulity so skilfully that when Louis XIV offered to place his Atlantic fleet at England's disposal James assured him it would not be necessary. Not until the end of September did James realize that Dutch military preparations were directed against him rather than Louis. By then it was too late to recall the French fleet from the Mediterranean and almost too late to prepare his own defences.

Instead, James attempted to prevent the invasion by political means. Abruptly he reversed the policies that depended on an alliance between Catholics and dissenters and which had rehabilitated the Whigs. At the end of September 1688 he announced that no Catholics would be allowed to sit in the upcoming parliament – a decision rendered superfluous two weeks later when he cancelled the session. To make amends with the Anglican hierarchy, James rehabilitated Bishop Compton, abolished the hated Commission for Ecclesiastical Causes, and restored the former fellows of Magdalen College. To make amends with the urban oligarchs, he reincorporated London and abrogated all of the charters imposed since 1679. This restored Tory mayors, aldermen and councillors to their places and effectively ended the campaign to secure a compliant parliament by controlling the electorate. In the counties, Tory JPs, Lord Lieutenants and militia officers were similarly reinstated, but they proved less eager than corporate officers to resume their places – 'some would think one kick of the breech enough for a gentleman'. Indeed, this new round of ejections left local government in a shambles at precisely the moment when the King needed to impose order. At court, James was buffeted between his hard-line Catholic ministers who urged defiance and the Tory time-servers who counselled compromise. He would heed the first if the invasion came, but for the moment his political volte-face might pay larger dividends.

The King's new domestic programme was forthrightly mendacious: 'to still the people, like plums to children', critics contended. So were his diplomatic overtures to the Dutch with offers of English neutrality. But both had the effect of undercutting the need for an invasion to 'preserve and maintain the established laws, liberties and customs' of England, as William claimed was his intention in the declaration he issued in October.

The declaration was a masterpiece of propaganda, the culmination of decades of Dutch manipulation of English public opinion. In it William disingenuously emphasized that he had been invited to come to England to inquire into the condition of civil and religious liberties. He did not mention his military objectives or his alliance with the Whigs, stressing instead the need to protect established religion, ensure the independence of the judiciary, and secure the election of a free Parliament. He gave no details as to how this might be accomplished. The declaration also hinted darkly at the circumstances of the birth of James's heir, invigorating the rumour that the Prince had actually been slipped into the Queen's bedchamber in a warming-pan. William called for an investigation to protect the hereditary rights of his wife. Sixty thousand copies were printed for distribution, and were kept so secret that it was not until weeks later that James II learned of its existence.

William's declaration was the political arm of an impressive amphibious operation. He assembled a force of over 20,000 soldiers, including his most reliable veterans. He provided the cavalry with 5,000 horses and the heavy equipment with an additional 2,000 draught animals. A flotilla of nearly 500 vessels was to supply logistical support on the long march towards London. Though William had been assured of English support once he landed, his plans did not rely upon it: his operation was self-sufficient. Preparations were minutely detailed and William left only one thing to chance: the wind which would propel him across the Channel. He intended to make an attempt in mid-October, but a storm battered the Dutch coast and drove the fleet back to port with minor damage. This would have been an opportunity for the English to strike first – a thought which crossed the mind of Admiral Lord Dartmouth – but the moment passed. There was still consternation at the audacity of William's plan to cross the Channel in the autumn and confidence that it could not succeed – 'I cannot see much sense in their attempt,' Dartmouth wrote. If they were not battered in port they were certain to be blown off course. This conventional wisdom would have been true enough had William a single destination. Instead he let the wind be his guide. He encouraged his English supporters in both the North and the West to expect his arrival, and waited until he was in open sea before choosing. The so-called 'Protestant wind' drove the Dutch at racing speed to the West Country while holding the English fleet at bay. On 5 November 1688 English Protestants had more to celebrate than the failure of the Gunpowder Plot: William had landed at Torbay in Devonshire.

All the while that William staked his life and the fate of his country on the open seas, James attempted to shore up his support. He convened a meeting of his Privy Council and other political notables, which included dismissed Tories like the Earl of Clarendon, to present incontrovertible proof of the legitimacy of his son. He launched an investigation to identify the signatories of the invitation to William, though most were already safely out of the country. Only Bishop Compton was directly confronted, and he replied casuistically. While his Catholic counsellors were preparing for war, James twice summoned the bishops and pressured them to issue an 'abhorrence' of the imminent invasion. With delicious irony, Archbishop Sancroft informed the King that they had recently been imprisoned for meddling in 'matters of civil government' and had learned their lesson. They could offer the King no help other than their prayers. Finally James concluded, 'I must stand upon my own legs, and trust to myself and my own arms.'

Superficially, James's arms and legs were strong enough. His professional army numbered over 25,000, and the county militias were at least as large. Although William brought a large professional army, he had the logistical problems of an invasion. He took two weeks to disembark and supply his forces, setting up headquarters at Exeter for the purpose. The mass defections of English soldiers that he had anticipated – one of his ships carried arms to be distributed to English recruits – never materialized, and there was at least a moment when it appeared that a winner-take-all battle between evenly matched forces would take place. For James, against the advice of his Catholic confessor and his leading privy counsellors, had left London on 17 November for Salisbury, where his army was encamped. But once he arrived he completely lost his nerve. Suffering from insomnia and severe nosebleeds, he mistakenly concluded that his army was too unreliable to be sent into battle. The next day two of his leading commanders, John Churchill and the Duke of Grafton, went over to William.

On 23 November James returned to London, where even worse news awaited him. His daughter Anne had fled to the Midlands, where insurgents for William had successfully captured many major towns. The King summoned all of the peers who remained in the capital, and they advised him to call Parliament and offer a pardon to William and his supporters. Distraught and humiliated, James sent Halifax, Nottingham and the Earl of Godolphin to negotiate while he raged Lear-like against the perfidy of Churchill and the ingratitude of his daughter. Secretly he began to make plans for flight.

The negotiators received a cool reception in William's camp. Halifax and Nottingham had refused to sign the letter of invitation and had thus lost most of their credit with William's English entourage. Despite the fact that the calling of a 'free parliament' had been the first of William's promises, there was now much opposition from the Whigs, who had not had time to canvass for seats. In the short, wet December days, amid sputtering camp-fires and contradictory advice, William had his first glimpse of what would become years of impenetrable English political rivalries. He offered concessions designed to avoid a war – his army would remain as far from London as James's if the King would surrender the Tower and the Thames forts – and declared himself for a free parliament.

At this moment William still did not know the strength of his military position nor the complexity of his political situation. Both were dramatically brought home with the news that James had fled London. He had secreted the Queen and his son aboard a French ship, and once he was sure they were safe he had taken flight himself. Before leaving he ordered the disbandment, but not the disarming, of his forces;

destroyed the writs for a parliamentary election; and tossed the great seal of England into the Thames. This would create the maximum amount of chaos for his opponents. London exploded when it realized the King was gone. Every Catholic chapel in the City was attacked, and some were demolished to the 'girders and joists'. The resident peers and City governors became self-appointed policemen and barely re-established order.

It is unclear who was more disconcerted by what happened next, James or William. Heavily disguised, the King made his way to the Kentish coast, where a small vessel awaited his arrival. But, before he could get away, a party of fishermen trawling for escaping priests netted the King and his companions. They were none too delicately strip-searched – the King's prize crucifix was confiscated – and were subsequently frog-marched to the nearest town. It was only then that James was recognized.

News that James had escaped to France had already reached William's quarters, along with an invitation from the Court of Aldermen to come to London. This was a totally unexpected develop-ment, with complex constitutional ramifications. Almost immediately his Whig supporters urged him to take the crown, and he was marching towards the City when the unexpected report of James's capture arrived. William soon knew that James had returned to London amid cheering crowds, and he halted his own progress to avoid a confronta-tion. But the Dutchman would not now be denied his triumph. He sent an imperious order that James vacate the City within ten hours and then dispatched an escort (but not a guard) of Dutch troops to speed him on his way to Rochester. They proved conspiratorially incompe-tent, as James easily escaped and for the second time found himself in a small boat on the Kentish coast. This time he succeeded in sailing to France.

Events had moved much faster than anyone could have imagined. Even if he wished it, William had not invaded England with the inten-tion of becoming king; nor would he have received the enthusiastic support of Anglicans and Tories if he had. The Tories' backing was proleptic – they had not thought out the consequences of their actions: 'how these risings and associations can be justified, I see not; but yet it is very apparent had not the Prince come and these persons thus ap-peared our religion had been rooted out'. But neither were the Whigs united. Some wished William to take the throne as a conqueror and to establish parliamentary, if not popular, sovereignty. Others simply wished for an assured Protestant succession, to set aside James and install Mary. William refused to be tied by 'apron-strings', as he put it, and would not follow the precedent of Philip II and serve only as his wife's consort. His demands were crucial, for, as Halifax observed, 'as nobody knew what to do with him, so nobody knew what to do without him'. Now it was necessary for everyone to find a way to fit reality within their principles. James's flight created a constitutional crisis of the first order.

When he arrived in London, William summoned a meeting of members of the parliaments of Charles II who were in the capital. By excluding representatives of James's parliament, this assembly was strongly Whig, but there was no precedent for its existence or its authority. It was a fig-leaf for William's naked power – as was the Convention which, on their advice, he summoned to meet on 22 January. The elections for the Convention came off quietly; neither the populace nor the gentry held strong convictions as to the best course of action, and communities did not even divide along party fault-lines. Despite their foreboding, the Whigs secured a majority in the Commons, but the Tories were well represented and from the first a spirit of compromise was manifest. There was still the possibility of civil war or foreign invasion; still the chance that Ireland or Scotland would erupt in rebellion. No one wanted an impasse – William least of all. Indeed, the most remarkable aspect of the Convention was that it solved the knottiest constitutional crisis in English history in little more than two weeks.

There was a wide divergence of opinion as to what should be done. In the House of Lords there was a core of Jacobites who would accept no solution other than the immediate restoration of James II. They were led by Archbishop Sancroft and four others of the seven bishops who had opposed James's ecclesiastical policies as a breach of law and could hardly support an even greater breach of law to overturn them. They adhered to the doctrines of non-resistance and indefeasible hereditary succession, and gave no comfort to those Tories who believed they could have both William and their principles. A much larger group of lords favoured a regency. Mary and William would rule as regents during the life of James II and as monarchs thereafter. A regency salved the consciences of those who did not wish to break the line of succession. Nearly everyone affected amnesia about the Prince of Wales, preferring to call him 'the little gent' or 'the little brat' on the few occasions he was mentioned at all. Thus the regency would restore the succession as it existed up to 10 June, and it would allow those who supported Mary's rights to pretend that she was the lawful monarch. This proposal might have carried in the Lords had not William, Mary and Anne all made known their opposition to it. As it was, it lost by only three votes.

In the Commons the spectrum of opinion was narrower, and the Whigs quickly devised the argument that James II had broken his contract with the people, subverted fundamental law, and 'having withdrawn himself out of this kingdom, has abdicated the government; and that the throne is thereby vacant'. This formulation contained a number of dubious constitutional arguments that became the core of debate at the end of January. Moderates in the Commons objected to the notion that government was by contract between the king and the people – a view that would soon receive its quintessential expression in the second of John Locke's *Two Treatises of Government* (1690). Others objected to the word 'abdicated'. This was not a word known in English constitutional law – an effort was made to substitute the more proper 'demised' – and it did not fit the circumstances after letters were received from James declaring his willingness to rule if Parliament would guarantee his safety. But the sharpest conflict was over the circumlocution that the throne was vacant. The whole premise of hereditary succession was that the throne was never vacant: it passed instantaneously from holder to heir: 'The King is dead, long live the King!' If the throne was vacant, and if Parliament could fill it, then the nation had passed to elective monarchy. The Whigs denied this conclusion: they were simply dealing with the practical effects of the situation. As the London lawyer Sir George Treby summarized the case, 'We have found the crown vacant. We found it so, we did not make it so.' This was the heart of the matter: the denial of revolutionary intent and of revolutionary responsibility. However dangerous was the formulation of abdication and vacancy, it was far less dangerous than the formulation of deposition and rebellion.

This was how the Commons argued the case when it sent its resolution to the Lords. The Lords debated it for an entire day and night without conclusion. On 30 January – the anniversary of the execution of Charles I – the Lords attempted several amendments, including substituting the word 'deserted' for 'abdicated' and subsequently deleting the clause declaring the throne vacant. This again expressed the predilection in the Lords for Mary's rights, as either queen, regent or consort, but it broke apart the careful consensus between Whigs and Tories crafted in the Commons. Two days later the Lower House adhered to its own resolution and in conference pressured the Lords to accept the original wording. For four days there was impasse as each House refused to give way. The Commons continued to insist on the ambiguity of the words it had chosen, denying that it intended to initiate an elective monarchy. The pressure on the Lords became excruciating after William threatened to return to Holland rather than accept a regency. Finally, on 6 February, the Upper House cracked. The Lords accepted the Commons' resolution and declared William and Mary king and queen of England.

In the end, agreement was reached because the largest numbers of Lords and Commons could interpret the resolution in their own way. For the Tories, the abdication consisted of James's flight, the vacancy of his physical absence. For the Whigs, the abdication consisted of his violation of the fundamental laws, the vacancy of his failure to fulfil the contract between ruler and ruled. The glory of the Revolution settlement was that it drove people with incompatible views towards each other despite the passion of beliefs and the heat of the moment. The London riots in early December had been as much a demonstration as a rampage, but there was genuine fear of mob violence and foreign invasion throughout the winter. The memory of the English Revolution was fresh in mind as members of the Convention struggled to fit political reality into the grid of constitutional theory. Even most of the radical Whigs believed that they were completing the work of 1660 rather than of 1649, and reports that the regicide Edmund Ludlow had returned to England led to a warrant for his arrest.

Thus, while the debates on the succession proceeded, the politicians were also at work producing a Declaration of Rights which would affirm the political principles to which they could all adhere. These debates, too, were contentious, for those who adhered to the contract theory of government saw the Declaration as an opportunity to add clauses that would bind the king. But in order to achieve consensus within the press of time it was agreed that the purpose of the Declaration was 'not for making new laws but declaring old'. Again the lawyers who drafted the Declaration chose ambiguous language that would allow radical Whigs and conservative Tories to support a single set of rights and allow king and Parliament to agree to them. The dispensing power, the abuse of legal proceedings, the standing army were all swept away. Rights of petition, of free elections and of consent to taxation were all confirmed.

Acceptance of the Declaration of Rights was not a requirement for William and Mary to receive the crown. Not only would William have rejected any quid pro quo, but such a condition would have been a more forceful statement of elective monarchy than even the most extreme interpretation of the words 'abdicate' and 'vacant'. Rather, the elaborate ceremony in which the monarchs were installed included a reading of the Declaration before the crowns were offered and a statement about it by William afterwards. 'As I had no other intention in coming hither than to preserve your religion, laws and liberties, so you may be sure that I shall endeavour to support them.' Less than two months before, William had entered London 'led by the hand of heaven and called by the voice of the people'. Now he was king.

12

A European Union
1689–1702

William III gazed through his field-glass at the Jacobite positions across the River Boyne on the afternoon of 30 June 1690. Here he intended to fight, just weeks after landing his army near Belfast. He had brought over 15,000 soldiers, including crack cavalry regiments, his Dutch guards and a detachment of hardened Danish mercenaries. These joined the 20,000 men that the Duke of Schomberg had commanded for the past year – a collection of Germans, Dutch, English volunteers and the Scottish and English planters who had held off the offensive of James II the previous summer. James had landed in Ireland in March 1689 with a French expeditionary force led by the comtye de Lauzun. He was the first English king to set foot there in 300 years, and Catholic Ireland flocked to his colours. It was said that he could command over 100,000 soldiers, though most were raw country lads – unfed, un-equipped, unsupplied – and his actual strength was nearer 25,000 as the day of battle approached.

James arrived at the Boyne first, and made his encampment on the Dublin side of the river. Lauzun discouraged him from making a stand at the Boyne, urging a retreat to Dublin and beyond, where high walls rather than low tides might provide protection. But James believed, as did his opponents, that the Boyne was the walls of Dublin, for if he could not stop William there his forces would be swept away. More-over, he held the better position both for bombarding an enemy and for repelling an attack. Mortars placed on Donore Hill would create havoc among advancing infantry, while the stone farmhouses on the river-bank provided perfect cover for sharpshooters. Three bridges crossed the river, though James's forces had demolished the southernmost one near Slane and could hold the northernmost one with their forces at Drogheda. The battle would come in the centre. James therefore con-centrated his army in the great bend of the river at Oldbridge, setting *field-pieces on the hill and snipers on the river-bank, and concealing his army in the folds of the sloping terrain.*

This array made reconnoitring difficult, and neither William nor his scouts had been able to estimate the size or disposition of the forces they would face. Thus, after viewing the scene from the rise on the river's northern bank, William descended to the shore for closer inspection. After dismounting to rest, he and his generals were recognized by sentinels on the other bank. A troop of James's horse drew up opposite, but the Jacobites kept their distance and seemingly showed no inclination to fight. Their presence, however, diverted attention from the placement of two artillery pieces to cover the path that William would have to take back to his headquarters. When the King retraced his steps, two shots boomed out. The first passed overhead and felled some horses a hundred yards away. The second struck short, hitting the river-bank and ricocheting high in the air. As William heard the equine agonies and turned to see the puffs of smoke, his coat and doublet ripped away from his shoulder and blood specked his linen. A great shout rose from James's camp, and a French emissary dispatched tidings of William's death to Paris, where it was greeted with bonfires in the street. On both sides of the river it was believed the King had been killed.

But the reports of the death of William III were greatly exaggerated. 'It's well it came no nearer' were William's first words after he realized that the ball had missed piercing his chest by inches. His shoulder was grazed, but the damage was no greater than that. He spent the next few hours riding among his army to demonstrate both his existence and his fitness. His bravery was in sharp contrast to James's conduct in 1688.

That night William plotted strategy with his council and determined upon a two-pronged assault. A quarter of his army, with Schomberg in command, would march two miles south, ford the river, and circle behind the enemy. The bulk of his force would charge straight across at Oldbridge.

By six o'clock on the morning of 1 July, Schomberg was in the water and, at the cost of his own life, his troops had reached the other bank. Thousands of Williamite soldiers followed, which forced James to shift his reserves up-river to prevent his being outflanked. At 10 a.m. William's famed Dutch guards waded into the Boyne at Oldbridge. Four hours of artillery shelling had demolished the farmhouses and James's advance guard. Still the attempt to cross the river met stout resistance, and over 250 men on both sides were killed. After nearly an hour of fierce hand-to-hand combat, almost 20,000 of William's men had crossed to the south side of the river. William himself had made the crossing to the north of Oldbridge and was soon in the thick of the fighting, bombarded by the Irish in front and his own troops from behind. His flanking action had surprised everyone and had put James's forces in mortal danger as they faced assault from three sides at once. As his Irish regiments bravely defended the face of Donore Hill, the greater part of James's infantry stood helpless behind it. What had begun as a closely contested battle, with heroic bravery on both sides, now changed into a rout. The Jacobite army stampeded south, and an orderly retreat was enforced only after commanders fired upon their own regiments. None flew faster than James II. He stayed overnight in Dublin, raced to Duncannon the following day, and put to sea, leaving his kingdoms for ever. The largest pitched battle in Ireland's history was over. So, too, was the only serious challenge to William's rule.

It was a tribute to the fear and loathing that James II had inspired that Englishmen would turn to a foreigner for a replacement. Throughout his reign William III had to overcome the disability of being foreign. There was constant suspicion that he was concerned more with the welfare of Holland than of England, that his countrymen came as locusts to impoverish the land, that he was another William the Conqueror. He spent much of each year out of England, and his returns were timed to parliamentary sessions where he asked his subjects for ever-greater taxes to support ever-larger armies.

William's first challenge was to survive. His accession initiated brutal warfare in Ireland and Scotland. The threat of James II's restoration hung constantly over his head, and many of his leading ministers were in secret correspondence with the deposed king. Not trusting anyone other than his Dutch companions, William conducted British foreign policy in secrecy from the British. War dominated ten of the thirteen years of his reign, and his great achievement was to battle Louis XIV to a stalemate. To achieve even this he had to turn the English gaze outward, to Europe and to a larger role in world affairs. It was William III who made Britain a military power and who created its first European union.

William's reign was notable for three developments, none consciously pursued by the King. The first was the creation of a parliamentary monarchy. While there were radical Whigs who wished to embody principles which restricted royal prerogatives in the Declaration and then the Bill of Rights, the milestones were in fact quite different. Yearly sessions of Parliament were necessitated by near-constant warfare and the fact that Parliament would only vote military supply annually. Parliament assumed responsibility for royal income through the creation of the civil list, which made the king a parliamentary dependant. Finally, Parliament established the contractual nature of royal government in the Act of Succession, which not only specified the line of descent but attempted to restrict the prerogatives of William's Hanoverian heirs.

The second development was a corollary of the first: the coalescence of party divisions. Whatever their origins, political parties took shape in the reign of William III, when Whigs and Tories battled each other for power and influence. If the purse was the lever by which Parliament controlled the King, party was the lever by which the King controlled Parliament. The usefulness of ministers and ministries was in direct proportion to their ability to pass William's programmes. His willingness to discard one party in favour of the other – though he personally decried party division – effectively controlled both parties and restrained parliamentary independence.

The final development began the process by which Britain became the financial centre of the world. Public confidence in the long-term stability of the monarchy and belief in its bonds and notes allowed for the expansion of credit that financed the European wars. The Bank of England and the national debt – fortuitous innovations that they were – catapulted Britain into the vanguard of world commerce.

*　　*　　*

It was easier for William III to acquire the English crown than it was for him to hold it. The spirit of compromise that had allowed the Convention to find points of agreement passed with the constitutional crisis. The scramble for office and the jealousies it entailed caused one kind of political division; opposing views of the monarch and the monarchy caused another. William was confronted by bewildering paradoxes. His Whig supporters believed in parliamentary sovereignty; his Tory opponents believed in the divine right of kings. The radical Whigs, who were republicans, had sponsored William's kingship; the radical Tories, who were loyalists, had acquiesced in James's removal. The principles which had brought the parties into existence – Exclusion for the Whigs and passive obedience for the Tories – were now altogether irrelevant, and the parties were held together only by past experience and personal loyalties. This gave the King the opportunity to use them to his own advantage.

In the government that William appointed after he and Mary were formally crowned in April 1689 he fell back upon those who had served Charles II. The Marquis of Halifax emerged as the King's closest confidant. He had been dismissed by James, and his aloofness from party politics exactly fitted William's desire to balance Whigs and Tories. Though Halifax had refused to sign the invitation to invade, he had smoothed William's path to the throne by chairing debates in the House of Lords during the Convention. There he had opposed a regency and had brought the peers into line with the Commons at the crucial moment in support of William's kingship. Halifax was admired for his intellect, feared for 'his piercing wit and pregnant thought', and distrusted for his independence. He became Lord Privy Seal, with constant access to the King. The Earl of Danby was also exhumed from the graveyard of discarded politicians. Danby had avoided the bitter party strife of the previous decade because he had spent so much of it in prison. He had impeccable anti-French credentials, was the ablest English Treasurer of the century, and had arranged the marriage of William and Mary. He was also an intolerant Anglican and an inveterate meddler. Danby had signed the invitation to William and had organized a rising in Yorkshire which, were it not for the westerly gales, would have welcomed the Dutchman to England. After supporting the bill for a regency, Danby tacked behind the winds that blew for kingship, and the support of his small faction made clear sailing in the Lords for the proposal to offer William the crown. Danby was frustrated when the Treasury was put into the hands of commissioners and he had to settle for the presidency of the Council. For his Secretaries, William balanced the Tory Nottingham and the Whig Shrewsbury. Alongside this motley foursome, the King relied upon members of his Dutch entourage, especially his favourite William Bentinck, whom William created Earl of Portland at his accession. At the xenophobic English court, Portland became a whipping-boy in the style of James I's Scottish favourites, and the wealth he amassed diminished the King's credit.

None of these officers had a powerful grip on English politics – Halifax, Shrewsbury and Sidney Godolphin, the ablest of the Treasury lords, resigned within the year – and this could be seen in the independent line taken by the Convention after it declared itself a parliament in February 1689. Predictably, the first issue combined religion and politics. Just as after the Restoration, William's desire for religious comprehension clashed with the interests of the Anglicans. It was Nottingham who cut through the thicket of the new oaths of allegiance by devising a formula that avoided the question of whether William and Mary were rightful sovereigns – though not even this formulation could persuade Archbishop Sancroft, seven other bishops and about 400 clergymen to abjure their allegiance to James, an upheaval in the church unknown since the Restoration settlement. By refusing to pledge obedience to the supreme governor of their church, they became known as nonjurors, a profound theological oxymoron, and were suspended from their duties and ultimately removed.

At the same time, Nottingham worked to steer bills for comprehension and for toleration through Parliament: the first to relax the terms of membership of the Church of England, the second to grant limited toleration to nearly all the rest. Even bigoted Anglicans believed that most Protestant dissenters had earned the right to worship as they pleased, though not even liberal Tories wished to see them enabled to hold public office. Thus the bill for comprehension, which would have brought the largest group of dissenters within the church, raised religious opposition from the Anglican hierarchy and political opposition from the Tories. In the Commons it was met with the procedural suggestion that its second reading be put off till 'Doomsday'; in the Lords the bishops opposed it. The King himself urged the abolition of the Test and Corporation Acts, which would have brought Britain more in line with Dutch practice, and this intervention was sufficiently resented to ensure the failure of the Comprehension Bill. The Toleration Bill (1689), which did pass, was a cruel misnomer. Though it permitted non-Anglican Protestant chapels – dissent ceased and Nonconformity began – it did nothing to remove the civil disabilities for those who worshipped in them. Its principal impact, though unintended, was to tolerate those who attended no church at all. William did all he could to practise a toleration for which Parliament refused to legislate, declining to prosecute Nonconformists and Catholics – whose security he had guaranteed to his European Catholic allies – whenever he could.

While bishops opposed William's liberalism, politicians were working to frustrate his conservatism. The Declaration of Rights, which had been read when he and Mary had been presented with the crown, was in August 1689 converted into a Bill of Rights. Though the framers of the Bill of Rights argued that it was declarative only – enunciating only what already existed – it uniformly declared for people and Parliament against the crown. The bill pronounced the suspending power illegal and forbade a standing army in peacetime. It struck down the exercise of prerogative in judicial matters, and the king was forbidden to create ecclesiastical commissions or to raise money outside Parliament. The people had the right to bear arms, to hold free elections, and to have frequent parliaments in which members could speak openly. They were not to be subjected to excessive bail, exorbitant fines, or cruel and unusual punishment. The Bill of Rights also established the new line of succession if Mary continued childless, excluding James and his son and favouring Anne and her heirs over any of William's children should he have a subsequent marriage. In excluding James, the bill set out two new principles: that no Catholic could rule and that no ruler could be married to a Catholic without forfeiting the crown. This second prohibition would have disabled every previous Stuart king and was so great an encroachment upon royal prerogative that Queen Elizabeth had once dissolved a parliament and imprisoned her own counsellors at its suggestion. Besides its maddening intrusion into the monarch's personal life, it was a diplomatic straitjacket. Finally, declarative or innovative, the Bill of Rights had the appearance of a contract and tacitly implied that William III and his successors were constitutional monarchs.

As the Convention debated religion and the constitution, William plotted war. Even before he had become king he had directed his admirals to pummel French shipping, and with spring came his official declaration of hostilities. Louis XIV not only refused to recognize William's accession to the British thrones, he financed the invasion of Ireland in March 1689 with a reluctant James II at its head. Only Ireland had not deserted James in 1688. There a very different revolution had taken place. Under the determined leadership of the Earl of Tyrconnell, Ireland's government had been taken over by Catholics. In the courts Catholic judges presided, in the counties Catholic sheriffs. The army, which for generations had protected Protestant planters, now defended the dispossessed majority. In the year since William had landed in England, Ireland had governed itself, and there was no question of recognizing the Dutchman's claim unless he was willing to accept Catholic power-sharing. Such a prospect was not inconceivable, for William's attention was fixed across the English Channel rather than the Irish Sea and even the aged Tyrconnell seemed willing to turn swords into ploughshares if Catholics could keep their land to plough. James's invasion scuttled negotiations. In derisive imitation of his Orange nemesis, the Stuart king with his French armada outran English defences to Kinsale, where he made the difficult landing in high seas. In less than twelve days James was in Dublin; in less than twelve weeks he controlled all but a few besieged garrisons in Ulster.

Irish Catholics poured into Tyrconnell's army despite the lack of food, clothing and pay and the fact that there was nothing for them to do. This was the opportunity to reverse the conquest and break the Protestant English stranglehold on their country. The Irish parliament that James summoned in May to raise money to clear the North came with a revolutionary agenda. In quick succession it repealed the Act of Settlement, which had driven Catholics from their lands, and established Ireland's independence from the English Parliament; and it would have revoked Poynings' Law if James had not refused to sign the bill. It would also have established the Roman Catholic Church; but James would go no further than to grant a full toleration of all religions.

The King was in a quandary. Never had the problem of multiple monarchies led so directly to royal schizophrenia. James had no desire to be king of Ireland without also being king of England, and of the two he made no secret of which he preferred – 'his heart is too English,' wrote his French political adviser, as if describing a genetic disorder. But James needed men, arms and money to be king of either, and he needed to complete the reconquest of Ireland quickly. His siege of Londonderry had already lasted over a month – the city would eventually hold out for 105 horrific days – and William III was coming to see the importance of securing Ireland before dispatching his regiments to the Continent.

The initial English campaign was calamitous. A boom placed across the mouth of Lough Foyle repulsed the first relief expedition sent to Londonderry. For two more months the garrison starved while waiting for aid. Seven thousand defenders were reduced to 3,000 before a determined effort to crash through the barricade succeeded. But the relief of Londonderry was a symbolic victory only, for the grim wraiths who survived the ordeal were only marginally more useful than those who hadn't. They needed more succour than food and ammunition, and an expedition of 14,000 under the command of the Duke of Schomberg landed in Belfast in August 1689. Schomberg was a soldier of fortune whose military exploits had made him an Imperial count, a French marshal and an English duke. For six decades he had fought in every theatre of European war and had survived through a combination of prudence, caution and luck. Once landed, Schomberg was undersupplied and in doubt as to whether to protect the Protestant communities that had withstood the Catholic onslaught or to engage the enemy in its strongholds. For two months he did nothing while camped beside a fetid bog. 'Our men died like rotten sheep,' an English commander reported as disease felled nearly half the army until cold weather killed the germs and unleashed its own miseries. James II retired to winter quarters in control of nearly all of Ireland.

In London the Convention Parliament was called back into session and voted £2 million for the reconquest; at Kensington, where the King escaped the noxious air of the capital, which made him physically ill, William took the decision to head the expedition himself. It was a difficult choice, for he had hoped to lead his forces into the European conflict rather than to be stuck in Ireland, as he put it, 'out of knowledge of the world'. But, once the decision was taken, the King immersed himself with characteristic thoroughness. He hired 7,000 troops from the King of Denmark and constructed his own polyglot force out of the Dutch and German regiments he had brought to England and the English volunteers who had joined him. These 15,000 men came properly fitted and well supplied from a flotilla of 300 ships. After landing near Belfast in June 1690, they joined with Schomberg's force, by now 20,000 strong. William's strategy was as subtle as a cannonade. He made straight for James's army, which camped not far from Drogheda, on the southern bank of the River Boyne. As we have seen, on 1 July William's troops bravely forded the river and, at great sacrifice, established the beachhead that made their victory inevitable. James and his senior commanders fled the Battle of the Boyne to Dublin, and two days later James took ship once again to France.

Though the Battle of the Boyne ended any effective threat that James would reconquer his kingdoms, it did not end the Irish wars. The suffering that the Catholics had inflicted upon Protestant garrisons in

Ulster now had to be repeated in reverse in Munster and Leinster. Despite his superior artillery, William was unable to batter Limerick into submission and was obliged to withdraw. He returned to England in August without the total victory he assumed would follow the Battle of the Boyne. In his place came John Churchill, Earl and later Duke of Marlborough. Marlborough had been a key defector to William when he landed in England in 1688, and William rewarded him with a peerage and appointment to command the English army. An incisive strategist and an aggressive commander, Marlborough was always straining against the reins of more cautious superiors. He was thus a perfect soulmate for the hyperactive William, had the Dutchman had much soul. Marlborough's plan to capture the fortified strongholds of Munster was opposed in the English privy council but approved by the King, who allowed him an independent command in Ireland. It was a critical decision. Marlborough took Cork within two days and summoned Kinsale to surrender. But the defenders set fire to the town and retreated to its forts. Again, Marlborough made quick work of the siege. Five weeks after setting sail he was back in England accepting the laurels of a grateful King.

The war lasted through one more campaign which demonstrated how much Ireland had become a theatre of the Europe-wide conflict. In July 1691 Irish forces under the French commander Saint-Ruth were decisively beaten by English forces under the Dutch commander Ginkel at Aughrim. Aughrim was the Jacobites' last stand, and among the 7,000 slaughtered that day were many heads of the most prominent Catholic families. Patrick Sarsfield, the heroic Irish general who had slightingly been given command of the reserves, was left to barter an agreement that did not totally dispossess Irish Catholics. The Treaty of Limerick (1691) restored the ambiguous *status quo* of the reign of Charles II, allowed those in arms against William either to join his service or to be transported to France – over 12,000 left to fight for Louis XIV – but did not preclude the introduction of new civil disabilities against Catholics. Test Acts for members of the Irish parliament permanently transformed it into a Protestant body and set the stage for comprehensive anti-Catholic legislation that completed the Protestant ascendancy in Ireland.

Though less bloody than in Ireland, the Revolution settlement in Scotland was no less decisive in shaping that country's future. Despite the rigours of James II's reign in Scotland, the collapse of his

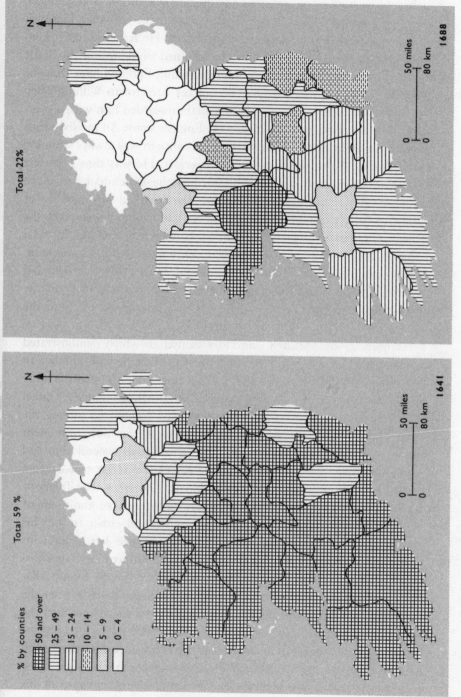

Total 22%

1688

Total 59 %

1641

% by counties

50 and over
25 – 49
15 – 24
10 – 14
5 – 9
0 – 4

50 miles
80 km

0

0

Ireland: Catholic Landholding, 1641 and 1688

government in England was not an occasion for rebellion in the North. For one thing, the Stuarts were Scots, and many heads of Scottish families were personally loyal to them. For another, the experience of the Interregnum would not bear repeating. The Revolution had impoverished the great landed families and weakened the powers by which they had resisted centralization. After thirty years they were still recovering, and, apart from a few extremists who had fled to Holland after the failure of Argyll's rebellion, most of the nobility had made their peace with James II. Scottish institutions, whether the clans, the burghs or the kirk, had ways to moderate the absolutist tendencies of their monarchs. Indeed, though the Scottish Estates had been sorely tempted, they refused James's demands for Catholic emancipation in exchange for a promise of free trade with England. Thus in 1688 the news that James had fled to France caused more perplexity than joy. All of those with a claim to stake on the new monarch made their way to Westminster, where William, fresh from his triumphal acceptance by the English Convention, authorized the calling of a Convention parliament in Edinburgh.

This met in March 1689, but it contained at least as many Jacobites as supporters of the new government. For a month the Scottish Convention wavered, and it was only James's arrogance that led to his deposition. While William issued a conciliatory address asking for advice on central questions of civil and ecclesiastical government, James declared traitors those who contemplated giving it. This led to the withdrawal of his supporters and the declaration by the remnant of the Scottish Convention on 4 April that James had forfeited his crown. The declaration went further than had the temporizing formula worked out in England, as did the Claim of Right which followed the next week (11 April). Alongside a litany of James's tyrannical acts, the Claim of Right asserted constitutional principles that restricted monarchical power, made Parliament an independent institution – especially in regard to supply – and condemned episcopacy. The Claim of Right and a separate set of Articles of Grievances were presented to William and Mary on 11 May, when they received the crown of Scotland. Though the leaders of the Scottish Convention believed that the taking of the one meant the acceptance of the other, as with the English Declaration of Rights there was no quid pro quo. This was soon seen when William refused to accept the abolition of the Lords of the Articles, the most important point in the Articles of Grievances. The Lords were the royally appointed steering committee that controlled the work of the Scottish parliaments. Not only did they voice the will of the monarch, they also represented the interests of their class against those of the lairds and the burghs. William offered to compromise on the composition of the Lords of the Articles, though it was not until the following year that he was forced to accept their elimination.

He was also pressured into the reconstitution of the Scottish Presbyterian kirk. Since the Restoration, those ministers who would not take the oaths of allegiance to the episcopal church had been systematically deprived of their livings. Simultaneously, the power of the Scottish bishops had grown. When James II acceded, he officially proscribed Presbyterianism. By then the Presbyterians had split between quietists, who maintained their faith in community-based congregations that largely escaped the government's persecution, and radicals known as Cameronians after their first charismatic leader. The Cameronians were viciously subjugated, and it was their communities that had suffered occupation by the Highland host in 1678. When James II embarked upon his short-lived policy of indulgence, the Cameronians refused to be pacified, though Presbyterian ministers of all stripes were let out of prison. While Scottish politicians manœuvred cautiously in the uncertain first months of the Revolution, churchmen were less restrained. One of the first acts of the Scottish parliament of 1689 was the abolition of episcopacy, and this was followed by legislation limiting the purchase of church livings by laymen. The general assembly that convened in 1690 encouraged the process of 'rabbling', which ultimately deprived over 500 pro-episcopalian ministers of their places, and purged the universities, despite William's directives against both.

The King's initial weakness in Scotland derived from two factors: his unfamiliarity with Scottish affairs and the danger that Scotland would join the Jacobite rebellion in Ireland. Ignorance caused William to stumble in the faction-riven environment of Scottish politics. Every appointment he made was a disappointment to someone else. His selection of the Duke of Hamilton as commissioner to the Convention alienated Viscount Dundee, who had once rescued William on the battlefield. William's decision to retain in office some of those who had served James II – especially Sir John Dalrymple, who became William's Scottish Secretary of State – also met with great hostility. So did the restoration of Archibald Campbell, tenth Earl of Argyll, to his

Highland estates where the fortunes of the Stuart monarchy for the past half-century had served as little other than backdrop for the struggle between clans Campbell and Macdonald. In Edinburgh a group of opposition lords and commissioners formed 'the Club' to harass William's ministers and frustrate his political programme. The Club was the first organized opposition movement in Scottish politics, demonstrating both the increasing importance of the Scottish parliament and the decreasing importance of individual lords.

In the country, opposition took the form of rebellion. Believing himself betrayed, Viscount Dundee accepted a commission from King James to raise an army. Dundee was a professional soldier who modelled his life on that of his kinsman, the Marquis of Montrose. He had served William in the European wars and Charles II in the suppression of the Cameronians. Then known as Sir John Graham of Claverhouse, he was denounced for the severity with which he carried out his orders and was thus a perfect foil for James II, who ennobled him and made him wealthy. Dundee had marched a regiment from Edinburgh to London in 1688 to join James's army and urged him to make a stand against William III. But after James's flight Dundee accepted a safe conduct, falsely pledging support for the new king. He was outmanœuvred in the Scottish Convention – not least through the incompetence of James II – and he fled only steps ahead of would-be assassins. Now Dundee rallied his own host in the Highlands, comprised partly of Jacobite loyalists and partly of clansmen settling feuds. Though outnumbered, in July 1689 they stormed through the pass of Killiecrankie and routed a force of trained troops. But for Dundee's battlefield death, Scottish and Irish Jacobites might have reinforced each other. As it was, his fall removed effective leadership from a force only tenuously united in purpose and sentiment.

Dundee's victory was far from decisive, and, as command of the force fell to an outsider sent from Ireland, it was not likely to be repeated. Two years of raid and counter-raid, atrocity and retaliation, followed until both sides had exhausted their resources. Thus William was persuaded to offer an amnesty to the rebellious Highland clans if they would take the oaths of allegiance by the first day of 1692. The offer was sweetened by bribes paid to the clan leaders in proportion to their stature. They were also allowed to seek James's consent to the pacification, which he granted from exile in France after his defeat at the Boyne.

The terms satisfied no one. The chiefs of the Highland clans bickered over money, pre-eminence and power. Most believed that the offer was born of weakness and that war would be more profitable than peace. William's Scottish advisers were equally discontented, for the opposite reasons. They were either Lowlanders or Campbells, conditioned to treat the rebels as they would beasts of prey. They thought the terms too generous and that leniency would be ineffectual.

As the deadline neared the Highlanders came in, family after family swearing the oaths. But not all swore on time, and it was determined in London and Edinburgh to speak to the Highlanders in a language they would understand. The MacIains of Glencoe were hardly lambs, though they were chosen to be led to slaughter. Their capitulation had come six days late, and Sir John Dalrymple decided to ignore it altogether. Under William's signature, he sent orders to 'extirpate' this branch of the Macdonalds, and he sent a Campbell to do it. The MacIains were murdered by those to whom they had given hospitality – a brutal violation of one of the basic codes of social conduct in Scotland. For the government, this massacre at Glencoe had the opposite of its intended effect. Though he knew little of its details, the cowardly deed stained William's reputation, especially after he refused to punish those responsible. The Highlands remained ungovernable, the staging-ground for Jacobite rebellions during the next half-century, and Glencoe became a rallying-cry for all of those who held out against the centralizing demands of the English crown. Throughout his reign, William III faced an intractable political situation in Scotland, and his proposals for a union fell on stony ground in both parts of Britain.

In England, William ruled jointly with his wife, Mary, who was a willing cipher for her husband's programme. She had stayed conveniently out of the way during the negotiations in 1689, and made it clear to all who gave their allegiance because of her hereditary right that she had no political existence separate from her husband. During William's frequent absences, Mary was a figurehead regent, controlled by a Council of Nine and managed by William's detailed directives. She disliked political responsibility and the details of government: '[it] does but break my brains the more and not ease my heart.' Mary's passions were domestic, a psychological shelter from the traumas of having rejected her father and fallen out with her sister, Anne. The comforts of home – 'the vanities I was most fond of' – also compensated for her fears for William's safety. Mary was drawn especially to architecture and horticulture, and worked with Sir Christopher Wren in the extensive remodelling of Hampton Court and Kensington Palace. Her other refuge was an intense religious devotion that drew her towards Tory Anglicans like the Earl of Nottingham. She took an active role in the promotion of bishops, patronized a host of uplifting charities, established the naval hospital at Greenwich, founded a college in America, and supported the movement for the reformation of manners and morals into which Puritan sensibilities were now channelled. After only five years on the throne, at the age of thirty-two, she succumbed to smallpox.

Mary's death was a grievous blow to William. Increasingly he craved the stability she had once provided. His health was deteriorating under the pressure of near-constant warfare. Twice since coming to England he had been so ill as to fear for his life. Assassins on the French payroll hunted him, and his brush with death at the Boyne was only the first of three close calls on fields of battle. To the strain of war was added the stress of office. William III constantly juggled incompatible roles. He was king of England, Ireland, and Scotland, stadtholder and captain-general of the Dutch United Provinces, and leader of the Grand Alliance of European states that opposed Louis XIV. Indefatigable though he was, it was less surprising that William governed badly than that he governed at all. The Holy Roman Emperor Leopold of Austria and the north-German princes who composed the Alliance were only slightly less jealous of his power than they were of Louis's. The Dutch regents cared more for mercantile profits than for military victories, while the xenophobic English, safe in their island fastness, opposed a European land war that promised to return little wealth, power or glory. They refused to acknowledge that it was a war fought to defend their crown and their religion. In these circumstances William's accomplishments were remarkable.

The parliament of 1690–95 provided over £2 million for the Irish wars to secure the dynasty, but it also embarked upon efforts to limit the power of the monarchy and the government. Though Whigs and Tories still dominated the landscape, William professed a desire to remain aloof from party conflict – a position made tenable by his incomprehension of the animus that had divided England's governing class. His initial refusal to embrace the principle of party or to allow one party to exclude the other from government strengthened the anti-party sentiment of members of the Commons who identified themselves with the 'country' interest that had once coalesced in the reign of Charles II. They castigated the overbearing political influence of great men, excoriated the venality of office-holders, and lamented the inevitable corruption of those through whose hands passed the coin of the realm. There was a strong moral component to their politics – a component with which it was difficult to argue. When they were not attacking admirals for incompetence or flaying excise commissioners for peculation, they were backing bills to punish 'debauchery'. 'Country' attitudes were a thorn in the side of the King, of the regency councils and of the leadership of both parties. In the House of Commons, Robert Harley of Herefordshire and Paul Foley of Worcestershire rallied back-bencher support for a 'country' programme of reforms to limit the discretionary power of government and to make government accountable to those who bore the burden of increasing wartime taxation.

The 'country' cut across party lines, as did its counterpart the court. Its influence lay in an ability to galvanize independent MPs around specific issues. Its success, limited though it was, derived from the fact that both parties found themselves in agreement with differing aspects of this 'country' platform. 'Country' Whigs supported constitutional checks upon the monarchy and the institutional autonomy of parliament. 'Country' Tories supported fiscal restraints and attacked the standing army as part of their opposition to the expense and seeming futility of a European land war. 'Country' interests revived a Triennial Bill that not only ensured the continuation of parliamentary sessions but restricted their length. Though William vetoed it in 1693, he was forced to accede to both principles the following year. More damaging to the work of government was the passage in the Commons of a Place Bill in 1693. This would have disabled members from holding ministerial office and removed the king's principal means of managing Parliament. While the Triennial Bill had united the 'country' with the Whigs, the Place Bill passed in concert with the Tories. It too was vetoed by William, who rejected more legislation than had any of his predecessors. Further measures to reform the electoral process never made it out of the Commons, though they indicated the 'country's' constitutional platform. Its administrative programme resulted in the creation of the Commissioners of Public Accounts in 1691, the pad from which Harley's public career was launched. The commissioners were given free rein to investigate the way in which parliamentary grants were spent. They browbeat department heads, terrorized junior ministers, and uncovered scandals in procurement and supply.

As influential as were 'country' ideas, William could govern only through the use of ministers attached to the two parties, and, from the beginning of the reign, party conflict flared. In 1690 the King allowed Danby to head an administration that was predominantly Tory. Danby was an effective parliamentary leader and was free of any taint of Jacobitism. His elevation over Nottingham was thus more palatable to the Whigs with whom he had to work on the Council of Nine that governed during William's long absences. Danby was a buttress rather than a pillar. He did not function as a chief minister, and when William created a small 'cabinet council' he also rigorously segregated its various functions. Danby was pointedly excluded from Treasury affairs and was only marginally involved with the military. His achievement was to obtain large parliamentary grants for the war in Europe. He pushed through Parliament increases in the excise and the introduction of a land tax, and these financed the largest English military establishment since the Protectorate. They were accompanied by sharp attacks from 'country' members and the Whigs. Investigations of a naval disaster off Beachy Head in 1690 shook the Tory-dominated Admiralty, while audits of army accounts ruffled the Treasury. The Tories struck back. Marlborough was cashiered for moving a resolution that English troops be commanded only by English officers, and Henry Sidney, the Whig Secretary of State, was shuffled off to Ireland. Even the most successful of English admirals, Edward Russell, eventually lost his place when he contested orders from the Tory Earl of Nottingham. Yet there was something fundamentally contradictory in a Tory government backing a European land war, and throughout his reign William changed parties as he changed uniforms, choosing whichever one gave greatest advantage at the moment.

Following his success in Ireland, William III spent the better part of each of the next six years campaigning on the Continent. The Grand Alliance he had built against Louis XIV was even more fragile than his grip on English politics. He held together Habsburg monarchs and German princes by the force of his personality and his willingness to finance the opposition to Louis XIV from his treasuries in London and The Hague. His goals were essentially defensive, and mostly short-term. Having no direct heir, William was not under the same pressures as Louis XIV or the Emperor Leopold. He had no interest in sacrificing today what might be recouped tomorrow. This was one reason why he treated every French probe as if it were the beginning of Armageddon. But it also meant that William was the perfect intermediary to broker a solution to the Spanish succession, the central problem of European diplomacy and the cause of the Nine Years War that had begun in 1689.

In little more than a century the vast Habsburg Empire of Charles V had disintegrated. Its great territories had been split between Austrian and Spanish houses, and both had dissipated their fortunes. For the Spanish, the gold and silver of the New World financed fruitless wars of imperial conquest and a half-century of extravagance known as the Golden Age. For the Austrians, the weight of the Holy Roman Empire proved unbearable during a century of religious warfare. The calamities of the Thirty Years War had included the loosening of the political ties of the Empire, the reduction of its revenues, and unprecedented social and economic dislocation. Ominously, the greatest challenge was just ahead. From the moment he acceded to the Spanish throne in 1665, everyone regarded Carlos II as a condemned man. Physically decrepit and mentally unstable, for thirty-five years all believed that his death was imminent. Despite two marriages, to a French and then an Austrian princess, he had produced no son. The nearest male claimant to the Spanish empire was either the heir to the kingdom of France or the heir to the Imperial throne, depending upon which clause of which marriage treaty one favoured. But the fact of the matter was that absorption of the Spanish empire into either France or the Holy Roman Empire would so upset the balance of power in Europe as to make continuous warfare a certainty. It was in preparation for a diplomatic settlement that Louis XIV started a new round of warfare in 1689 by striking against Spain and the Empire.

The Nine Years War did not go well for William III. Louis began with a devastating assault on the Palatinate, demolishing Mannheim 'stone by stone' and burning most of Heidelberg to the ground. His fearsome armies then moved into the Spanish Netherlands, where his objectives were conquest rather than destruction. In 1690 French forces defeated the allies at Fleurus; in 1691 Louis personally invested the fortified town of Mons and accepted its surrender. For the campaign of 1692 William induced his ministers to raise and support a land force of 65,000. Yet the only tangible result of this vast expenditure was Russell's naval victory off La Hogue in May, when a joint Anglo-Dutch fleet turned back the vaunted French navy and ended fears of a French invasion. Though it was a considerable achievement, it stood alone.

On the ground, disaster was followed by catastrophe. William's intense efforts to reinforce the strategically important town of Namur failed as torrential rains enveloped his relief columns in mud. Thought impregnable because of its heavy fortifications, Namur surrendered at the end of June 1692. William now decided to give chase to the main French army under the command of the duc de Luxembourg, the greatest general of the age. William caught him near Steenkirk at the end of July and, through a ruse, surprised the French with a sudden attack. But no tactical advantage could outweigh superior French manpower. The English component of William's army took the brunt of the fighting – its first Continental campaign – and its valour was matched only by its losses: more than a third of the whole. The best that could be said about Steenkirk is that the vastly outnumbered raw English infantry fought veteran Frenchmen to a standstill. The worst that was said was that more men and money had been wasted to no purpose.

This was the keynote of a chorus of complaint in the parliamentary session at the end of 1692. 'Country' members and Tory back-benchers rehearsed the all-too-familiar arguments in favour of a 'blue water' policy of fighting only at sea and against a prohibitively expensive standing army and land war, though this would hardly have stemmed French ambitions. It could not be realized that the size of armies had already peaked and was about to begin a century-long decline. A dispute over the direction of naval policy between Admiral Russell and the Earl of Nottingham led to Russell's dismissal and attacks on Nottingham's allegiance. Members introduced bills in the Commons to impose loyalty oaths on office-holders – Whig snares to catch Tory consciences. In truth, prudent politicians of both parties were purchasing insurance against a French triumph by opening communication with James's court at Saint-Germain-en-Laye. But it was the Tories who were reluctant to impose ever-larger fiscal burdens on the country and the Whigs who were willing to use their influence among city moneylenders. At the Treasury, Charles Montagu, the youngest of the commissioners, devised a scheme for the loan of £1 million to be repaid as annuities from specially designated customs duties. This was the beginning both of 'the funds', the gilt-edged securities of so many middle-class families in the eighteenth century, and of the national debt which was essential for the continuation of the European conflict. After the dissolution of Parliament, William moved several Whigs on to the Privy Council, effectively ending Tory domination of English government. In the following year he rehabilitated the Earl of Sunderland, James II's most trusted adviser, though he did not yet grant him formal office.

Nor was 1692 the darkest hour of King William's wars. The peace proposals that William received were offers of a French victory that included the eventual accession of the young Prince of Wales to the English throne. Despite irreconcilable differences between Mary and her sister, Anne, William never gave a thought to abandoning the established succession and he had no choice but to lead another inadequate army into Flanders. This one fought more stoutly than the last, against even greater odds. In the middle of July near Neerwinden a giant pitched battle occurred in which 80,000 French troops only just managed to drive 50,000 of the allies from the field. Even worse, Anglo-Dutch naval superiority could not prevent the French capture of the Mediterranean merchant fleet with its rich cargoes bound for the Levant.

Members of Parliament cried treason at the incompetence of the Admiralty, and revelations that the military was costing over £3 million a year shocked them. More Whigs were brought into government, and from 1694 it was dominated by a group known as the Junto. A confederacy led by Shrewsbury in the Lords, Admiral Russell in the Commons and Charles Montagu at the Treasury, the Junto introduced a new passion to party politics. Lord Somers, who as Lord Keeper advised the crown on judicial appointments, began a thorough purge of the bench. Somers possessed one of the sharpest minds of the age. His legal career had been capped as barrister for the seven bishops prosecuted by James II, his parliamentary career as principal author of the Declaration of Rights. These were impeccable Whig credentials, and for all of his broad-mindedness as a patron and his public-spiritedness as a philanthropist Somers was also a petty party politician. The Whigs took advantage of every opportunity, and none was greater than the revelation of a plot to assassinate William III in 1696. Though the plot was foiled and the King's life never in danger, an Oath of Association to protect William and avenge his death was mandated by Parliament. The oath contained the assertion that had been avoided since the Revolution: that William was the 'rightful and lawful' monarch. All members of Parliament and office-holders were required to swear to the

Association, and over 150 Tories were put out of the commissions of the peace for refusing to compromise their principle of hereditary monarchy. The Whigs portrayed themselves as the only secure haven for the King, and increased their power at Westminster.

The war ground on until 1697. In 1695 William succeeded in recapturing Namur, but the campaigns of the following two years were half-hearted. French diplomacy succeeded where French arms had failed, and through a combination of threats and bribes Louis XIV managed to drive one enemy after another into neutrality and to diminish the grandeur of the Grand Alliance. William's sense of betrayal was all the greater in that the one concession that Louis had refused to make was to recognize him as king of Britain. But continued warfare was becoming untenable to both sides. Dutch merchants could not endure the disruption of trade; the English gentry could not tolerate the burden of the land tax. The French economy was in ruins. It was no longer clear to Louis that negotiation would not be as effective as battle in ensuring his claim to significant parts of the Spanish empire. At the Peace of Ryswick (1697) France abandoned territorial gains in Spain, Germany and the Netherlands and recognized William's rule in Britain. In return, William agreed to act as broker to a series of Partition Treaties that were designed to redistribute the Spanish empire. For the next three years European diplomats redrew the map of the world in an unsuccessful effort to avoid another war.

The constant warfare of the first decade of William's reign had a profound effect upon England. As income from the dissolved monasteries had once made for an administrative revolution in the reign of Henry VIII, so the unprecedented levels of taxation transformed William's government. Royal income rapidly doubled after 1688, and tax receipts alone averaged over £4 million a year in the last decade of the century. The major source of revenue was the land tax, which from its introduction in 1692 outstripped income from customs and the excise. The land tax, which yielded £500,000 per shilling assessed – four shillings in the pound being the normal wartime rate – replaced the old parliamentary subsidies and contained some of their defects. It was collected by local commissioners on self-reported values, so real rates remained artificially low. On the other hand, there was a high degree of compliance, and county magnates resolved local disputes and rectified inequities. This co-opted them into the process whereby the state extracted local wealth for national purposes. In addition to the land tax the excise expanded dramatically, with yields a third higher after 1688 than before. An innovation of the 1640s, the excise had survived the Restoration mostly as a tax on alcohol. Under William III it expanded to include almost all popular items of consumption: coal, leather, salt, spices, tea, coffee and tobacco among them. William's ministers were nothing if not innovative, and they experimented with a glass tax, a building tax, a stamp tax, a registry tax – even a tax on bachelors.

All of this increased revenue had to be administered, and here William benefited from developments in the reigns of his two predecessors. Beginning in 1667 the Treasury had been run by commissioners and was largely out of the hands of the politicians (though Danby interrupted the trend). Through streamlined accounting and effective auditing, the Treasury gradually gained control over royal income if not royal expenditure. The farming of customs and excise ceased, increasing yields and the independence of royal tax collection. This centralization was explicitly repudiated both in the establishment of the land tax and in the refusal of Parliament to adopt either a universal income tax or a comprehensive excise. The increasing power of treasury officials, customs officers and excise collectors was resented in the local communities, both urban and rural. Efficient taxation was one of the hallmarks of absolutism, yet the sheer quantity of money that was necessary to finance William's huge armies necessitated efficiencies. As a result, London monied men were appointed to the revenue boards and became the source of substantial capital advances which were repaid both in cash and in influence over crown fiscal policy.

Their presence within the fiscal apparatus of administration was testimony to the other significant result of William's wars: the creation of a national debt. While early Stuart monarchs had consistently run a deficit, theirs had been the result of profligacy rather than policy. The need to pay and supply soldiers kept William III desperately short of money, and his ministers made borrowing an art. They organized lotteries and annuities to attract creditors large and small. Beginning with the 'Million Loan' of 1692, it became government policy to tie future collection of specific taxation guaranteed by Parliament to the interest due on specific loans – an innovation known as 'funded debt'. Soon all of these separate funds would be consolidated into a single national debt. War finance provided the King's redcoats and the Treasury's red ink. In 1693 the coffers were bled dry in the middle of the campaign season. Three years later the shortage of specie was so severe that the government risked recoinage to restore confidence. By 1698 the national debt stood at £17 million, and roughly 30 per cent of annual revenues went to service it.

Like income, debt demanded administrative efficiencies, and the one that proved in the long term to be most successful was the establishment of the Bank of England in 1694. This was a chartered corporation made up principally of London Whigs who had agreed to raise £1.5 million and oversee its repayment. The Bank took over military disbursements through a branch established in Holland, and soon became a clearing-house for public credit. Ultimately the bank issued its own notes, which gradually were established as a medium of exchange.

All of this shifted the balance of power in London from commerce to finance. In a world at war, the security of funded debt was more prudent than the risk of overseas trade.

The end of the Nine Years War eroded the power of the Whigs. Their pre-eminence lay in their ability to tap the spring of urban wealth and their willingness to support William's militaristic foreign policy. Though a number of leading Whigs held secret correspondence with James II, they still had the most to lose from a Jacobite restoration. But peace found the country weary of debt and taxes, and the parliament returned in 1698 was more evenly balanced than its predecessor, with a number of leading Whigs failing to be selected. For his service to the crown, William elevated Russell to the peerage, depriving the Junto of a key leader in the Commons. The result was the revival of the 'country' interest in combination with the Tories. Under the leadership of Robert Harley, the land tax was halved, the standing army was drastically reduced, and the peculation of the Whigs was punished. William's beloved Dutch guards were disbanded, his generosity to the Earl of Portland, the Dutchman who was always at his side, came to an end, and the Junto leaders were impeached by the Commons. Though the King was inclined to dismiss parliamentary independence as petulance, it couldn't have come at a worse time for the monarchy. In the summer of 1700 Princess Anne's only son, the Duke of Gloucester, died, and in the autumn Carlos II of Spain finally gave up the ghost. The first created turmoil for the British; the second for all of Europe.

The succession to the British crowns had been established in 1689 to favour Princess Anne and her heirs. Though she had had seventeen pregnancies, only one of her children had survived long enough to figure in the succession, William, Duke of Gloucester. In the interim it became clear that William III would sire no heir and that James Stuart, now twelve years old, would survive his youth. The death of the Duke of Gloucester unhinged what had once been a tidy settlement. After Anne, the next Protestant heirs were the children of Sophia of Hanover, and this meant that Britain would eventually come under the rule of another foreign monarch. The Act of Settlement (1701) did not simply declare this succession: it sought to limit the rights of the Hanoverian successors. In future, the monarch could not make war to defend his foreign possessions or leave England to fight on the Continent without the consent of Parliament. No foreigner was to be admitted to any English office or be rewarded with any English land. Judges were to be detached from the crown, both in that their salaries would be paid from the civil list and in that they could be removed only by vote of Parliament. Most of these clauses were explicit critiques of William's government, the hobby-horses of the 'country' and the Tories. With another war imminent in Europe, William had no choice but to accept the Act of Settlement – although many of its most radical provisions would ultimately be repealed – especially since when James II died in 1701 Louis XIV violated the Peace of Ryswick by declaring James III the lawful king of Britain – one in a series of steps that led to the War of the Spanish Succession.

The War of the Spanish Succession once again put William in need of a Whig ministry. The deep cuts in the military establishment and the lower rates of land tax were obviously popular, though they were also dangerous now that Louis XIV had again unleashed his armies. Fear of a renewed invasion of Ireland and resurgence of Jacobites in Scotland heightened immediately following James II's death. A public debate over Britain's responsibility in Europe dominated the winter of 1701–2 – a debate from which the Whigs gained most. The criticism of William's foreign policy, especially in the secret negotiation of the Partition Treaties, was muted by the realization that it had provided Britain with a much needed breathing-space. Preparations for war were well under way when news came of William's sudden demise. A riding accident at first believed inconsequential had on 8 March proved fatal to the 52-year-old monarch, whose constitution had already been sapped of most of its recuperative powers. He had no time to put his affairs in order – one of his deathbed wishes was for a union of Scotland and England – and no way of knowing that his successor would attain his life's ambition: the containment of France and the prosperity of Britain and Holland.

13

Great Britain
1702–1714

Queen Anne was Anglican. That much was certain. She had been in-
structed by Bishop Compton, had defied her father's attempts at con-
version, and had remained aloof from the changes William III had
made in his church. No one could doubt her personal piety nor her
commitment to the church by law established. Had she not provided
for the relief of impecunious country parsons, and was this not known
ever after as Queen Anne's Bounty? Had she not revivified Convocation
to govern the church? Was not the new St Paul's finally completed and a
bill passed to fund the building of a further fifty churches in London?
By word and by deed she was as staunch an Anglican as it was possible
for her to be. Yet from the moment of her accession the cry echoed
from parsonage, pulpit and episcopal palace that the church was in
danger. Not only did wolves ring about its flock – Quakers and Bapt-
ists, Presbyterians and Unitarians – but some penetrated it in sheep's
clothing, occasional conformists who took Anglican communion all
the better to devour places reserved for the truly faithful.

To those who thought about it seriously, church in danger was no
delusion. The Toleration Act of 1689 had had two different con-
sequences. First, it legitimated Nonconformity by licensing nearly 4,000
meeting-houses, and dissent grew steadily, if slowly. Secondly, it en-
abled the irreligious to attend no church at all. Scepticism flourished
among intellectuals; indifference among the masses. Attendance at
Anglican services declined, and bishops complained of 'a settled con-
tempt of religion and the priesthood'. Moreover, the elimination of
censorship after the Licensing Act lapsed in 1695 was succeeded by a
war of words in which Anglican divines were routed time and again.
Rationalists bombarded the church with fashionable theories of deism
and agnosticism, assaulting first the prescribed forms of worship and
then their object. Anti-clericalist snipers found their marks with lurid

stories of the misconduct of ministers. More damaging still was the internecine skirmishing. Disputes between high and low churchmen – sometimes mirrored in the opposition of Tories and Whigs – sapped the Anglican church.

The internal divisions were extremely serious. Since 1689, the most conservative Anglicans had refused to take the oaths of allegiance to what they regarded as monarchical usurpers. These nonjurors were deprived of their offices, but through their self-sacrifice they gained in moral authority what they had lost in administrative power. Next to them stood the so-called 'high-flyers', who had swallowed the oaths yet strained at their implications. Led by Francis Atterbury, later Bishop of Rochester, the high-flyers provoked Queen and ministers by demanding enforcement of the Test and Toleration Acts to the letter. Three times their allies in Parliament proposed an act prohibiting the practice of occasional conformity whereby dissenters took Anglican communion annually to avoid the civil disabilities attached to Nonconformity. Three times the bill was defeated, despite once being tacked to a money measure in an attempt to prevent its rejection in the House of Lords. Those who stood their ground were known as low churchmen or latitudinarians. Led by Archbishop Tillotson and other Williamite bishops who accepted that the Anglican church had been partially disestablished, they were willing to embrace any who came within arm's length of conformity. In 1705 low-church supporters passed a resolution that the church was not in danger; in 1707 they supported the union which sanctioned Presbyterianism in Scotland.

Without support from either Queen or hierarchy, the high-flyers became increasingly desperate and their rhetoric increasingly violent. In 1709 one of their number preached a sermon at St Paul's so inflammatory that the Whig ministry decided to impeach him for 'sedition and subversion'. Henry Sacheverell DD was not a man to do things by halves. He held a Manichean view of the universe in which his enemies were evil incarnate. At Oxford he was remembered for his hard drinking, violent temper and ability to swear like a trooper. In the pulpit his florid face – domed forehead and double chin forming a perfect oval – and his beautiful voice honey-coated the invective that he spewed.

On 5 November 1709 – a day doubly sacred to the entire Protestant community in that it commemorated God's rescue of James I and rejection of James II – Sacheverell preached against 'The Perils of False Brethren'. He characterized low churchmen and occasional conform-

ists as 'double-dealing, practical atheists', 'bloodsuckers that had brought our kingdom and government into a consumption', 'a brood of vipers'. Shortly 100,000 copies of Sacheverell's sermon were in print, and his trial rivalled the seven bishops' in excitement and Charles I's in spectacle. Over £3,000 was spent so that Westminster Hall could accommodate 2,000 spectators. Polite society was more bitterly divided for and against the 'doctor' than political society was into Whigs and Tories. In London, the trial was accompanied by unprecedented rioting that forced the government to call out regular-army troops to quell organized mobs who were intent on burning dissenting meeting-houses and even the Bank of England. The level of violence was unprecedented – worse than anything London had experienced during the Civil Wars or the Exclusion Crisis, and all the more remarkable in that many rioters were members of the respectable middling sorts.

The violence in London turned to euphoria in the country when Sacheverell was convicted of high crimes and misdemeanours but only lightly punished. Everywhere the doctor's health was drunk to the accompaniment of the sound of windows being smashed in dissenting meeting-houses. When he was appointed to a lucrative living in Shropshire, Sacheverell journeyed to it as if on a royal progress. He was received with all pomp in town and city. Public feasts, civic rituals, a shower of gifts greeted the doctor wherever he chose to alight. Mostly he appeared in parliamentary boroughs where he publicly aligned himself with Tory candidates to Parliament and, though banned from public preaching, made his high-church sentiments the cri de cœur of a populace wearied from years of inconclusive wars, of an uncertain monarchical succession, and of an unpredictable future. It was not just the church that was in danger.

There could be no premonition in 1702 that the next decade of English government would be the most successful of the Stuart century. William III's untimely death – the Jacobites toasted 'the little gentleman in the velvet coat', as they called the mole whose hole the King's horse had struck – had left everything suspended in mid-air. Yet in little more than a decade French militarism had been crushed, an English general was the toast of Europe, and Great Britain – formally created by an incorporative union with the Scots – could lay claim to be being the greatest commercial and financial centre in the world. Its constitution was strengthened not only by Anne's peaceful accession but through the guarantee and then achievement of the Protestant, Hanoverian, succession. Though most of Anne's policies merely continued those of William – security from French domination in Europe, union with Scotland, the Protestant succession, and monarchical independence from party strife – for her people, the contrast between the two monarchs could not have been greater.

* * *

Anne Stuart was only thirty-seven when she acceded to the thrones of England, Scotland and Ireland in 1702, but she was already an old woman, carried to her coronation in a sedan chair. She had been physically depleted by seventeen pregnancies and psychically debilitated by their futility – not a single child had survived. Anne, the daughter of James II and Anne Hyde, who had died when the Princess was just six, grew up without any strong female influence. Her elder sister, Mary, whom she adored as a child and hated as an adult, was removed to Holland to marry William III just as Anne entered puberty. Her sense of loss and isolation had important consequences for the Queen's political development. Her frayed familial ties allowed her to ignore her Hyde relations, maintain her distance from William and Mary, and reject her father and half-brother. Anne's craving for friendship led to an intense, stormy relationship with Sarah Churchill, one of the most important figures in her private life. The influence of the royal household, especially in the person first of Sarah and then of Abigail Masham, was every bit as strong under Anne as it had been under James I.

Anne was dull, taciturn, stubborn and unattractive. Her conversation was mind-numbing, her taste insipid, her pleasures limited to gambling and dining, losing pounds at one set of tables and gaining them at the other. The Queen had the good fortune to marry below her, for George of Denmark was, if anything, less impressive, and their union was blissful. Despite all of her obvious deficiencies – or perhaps because of them – Queen Anne was a monarch beloved. She desired nothing so much as to be a mother, and if she couldn't achieve this with her children then she would with her subjects. Her pitted face and bulging, watery eyes that limited her vision, her ailments and constant pain, all made her seem a monarch of the people. Anne revived the practice of touching for the king's evil – a monarch's special power to heal scrofula – and this was a stroke of genius. She touched thousands in the royal banqueting-hall, the scene of the execution of Charles I, who was elevated into a cult figure during the reign. Her association with her martyred grandfather who had suffered for his people and his church was one the Queen cultivated. But the most deliberate parallel she drew was between herself and Queen Elizabeth I. Anne adopted Elizabeth's motto, *Semper Eadem*, as her own, and even dressed in imitation of portraits of England's last ruling queen. As her generals recaptured the military grandeur paradoxically associated with Gloriana, in whose reign England had never won a battle, the comparison grew stronger.

Anne was not just adored, she was supported. Her principles were an amalgam of those which underlay both Tory and Whig parties and if held by anyone except the monarch would have exploded in contradiction. She was what the Tories longed for: an Anglican Stuart whose commitment to the church was unswerving. She was what the Whigs cherished: a contractual monarch who explicitly denied divine right and repudiated an indefeasible hereditary succession. She consistently chose Tory ministers to effectuate Whig policies, associated herself with the landed interest while accelerating the financial revolution, and from her little-England perspective presided over the creation of an empire. Thus Anne was able to govern through the ministerial coalitions that had always eluded William III and avoided becoming captive to the rage of party that whirled not only in the coffee-houses and elegant clubs of London but throughout provincial England as well.

Party politics came of age at the beginning of the eighteenth century. The process, whose ideological roots lay in the Civil War but whose forms took shape gradually after the Exclusion Crisis, was completed by the development of sets of coherent principles, enduring institutions, and procedures for mobilization and discipline of supporters. Whigs and Tories were no longer opprobrious labels (after Scottish and Irish brigands respectively): they were organizations whose opposition dominated the political life of the nation everywhere except in the tiny circle that surrounded the Queen. Indeed, the rage of party was strongest outside Westminster, where local officials were purged and repurged, where electoral contests for borough offices gradually replaced rotational systems, and where party affiliation infected every aspect of social life from patronage to friendship and distorted every market from commodities to matrimony. Though not everyone followed a whip (who first appeared in this period to calculate support and actuate it), party conflict politicized England. Whigs commemorated 5 November; Tories 30 January. In London, Whigs took their coffee and chocolate at St James's Coffee House and their whisky and wine at the Kit-Cat Club; Tories took theirs at the Cocoa Tree and the Society of Brothers. Whig authors wrote in the *Observator* or the *Spectator*, Tories in the *Rehearsal* or the *Examiner*, and they alternately edited the semi-official *London Gazette* when their party was in power. Whigs read Rushworth's *Historical Collections*; Tories Clarendon's *History of the Civil Wars and Great Rebellion*. Whig progeny learned the morals of *Aesop's Fables* from Samuel Croxall; Tory sons and daughters from Sir Roger L'Estrange.

The parties were divided over matters of outlook, principle and instinct. There was remarkably little overlap. Tories – more numerous by having appropriated the symbols of church and king – represented Anglicanism, the country landed interest and a xenophobic view of England's destiny. Their intellectual heritage derived from loyalty to the Stuart monarchy; their self-justification from having been right in 1649. Whigs – the rising tide – stood for dissent, the urban monied interest and an internationalism that had once been the heart of the Protestant cause. Their intellectual heritage derived from the defence of liberties; their self-justification from having been right in 1689. Ten times between 1695 and 1715 the country went to the polls, and progressively each election was framed as a choice between Tories and Whigs. In 1702 the Tories were buoyed by the Anglican succession; in 1705 they sank under the weight of the Queen's rejection of occasional conformity. In 1708 the Jacobite invasion of Scotland brought in the Whigs; in 1710 the Sacheverellite Tories chased them back out. In the House of Commons the party conflict slowly assumed the shape it had already taken in the country. The 'country' gradually disappeared as a separate political force, though 'country' issues continued to be co-opted by whichever party could make best use of them. Nor did that group of office-holders who saw job security in neutrality enlarge as the parties quickly realized the power of political patronage.

What slowed down party development at Westminster was the Queen. Anne had her own complex reasons for remaining aloof. The Tories were too tainted by Jacobitism and the Whigs by contract theory to make either a safe haven for her monarchy. Moreover, she had chosen her confidants for their personal rather than their political qualities, and in Godolphin and Marlborough and his wife, Sarah Churchill, she possessed a trio with divided loyalties. Godolphin, who possessed an impeccable Tory ancestry and the conservative instincts of an accountant, had spent most of his career massaging London's largely Whig financial interests. He was sound, rather than committed. Marlborough had the soldier's disdain for politicians, and throughout his career he allied with anyone who would advance his own interests. Sarah, on the other hand, was a devoted Whig, her abrasive character suited to the confrontational aspects of Whiggism. But most of all the Queen despised the divisiveness inherent in party conflict. 'I pray God keep me out of the hands of both of them' was her constant lament, and thus she never learned how to manipulate the new structure of politics. Indeed, Anne insisted that her main ministers remain above the fray, and throughout her reign she saw no need to adapt her administrations to the results of parliamentary elections.

At her accession, Parliament and Privy Council were put in the hands of the Tories. Whatever the Queen's shortcomings in understanding policy, her knowledge of personalities was acute. She cordially disliked all of the leaders of the Whig Junto except Lord Wharton. Wharton she passionately detested. Thus her first government was composed of Tory stalwarts like her uncle the Earl of Rochester, the Earl of Nottingham and Sir Edward Seymour. Godolphin was made Treasurer, and Marlborough was given *carte blanche* in military matters. Only Sarah Churchill leavened the Tory lump, and she was able to do little other than protect her husband's diplomatic efforts from conventional Tory hostility to a land war in Europe.

Sarah and Anne were intimates whose relationship was based on conflict rather than compatibility. Their private language and shared experiences made them more like a married couple than a mistress and her servant. They delighted in irritating each other, and it was hard even for them to know where one quarrel ended and another began. 'I desire nothing but that she will leave off teasing and tormenting me,' the Queen once wrote to Marlborough about his wife. It seems clear that, while Anne was psychologically dependent upon the relationship, Sarah was playing an extremely dangerous political game. She was equally capable of domination or submission, and for a time her alternations were in rhythm with Anne's needs. But there was never any question of a gradual estrangement. When Sarah fell it was into a bottomless abyss, and her screams are still heard in the vicious memoirs she penned after the Queen's death.

Initially Tory policy centred on deflecting the Queen from a land war and repairing the breaches in the Anglican church. Towards the first end Tories advocated their traditional 'blue water' strategy of naval dominance and fiscal retrenchment. The years of peace had seen a reduction of the land tax and an increase in trade, and the Tories would have welcomed a continuation of both. But, before the parliament of 1702 had convened, Marlborough had already engaged French forces in Flanders and the outcome had not been unsatisfactory. Rochester's jealous carping against the Earl resulted in his own forced resignation from office and signalled the Queen's support for war in Europe.

Frustrated, the Tories turned to the church. In early 1703 they brought in a bill against the practice of occasional conformity. Large fines would be assessed on those who took the Anglican sacrament and afterwards attended the services of dissenting churches. The bill had the fervent support of the Queen, though it split the bishops along the fault-line of high and low church. It passed the Commons easily, and was defeated only by wrecking amendments in the Lords that removed its teeth. But the bill was revived in the next session of Parliament with even greater pressure mounted to force its acceptance as the ardour of the Queen had noticeably cooled.

Between sessions the issue had stirred passions within the burgeoning political community. Daniel Defoe was pilloried for writing a biting attack upon the bill, *The Shortest Way with the Dissenters* (1703), and the Queen was concerned as much with the turmoil as with the fact that her husband – technically a dissenter – would be deprived of his military command of the English armies. The second bill was rejected in the Upper House. Again the Tories in the Commons were stymied, and from their frustration developed a desperate resolve. They would again pass their bill, only this time they would 'tack' it to the annual authorization of the land tax. This would have two different results: it would neutralize those Whigs for whom the war was the chief issue, and, because it was a money bill, it would make it procedurally impossible for the Lords to reject it. The tack stirred opinion more violently than the bill itself. The Queen publicly opposed it as inimical to the nation's interests. Its proponents were denounced as traitors, its opponents as hypocrites. It failed in the Commons by over 100 votes – many provided by apostates who were reviled as 'sneakers'. The gradual erosion of Tory domination at Westminster and the defeat of the tack was magnified by England's continued victories in Europe.

The War of the Spanish Succession lasted almost the Queen's entire reign. It was a continuation of the struggle to contain the power of France that had dominated European politics for nearly a half-century. British objectives were threefold: to maintain a balance of power in Europe that would protect Britain against invasion and conquest; to secure recognition of both Anne and the Hanoverian succession; and to protect Britain's commercial interests. The first was a national concern that fed on memories of James II's invasion of Ireland and on threats of a Jacobite rebellion in Scotland. As both William and James had recently made successful amphibious landings, there appeared to be little security in the moat of the English Channel. Were France to conquer the Continent, there was little doubt that Britain would be next. The second resulted from Louis XIV's recognition of James III as rightful king. Ironically, this cemented Tory support for a war they detested. However much many Tories may have secretly wished the Stuart line to continue, they would not have it imposed and they would not accept a Catholic monarch. With each passing year more Tories found it easier to take the oaths that established the rights of hereditary Protestant descent, and it was the Tories who insisted that the second Grand Alliance make no peace without recognition of Anne and her Hanoverian heirs. Finally, the threat to England's commercial interests motivated the Whigs. Cooperation between France and Spain would cut deeply into England's Atlantic trade and threaten its access to the Mediterranean. A threat to trade was a threat to finance, and without finance Britain would be impoverished and impotent. Thus the country remained united behind a military effort even more massive than that launched by William – an effort which this time would more than repay its costs.

Since the conclusion of the Nine Years War, European diplomats had been working to prevent renewed bloodshed. Every major power except one agreed that on the death of Carlos II the Spanish empire would be partitioned. The disagreement was over how to do it. A first plan was made obsolescent by the demise of the principal beneficiary, a German prince; a second by Carlos's last-minute will. For the one European power that did not agree to partition was Spain, and it was willing to set the entire Continent ablaze rather than divide up its territories in the Netherlands, Italy or the Indies. A month before his death on 1

November 1700, Carlos cast his own apple of discord among the princes of Europe in the form of a take-it-or-leave-it will. All of his empire was left to Philip de Bourbon, grandson of Louis XIV, on the condition that he accept it intact. Otherwise all of the empire was left to the Archduke Charles, younger son of the Holy Roman Emperor Leopold of Austria.

Before Carlos made his will, Louis XIV had not only agreed to the principle of partition, he had accepted the fact that most of Spain and its possessions would fall to the Austrian heir. Now he was suddenly presented with the entire prize if only he would accept it. Though Louis was a monarch of big dreams, Carlos's will must have seemed a hallucination. In the following months he installed Philip V in Madrid, recognized James III as king of England – so throwing Tories and Jacobites into conflict – and quickly moved French troops into the barrier towns of the Spanish Netherlands whose neutrality, according to the Peace of Ryswick, was to be guaranteed by the Elector Max Emanuel of Bavaria. Max became Louis's first ally, turning his coat in return for territorial concessions in Germany and appointment as governor-general of the Netherlands.

Greed was the downfall of Louis XIV. Though the Emperor disputed Philip's inheritance and sent troops to Spanish Italy, England and Holland had been willing to recognize Philip's rule over Spain and the Indies, for they were reluctant to sacrifice the prosperity of the last few years of peace. But the occupation of the barrier towns and the gratuitous recognition of James III were as good as a declaration of war. In the last months of his life, William III had entrusted the task of building another anti-French coalition to the Earl of Marlborough, tacitly recognizing that he would be Anne's principal soldier and statesman. At the age of fifty-two, Marlborough was entering upon his first supreme command. He had risen to power on his good looks, his marriage to the Queen's confidant and his own talents. By 1702 he had not risen very far. His two best-known military achievements were to desert James II in 1688 and to reduce Munster in 1690. Throughout a decade of European warfare Marlborough saw only one brief campaign. William neither liked him nor trusted him, and in 1692 Marlborough was stripped of his offices and briefly committed to the Tower. It was not until the end of the century that the Earl regained influence at court. Thus while British commanders fell in the fruitless Flanders campaigns, Marlborough and his wife tightened their hold on Anne.

Marlborough's character was a mixture of rare talents and common faults. Like Cromwell, he had an intuitive military genius that allowed him to gamble against the odds and win. His introduction of the forced march and the massed cavalry charge had a lasting effect on European warfare. He was aggressive and bold, but he was not impetuous, and this was the key to his military success. If anything, Marlborough was a greater diplomat than general. He led a reluctant coalition into decisive engagements, using cajolery to gain some ends, chicanery to gain others. The Dutch and Imperial forces he had to coordinate were a personal albatross whose weight denied him even greater fame and glory; yet to achieve the common purpose he bowed under it. Marlborough inspired so much confidence that the arrogant Hollanders deferred to him, as did Prince Eugène of Savoy, who was his better in birth, breeding and experience. Marlborough's defects, too, were larger than life. 'His ambition was boundless and his avarice insatiable' was Lord Somers's assessment. His political interventions were self-serving whether he was in or out of power. He hedged his loyalty first by treacherous communication with William of Orange and then by treasonous correspondence with the Jacobite court in France. At the end of his career he even sought favours from Louis XIV. Buckingham and Albemarle may have risen more quickly, but no Stuart shooting-star had Marlborough's trajectory. He made his first fortune as the Duchess of Cleveland's gigolo and parlayed it into the greatest wealth that any British subject had ever achieved. He was made an English duke and an Imperial prince, and was presented with the royal estate at Woodstock and a blank cheque to build the greatest prodigy house of the age, Blenheim Palace. For a time, Marlborough was the most famous man in the world.

His palace was named after the site of his great victory on the Danube. The Battle of Blenheim was significant in that it represented Britain's willingness and ability to conduct a land war in the heart of Europe. It represented the first time that British troops had defeated a French army for centuries, and the first time in fifty years that a French army was decisively beaten. The strategy was Marlborough's alone. His Dutch confederates presumed that he would mass their joint forces in Flanders, his Austrian allies that he would besiege towns in the Palatinate. But Marlborough understood that Bavaria was the key to the war in Germany. With so powerful an ally, Louis could hope to threaten Vienna itself; without it France would be reduced to defending the Rhine. Thus in June 1704, while the French languidly shadowed his army eastward, Marlborough feinted south and then raced into Bavaria. By doing so, he forced the convergence of an undersupplied and exhausted French army with the cream of Max Emanuel's soldiers. Marlborough left no doubt that he intended to fight. The initial encounter was on 2 July 1702 at the fortified town of Donauworth, where Marlborough led the Anglo-Dutch forces into a near-suicidal assault in which a third of his British troops perished. At the critical moment he directed his Austrian allies into a flanking attack that routed the defenders.

All of Bavaria now lay open to the allies, and even Louis XIV expected that Max Emanuel would turn his coat again. Instead he reformed his defences and joined his forces to the main French army, led by Marshal Tallard. There, at Blenheim, on the morning of 13 August 1704, Marlborough surprised them in their camp on high ground beyond the bank of the Nebel river. Tallard's position was so advantageous that he slept peacefully as the allied forces were deployed, and doubted the reports read to him that battle was at hand. His strength was 60,000 – slightly larger than the army of 52,000 that opposed him. The battle was a titanic struggle of attack and repulsion. Marlborough had ordered his host with the precision of one who had thought out events before they unfolded. He remained in the centre of the field, where the fighting was fiercest and the outcome long in doubt. His tactic of alternating lines of infantry and cavalry eventually took its toll on Tallard's defenders and sapped their resistance to the final massed cavalry charge that swept them from the field. In the meantime over 10,000 French infantrymen were trapped inside the town of Blenheim, and after being subjected to murderous fire surrendered *en masse*. Tallard and two of his generals were captured, and dispatches which proclaimed 'the Duke has saved the empire' did not exaggerate.

The victory at Blenheim allowed the British ministry to prosecute the war on more ambitious terms. While Marlborough was massing on the Danube, the English navy took the island of Gibraltar and escorted Archduke Charles to Portugal, where supporters proclaimed him Carlos III, king of Spain. From then on, the War of the Spanish Succession was fought primarily on two fronts: in the Netherlands, to secure Holland's barrier against French aggression, and on the Iberian Peninsula, to conquer Spain. 'No peace without Spain' became the battle-cry of those who sought an end to French militarism.

The war in the Netherlands reconfirmed Marlborough's gifts. Though William III had fought French armies on this ground year in and year out, his victories were all draws. In 1706 at Ramillies Marlborough won the first massed battle on the Netherlandish plains as decisively as he had won Blenheim. His army of 40,000 bested that of the duc de Villeroi, taking thousands of prisoners and leaving the remainder incapable of regrouping or fighting. By the end of the year the French presence in the Netherlands was limited to positions within their fortified towns, the strongest of which, Lille, was taken two years later. In 1708, at Oudenarde, Marlborough earned another decisive victory – one which definitively ended the threat of a French invasion of Holland.

But the war in Spain was not nearly as successful, despite promising beginnings. Gibraltar was seized and held, and a combined Anglo-Dutch force under the Huguenot Earl of Galway was entrenched in Lisbon, from which he could mount offensives from the west. In 1705 the mercurial Earl of Peterborough unexpectedly took Barcelona, from which he could mount offensives from the east. Both armies were seemingly in service of Carlos III, the Austrian claimant to the Spanish throne, though from the beginning of the war Carlos did everything possible to restrain his aggressive allies, and his half-hearted attitude at the height of allied success presaged the quagmire into which the Peninsula War was to turn. His quarrels with Peterborough – who was more than his match in arrogance and obstinacy – prevented the allies from consolidating their gains through control of Madrid and the heart of Castile. After 1706, French forces under the command of Marlborough's half-brother, the Duke of Berwick, took the offensive and inflicted a crushing blow at Almanza (1707), where over 5,000 allied forces were either killed or captured.

While the outcome of the war remained in doubt, the Queen and her ministers continued to fear a back-door French assault upon England through Scotland. On his deathbed, William III had commended a political union of England and Scotland to his ministers. His relations with his northern subjects had not been happy. Though he had spent his entire life negotiating treaties and settlements – and not often from positions of strength – no one had ever driven a harder bargain than the Scots. The concessions he made to secure the crown had created a virtually independent Scottish parliament which his perpetual need for money and manpower prevented him from restraining. It had gained control of determining its membership, its procedures and its agenda, creating a problem of management that had not existed since the Union of Crowns in 1603. It became the playground of a factionalism so cross-hatched by issues of geography, clan, religion and politics as to be incomprehensible to the outsiders who were William's principal advisers. It was impossible to know what scores were being settled, and it was this that had led to the first disaster of William's rule in Scotland, the Glencoe massacre. Glencoe left a bitter legacy and reinvigorated the Jacobite party in Scotland. It was viewed as an act of conquest carried out by English oppressors, even though it was ordered and implemented by Scots.

Glencoe stirred the anti-English sentiment never far below the surface in Scotland and thus fed the anti-Williamite hostility that was to emerge after the Darien débâcle. Just as the king of Spain regarded the Indies as a possession of Castile, so the Stuarts regarded their colonies as English. Scotland and Ireland were prohibited from creating their own overseas mercantile companies and were subject to the Navigation Acts, which restricted their shipping. As the benefits of overseas trade were made manifest, Scottish speculators tried their hand at a number of ventures, including fisheries in Canada and plantations in America, though they came to little. Petitions for joint Anglo-Scottish ventures were rebuffed at Westminster. In 1695 the Scottish parliament licensed a group of merchants to form a company to promote trade to Africa and the Indies, stipulating that at least half the money should be Scottish. The scheme that attracted attention was to settle a trading factory on the Isthmus of Panama at Darien, to engage simultaneously in the Atlantic and Pacific trade. Initially, London merchants oversubscribed their share, and this encouraged wealthy Scots to do the same. Nearly a quarter of all the liquid capital in Scotland poured into the venture. But it soon went badly wrong. English monopoly companies petitioned Parliament against a new Scottish company, and this forced English speculators to withdraw their subscriptions. The King himself opposed the Darien venture, as it threatened his delicate negotiations with Spain, which had ruled Panama since its discovery. Two expeditions were allowed to perish unaided, the company's debts multiplied, and many prominent Scots traders and politicians were nearly ruined.

Darien demonstrated – if demonstration was needed – that the Scottish economy was held in an English vice. Scotland was 'like a farm managed by servants, and not under the eye of the master'. Over half of its commodities were exported to England encumbered by disadvantageous tariffs, and its internal industries were strangled by English competition. King William's wars brought no benefit to Scotland. Taxation flowed south, while the embargo against France cut Scotland off from an important Continental trading partner. A series of harvest failures at the end of the century compounded the misery. All the while, intensive Scottish efforts to achieve commercial relief in the form of an economic union foundered on English indifference. To manage increasingly unruly Scottish parliaments, William lurched from ministry to ministry, replacing the Duke of Hamilton with Viscount Stair, Stair with the Marquis of Tweeddale, Tweeddale with the Duke of Queensberry, and Queensberry with a coalition. None was more suitable than the last, for each was given the impossible task of subjugating Scottish to English interests. Each succeeded, in so far as they did, by what was coming to be known as 'management' – that is, by liberally rewarding themselves and their friends. 'Country' voices not dissimilar to those which opposed corruption in English politics were now heard in Scotland, joining the Jacobite attack upon successive governments.

The crisis in Anglo-Scottish relations that had been looming since the Revolution of 1689 came with the death of the Duke of Gloucester. The English Act of Settlement, which passed the throne to the Protestant heirs of Sophia of Hanover, was not ratified by the Scottish parliament. Although fears of a Jacobite rebellion were overblown, Anne's peaceful accession in Scotland was accompanied by a political struggle over the succession. 'If we live free, I little value who is king,' declared Andrew Fletcher in the debate over the Act of Security (1704), which first passed the Scottish parliament in 1703. The Act of Security reasserted the power of the Scottish estates to determine their own monarch and declared that, unless negotiations were concluded to secure Scotland's political and economic liberties, that monarch would not be the king of England. Moreover, a further act was passed devolving the power to declare war and make peace on to the Scots parliament (Act Anent Peace and War 1703).

At Westminster the Act of Security was regarded as a radical attack upon royal prerogative, but in Edinburgh it had been the compromise position. The 'country' opinions espoused by Fletcher were nearly republican, while the Jacobites clamoured for the restoration of the Stuarts. Anne refused to accept the Act of Security, and in retaliation the Scottish parliament refused to vote supply and passed the Wine Act

(1703), which allowed trade in that commodity with France despite the English embargo. The withholding of supply, the assertion of independent diplomatic power, and commerce with the enemy all suggested that Scotland was playing its traditional French card in its relations with England. But Anne's ministers saw the pattern as nothing less than treason at a moment when the fate of Europe hung in the balance. False reports of an active Jacobite conspiracy in the Highlands exacerbated these tensions, and less restrained members of the English parliament began to recall Cromwell's solution to his Scottish problem. In 1704 Anne's need for supply forced English acceptance of the Act of Security, and the concession was another red rag in front of those bullish to force the Scots to submission. Godolphin, at the head of the Queen's government, chose a scalpel rather than a bludgeon. The English parliament passed an Alien Act (1705) which threatened that, unless the Hanoverian succession was accepted by legislation, Scotland would be regarded as a foreign nation. Scots would be denied rights of English citizenship, all trade would be interdicted, and Scottish ships trading with France would be captured or sunk. The Scots were given fifteen months to decide.

The Alien Act ultimately forced the union of the two kingdoms. The Scots could not prosper without English trade, nor the English without security on their northern border. For centuries the question for Scotland was whether to ally with England or with France, and now it was finally to be settled. Commissioners had begun work on treaties for union in 1705, and with this edict of doom hanging over them they redoubled their efforts. The first principle established was that union would be incorporative, the creation of Great Britain. The second principle was that there would have to be large exceptions to the first. Political institutions might meld together, but legal ones would not. As the common lawyers had argued a century earlier, there was English law and there was Scottish law but there was no British law, and there could be none without the abolition of the other two. Nor did anyone need a history lesson to know why the Scottish kirk and the Anglican church could not worship the same God in the same way. Not even free trade – so much desired on both sides of the border – was uncomplicated. Scottish cattle barons and linen manufacturers could not survive without free trade, but Scottish colliers and saltmakers could not survive without protection. Thus the incorporative union took shape. There would be one flag, one coin, one measure, one seal of Great Britain. With specified exemptions, trade would be free and taxation equal and uniform. The Act of Union (1707) provided for one British parliament, at Westminster, with forty-five Scots returned to the Commons and sixteen Scottish peers to the House of Lords. The Hanoverian succession was secured, and the navies and militias were combined into one British military establishment. A separate act secured the Presbyterian church in the form in which it then existed.

There was no architect of what Swift would call 'this crazy double-bottomed realm', and little enthusiasm in either kingdom for the result. There were riots in Edinburgh, and for a time a curfew was imposed so that the Duke of Queensberry, whom the citizens judged responsible, could travel through the streets. In the short term Anne gained the elimination of a troublesome legislative body and support for the war against France. But in the long term the promise of political conformity had to be purchased in blood. The Scots gained economic security at the cost of their new-found political independence. The Union of Crowns in 1603 had brought little benefit; a political and economic union might bring little more. Indeed, despite the fact that each parliament had forced the other to the table, it was not clear that either would agree to the results. English Tories feared that the union would bring a bloc of Whigs into both Houses of Parliament, and only the recent realignment of court politics allowed the act any chance of passage. In Scotland it was discovered – not for the first time – that as a means of persuasion bribery was more effective than reason. Under cover of incorporating the trading companies of the two nations, the English agreed to repay the losses of Scots investors in the Darien colony. A large payment was made directly to offset Scottish responsibility for the English debt, while a smaller sum was given to those whose offices would be abolished. Money found its way into the pockets of the leaders of the Scottish factions crucial to carry the vote. Still, two of the three Scottish estates passed the article creating a unified state (with a majority of only four), and accusations that they were 'bought and sold for English gold' never disappeared.

The military achievements in Flanders and the union were accomplished by a parliament in which the parties were evenly matched and the government held the balance by votes of placemen. Through concessions to the Whigs – which the Queen was loath to make – Marlborough achieved a free rein in Europe and Godolphin gained control over the Scottish negotiations. They were called the 'Duum-virs', and were distrusted by party leaders in both Houses because of their ideological flexibility. By 1706 Godolphin saw that it was easier to rule with the support of the united Whigs than of the divided Tories. This strategy was aided by the self-destructive impulse of the high Tories, who set out to spite the Queen both by reviving claims that the church was in danger and by introducing a motion to invite Electress Sophia to reside in England. Anne, who lived in constant fear of a Jacobite coup, was no more receptive to a resident Protestant ruler-in-waiting. She allowed her opposition to be widely bruited and attended the debate in the House of Lords, where she was mortified to hear her dotage described. Sophia's residence in England had initially been Whig policy, and it was all Godolphin could do to stave it off through the introduction of a Regency Act (1706). This provided for the con-tinuation of government in the period between Anne's death and the arrival of the Hanoverians through a council composed of the leading officers of state.

The move of the Duumvirs towards the Whigs was completed by the reports of an abortive Jacobite invasion of Scotland in 1708. Though there was hardly a prominent English politician who had not kept some line open to Saint-Germain in the 1690s, Jacobitism was the bane of the Tories, who were poisoned by it in the spring elections. Even before the first session of Parliament, Godolphin had switched his allegiances en-tirely, and this led to the resignation of Robert Harley and his move towards the Tory party.

Harley was the first of that breed of politicians who would never take a short, straight path when there was a long and winding road. He raised backstairs intrigue to an art form, though his subtlety was often too profound for his age. Harley's political career, which began on the Commission of Accounts, spanned every imaginable position. He came from pure dissenting stock, and his relatives, who included his Foley wife and Hampden in-laws, read like an honour roll of True Whiggism. His True Whig phase, however, was brief as he began to play a prominent role in the 'country' interest that coalesced against William III's foreign policy and fiscal expedients. Harley remained aloof from the struggle between the Junto and the Tories that domin-ated the 1690s, and he mastered the language of unity and national interest that excoriated the development of the party system. He was elected Speaker in 1701 – a position he held in three consecutive parliaments. In 1704 he accepted appointment as Secretary of State, forfeiting the independence he had built by refusing crown office.

Harley expected to supplant Godolphin in the Queen's confidence, and made elaborate preparations to become chief minister by building bridges to span Tory divisions. He realized that in order to combat the Duumvirs he too needed access to the bedchamber, and he found the perfect foil in his cousin Abigail Masham, who had begun to replace Sarah Churchill in Anne's affections. Sarah's hysterical accusations against Abigail and Harley contributed to Godolphin's own suspicions, and in 1708 he forced the Queen to choose by threatening his own and Marlborough's resignations. Harley was dismissed.

Anne was reluctant to part with Harley or to accept the continued infiltration of her ministry by Whigs. But her will was broken by the death of Prince George in October 1708, and, grief-stricken, she acceded to the return of the Junto – even elevating Wharton to an earldom. Though complete, the Whig triumph was short-lived. The European war ground on, and each campaign no longer brought tidings of allied victories. Almanza in 1707 had been a disaster, the siege of Lille had cost 15,000 lives, and Malplaquet could be called a victory only by ignoring the enormous cost in lives of the bloodiest battle of the eighteenth century. Philip V had not been driven from the Spanish throne and, despite expectations, France had been contained rather than defeated. Beginning in 1708 war weariness swept the nation, and each renewed campaign was less popular than the last. The Whigs took the brunt of the criticism, the charges ranging from military incompetence to political treachery. The idea that they profited personally from the war was widely canvassed, and the run on the Bank of England in 1708, though occasioned by fear of a Jacobite rebellion in Scotland, contributed to uneasiness over Whig management. The war was costing nearly £13 million a year, and the rewards heaped upon Marlborough were becoming a symbol of Whig profiteering, always suspected though never proved.

It was in this context that Dr Sacheverell preached his sermon and, as we have seen, Godolphin and the Whig leaders overstepped themselves by prosecuting him. Behind the scenes, the Marlboroughs had lost the struggle for the Queen's heart. Sarah wildly accused Anne of a lesbian relationship with Mrs Masham, while the Duke unwisely demanded that he be made captain-general for life. In April 1710 Anne granted Sarah her last interview, and the two parted bitterly. The Queen made it known that she leaned towards a light sentence for Sacheverell and was horrified at the riots that took place in London. Immediately afterwards she began to dilute the Whig administration with appointments recommended to her by Harley. Finally, in September, Anne dismissed Godolphin, though she lacked the courage to tell him to his face. The election which followed returned the Tories in triumph, with a two-to-one majority over the Whigs. Harley was first made Chancellor of the Exchequer, and then Lord Treasurer and Earl of Oxford.

Harley had won his battle by preaching a sermon that the Queen knew by heart. Government had to be above party, for the common good. 'If the gentlemen of England are made sensible that the Queen is the head, and not a party, everything will be easy.' But this was simpler to preach than to practise. With the exception of Marlborough, the leading Whigs who did not resign were purged. Despite the rhetoric of moderation, Harley led a Tory government – albeit one whose divisions mirrored those of the Tory party. At one end were the high churchmen, who immediately revived their campaign against dissent. On the positive side they funded the building of additional churches in London; on the negative they finally achieved the Occasional Conformity Act (1711), which punished those whom Sacheverell had branded 'a brood of vipers'. Harley had little sympathy for the Anglican high-flyers, for they made moderate counsel more difficult. They also supported his chief political rival, Henry St John, ultimately Viscount Bolingbroke. Bolingbroke was everything Harley was not: brilliant, charming and transparent on the one hand; erratic, bigoted and amoral on the other. He had been secretary of war in Godolphin's government, and he maintained a close relationship with Marlborough. Purged by the Whigs in 1708, Bolingbroke spent the next two years in solitude, contemplating politics and his revenge. Back in power as Secretary of State from 1710, he vied with Harley for leadership by allying himself with the Tory extremists. He openly supported the high-flyers and did everything possible to push Harley in a more conservative direction.

The key issue for Harley's government was peace in Europe. Though Marlborough still believed that a successful invasion of France was possible, war fever had run its course in England. Parliamentary investigations into fiscal irregularities undermined confidence, while the military situation in Spain continued to deteriorate. The policy of the Whigs had been 'no peace without Spain', but they could not achieve it either by arms or by diplomacy. The Tories had come to oppose the

Peninsula War and they were now determined to find a means of extrication. This involved abandoning England's allies, the Austrians, Dutch and Germans. In 1711 Harley entered into secret negotiations with Louis XIV to achieve three objectives: the division of the Spanish empire among the rival claimants, a new barrier agreement to protect Holland, and concessions to English traders in Spanish America. In 1709 England had pledged to make no separate peace in the face of efforts by Louis XIV to break the Grand Alliance through generous concessions to the Dutch and Germans. Now the Tories were determined to grab the lion's share of the spoils.

These terms repudiated the sacrifices of the past six years as much as they repudiated England's allies. They might have been impossible even to broach were it not that the same year saw the fortuitous death of the Emperor Joseph, who had succeeded Leopold in 1705, and the accession of his brother, Archduke Charles (Carlos III), to the Imperial throne. This made a compelling case for the dissolution of the Spanish empire, for there was now as much reason to fear Habsburg domination of Europe as Bourbon. Yet when the articles of the treaty became known – Harley blamed Bolingbroke for leaking them to Marlborough – there was a fire-storm of opposition. Marlborough was enraged. He had given his word there would be no separate peace, and he gambled his prestige on a move to block it. Through an unusual coalition in the House of Lords – the Earl of Nottingham sold his vote in return for passage of the Occasional Conformity Bill – a resolution was narrowly passed that there would be no peace without Spain. But Marlborough's position had been significantly weakened by the investigation of military accounts which revealed huge shortfalls. Anne made one attempt to persuade him to support the peace, but after that she threw him to the wolves in much the same way she had Godolphin. He was savagely attacked by Jonathan Swift in *The Conduct of the Allies* (1711), a pamphlet which brilliantly played the stops of English xenophobia. In December, Marlborough was dismissed from his offices, and in the following month Anne blatantly packed Parliament by creating twelve new peers, all of whom were pledged to vote for what was to become the Treaty of Utrecht (1713). The treaty provided that Britain would retain Gibraltar and Cape Mahon in the Mediterranean, Newfoundland in Canada, and St Kitts in the West Indies. English merchants were awarded the Asiento, a thirty-year monopoly on the Spanish slave trade. The Spanish Netherlands were ceded to Austria, making an even more effective barrier against the French than the original fortified towns. Finally, the pretender, James III, was expelled across the French border, out of the vortex of intrigue.

There could be no doubt that from the British point of view the peace was as successful as the war. At a stroke, it made Britain the greatest maritime power in the world. Naval bases in the Mediterranean ensured the Levant trade and made English merchantmen competitive with the Portuguese. The acquisition of the Canadian fisheries supported the burgeoning North American trade and weakened the French position in the New World. The exclusion of the Dutch from all aspects of the South American trade completed the sweep against European rivals. The newly created South Sea Company – Harley's Tory rival to the Whig Bank of England – was given what amounted to a licence to print money, for the barbarous slave trade was believed to be immensely profitable. Though it was labelled betrayal abroad, at home the treaty was wildly popular. Britain had made the financial sacrifices during nearly a quarter century of war; a British commander had finally broken the military deadlock. What the British gained in trade, the Europeans gained in security. Holland, Austria and the German states were no longer at the mercy of French expansionism, and everyone had got something from a war in which they might very well have been conquered. Thus did might make right; thus was perfidy rationalized.

The Treaty of Utrecht did not officially end the War of the Spanish Succession. The Emperor and his German allies held out for another year, though without Britain and Holland their opposition was futile. Among the Germans, however, was Prince George, Elector of Hanover, who had made public his opposition to the Tory peace in 1711. Like every other observer of the European scene, once the British terms became known the Elector George assumed that they were prelude to the restoration of James III after Anne's death. Harley and latterly Bolingbroke, who, as Secretary of State, took over the management of the negotiations, had used known Jacobites as go-betweens. Though the number of committed British Jacobites was small – less than 10 per cent of the Tories in the House of Commons – Jacobitism as an amalgam of views about hereditary succession, opposition to Whig principles and fear of a foreign monarchy was potent. Harley and Bolingbroke both maintained indirect contact with the court at Saint-Germain, and both knew that George's accession would put an end to

Tory rule. Harley, as was his wont, played a triple game, anticipating the succession of either a Hanoverian or a Stuart while at the same time exploring the possibility that, like Henry IV, James III might change his religion and conclude that he was predestined to rule Britain. Bolingbroke, as was his wont, played a complicated bluff while he worked for a French alliance and for the succession of James III. The Queen vigorously denied that there was any connection between the articles of peace and Jacobitism, though she was largely in the dark about the machinations of her ministers. As the negotiations moved forward, Anne's health deteriorated.

Her final year was dominated by the question of the succession. As she moved closer to the Tories, and as the Tories moved closer to the Jacobites, there was continual speculation that Anne would overturn the Act of Succession by a deathbed declaration. In 1714 Harley firmly made his commitment to the Hanoverians after learning definitively that James III would remain Roman Catholic. He won the temporary support of a segment of the Tory parliamentary party, including the Speaker, Sir Thomas Hanmer, who were ominously called the 'whimsicals' for their avowed support of Hanover. But Harley was a shell of his former self, his body wracked with pain, his concentration noticeably failing, his power ebbing with his strength. Bolingbroke, who now opposed him with all of his might, was openly in communication with the Jacobite court at Saint-Germain and was negotiating a formal treaty of mutual defence with the French. The struggle between him and Harley had been fought around a single refrain: government could not live by party alone. Harley believed in leavening the Tory mass and Bolingbroke did not. Harley could not purge junior ministers or military commanders, and he would not exert party discipline. In Bolingbroke's view, Harley had undermined the Tory interest and had ensured that along with Hanover would come the Whigs. This was no fantasy, for when the Electress Sophia died in May 1714, just months before Anne, her son George altered the regency council so that it would be dominated by Whigs. Bolingbroke's only hope was the Queen, but Anne was sinking fast. In one of her last official acts, she dismissed Harley from office; but in one of her last private ones, she allowed Marlborough to return from his self-imposed exile. He had already been appointed by the Elector to command any troops that were necessary to suppress a rebellion. Yet – much to everyone's relief – the crown passed as peacefully as the Queen, who died in her sleep on 1 August 1714.

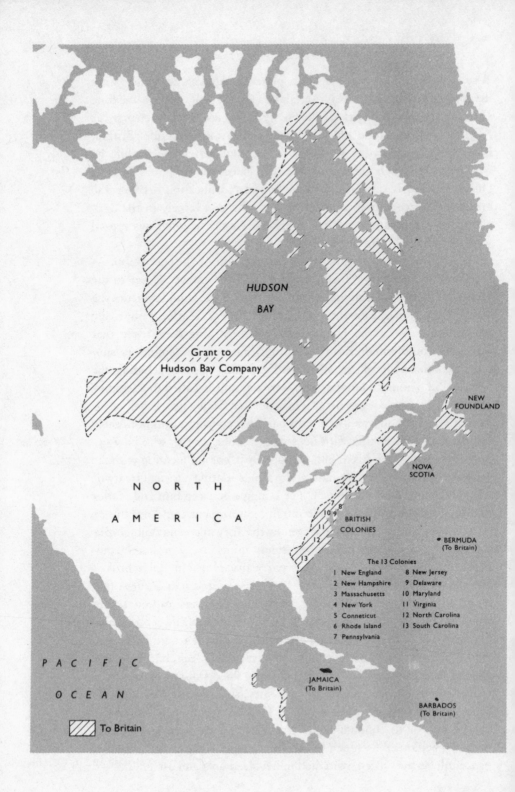

HUDSON
BAY

Grant to
Hudson Bay Company

NEW
FOUNDLAND

NORTH

AMERICA

NOVA
SCOTIA

7
4 3
5 6
2
10 8
9
BRITISH
COLONIES

● BERMUDA
(To Britain)

11

12

13

The 13 Colonies

1 New England	8 New Jersey
2 New Hampshire	9 Delaware
3 Massachusetts	10 Maryland
4 New York	11 Virginia
5 Conneticut	12 North Carolina
6 Rhode Island	13 South Carolina
7 Pennsylvania	

PACIFIC

OCEAN

JAMAICA
(To Britain)

BARBADOS
(To Britain)

To Britain

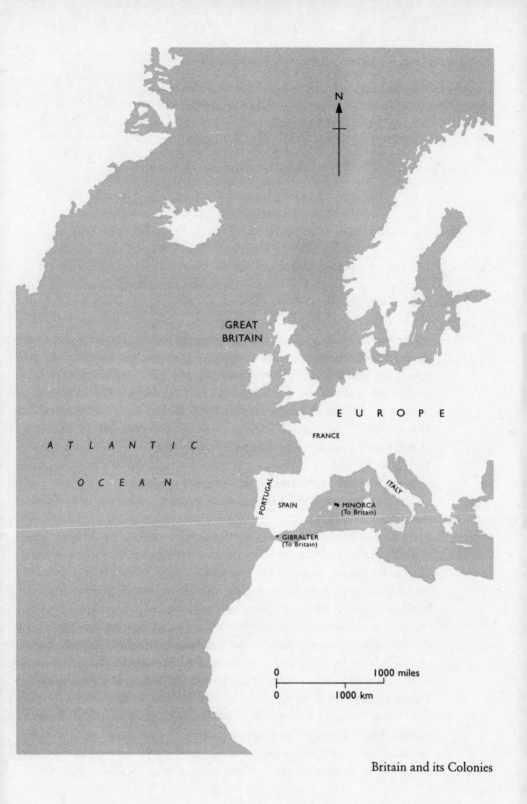

Britain and its Colonies

Epilogue

The peaceful death of Anne ended the tempestuous rule of the Stuarts. The crown passed to a German prince, who, predictably, faced a rebellion after his first year on the throne as James I had faced a plot after his.

The century of Stuart rule had clarified the role of the monarchy, the development of the central institutions of state and the position of the governing élites in both town and country. The process had been neither gradual nor evolutionary. Two revolutions had been necessary to alter the relationship between the crown and its subjects, though the alterations were in ways that neither would have imagined. By the end of the Stuart century there was a partnership between ruler and ruled cemented by the interdependence of king and Parliament and the independence of centre and locality.

The central problems of the reign of James I – religion, finance and the union with Scotland – had all been solved in unexpected ways. Religion had been the most contentious, beginning with an attempt by Catholics to assassinate the monarch and ending with the principle that only a Protestant could wear the crown. The Anglican church had established itself as the bulwark against Roman Catholicism on the one hand and against Nonconformity on the other, but it took the effects of two different revolutions to achieve this result. In the first, the possibility that radical Protestantism could form the basis of further reformation was fully explored and found wanting. The rule of the saints was brief and unsuccessful. Without the strong hand of central institutions, Protestantism had disintegrated into a *mélange* of churches and sects that created more problems for doctrine and discipline than it had solved. The subsequent attempt to incorporate Catholicism had run aground on the rocks of a prejudice so firmly entrenched in the British psyche as to be impervious to reason, blandishment or power. When the

Stuarts attempted to illustrate the dictum that, while Protestantism was the religion of princes, Catholicism was the religion of kings, they discovered that Protestantism was the religion of their people. Charles II, who always knew which way the wind blew, kept his Catholicism secret. His brother, who usually had the wind blowing against him, suffered for his.

Royal finance, which so bedevilled the early Stuarts, had a happier ending. The antiquated principle that the king should live of his own was replaced by the responsibility of the people to maintain a solvent government. Landowners overcame their reluctance to pay their share both through their experiences during the revolutionary period and through the realization that a stable monarchy was a bulwark against anarchy. New forms of revenue replaced subsidies, benevolences and feudal prerogatives. Taxes on land, wealth and commerce spread the pain evenly and gave the monarch an incentive to increase the prosperity of his subjects in order to augment his own revenues. But the transformation of royal revenue had significant consequences beyond ensuring the solvency of the crown. Administration grew as revenue agents, customs inspectors, tax collectors, auditors and receivers all became a permanent interest of a kind very different from property-holders. In the next century, they would form a vital part of parliamentary government and become a recognizable special interest. Similarly, the power of the House of Commons increased in proportion to the crown's dependence on the excise and the land tax to fund its policies and the civil list to fund its expenses. The commercial and then the financial sectors also enhanced their influence over both Parliament and crown as their expertise and access to ready cash made them the paymasters of British government.

James I's dream of a union of his kingdoms was also finally realized, though it remained for decades to come an unsettled amalgamation. Scotland's geopolitical position meant that it would always be caught between the ambitions of two more powerful nations, France and England. Throughout the early modern period, alliance with one was tantamount to war with the other, and the independent development of a powerful native Protestantism did little to change this fact of life. Not even the pro-French foreign policy of Charles II eased the difficulties the Scots had in retaining their independence. If they were not being strangled militarily, they were being bled economically, and it was the realization that their relative position could only grow weaker that led at least some of their leaders into the acceptance of the incorporative union that was achieved in 1707. Whether as a result of the infusion of resources and a new sense of security or as the final shudder of a people who had lost their liberty, there followed in Scotland an efflorescence of cultural, intellectual and social achievements never duplicated before or since.

The central problem of the reign of Charles I had been Britain's martial inadequacies. Neither army nor navy had been modernized, the crown was dependent upon emergency finance to raise troops, and an aristocratic ethos dictated the choice of commanders. Charles's early political difficulties could all be traced to his inability to make war, which, in the uncertain circumstances of the seventeenth century, meant an inability to defend his kingdoms and therefore an inadequacy as a king. War dominated seventeenth-century Britain from Charles's reign forward. His wars with Spain and France were succeeded by the Wars of the Three Kingdoms, the Commonwealth's wars with Holland and Spain, and the Anglo-Dutch wars of the reign of Charles II. James II faced two rebellions in three years, and constant warfare marked the reigns of both William III and Anne. The military capacities of the monarch developed of necessity. Professional officers led well-drilled and properly equipped soldiers. Despite an anti-army ideology that emerged during the revolutionary period, the later Stuart monarchs all maintained a standing army, and all increased the amount of money that was spent on military preparations. War finance was no longer an extraordinary expense that members of Parliament were occasionally summoned to provide: it was central to the workings of the royal budget, and drove the modernization of taxation, credit and finance. Charles I presided over the tragedy at Rhé; his granddaughter over the triumph at Blenheim.

The central problem of the Revolution, the distrust of the monarch and the monarchy, had also been resolved by the realization that, though the cure was as likely to be fatal as the disease, there were times when it was necessary to attempt it. The revolution of the mid-century left a legacy that nourished two political traditions. The first – conservative and loyal – kept the memory of the Revolution alive so that glimpses of the dark, churning underside of British society could always be seen, in the way that the owner of a castle might take visitors on a tour of the dungeons. It magnified the social and economic dislocation of the revolutionary decades, exaggerated the brutality and atrocities, painted the revolutionary leaders in monochrome. After the Restoration, believers in this tradition clung to church and king and joined the Tory party or imbibed 'country' ideology. After the revolution of 1688, if they were not tainted by Jacobitism, they melded quietly into that mainstream Whiggism which propped up the Anglican church and came to equate the ministry with the crown. The other political tradition of the Revolution long lived underground – among dissenters in the Restoration period, Exclusionists in the 1680s, opposition Whigs in the eighteenth century. Its adherents saw the light briefly as True Whigs in 1688, but their touchstones remained distrust of the monarchy and dissent from the established church. Liberty was their shibboleth, and they became torch-bearers to the great revolutionary movements of the late eighteenth century – one of the few examples of to the losers belong the spoils.

By the nineteenth century there was no doubt of the political legacy of the seventeenth. Tyrants had been tamed, liberty defended, religious toleration established, the British constitutional monarchy born. These were landmarks so clear as to need neither identification nor examination. But they were the landmarks of a later age. In 1714 the potential theoretical power of the monarch had been greatly diminished, its real practical power greatly enhanced. The liberty of the subject to be secure in property and person was inviolable as long as he paid his land tax and excise and did not fall foul of nearly 200 capital offences or come too near the insatiable press-gangs. Religious toleration was a chimera of the salons, a liberal daydream in a world which, having endured the mass hysteria of the Popish Plot, could be congratulated only on having avoided the mass violence of the Gordon Riots which were yet to come. The beliefs of Catholics, Unitarians, deists and atheists were still proscribed, and nonconforming Protestants were still penalized. The constitutional monarchy was, in one sense, real enough. Parliament had determined the line of succession and made itself an indispensable ally of the king. But the constitutional relationship between them was in its infancy, and George I and his immediate successors would not have the leverage of competing political parties to manage their parliaments. They would turn to corruption instead.

But the Stuarts did leave enduring legacies to their successors. Great Britain was one of the military, commercial and financial centres of the world. Though deeply in debt, the crown was solvent and its obligations were backed by public faith. It had thriving colonies in North

America and lucrative trading partners in Asia. The navy maintained strategic control over the Mediterranean from bases in Gibraltar and on the North African coast. The threat of a Spanish invasion – the bane of the sixteenth century – and the threat of French domination – the bane of the seventeenth – were both past. The Stuarts inherited a nearly bankrupt crown, social and economic crisis, and kingdoms imperilled by their neighbours. They passed on prosperity, security and a sense of national pride. There could be no better measure of their accomplishments than the fact that eighteenth-century Frenchmen came to envy the achievements of seventeenth-century Britain.

For Further Reading

The literature on Stuart Britain is so extensive that it has already outdated several volumes of bibliography. The suggestions that follow are designed to help readers locate good starting-points and to sample some of the best products of recent historiography. The list is not intended as either a critical appraisal or a full one. It includes only published books that are generally available in shops or college and university libraries and omits all references to specialist articles, which can easily be found through the bibliographies of the introductory surveys that are listed at the beginning of each section.

The Social World

The literature on social and economic history is so impressive that a separate volume of a companion series is devoted to synthesizing it. All that can be done here is to identify some recent work on major topics. The best general work on the entire period is Christopher Clay, *Economic Expansion and Social Change: England 1500–1700* (2 vols., 1984), which is unsurpassed in the range of material covered, the clarity of explication and the soundness of judgement. J. A. Sharpe, *Early Modern England: A Social History* (1987) is very good on social relations, crime and education. Keith Wrightson, *English Society, 1580–1680* (1982) bristles with insights and is strongest on social organization and personal relationships. There are numerous collections of primary materials on various aspects of social life. Ralph Houlbrooke, *English Family Life 1576–1716* (1989) contains excerpts from diaries covering an array of family relations, while Linda Pollock, *A Lasting Relationship: Parents and Children over Three Centuries* (1987) samples changing attitudes towards parenting. The experiences of women have been collected in Elspeth Graham et al. (eds.), *Her Own Life: Autobiographical Writings by Seventeenth-Century Women* (1989). One of the best eyewitness accounts is William Harrison, *The Description of England*, ed. Georges Edelen (1994).

Economic history, once buoyant, has sunk in recent years as practitioners have turned their attention to other periods and to methods less suitable for the surviving records of the seventeenth century. D. C. Coleman, *The Economy of England 1450–1750* (1977) remains the best single-volume survey for England, and Raymond Gillespie, *The Transformation of the Irish Economy* (1991) the best for Ireland. Though it begins towards the end of the period, L. M. Cullen, *An Economic History of Ireland since 1660* (1972) is also valuable. There is much of interest in L. A. Clarkson, *The Pre-Industrial Economy in England 1500–1750* (1971) and Joan Thirsk, *Economic Policy and Projects* (1978). Charles Wilson, *England's Apprenticeship* (2nd edn, 1984), though dated, is a treasure trove of information. Joan Thirsk and J. P. Copper (eds.), *Seventeenth-Century Economic Documents* (1972) provided a vast array of primary materials.

The topographical and geographical features of early modern Britain can be studied in H. C. Darby (ed.), *An Historical Geography of England before 1800* (1936); R. A. Dodgshon and R. A. Butlin (eds.), *An Historical Geography of England and Wales* (1978); G. Whittington and I. D. Whyte (eds.), *An Historical Geography of Scotland* (1983); A. R. Baker and R. A. Butlin (eds.), *Studies of Field Systems in the British Isles* (1973); and W. G. Hoskins, *The Making of the English Landscape* (rev. edn, 1992). The best starting-point for demographic history is still Peter Laslett, *The World We Have Lost: Further Explored* (3rd edn, 1984) but it has been surpassed by the quantitative work of the Cambridge Group that he helped to found. The comprehensive study is E. A. Wrigley and R. Schofield, *The Population History of England 1541–1871* (1981). An excellent brief introduction that includes Scotland and Ireland is R. A. Houston, *The Population History of Britain and Ireland 1500–1750* (1992). Roger Finlay, *Population and Metropolis: The Demography of London 1580–1650* (1981) studies the most significant case of population growth. Paul Slack, *The Impact of Plague in Tudor and Stuart England* (1985) examines one dimension of mortality crises; C. Gittings, *Death, Burial and the Individual in Early Modern England* (1984) another.

Family history has been the subject of much contention as the result of Lawrence Stone's massive *The Family, Sex and Marriage in England 1500–1800* (1977). Among those who have taken exception to the Stone thesis is Alan MacFarlane, *Marriage and Love in England: Modes of Reproduction 1300–1840* (1986). A good survey of family history is Ralph Houlbrooke, *The English Family, 1450–1700* (1984), but the best reconstruction remains A. MacFarlane, *The Family Life of Ralph Josselin: A Seventeenth-Century Clergyman* (1970). Anthony Fletcher's *Gender, Sex and Subordination in England 1500–1800* (1995) surveys a vast literature on gender relations. The varying experiences of children are the subject of Ilana Ben-Amos, *Adolescence and Youth in Early Modern England* (1994), while the particular experiences of agricultural servants are analysed by A. Kussmaul, *Servants in Husbandry* (1981). One aspect of marriage is treated in L. Stone, *Road to Divorce: England 1530–1987* (1990).

Urban history has been the subject of a host of monographs and collections of essays. Among the best are A. D. Dyer, *The City of Worcester in the Sixteenth Century* (1973); J. Patten, *English Towns, 1500–1700* (1978); C.

Phythian-Adams, *The Desolation of a City: Coventry and the Urban Crisis of the Later Middle Ages* (1979); D. H. Sacks, *The Widening Gate: Bristol and the Atlantic Economy, 1450–1700* (1991); Michael Lynch, *The Early Modern Town in Scotland* (1987); R. A. Butlin (ed.), *The Development of the Irish Town* (1977); and P. Clark and P. Slack (eds.), *Crisis and Order in English Towns 1500–1700* (1972) and *English Towns in Transition* (1976). Peter Borsay, *The English Urban Renaissance: Culture and Society in the Provincial Town 1660–1770* (1989) surveys town history in one of the great periods of transformation. There are a number of studies of London, beginning with the influential essays in F. J. Fisher, *London and the English Economy, 1500–1700* (1990). Ian Archer, *The Pursuit of Stability: Social Relations in Elizabethan London* (1988); Steven Rappaport, *Worlds Within Worlds: Structures of Life in Sixteenth-Century London* (1989); and Jeremy Boulton, *Neighbourhood and Society: A London Suburb in the Seventeenth Century* (1987) all complement each other. Another important collection of essays is A. L. Beier and Roger Finlay (eds.), *London 1500–1700: The Making of the Metropolis* (1986). R. A. Houston, *Social Change in the Age of Enlightenment: Edinburgh, 1660–1760* (1994) is the best work on the Scottish capital, and Maurice Craig, *Dublin 1660–1860: A Social and Architectural History* (1952) still the best for Ireland's.

The starting-place for early modern agriculture is Joan Thirsk (ed.), *The Agrarian History of England and Wales*, Vol. 4, *1500–1640* (1967) and Vol. 5, *1640–1750* (1984) and I. D. Whyte, *Agriculture and Society in Seventeenth-Century Scotland* (1979). Thirsk's collected essays, *The Rural Economy of England* (1984), are among the finest studies of farming and life on the land. The work that has generated the most controversy is Eric Kerridge, *The Agricultural Revolution* (1967), which presents a case for technological innovation in the seventeenth century. The classic work on agrarian change is R. H. Tawney, *The Agrarian Problem of the Sixteenth Century* (1912), the most complete study of enclosures J. A. Yelling, *Common Field and Enclosure in England, 1450–1850* (1977). There are a number of valuable local studies which chart change in the lives of the rural population and reconstruct the web of social and economic relationships within them: W. G. Hoskins, *The Midland Peasant* (1957); D. G. Hey, *An English Rural Community: Myddle under the Tudors and Stuarts* (1974); Margaret Spufford, *Contrasting Communities* (1974); Victor Skipp, *Crisis and Development* (1978); K. Wrightson and D. Levine, *Poverty and Piety in an English Village* (2nd edn, 1995); K. Wrightson and D. Levine, *The Making of an Industrial Society: Whickham, 1560–1765* (1991). An important collection of essays on a variety of social history topics is R. A. Houston and I. D. Whyte (eds.), *Scottish Society 1500–1800* (1989), while L. M. Cullen, *The Emergence of Modern Ireland 1600–1900* (1981) is invaluable on Irish society. The relationship between wages and prices is established in H. Phelps Brown and S. Hopkins, *A Perspective of Wages and Prices* (1981), and the literature on the subject is surveyed in R. B. Outhwaite, *Inflation in*

Tudor and Early Stuart England (2nd edn, 1982). The most dramatic consequences of economic dislocation can be seen in Andrew Appleby, *Famine in Tudor and Stuart England* (1978). Social change among the more fortunate is the subject of Mildred Campbell, *The English Yeoman under Elizabeth and the Early Stuarts* (2nd edn, 1967), while excerpts from the gentry controversy can be found in L. Stone (ed.), *Social Change and Revolution in England 1540–1640* (1965), whose bibliography is a guide to the full texts. Stone's own *The Crisis of the Aristocracy 1558–1641* (1965) is one of the great works of English social history. The transformation from the landed to the monied is the subject of P. Earle, *The Making of the English Middle Class: Business, Society and Family Life in London 1660–1730* (1989).

Trade and industry have long attracted interest for their impact on industrialization in the eighteenth century. There are many specialist studies and a number of good synthetic works. For the most important industry of all, the classic work is P. J. Bowden, *The Wool Trade in Tudor and Stuart England* (1962), which should be read with B. Supple, *Commercial Crisis and Change in England 1600–1642* (1959). D. C. Coleman, *Industry in Tudor and Stuart England* (1975) and Sybil Jack, *Trade and Industry in Tudor and Stuart England* (1977) provide good surveys, while L. A. Clarkson, *Proto-Industrialization: The First Phase of Industrialization?* (1985) presents the results of the debate over the putting-out system. Foreign trade is treated in G. D. Ramsey, *English Overseas Trade during the Centuries of Emergence* (1957); Ralph Davis, *The Rise of the English Shipping Industry* (1962); his succinct *A Commercial Revolution: English Overseas Trade in the Seventeenth and Eighteenth Century* (1967) and Kenneth R. Andrews, *Trade, Plunder, and Settlement: Maritime Enterprise and the Genesis of the British Empire, 1480–1630* (1984). The greatest of the seventeenth-century trading companies is the subject of K. N. Chaudhuri, *The English East India Company* (1965). Robert Brenner, *Merchants and Revolution: Commercial Change, Political Conflict, and London's Overseas Traders, 1550–1653* (1993) studies conflicts within the London merchant community.

The problem of poverty and social control has been studied from a number of different perspectives. A. Fletcher and D. Stevenson (eds.), *Order and Disorder in Early Modern England* (1985) contains important essays which stake out conflicting positions. On vagrancy, see J. F. Pound, *Poverty and Vagrancy in Tudor England* (1971); Lee Beier, *Masterless Men* (1985); and Paul Slack, *Poverty and Policy in Tudor and Stuart England* (1988). There are a number of important studies of Puritan attitudes, including Christopher Hill, *Society and Puritanism in Pre-Revolutionary England* (1964); Paul Seaver, *Wallington's World* (1985); and David Underdown, *Fire from Heaven* (1992). Popular assumptions about the social order and its violation are the subject of D. Underdown, *Revel, Riot and Rebellion* (1985) and Susan Amussen, *An Ordered Society* (1988), which also treats the ambiguous role of women in local society. Work on women's lives has revived in the last decade, though the classic study remains Alice Clark, *Working Life of Women in the Seventeenth Century* (1919). A good general introduction is A. Laurence, *Women in England 1500–1760: A Social History* (1994). Margaret Sommerville carefully surveys attitudes towards women in *Sex and Subjection* (1995). Amy Erickson has written an important monograph, *Women and Property in Early Modern England* (1993), and there is much of interest in Sarah Mendelson, *The Mental World of Stuart Women* (1987). P. Crawford, *Women and Religion 1500–1720* (1993) is useful, though the outstanding book on the subject is Phyllis Mack, *Visionary Women* (1992). The collection of essays edited by Mary Prior, *Women in English Society 1500–1800* (1985), continues to be a touchstone. The prosecution of women is among the topics of Martin Ingram, *Church Courts, Sex and Marriage in England 1570–1640* (1987). For crime in general the best place to start is J. A. Sharpe, *Crime in Early Modern England 1550–1750* (1984). Though much of it falls beyond our period, J. M. Beattie, *Crime and the Courts in England, 1660–1800* (1986) is definitive. Witchcraft, the criminal activity that has received most scholarly attention, is one of the subjects of K. V. Thomas's seminal work, *Religion and the Decline of Magic* (1971).

Popular attitudes and culture have largely relied upon written sources. David Cressy has studied the probable proportion of people who could write and read in *Literacy and the Social Order: Reading and Writing in Tudor and Stuart England* (1980). What was available to them is the subject of B. S. Capp, *English Almanacs, 1500–1800* (1979) and Margaret Spufford, *Small Books and Pleasant Histories: Popular Fiction and its Readership in Seventeenth-Century England* (1981). Barry Reay has edited a good collection of essays, *Popular Culture in Seventeenth-Century England* (1985), and for Ireland there is Edward MacLysaght, *Irish Life in the Seventeenth Century* (3rd edn, 1979). Three studies that delve into the popular imagination are Michael MacDonald, *Mystical Bedlam: Madness, Anxiety, and Healing in Seventeenth-Century England* (1981); Keith Thomas, *Man and the Natural World* (1983); and D. Cressy, *Bonfires and Bells: National Memory and the Protestant Calendar* (1989).

The Political World

The outstanding survey of sixteenth-century political history is J. A. Guy, *Tudor England* (1988). It can be read in conjunction with Penry Williams, *The Tudor Regime* (1979), which is strong on administrative matters, and the classic *England under the Tudors* (2nd edn, 1974) by Sir Geoffrey Elton. The Elizabethan period, sandwiched between the age of Reformation and the reign of the early Stuarts, has suffered comparative neglect and is best approached through the relevant chapter in Penry Williams, *The Late Tudors: England 1547–1603* (1995). Two good recent biographies are by Wallace MacCaffrey, *Elizabeth I* (1993), and Christopher Haigh, *Elizabeth I* (1988), but the best work remains J. E. Neale, *Queen Elizabeth* (1934). Haigh has led a group of younger revisionists who have questioned the achievements of Gloriana and has edited an important collections of essays, *The Reign of Elizabeth I* (1984). The most complete history of the reign is MacCaffrey's trilogy, *The Shaping of the Elizabethan Regime* (1968); *Queen Elizabeth and the Making of Policy 1572–1588* (1981); and *Elizabeth I: War and Politics 1588–1603* (1992), all of which are very strong on foreign policy. For Elizabeth's other kingdoms the best introductory volumes are Steven Ellis, *Tudor Ireland: Crown, Community and the Conflict of Cultures 1470–1603* (1985) and Jenny Wormald, *Court, Kirk and Community: Scotland 1470–1625* (1981). There are several new collections of essays that attempt to view Britain and Ireland as a single unit, including S. Ellis and S. Barber, *Conquest and Union: Fashioning a British State, 1485–1725* (1995) and B. Bradshaw and J. S. Morrill, *The British Problem 1534–1707* (1996).

One has to go back to J. N. Figgis, *The Divine Right of Kings* (1886) to find a study devoted entirely to the theory of monarchy in the early modern period. Glenn Burgess, *Absolute Monarchy and the Stuart Constitution* (1996) is one attempt to fill this gap, and Howard Nenner, *The Right to be King: The Succession to the Crown of England 1603–1714* (1995) another. There are a number of outstanding works of political theory that survey both royalist and constitutionalist thought: J. W. Allen, *English Political Thought 1603–60* (1938); Margaret Judson, *The Crisis of the Constitution* (1949); J. G. A. Pocock, *The Ancient Constitution and the Feudal Law* (2nd edn, 1987); Johann Sommerville, *Politics and Ideology in England 1603–40* (1986); J. H. Burns (ed.), *The Cambridge History of Political Thought 1450–1700* (1991); and Glenn Burgess, *The Politics of the Ancient Constitution* (1992). Political culture more broadly conceived is the subject of the essays in the collections of P. Lake and K. Sharpe (eds.), *Culture and Politics in Early Stuart England* (1993) and S. Amussen and M. A. Kishlansky (eds.), *Political Culture and Cultural Politics in Early Modern England* (1995). Standard editions of key political texts are Sir Robert Filmer, *Patriarcha and Other Writings*, ed. J. P. Sommerville (1991); John Locke, *Two Treatises of Government*, ed. Peter Laslett (2nd edn, 1967); and Thomas Hobbes, *Leviathan*, ed. C. B. Macpherson (1985).

Treatments of the English church or the royal court as a political institution are uncommon, though there has been much recent interest in the court as a cultural construct. Andrew Foster's *The Church of England 1570–1640* (1994) and S. Doran and C. Durston, *Princes, Pastors and People* (1991) are good overviews of the ecclesiastical establishment. The best introduction to the court are the essays by Neil Cuddy and Kevin Sharpe in D. Starkey (ed.), *The English Court* (1987). The administrative side of the court in the early seventeenth century has been definitively studied by G. E. Aylmer in *The King's Servants* (2nd edn, 1974) and *The State's Servants: The Civil Service of the English Republic* (1973), while its political impact at the other end of the century is the subject of R. O. Bucholz, *The Augustan Court: Queen Anne and the Decline of Court Culture* (1993). The vexed question of corruption at court has been addressed by Joel Hurstfield, *Freedom, Corruption and Government in Elizabethan England* (1973) and Linda Peck, *Court Patronage and Corruption in Early Stuart England* (1990).

There are nearly as many studies of individual counties as there are counties to study. Among the best for political and administrative history are T. G. Barnes, *Somerset 1625–40: A County's Government during the 'Personal Rule'* (1961); Mervyn James, *Family, Lineage and Civil Society: A Study of Society, Politics and Mentality in the Durham Region 1500–1640* (1974); A. Hassell Smith, *County and Court: Government and Politics in Norfolk 1558–1603* (1974); Diarmaid MacCulloch, *Suffolk and the Tudors* (1986); Philip Jenkins, *The Making of a Ruling Class: The Glamorgan Gentry 1640–1790* (1983); and Clive Holmes, *Seventeenth-Century Lincolnshire* (1988). Anthony Fletcher, *Reform in the Provinces* (1986), studies the overall shape of Stuart local administration. There is no work on the office of sheriff, adequate or otherwise. Lord Lieutenants have been treated in Lindsay Boynton, *The Elizabethan Militia 1558–1638* (1967) and more centrally by Victor Stater, *Noble Government* (1994). The classic work on justices of the peace is J. P. Dawson, *A History of Lay Judges* (1960). For seventeenth-century JPs see J. H. Gleason, *Justices of the Peace in England* (1969); Lionel Glassey, *Politics and the Appointment of Justices of the Peace 1675–1720* (1979); and N. Landau, *The Justices of the Peace, 1679–1760* (1984). An important book on crime and criminal justice is Cynthia Herrup, *The Common Peace* (1987), while the best work on assizes is J. S. Cockburn, *A History of English Assizes, 1558–1714* (1972). There are interesting chapters on the gentry's role in local government in Felicity Heal and Clive Holmes, *The Gentry in England and Wales 1500–1700* (1994).

Parliament and its place in English government and politics have been the subject of numerous studies, mostly concerning the House of Commons. For the Lords the outstanding book on practice is Elizabeth Foster, *The House of Lords 1603–49* (1983) and, on a specific parliament, C. H. Firth, *The House of Lords During the English Civil War* (1910). For the Commons, the best introduction is the first chapter of C. S. R. Russell, *Parliaments and English Politics* (1979). J. E. Neale, *The Elizabethan House of Commons* (1950) explains the basic workings, while Derek Hirst, *The Representative of the People?* (1975) and M. A. Kishlansky, *Parliamentary Selection: Social and Political Choice in Early Modern England* (1986) offer differing views of the ways in which members were chosen. There are as yet no volumes of the history of Parliament for the early seventeenth century, but M. F. Keeler, *The Long Parliament* (1954) offers biographical information and D. Brunton and D. H. Pennington, *Members of the Long Parliament* (1954) offer analysis for the Civil War parliament. B. D. Henning, *The House of Commons 1660–1690* (3 vols., 1983) is invaluable for the later Stuarts.

James I

The starting-point of all narratives of early-seventeenth-century political history is Volumes 1–5 of S. R. Gardiner, *History of England 1603–42* (10 vols., 1883–4). There are valuable chapters on James's reign in Derek Hirst, *Authority and Conflict: England, 1603–58* (1986) and Barry Coward, *The Stuart Age: England 1603–1714* (2nd edn, 1994); and especially Roger Lockyer, *The Early Stuarts: A Political History of England, 1603–1642* (1989). For Ireland, the best single volume is Brendan Fitzpatrick, *Seventeenth-Century Ireland* (1988); for Scotland, Gordon Donaldson, *James V–James VII* (1965); and for Wales both Glanmor Williams, *Recovery, Reorientation and Reformation Wales c. 1415–1642* (1987) and W. S. K. Thomas, *Stuart Wales* (1988) should be consulted. Maurice Lee's *Great Britain's Solomon* (1990) is an insightful study of various aspects of the reign. Christopher Durston, *James I* (1993) is a brief guide to recent literature. Though the era is renowned for its literary masterpieces – including the mature works of Shakespeare, the drama of Jonson, the poetry of Donne and the Authorized Bible – only Bacon qualifies as a significant political theorist: *The Essayes or Counsels, Civill and Morall of Francis Bacon*, ed. Michael Kiernan (1985). The King, of course, might have placed himself in this category, and much of James's work has been printed: *Letters of King James VI & I*, ed. G. P. V. Akrigg (1984) and *The Political Works of James I*, ed. C. H. McIlwain (1918). A fascinating compendium of portrayals of James is found in R. Ashton, *James I by his Contemporaries* (1969). A selection of constitutional documents can be found in G. W. Prothero (ed.), *Select Statutes and other Constitutional Documents Illustrative of the Reigns of Elizabeth and James I* (4th edn, 1913) and J. P. Kenyon (ed.), *The Stuart Constitution* (2nd edn, 1986). Finally, one of the most notable court gossips in English history can be savoured in N. E. McClure, *The Letters of John Chamberlain* (2 vols., 1939).

There is no adequate biography of James, as D. H. Willson's *King James VI & I* (1956) has not worn well. His early career is best studied through histories of Scotland of which Jenny Wormald's *Court, Kirk and Community: Scotland 1470–1625* (1981) is the best on James VI & I. M. Lee's *Government by Pen* (1980) is a reliable narrative of Scottish politics during this period. The Jacobean court has attracted the attention of cultural historians like Graham Parry, *The Golden Age Restored* (1981) and Malcolm Smuts, *Court Culture and the Origins of a Royalist Tradition in Early Stuart England* (1987), as well as in an interesting collection of essays, L. L. Peck (ed.), *The Mental World of the Jacobean Court* (1991). Courtiers have received less sustained attention, and we are in desperate need of a biography of Salisbury. There are two good studies of subsequent Jacobean ministers: Linda Peck, *Northampton: Patronage and Policy at the Court of James I* (1982) and M. Prestwich, *Cranfield: Politics and Profits under the Early Stuarts* (1966). As always, Parliament takes the laurel for the greatest number of works, and every Jacobean parliament has been studied individually, beginning with Wallace Notestein's posthumous *House of Commons 1604–10* (1971). C. S. R. Russell's *Parliaments and English Politics* (1979) is useful on 1621, as is Robert Ruigh, *The Parliament of 1624* (1971) on James's last assembly. Thomas Cogswell, *The Blessed Revolution* (1989) is outstanding for the impact of foreign policy on parliamentary politics.

Jacobean finance remains *terra incognita*, the only map being F. C. Dietz, *English Public Finance 1558–1641* (1932). R. Ashton, *The Crown and the Money Market* (1960) and *The City and the Court 1603–43* (1979) are both good on debt and debtors in London. R. W. Hoyle (ed.), *The Estates of the English Crown, 1558–1640* (1992) contains valuable essays on royal land-holding. James's scheme for a union of two of his kingdoms has had recent treatments in B. Galloway, *The Union of England and Scotland 1603–1608* (1986) and Brian Levack, *The Formation of the British State* (1987). Keith Brown, *Kingdom or Province?: Scotland and the Regal Union 1603–1715* (1992) covers a longer period but is essential for the Jacobean developments. Religion and religious policy have been exceptionally well studied. The starting-point should be Patrick Collinson, *The Religion of Protestants 1559–1625* (1982). K. Fincham, *Prelate as Pastor* (1990) provides a careful analysis of the Jacobean bishops. A good short study of Catholicism is Alan Dures, *English Catholicism, 1558–1642* (1983). Peter Lake's *Anglican and Puritan?* (1988) calls into question the simple distinctions among Calvinists that formed the basis of William Haller's seminal *The Rise of Puritanism* (1938). *Society and Puritanism in Pre-Revolutionary England* (1964) by Christopher Hill has a greater range than the Jacobean period, but is a stimulating work. K. Fincham (ed.), *The Early Stuart Church 1603–42* (1993) is a valuable collection of essays. Foreign policy has been neglected, but there are outstanding studies from the perspective of the Continent, including Geoffrey Parker (ed.), *The Thirty Years War* (1984) and C. V. Wedgwood's classic *The Thirty Years War* (1939). There is no adequate life of the great jurist Sir Edward Coke, though there are many books on his rival, Sir Francis Bacon: Anthony Quinton, *Francis Bacon* (1980) is an excellent brief introduction. There is some outstanding work on Jacobean legal history, including W. J. Jones, *Politics and the Bench* (1971) and Wilfred Prest, *The Inns of Court under Elizabeth I and the Early Stuarts 1590–1640* (1972) and *The Rise of the Barristers: A Social History of the English Bar, 1590–1640* (1986).

Charles I

No period of English political history has been as intensively studied as the reign of Charles I. The following works are but a small sample of the general and monographic literature. There remains no substitute for Volumes 6–10 of S. R. Gardiner's magisterial *History of England 1603–42* (1883–4). There are good chapters in Derek Hirst, *Authority and Conflict: England 1603–58*

(1986); Roger Lockyer, *The Early Stuarts: A Political History of England, 1603–1642* (1989); and Barry Coward, *The Stuart Age: England 1603–1714* (2nd edn, 1994). Christopher Hill, *The Century of Revolution, 1603–1714* (2nd edn, 1980) is still worth reading. For Ireland the best single volume is Brendan Fitzpatrick, *Seventeenth-Century Ireland* (1988) and for Scotland, Gordon Donaldson, *James V–James VII* (1965). The best short survey, however, is Brian Quintrell, *Charles I, 1625–1640* (1993). There are many collections of specialized essays, including Conrad Russell (ed.), *The Origins of the English Civil War* (1973) and Kevin Sharpe (ed.), *Faction and Parliament: Essays on Early Stuart History* (1978), both of which have worn well. R. P. Cust and Ann Hughes (eds.), *Conflict in Early Stuart England* (1989) is important. The landmark political and constitutional documents of the period are conveniently presented in J. P. Kenyon (ed.), *The Stuart Constitution* (2nd edn, 1986), while the debate over the Petition of Right can be followed day to day in Robert Johnson et al. (eds.), *Commons Debates, 1628* (6 vols., 1977–83). Though it was not published during his lifetime, Filmer's *Patriarcha* was written in the late 1620s and is the outstanding work of political theory of the period: see Sir Robert Filmer, *Patriarcha and Other Writings*, ed. J. P. Sommerville (1991). Contemporary sketches of some of the leading figures of the age are incomparably drawn in John Aubrey, *Brief Lives*, ed. Richard Barber (1983).

There are two modern biographies of the King, neither of which is altogether satisfactory: Pauline Gregg, *King Charles I* (1981) and Charles Carlton, *Charles I, the Personal Monarch* (1983). There is no modern life of the Queen that can be recommended. Charles's courtiers and counsellors have been well studied. The key figures are covered by Roger Lockyer, *Buckingham: The Life and Political Career of George Villiers, First Duke of Buckingham, 1592–1628* (1981); C. V. Wedgwood, *Thomas Wentworth, First Earl of Strafford, 1593–1641: A Revaluation* (1962) and a recent collection of essays, J. F. Merritt (ed.), *The Political World of Thomas Wentworth, Earl of Strafford* (1996); H. R. Trevor-Roper, *Archbishop Laud* (3rd edn, 1988); and Michael Van Cleave Alexander, *Charles I's Lord Treasurer: Sir Richard Weston, Earl of Portland (1577–1635)* (1975). Away from the centre there are numerous county studies, of which Thomas G. Barnes, *Somerset, 1625–1640: A County's Government during the 'Personal Rule'* (1961); John Morrill, *Cheshire 1630–1660: County Government and Society during the English Revolution* (1974); J. T. Cliffe, *The Yorkshire Gentry from the Reformation to the Civil War* (1969); Anthony Fletcher, *A County Community in Peace and War: Sussex 1600–1660* (1975); and William Hunt, *The Puritan Moment: The Coming of Revolution in an English County* (1983) can all be recommended. Among the many works on political subjects are three outstanding accounts: Richard Cust, *The Forced Loan and English Politics, 1626–28* (1987); Kevin Sharpe, *The Personal Rule of Charles I* (1992); and Conrad Russell, *The Fall of the British Monarchies, 1637–42* (1991).

Charles's religious policies have been intensely studied, even if the King's own views remain elusive. The modern starting-point is the debate over Arminianism, which can be followed by reading Peter Lake, *Anglican and Puritan?* (1988); Nicholas Tyacke, *Anti-Calvinists: The Rise of English Arminianism* (1987); Peter White, *Predestination, Policy and Polemic: Conflict and Consensus in the English Church from the Reformation to the Civil War* (1992); and the lengthy chapter on religion in Kevin Sharpe, *The Personal Rule of Charles I* (1992). While controversy over Arminianism rages, the debate over Puritanism is currently stilled. There are innumerable studies. The classic accounts are William Haller, *The Rise of Puritanism* (1938) and Christopher Hill, *Puritanism and Revolution: Studies in Interpretation of the English Revolution of the 17th Century* (2nd edn, 1995). Patrick Collinson, *The Religion of Protestants 1559–1625* (1982) challenges old definitions, despite concentrating on the earlier period. David Underdown, *Revel, Riot and Rebellion* (1985) places Puritanism and its critics within a cultural context. The impact of Catholicism, real or imagined, is only now coming to be recognized. Three valuable works are John Bossy, *The English Catholic Community 1570–1850* (1975); Caroline Hibbard, *Charles I and the Popish Plot* (1983); and Anthony Milton, *Catholic and Reformed* (1995).

Work on Ireland and Scotland, though less copious, is still substantial. Two good introductory volumes are Karl S. Bottigheimer, *Ireland and the Irish* (1982) and Nicholas Canny, *From Reformation to Restoration: Ireland, 1534–1660* (1987). T. W. Moody et al. (eds.), *A New History of Ireland*, Vol. 3, *Early Modern Ireland 1534–1691* (1976) is an important collection of essays at a high level of synthesis. Two outstanding works on the Caroline period are Aidan Clarke, *The Old English in Ireland 1625–42* (1966) and Hugh Kearney, *Strafford in Ireland, 1633–41: A Study in Absolutism* (2nd edn, 1989). There are a number of good monographs that trace the history of Charles's rule in Scotland: Maurice Lee, *The Road to Revolution: Scotland under Charles I 1625–37* (1985); Allan MacInnes, *Charles I and the Making of the Covenanting Movement* (1991); and Peter Donald, *An Uncounselled King* (1990).

Civil War and Revolution

The starting-place for the political history of the period 1640–60 is the continuation of S. R. Gardiner's magisterial survey of the seventeenth century, *The History of the Great Civil War* (4 vols., 1883); *The History of the Commonwealth and Protectorate* (3 vols., 1894); and its conclusion by Sir Charles Firth, *The Last Years of the Protectorate* (2 vols., 1909). The best single-volume history is G. E. Aylmer, *Rebellion or Revolution? England 1640–60* (1986). There are good chapters in Derek Hirst, *Authority and Conflict: England, 1603–58* (1986) and Barry Coward, *The Stuart Age: England 1603–1714* (2nd edn, 1994). For the period to 1649 there can be no more enjoyable reading than C. V. Wedgwood's trilogy *The King's Peace* (1955), *The King's War* (1959) and *A Coffin for King Charles* (1964). The period from the execution of the King to the Restoration has not found its historian. Two brief surveys are T. C. Barnard, *The English Republic* (1982) and R. Hutton, *The British Republic 1649–60* (1990). The best treatment of the vast modern literature on the causes of the breakdown of Charles's government is Ann Hughes, *The Causes of the English Civil War* (1990), while R. C. Richardson, *The Debate on the English Revolution Revisited* (1988) traces interpretations through the centuries. There are any number of valuable essay collections, including Conrad Russell, *Unrevolutionary England 1603–1642* (1990); Christopher Hill, *The Collected Essays* (3 vols., 1986); J. S. Morrill (ed.), *Reactions to the English Civil War* (1982) and *The Nature of the English Revolution* (1993); and G. E. Aylmer (ed.), *The Interregnum* (1972). Selections from political sources can be found in J. P. Kenyon (ed.), *The Stuart Constitution* (2nd edn, 1986) and more fully in S. R. Gardiner (ed.), *Constitutional Documents of the Puritan Revolution* (3rd edn, 1906). There is a profusion of contemporary materials available from this period. On the royalist side the starting-place must be Clarendon, who can be sampled in *Selections from the History of the Rebellion and the Life*, ed. G. Huehns (1978). There is an interesting selection of lesser-known theorists in David Wootton (ed.), *Divine Right and Democracy* (1986). Lucy Hutchinson's life of her husband has been reprinted: *Memoirs of the Life of Colonel Hutchinson*, ed. James Sutherland (1973). There are many collections of the writings of the Levellers, of which G. E. Aylmer (ed.), *The Levellers in the English Revolution* (1975) is the most accessible. A. S. P. Woodhouse, *Puritanism and Liberty* (1992) contains the records of the Army debates at Putney and Whitehall. Cromwell can be approached through *The Speeches of Oliver Cromwell*, ed. Ivan Roots (1989); Milton's vast outpouring of prose can be sampled in *Selected Prose of John Milton*, ed. C. A. Patrides (1985), while D. Lagomarsino and Charles Wood have edited the documents of *The Trial of Charles I* (1989).

Two very different works should be the starting-point for study of either long- or short-term causes of the events of the mid-century: Lawrence Stone, *The Causes of the English Revolution* (1972) and Conrad Russell, *The Causes of the English Civil War* (1990). Gordon Donaldson, *The Making of the Scottish Prayer Book of 1637* (1954); David Stevenson, *The Scottish Revolution, 1637–1644* (1973); and Allan MacInnes, *Charles I and the Making of the Covenanting Movement* (1991) are all essential for the Scottish origins of the civil wars; Anthony Fletcher, *The Outbreak of the English Civil War* (1981); Conrad Russell, *The Fall of the British Monarchies, 1637–42* (1991); and Kevin Sharpe, *The Personal Rule of Charles I* (1992) narrate the English origins; and M. Perceval-Maxwell, *The Outbreak of the Irish Rebellion of 1641* (1994) and Jane Ohlmeyer, *Civil War and Restoration in the Three Stuart Kingdoms: The Career of Randal MacDonnell, Marquis of Antrim, 1609–1683* (1993) explain the Irish origins. J. S. Morrill, *Revolt of the Provinces* (1976) has been an influential interpretative essay.

The best single volume on the military aspects of the war is J. P. Kenyon, *The*

Civil Wars of England (1988). Peter Young has written numerous popular works, of which *The English Civil War: A Military History of the Three Civil Wars* (1974) and *Naseby 1645: The Campaign and the Battle* (1985) can be consulted with profit. The social history of the war is the subject of Charles Carlton, *Going to the Wars: The Experience of the British Civil Wars 1638–51* (1992). For the royalist armies the best studies are Ronald Hutton, *The Royalist War Effort* (1982) and P. R. Newman, *The Old Service* (1993); for the parliamentarians, C. H. Firth, *Cromwell's Army* (1902) remains unsurpassed and B. S. Capp, *Cromwell's Navy* (1989) is a thorough account of an important subject. There are few good studies of the military commanders. Maurice Ashley, *Rupert of the Rhine* (1976) and John Wilson, *Fairfax* (1985) present interesting contrasts. There are, of course, a host of biographies of Cromwell, but the best is still C. H. Firth, *Oliver Cromwell and the Rule of the Puritans in England* (1900). R. S. Paul, *The Lord Protector* (1955) is strongest on Cromwell's religion. B. Coward, *Oliver Cromwell* (1991) is up to date, if bloodless, and J. S. Morrill (ed.), *Oliver Cromwell and the English Revolution* (1990) has some important essays.

Civil War politics are the subject of Clive Holmes, *The Eastern Association* (1973); M. A. Kishlansky, *The Rise of the New Model Army* (1979); I. J. Gentles, *The New Model Army in England, Ireland and Scotland, 1645–1653* (1992); Austin Woolrych, *Soldiers and Statesmen* (1987); and David Underdown's classic *Pride's Purge* (1971). There is little on the royalist side apart from David Smith, *Constitutional Royalism and the Search for Settlement c. 1640–49* (1994). There is no satisfactory work on the Presbyterians, though William Haller, *Liberty and Reformation in the Puritan Revolution* (1955) is good on the pamphlet controversies of the 1640s and William Lamont, *Marginal Prynne* (1963) delves into the mind of a complicated thinker. For the radical congregations see Murray Tolmie, *The Triumph of the Saints: The Separate Churches of London, 1616–1649* (1977) and B. S. Capp, *The Fifth Monarchy Men* (1972). The Levellers have been studied by T. C. Pease, *The Leveller Movement* (1916) and H. N. Brailsford, *The Levellers and the English Revolution* (1961). Christopher Hill, *The World Turned Upside Down* (1972) is the classic account of radical religion in the 1640s and '50s, though it should be read alongside J. C. Davies, *Fear, Myth and History: The Ranters and Historians* (1986). Blair Worden, *The Rump Parliament* (1975) and Austin Woolrych, *Commonwealth to Protectorate* (1982) are outstanding on the politics of the 1650s.

The revolutionary period in Ireland is the subject of T. C. Barnard, *Cromwellian Policy in Ireland: English Government and Reform 1649–60* (1975); David Stevenson, *Scottish Covenanters and Irish Confederates: Scottish-Irish Relations in the Mid-Seventeenth Century* (1981) and the chapters by P. J. Corish in T. W. Moody et al. (eds.), *A New History of Ireland*, Vol. 3, *Early Modern Ireland 1534–1691* (1976). Jane Ohlmeyer (ed.), *Ireland from Independence to Occupation* (1995) is a valuable collection of essays. There is a brief biography of Ormond: J. C. Beckett, *The Cavalier Duke* (1990). Scotland is treated by David Stevenson in both *Revolution and Counter-Revolution in Scotland, 1644–1651* (1977) and *Alasdair MacColla and the Highland Problem in the Seventeenth Century* (1980). See also F. D. Dow, *Cromwellian Scotland* (1979). E. J. Cowan, *Montrose for Covenant and King* (1977) is a good study of the most royalist of the Scots, though for sheer pleasure it is hard to replace John Buchan, *The Marquis of Montrose* (1913).

There are numerous histories of the English localities during the revolutionary period. Alan Everitt, *The Community of Kent and the Great Rebellion* (1966) is credited with beginning the second great wave of county studies. Among the best of later works are David Underdown, *Somerset during the Civil War and Interregnum* (1973); John Morrill, *Cheshire 1630–1660: County Government and Society during the English Revolution* (1974); R. Howell, *Newcastle-upon-Tyne during the Puritan Revolution* (1967); and Ann Hughes, *Politics, Society and Civil War in Warwickshire, 1620–60* (1987). J. Eales, *Puritans and Roundheads: The Harleys of Brampton Bryan* (1990) is a history of both a family and a locality. Regrettably, there is no reliable full-length study of London.

Charles II

The reign of Charles II has recently attracted attention after a long hiatus. The classic work remains David Ogg, *England in the Reign of Charles II* (2 vols., 1956) which is best on foreign policy and the navy. There are valuable chapters in Geoffrey Holmes, *The Making of a Great Power* (1993) and Tim Harris, *Politics under the Later Stuarts* (1993). J. R. Jones, *Country and Court: England 1658–1714* (1978) is good on the 1670s and '80s. Wales, Scotland and Ireland remain the subject of few general surveys. G. H. Jenkins, *The Foundations of Modern Wales: Wales 1642–1780* (1993); Rosalind Mitchison, *Lordship to Patronage: Scotland, 1603–1745* (1983); and David Dickson, *New Foundations: Ireland 1660–1800* (1987) are good starting-points. There are detailed chapters in T. W. Moody et al. (eds.), *A New History of Ireland*, Vol. 3, *Early Modern Ireland 1534–1691* (1976). There is an outstanding selection of political and constitutional documents in A. Browning (ed.), *English Historical Documents, VIII: 1660–1714* (1953). The great diarists Evelyn and Pepys can be sampled in accessible modern editions: *The Diary of John Evelyn*, ed. John Bowle (1983) and *The Shorter Pepys*, ed. R. Latham (1985).

Two favourable recent biographies are John Miller, *Charles II* (1991) and Ronald Hutton, *Charles II: King of England, Scotland, and Ireland* (1989). The latter can be read with the same author's *The Restoration* (1985) for subtle shifts of emphasis. Godfrey Davies, *The Restoration of Charles II* (1955) remains indispensable, especially for political developments in 1659 which are also the subject of Austin Woolrych's long introduction in *The Complete Prose Works of John Milton*, Vol. 7, *1659–1660*, ed. R. W. Ayers (1980). Paul Seward,

The Restoration (1991) serves as a reliable guide to the history and historiography of the re-establishment of the Stuarts. Charles's court has largely escaped attention, and the starting-point for the most important figure remains B. H. G. Wormald, *Clarendon: Politics, History and Religion 1640–60* (1951). Maurice Lee, *The Cabal* (1965) treats the ministers who succeeded Clarendon. For the later period there are excellent studies, including K. D. H. Haley, *The First Earl of Shaftesbury* (1968) and Andrew Browning, *Thomas Osborne, Earl of Danby and Duke of Leeds* (3 vols., 1951). The careers of MPs can be found in B. D. Henning (ed.), *The House of Commons 1660–1690* (3 vols., 1983). There has been limited monographic work on Caroline politics, of which Paul Seward's *The Cavalier Parliament and the Reconstruction of the Old Regime, 1661–1667* (1989) is the best for the opening of the regime and J. R. Jones, *The First Whigs: The Politics of the Exclusion Crisis, 1678–83* (1961) for its close, though Jones should be read in conjunction with Mark Knights, *Politics and Opinion in Crisis, 1678–81* (1994). Keith Feiling, *A History of the Tory Party 1640–1714* (1924) remains valuable. Provocative reinterpretations of these years can be found in Jonathan Scott, *Algernon Sidney and the Restoration Crisis, 1677–83* (1991) and Richard Ashcraft, *Revolutionary Politics and Locke's 'Two Treatises on Government'* (1986). Crown finance has been exhaustively researched in C. D. Chandaman, *The English Public Revenue 1660–88* (1975). The church has been the subject of two excellent general studies and a useful collection of essays: I. M. Green, *The Re-Establishment of the Church of England 1660–63* (1978); John Spurr, *The Restoration Church of England, 1646–1689* (1991); T. Harris, P. Seaward and M. Goldie (eds.), *The Politics of Religion in Restoration England* (1990). R. Greaves's *Deliver Us from Evil* (1986) and *Enemies under His Feet* (1990) are compendious, if uncritical, accounts of religious radicalism. The best treatment of Catholicism is John Bossy, *The English Catholic Community 1570–1850* (1975), but the seminal work on attitudes towards Catholics is John Miller, *Popery and Politics in England 1660–1688* (1973). J. P. Kenyon, *The Popish Plot* (1972) is an outstanding narrative of complicated events. An excellent study of the Scottish church is Julia Buckroyd, *Church and State in Scotland, 1660–81* (1980). There has been no recent study of Caroline foreign policy, though there are up-to-date chapters in Jeremy Black, *A System of Ambition?: British Foreign Policy, 1660–1793* (1991). The standard works remain K. Feiling, *British Foreign Policy 1660–1672* (1930) and C. Wilson, *Profit and Power: A Study of England and the Dutch Wars* (1957). John Childs, *The Army of Charles II* (1976) is useful for the army, and Sari Hornstein, *The Restoration Navy and English Foreign Trade, 1674–1688* (1991) for the navy.

James II

There can be no better starting-place for the reign of James II than any segment of the first two volumes of T. B. Macaulay's *The History of England from the Accession of James II* (5 vols., 1849–61). D. Ogg, *England in the Reign of James II and William III* (1955) is surprisingly strong on social history. There are relevant chapters in J. R. Jones, *Country and Court: England 1658–1714* (1978); Tim Harris, *Politics under the Later Stuarts* (1993); and Geoffrey Holmes, *The Making of a Great Power* (1993). A brief survey of events is found in Michael Mullett, *James II and English Politics, 1678–1688* (1994). Two valuable collections of documents are A. Browning, *English Historical Documents, VIII: 1660–1714* (1953) and J. P. Kenyon (ed.), *The Stuart Constitution* (2nd edn, 1986). Among the most accessible sources are *Memoirs of Sir John Reresby*, ed. Mary Geiter and W. A. Speck (1991); *The Works of George Savile, Marquis of Halifax*, ed. Mark Brown (1989); and John Locke, *Two Treatises of Government*, ed. Peter Laslett (2nd edn, 1967).

There are two thorough biographies, both of which try to understand the King on his own terms: F. C. Turner, *James II* (1948) and John Miller, *James II: A Study in Kingship* (1978). James II's ministers have not been well served by historians. There are no studies of Clarendon or Rochester and no recent study of Halifax to replace H. C. Foxcroft, *A Character of the Trimmer: Being a Short Life of the First Marquis of Halifax* (1946). The truly outstanding political biography is J. P. Kenyon, *Robert Spencer, Earl of Sunderland* (1958).

J. R. Western, *Monarchy and Revolution* (1972) is one of the only works to focus on politics in the 1680s. The religious history of this period is treated in Douglas Lacey, *Dissent and Parliamentary Politics in England* (1969); Richard Greaves, *Secrets of the Kingdom: British Radicals from the Popish Plot to the Revolution of 1688–89* (1992); and John Spurr, *The Restoration Church of England 1646–1689* (1991).

The greatest attention given to James's reign has been to its end. A classic Whig view, still worth reading, is G. M. Trevelyan, *The English Revolution, 1688–89* (1938). The best overall work remains J. R. Jones, *The Revolution of 1688 in England* (1972), though some of its insights have been updated in books published during the tercentenary, of which W. A. Speck, *Reluctant Revolutionaries* (1988) and R. A. Beddard, *The Revolutions of 1688* (1991) are the most valuable. John Childs, *The Army, James II, and the Glorious Revolution* (1980) is an important study of why the revolution in England was bloodless. Two works which highlight the international dimensions of 1688 are John Carswell, *The Descent on England* (1969) and Jonathan Israel (ed.), *The Anglo-Dutch Moment* (1991), which contains several important revisionist essays. Though he took no part in the events and wrote his seminal work some years earlier, John Locke has always been associated with the revolution of 1688–9, John Dunn, *Locke* (1984) is a good short biography, but Maurice Cranston, *John Locke: A Biography* (1957) is the most compelling. J. Marshall, *John Locke: Resistance, Religion and Responsibility* (1994) is a learned study.

William and Mary

The classic work on the reign is T. B. Macaulay's *The History of England from the Accession of James II* (5 vols., 1849–61), one of the great achievements of English historiography. Macaulay's interpretation of events has not worn well, but his portraits of individuals, honed by dozens of entries for the *Encyclopaedia Britannica*, are unrivalled and his narrative is gripping. David Ogg, *England in the Reigns of James II and William III* (1955) is a useful corrective with a wider ambit than political history. There are relevant chapters in J. R. Jones, *Country and Court: England 1658–1714* (1978); Tim Harris, *Politics under the Later Stuarts* (1993); and Geoffrey Holmes, *The Making of a Great Power* (1993), but the reign continues out of focus. Much of its essential context is Continental, and J. B. Wolf's *Louis XIV* (1968) is a good antidote to an Anglocentric view of European warfare. Among Jeremy Black's numerous works on this period, *A System of Ambition?: British Foreign Policy, 1660–1793* (1991) is to be preferred. There are also valuable chapters in Jonathan Israel (ed.), *The Anglo-Dutch Moment* (1991). Accessible sources for the political history of the period include *The Diary of John Evelyn* (1983), ed. John Bowle; *Bishop Burnet's History of His Own Time: Selections*, ed. Thomas Stackhouse (1979); *Memoirs of Sir John Reresby*, ed. Mary K. Geiter and W. A. Speck (1991); *The Parliamentary Diary of Narcissus Luttrell, 1691–1693*, ed. Henry Horwitz (1972); and *The Illustrated Journeys of Celia Fiennes, c. 1682–c. 1712*, ed. Christopher Morris (1995).

The outstanding biography of the King is Stephen Baxter, *William III and the Defense of European Liberty* (1966). David Ogg, *William III* (1967) is brief and readable, while Henri and Barbara van der Zee's breezy *William and Mary* (1973) gives more consideration to the role of the Queen. The later Stuart period is not well served by political biographies, and William's reign is no exception. J. P. Kenyon's outstanding *Robert Spencer, Earl of Sunderland* (1958) continues useful, as does Andrew Browning, *Thomas Osborne, Earl of Danby and Duke of Leeds* (3 vols., 1951) and Henry Horwitz, *Revolution Politicks: The Career of Daniel Finch, Second Earl of Nottingham* (1968). W. L. Sachse's *Lord Somers* (1975) chronicles the life of one of the Junto lords, but there is no modern study of Halifax or Orford and, most regrettably, none of Portland. There are several good works on the politics of the period, including Henry Horwitz, *Parliament, Policy and Politics in the Reign of William III* (1977); B. W. Hill, *The Growth of Parliamentary Parties, 1689–1742* (1976); and Jane Garrett, *The Triumphs of Providence* (1980), which narrates the attempt on William's life. Geoffrey Holmes (ed.), *Britain after the Glorious Revolution, 1689–1714* (1969) includes a number of valuable essays. There are three outstanding books on the effects of war: P. G. M. Dickson, *The Financial Revolution in England* (1967); D. W. Jones, *War and Economy in the Age of William III and Marlborough* (1988); and John Brewer, *The Sinews of Power* (1989), but the best starting-point for beginners is Henry Rosevere, *The Finan-*

cial Revolution 1660–1750 (1991). J. P. Kenyon, *Revolution Principles* (1977) is a cogent work of intellectual history.

Coverage of Scotland and Ireland fares better for this reign than for those of Charles and James. William Ferguson, *Scotland: 1689 to the Present* (1968) is a reliable survey. Paul Hopkins, *Glencoe and the End of the Highland War* (1986) is difficult but worth the effort to understand clan relations and local politics before the massacre. M. Linklater and C. Hesketh, *For King and Conscience* (1989) can be recommended as a study of the Earl of Dundee. The most important monograph on the politics of this period is P. W. J. Riley, *King William and the Scottish Politicians* (1979). J. G. Simms, *Jacobite Ireland* (1969) is highly regarded, as are his chapters in T. W. Moody et al. (eds.), *A New History of Ireland*, Vol. 3, *Early Modern Ireland 1534–1691* (1976) and Vol. 4, *Eighteenth-Century Ireland 1691–1800* (1986).

Anne

The classic work on the reign of Anne is by G. M. Trevelyan, *England under Queen Anne* (3 vols., 1930–34). It is a full narrative of politics into which is interspersed an account of the development of a political culture. Trevelyan excelled at writing military history and there are concise studies of the main battles of the War of the Spanish Succession as well as maps and battlefield plans. There has been no competing narrative written since. There are relevant chapters in J. R. Jones, *Country and Court: England, 1658–1714* (1978); Geoffrey Holmes, *The Making of a Great Power* (1993); and Barry Coward, *The Stuart Age: England 1603–1714* (2nd edn, 1994). Tim Harris, *Politics under the Later Stuarts* (1993) is especially good on Jacobitism but otherwise lumps the reign together with the preceding one. There are a number of outstanding biographies, of which Edward Gregg, *Queen Anne* (1980) is exemplary – the best biography of any Stuart monarch. Frances Harris, *A Passion for Government* (1991) is an unsentimental life of Sarah, Duchess of Marlborough, and better than any of the recent studies of her husband. There is still much pleasure to be had in dipping into Winston Churchill's encomium for his ancestor, W. S. Churchill, *Marlborough: His Life and Times* (4 vols., 1933–8). Correlli Barnett, *Marlborough* (1974) is the best military study and J. R. Jones, *Marlborough* (1993) is the most recent. Two recent works that focus on the military history of the period are John Childs, *The British Army of William III, 1689–1702* (1987) and David Chandler, *The Art of Warfare in the Age of Marlborough* (1990). It is regrettable that there is no adequate life of Godolphin, but his rivals Harley and St John (Bolingbroke) have been well served: Angus McInnes, *Robert Harley, Puritan Politician* (1970); Brian Hill, *Robert Harley, Speaker, Secretary of State, and Prime Minister* (1988); and H. T. Dickinson, *Bolingbroke* (1970) are all valuable. G. V. Bennett, *The Tory Crisis in Church and State* (1975), a biography of Francis Atterbury, is a model study of an important ecclesiastic. There are innumerable editions of the works of the great political polemicists Defoe and Swift.

The political history of the reign was energized by the debate over the structure of Augustan politics. It may be followed in Robert Walcott, *English Politics in the Early Eighteenth Century* (1956); J. H. Plumb, *The Growth of Political Stability in England 1675–1725* (1967); and W. A. Speck, *Tory & Whig: The Struggle in the Constituencies, 1701–1715* (1970). B. W. Hill, *The Growth of Parliamentary Parties, 1689–1742* (1976) places the subject in a longer perspective and draws on a wealth of knowledge about the reign of Anne. But the great work on the subject is Geoffrey Holmes, *British Politics in the Age of Anne* (2nd edn, 1987). R. O. Bucholz, *The Augustan Court: Queen Anne and the Decline of Court Culture* (1993) argues for a more vigorous Queen. Holmes has also edited the best collection of essays, *Britain after the Glorious Revolution, 1689–1714* (1969), though Clyve Jones (ed.), *Britain in the First Age of Party* (1987) is also useful. Daniel Szechi, *Jacobitism and Tory Politics* (1984) is the best treatment of a much controverted subject, and his *The Jacobites, Britain and Europe, 1688–1788* (1994) expands the context. Paul Monod, *Jacobitism and the English People, 1688–1788* (1989) is an important monograph. There remain few local studies of the late Stuart period, but Gary De Krey, *A Fractured Society* (1985) is the ablest study of London for any part of the seventeenth century. Geoffrey Holmes, *The Trial of Doctor Sacheverell* (1973) is a gripping narrative which also has much to say about London politics and the politics of religion. P. G. M. Dickson, *The Financial Revolution in England* (1967) and John Brewer, *The Sinews of Power* (1989) are key works on government and military finance.

There is a vast literature on the union of England and Scotland. The classic narrative remains James Mackinnon, *Union of England and Scotland* (1896), but there are many modern studies, of which William Ferguson, *Scotland's Relations with England: A Survey to 1707* (1977); P. W. J. Riley, *The Union of England and Scotland* (1978); and P. H. Scott, *1707: The Union of Scotland and England* (1979) represent the cross-section of interpretation. Though brief, Christopher Whatley, *Bought and Sold for English Gold?* (1994) is an outstanding summary of the literature as well as of the author's own contribution to the debate over the economic dimensions of the union. Anne's reign is not usually viewed as a special period in Irish history, and the best introduction are the chapters by J. G. Simms in T. W. Moody et al. (eds.), *A New History of Ireland*, Vol. 4, *Eighteenth-Century Ireland 1691–1800* (1986).

Index

Portsmouth, Duchess of (Louise de
Kéroualle) 243, 252
Portugal 21, 22, 236, 237
postal service 2
'post-nati' (Scots born after James I's
accession to English throne) 81, 82
Poulett family of Somerset 50
poverty 26–9
Poynings' Law 47, 294
prayer-books: Book of Common Prayer
234; Scottish 130, 132, 138
preaching, control of 128–9
predestination 127
prerogative, royal: Parliament attempts to
restrict 106, 144, 150–51, 290, 293;
suspending power 275–6; *see also*
courts, judicial (prerogative) *and under*
individual monarchs
Presbyterianism 5, 33, 39, 49; James I and
74–5, 76, 227; in Civil War Parliaments
161, 168–9, 170–75; under
Commonwealth 192, 194, 203, 208; in
Convention Parliament 220, 232–3;
under Charles II 216, 232–3; under
Anne 313; Scots 49, (under James I) 39,
74–5, 76, 227, 268, (under Charles I)
129, 131, 227, (in Civil War) 168–9,
235, (under Charles II) 227, 267–8,
(William III reconstitutes) 299,
(recognized by union of 1707) 314, 328,
329
press 2, 257, 258, 272, 318
pressure cooker 2
Preston, Battle of 180
pretenders 40; *see also* Stuart, James
Edward
prices 16
Pride, Thomas 210; Pride's Purge 185,
192, 193, 194
printing 14
privacy, lack of 30
privileges: royal grants 34, 36, 37–8, 83;
see also under Parliament
Privy Chamber, Charles I's 42
Privy Council 42, 43–4, 57; Scottish 128,
227; *see also under individual*
monarchs
proclamations, royal 34
professional classes 23

progresses, royal 45
propaganda: under Charles II 247, 250,
259; Civil War 152, 164, 166–7;
Cromwell's, in Scotland 200; Dutch
247, 250, 279; religious 260, 273–4;
Tory 260; Whig 257
property 36, 192, 196
prostitution 28
protection, commercial 21, 23, 81, 326,
327; Navigation Acts 23, 201, 326
Protectorate 191, 206–12; Oliver
Cromwell's 206–12, 230; Richard
Cromwell's 212, 216–18; Army and
208, 209–11, 212, 215, 217;
constitutional reform 207, 211–12;
Council 207, 208–9, 211; finance 217–
18; Parliaments 207, 208, 211–12, 218;
public acquiescence 189; Spanish war
211, 217
Protestant League 117
Protestant Union 92
'Protestant wind' 280
Providence Island investors 138
Prynne, William 129
publishing 14, 55, 152, 197; censorship
229, 234, 313
punishments, judicial 13, 28, 38, 129, 293
Purcell, Henry 4
Puritanism 5, 31–3; anti-Catholic hysteria
126; clergy 40, 75, 137; culture 31–3
election, doctrine of 31, 33; and
English Revolution 190–91; under
James I 72, 73, 75–6; justices of the
peace 32, 55; Laud and 128–9; lay
movement 75–6; political impact 49,
63; preaching under Anglican control
128–9
purveyance 84, 85–6, 87, 120
Putney debates 176, 205
Pym, John 142–3; and Strafford's
attainder 143, 144; and The Incident
145; and Irish rebellion crisis 147, 148;
King's attempt to impeach 135–6, 150;
and Oxford Proposals 154; death 155;
printed speeches 152

Quakers 5, 209, 313; persecution 218–19,
231, 260, 274
Queen Anne's Bounty 313

government under William III 308–9;
Ireland 49; in kind 17; land 1, 230, 304,
308, 310, 311, 339; London resistance
114, 161, 219; Parliamentary approval
61, 286; royal power 34; Scotland 49;
subsidies 61; Union and 329; war
finance 115, 340; in Wars of Three
Kingdoms 160, 161, 164, 179
tea 2, 309
technology 2, 3
tethering ordinances 17
textiles 16, 20–21, 22, 84
Thames Valley 18
theatre 4, 14, 16
Thirty Years War 21; James I and 91, 92–
3; Charles I and 91, 103, 115–16; effect
on Empire 305; and merchant marine
22; see also Frederick V
Thirty-Nine Articles 68, 74
thought 2–3; see also political theory
Three Kingdoms, Wars of the 182–3, 340;
impact on civilians 160; see also
Bishops' Wars; Civil War; Ireland
(rebellion of 1641); Scotland (under
Charles I)
Thurloe, John 210, 218
Tillotson, John, Archbishop of
Canterbury 314
tithes 17, 192, 196, 203, 204, 206
tobacco 2, 21, 22, 120, 309
Tonge, Israel 241, 253
tonnage and poundage 84, 114, 115, 118
Torbay 280
Tory party: and James II 259, 263, 265,
266, 274, 276, 278–9; and William and
Mary's accession 282, 283; under
William III 285, 290, 303, 306, 307, 310,
311; under Anne 317–19, 320, 321, 330,
332–3, 334–5
    and Admiralty 304, 306, 320; and
Anglicanism 260, 302, 318, 330, 332;
'country' interest 303; formation 43,
257–8, 290; and landed interest 317,
318; in London 251, 259; memory of
Revolution 341; theory of monarchy
290; and wars, (William III's) 306, (of
Spanish Succession) 321, 332–3;
'whimsicals' 335; xenophobia 318
torture 1, 268

towns 15, 46; food supply 16; garden plots
17; growth 8, 13–16, 26; houses 2, 14,
19; mortality 14, 16; population 6;
Puritanism 31; sanitation 2, 14;
Scotland 46, 78; social order 26; Whigs
and monied interest 318; see also
individual towns
trade 20–23; American 11, 22, 23, 259,
261, 334; Baltic and Muscovy 22; Dutch
rivalry 23, 261; with East 261, 342; in
empire 1; joint-stock companies 22,
237; ports 14, 23; regulation 34, 43,
119; revival in 1630s 116, 117–18, 121;
transshipment 21, 23, 118; Union and
free 328–9; wars disrupt 245, 308;
wealth from 20, 23, 121, 259, 261
Trade's Increase (merchant vessel) 22–3
trained bands 150, 163, 169–70, 214, 235
transport 2, 6, 8, 16; see also individual
modes
transportation as punishment 271
transshipping trade 21, 23, 118
Traquair, 1st Earl of (John Stewart) 139,
140
treason, punishment for 38
Treasurer, Lord 40, 42–3, 44
Treasury 309
Treby, Sir George 284
Tresham, Francis 66
Tresham family 20
Turnham Green, Battle of 153
turnpike roads 2
Tweeddale, 1st Marquis of (John Hay)
327
Tyrconnell, 1st Earl of (Rory O'Donnell)
70–71
Tyrconnell, 3rd Earl of (Richard Talbot)
273, 293, 294
Tyrone, 2nd Earl of (Hugh O'Neill) 70–71

Ulster 48, 71, 197
unemployment, structural 28
Union of Crowns (1603) 68, 77–80, 81–2,
329, 338
Union of Great Britain (1707) 47, 59, 312,
325–9, 339–40
Unitarians 313
universities 14; Arminianism 127; clerical
education 40, 75; James II and 266,